W9-BXD-680

THE ELIZABETHAN RENAISSANCE
The Cultural Achievement

Books by A. L. Rowse

THE ELIZABETHAN AGE

The England of Elizabeth
The Expansion of Elizabethan England
The Elizabethan Renaissance: The Life of the Society
The Elizabethan Renaissance:
The Cultural Achievement

———————

William Shakespeare: A Biography
Shakespeare's Sonnets
(*A modern text, and prose versions, introduction and notes*)
Christopher Marlowe: A Biography
Shakespeare's Southampton: Patron of Virginia

———————

The Elizabethans and America
Ralegh and the Throckmortons
Sir Richard Grenville of the *Revenge*
Tudor Cornwall
The Cornish in America

———————

A Cornish Anthology
Cornish Stories
A Cornish Childhood
A Cornishman at Oxford

———————

The Early Churchills
The Later Churchills
The Churchills
The English Spirit (*revised edition*)
Times, Persons, Places (The English Past)

THE ELIZABETHAN RENAISSANCE

THE CULTURAL ACHIEVEMENT

A. L. ROWSE

✶✶

'So understand as to re-live' — GILBERT MURRAY

ჼ
BC

First published *1972* by
MACMILLAN LONDON LTD
London and Basingstoke
Associated companies in New York Toronto
Dublin Melbourne Johannesburg and Madras

SBN 333 13788 4

Printed in Great Britain by
R. & R. CLARK LTD
Edinburgh

I wish to inscribe upon these pages the names of
JAKOB BURCKHARDT
J. H. HUIZINGA

CONTENTS

LIST OF ILLUSTRATIONS

between pages 246 and 247

PREFACE

WITH this volume I complete the task I set myself more than twenty years ago of constructing a large canvas covering *The Elizabethan Age*, which was to be the title of the whole. From time to time friends have reproached me with my dilatoriness in completing the trilogy. In fact the delay turned out to be fortunate. For it is only in the last decade that it has become possible to tackle two of the subjects essential to this book. Owing to the work of Miss Auerbach, Dr. Roy Strong and others, we now have a clearer grasp of the still difficult subject of Elizabethan painting; while indispensable work on Elizabethan architecture has been accomplished by such scholars as Sir John Summerson and Mr. Mark Girouard. With regard to Tudor music much more work had been done already, but too exclusively from an English perspective. The present generation of historians of music have given us a European perspective, and I am as greatly indebted to their work.

Thus this volume portrays the cultural life of the age as its predecessor depicted its social life. The two are intimately bound together: without the background of the society, of which the activities here dealt with are expressions, the book could have been a succession of disparate chapters. In fact each subject is seen both arising out of its soil in society, and in its interrelations with each other. Only thus could the book be an organic whole, which is what a book should be. And this apart even from artistic integration – though it should be obvious to perceptive readers that my ultimate values are aesthetic.

This volume and its predecessor were planned as one book, *The Elizabethan Renaissance*, though for economic reasons it has had to be published in two halves. Those who do not embark on such large-scale projects can hardly conceive of the difficulties. For each subject, each chapter, I had collected, in more than twenty years, enough material for a small book. The determining problem was how to organise it all, give it a vertebrate structure. In the course of this a great deal of material could not be used: a sense of proportion must be the constant governor in deciding what to include and what not. No point in complaining that this or that is not here – what I care about is not that the book should be all-inclusive but that it should give a representative and significant portrait of the Age and its activities.

Over these years I have derived immense help from the institutions of which I have been a member, and friends too numerous to specify. In particular, at All Souls I am indebted to Professor Jean Seznec for helping me with the subject of Shakespeare's reception and influence in France; to Dr. J. S. G. Simmonds with that of Elizabethan physicians in Russia; to Sir George Clark for help at various points; and to Dr. A. C. Crombie on the history of science. Many years ago Sir Jack Westrup kindly allowed me to attend his class on Elizabethan Music; I am grateful to Mr. R. E. Davidson of Ripon Cathedral Choir School, for keeping me abreast with record performances of it. To Mr. John Buxton I am indebted for many discussions of Elizabethan literature, while he introduced me to the incised brasses of that New College connoisseur, Richard Haydock. My chief personal obligation is to Professor Jack Simmons of Leicester, who has accompanied me on many visits to historic houses and churches, and constantly alerted me to Elizabethan objects and material.

I cannot fully express all my obligations to the hospitable owners of historic houses who have helped my work by opening to me their manuscripts and treasures; but it would be churlish not to record what I owe, in particular, to the late Dowager Duchess of Devonshire at Hardwick, the Duke and Duchess of Buccleuch at Boughton, the Marquis and Marchioness of Salisbury at Hatfield, Viscount De L'Isle at Penhurst, Mrs. Luttrell at Dunster; to my friend Wyndham Ketton-Cremer, late of Felbrigg, and Mr. Norman Scarfe, who showed me many things of interest in East Anglia. Evidences of these and other kindnesses are frequent throughout these volumes.

At the Huntington Library in California the Librarian, Mr. Robert Dougan, the Curator of the Art Gallery, Mr. Robert Wark, and Miss Mary Isabel Fry were most helpful, and I am indebted to Dr. J. M. Steadman for literary and philosophic enlightenment.

Miss N. O'Farrell has long helped me with manuscript material as has Mr. G. A. Webb, of the Codrington Library, over books.

A. L. ROWSE

BOOK II

THE CULTURAL ACHIEVEMENT

CHAPTER I

THE DRAMA AS SOCIAL EXPRESSION

AFTER our survey of the life of Elizabethan society we are in a better position to appreciate the rôle of drama in it.* Life itself had a more dramatic quality, from the top to the bottom, when people were more direct and spontaneous, even in their insincerities and hypocrisies, their lying and cheating. Clever people, or educated upper-class persons, were not without sophistication; even so they were more themselves, more in the part. They were often conscious of playing a part – no one more so than that glittering specimen of disingenuousness, Leicester, though to some extent the rôle was forced on him by his position. Even the upright and honest Philip Sidney, the *preux chevalier*, was playing his part. It is never more obvious than when these people are taking leave of life: grandees, like Norfolk, Essex, Ralegh, dramatise their executions, Ralegh deliberately arranging his positively last appearance on the stage outside the Gatehouse at Westminster as a demonstration against James I. It has been well said that 'one actress of consummate skill appeared in Elizabethan England: the Queen herself.'[1] From the beginning to the end she never failed to appeal to the gallery, as conscious of playing a part as of the part she played.

This quality of directness, this lack of return upon oneself, of irony – even among the sophisticated, for sixteenth-century people were very different from us in this respect – encouraged the dramatic in their lives, their aspiring minds and reverberating falls, their bounding hopes and their refusal to be discouraged. It is the theatre of Marlowe and Shakespeare as against the theatre of Eliot and Samuel Beckett.

Here we are viewing the drama as an expression of the society, rather than as an art-form in itself. The drama as literature was a secondary matter to the earlier dramatists. It was not until the year of Shakespeare's death that Ben Jonson put forth his collected

* Cf. the previous volume, *The Elizabethan Renaissance: The Life of the Society.*

3

plays in folio as literature – and was laughed at by some for doing so. No less striking the other way is that Shakespeare displayed little interest in publishing his plays, though he took care with his poems. Jonson, of a younger generation, was the chief upholder of the view that the drama was literature. This differed from the earlier view and the low rating of playwrights compared with poets, mere craftsmen as against artists. The position Jonson always took up was in itself a strong indication (as well as vindication) of the upward movement of drama in literary esteem. By the end of the age it had become literature. The noticeable part Jonson took in forwarding the publication of the works of the theatre's greatest craftsman was in keeping with his campaign to advance its claims as art.

The specific Elizabethan drama that was, in retrospect, one of the glories of the age – a high peak of cultural achievement in the language for all time – was the work of a handful of men: the theatre entrepreneurs and proprietors, the actors and playwrights, with the necessary following of theatre workmen. These were a small number indeed. We might almost subsume the story of the Elizabethan drama under a very few names, the crucial figures in its brief and brilliant development: the Burbages, Philip Henslowe and his son-in-law, Edward Alleyn; Marlowe, Shakespeare, Ben Jonson. If to these we add a few more at either end – among actors, Tarleton, Kemp, Armin, among playwrights Lyly, Peele, Kyd, and Dekker, Webster, Middleton, Beaumont and Fletcher – we have a canvas covering the essential features of the achievement. To this we must add the theatres themselves, something new and specific to the age, and their special audience – primarily a London audience, along with the Court – which was an integral element in the creation of the Elizabethan drama. Even so, the theatre-audience was a minority of Londoners; the majority did not go to the theatre.

This drama has been regarded in too free a perspective as a culmination of a nation-wide entertainments activity; more precisely it was a precipitation of some elements out of all that, a concentration of them upon the London stage. It was essentially a creation of the capital: a highly coloured and significant expression of the increasing concentration of the nation's life upon the plane of London, with its growing wealth, sophistication and luxury, the secularisation of society consequent upon the Reformation, the specialisation that comes with a heightening of culture.

The moment was of supreme importance – such a moment can

4

never come again. Its rise, maturity and decline roughly coincided with Shakespeare's dramatic career. Not much more than a quarter of a century – but these were the years in which a small, highly tensed society braced itself for a tough struggle for its future with a more powerful opponent and won through, its integration much heightened by the struggle. After the strain was over and the heroic days departed – people were conscious of them as such – things began to fall apart. As with the society, so with the drama. Intelligent historians of it appreciate that it cannot be understood apart from the historical environment that gave rise to it.[2] Time and circumstance were propitious and brought forth the men – gave them their chance, and not only that, but inspiration.

We have already glimpsed something of the varied and customary spread of entertainments of a medieval society, in country and town, such as England remained up to and into our period. There were the mummings and disguisings, the dancing and jigs, the folk-plays, the miracles and mysteries performed in towns and in the countryside, pageants and royal entries, interludes of Court, castle and manor, the ritual drama of the Church. Much of this was enacted by the people themselves – one hesitates to use the word amateurs as anachronistic, since there was no strict dividing line. For centuries there had also been small troupes of strolling players – a medieval troupe would be only three or four. From the early years of the reign there was a growth of this strand in dramatic activity, partly filling the vacuum of the vanishing drama of the Church. It meant a notable increase in secular drama, though up to the end of the century these players sometimes played in the churches.

Meanwhile the 'storial shows' of towns like Coventry, Chester and York, which had their cycles customarily performed by their gilds, were declining – naturally with the Protestant decline of interest in the medieval presentation of religion and the professionalisation of the drama. Far more numerous visits from the touring companies, which took the name of their patron, protector, or even owner, filled the gap and gave better value. Look at the number of companies visiting Leicester, for which we have complete information – there is no reason to suppose that this town, under the wing of the Puritan Earl of Huntingdon, was specially addicted to plays. Yet during the reign, to go no further than 1603, nearly fifty companies visited it, many of them several

times.[3] After the formation of the Queen's company in 1583 with
a dozen of the best actors out of others, these were the most
frequent visitors, with over a score of visits. With this company
the reward given by the town council, over and above what it
collected, was increased to 20 shillings, and this had the effect of
gradually increasing the rewards for others. (The highest reward
given was £4 at Ipswich in 1599 to these same players, perhaps
for some special entertainment. Nottingham was more economical
and never gave them more than 20s. Other places varied.[4]) The
next favourites at Leicester were the Earl of Worcester's – in
which the famous actor, Edward Alleyn, began as a boy – who
visited the town some fifteen times. Next to them came Lord
Strange's players, out of which company ultimately was born
Shakespeare's fellowship, the Lord Chamberlain's men. Fourth
in favour at Leicester were Leicester's own – but they did not
continue as such beyond his death in 1588. In addition to this,
besides many visits by bearwards and musicians, we find Christopher Alexander being paid for certain plays – he was a townsman
– as well as a reward of 5s. to 'players that came out of Wales',
over and above their takings.[5] A career was evidently opening
out to talents.

The accounts of Bath for a slightly shorter period, 1568–1602,
entirely confirm this picture. Visited by some thirty companies,
the city's favourites were again the Queen's, fifteen times, followed
by Lord Berkeley's (but those would be local) and the Lord
Admiral's.[6] There were other plays, though very few compared
with the professionals. At Christmas 1601 and again in 1602 the
young men of the city put on plays; at Candlemas the children
performed a play.[7] In 1583 Mr. Long received a reward of 6s/d
for his play, and Will Tucker for playing on his instruments the
same time, 2s.; then Mr. Long was given 3s. 4d. for another
play.[8] Who was Mr. Long? – the schoolmaster, evidently having
coached his pupils to perform. This must have been familiar
enough, when we think of the much publicised performances of
Mulcaster, headmaster of Merchant Taylors, in London, or of a
remote schoolmaster, Mr. Kemp, with his boys at Plymouth. All
this represented recognised dramatics, rewarded by the authorities; there must have been much more that was not thus rewarded,
strolling players who got only their takings. And this fairly represents the situation over the country in general: the ubiquitous-
ness, along with the secularisation and professionalisation, of the
drama.

There is a tendency at present to overemphasise the medieval element, and even the traditional, in the drama: after all, what is specifically Elizabethan is what is new. Plays as such played a small part in medieval education, whereas the humanists of the sixteeenth century urged their use both at school and university. The statutes of new foundations at Shrewsbury, Westminster and Sandwich required the performance of plays;[9] humanist educational theory recognised their value not only in learning and speaking Latin but for elocution, bearing and 'audacity', i.e. self-confidence in public. Naturally there had been medieval school performances, as at Shrewsbury at the end of the fifteenth century, but it was the first headmaster of the new foundation, Hugh Ashton (1562–71), who made a regular thing of it. He not only wrote and produced plays in the Quarry but laid down that scholars of the first form were to declaim and play one act of a comedy every Thursday.[10] For the performances of 1569 Ashton obtained the publicity services of Thomas Churchyard, who wrote that ten or twenty thousand might conveniently be accommodated in the Quarry – another example of the contemporary unreliability for figures: perhaps two or three thousand would be present.

The grammar school at Hitchin had its plays earlier at mid-century: very forward-looking, for they were in Latin and English, and dealt in both ancient and modern subjects.[11] Winchester, too, which had its first recorded play in 1565, by 1573 has advanced scenic devices, little houses on the stage; and further performances there are recorded. It is natural to suppose that these things depended on the tastes and aptitudes of individual masters. Most gifted of all had been Nicholas Udall, headmaster of Eton, gifted as both dramatist and producer: all his plays are lost except *Ralph Roister Doister*, but records of his dramatic performances with his boys remain – as also of his non-dramatic, which made a scandal at the time. (His tastes were those apt to go with his gifts.) Udall was rather a favourite at Court and several times performed there. He died in 1556; but, when Elizabeth paid her state visit to Cambridge in 1564, his English play *Ezechias* was revived by King's men – thus it was probably an Eton play. In this we see obvious links between school-drama and that of Court and university.

These are at their most significant in the case of the London schools. From 1561 Westminster boys were to the fore – probably other scholars along with the choristers – with performances before the Merchant Taylors Company, then the Parish Clerks, then the Ironmongers.[12] In 1567 they appeared before Bishop Grindal at Fulham Palace – Bucer, who took upon him to be mentor of the English Church, had no objection to religious drama – and from 1568 to 1574 the Westminster boys were appearing at Court. From 1573 to 1583 they were out-played and their place taken by the Merchant Taylors boys, under the direction of Mulcaster. We have, in a previous volume, seen something of Mulcaster's progressive educational ideas;[13] but he was also a strong believer in the value of acting, in the future of the English language, and in the unity of society and government.[14]

With the choristers of St. Paul's, the 'Children of Paul's', we observe the transition from amateur to professionals. From the first year of the reign they were performing before the Queen – at Nonsuch in the summer of 1559 – under the direction of their Master, Sebastian Westcott.[15] He was really a Catholic, and as such gave heart-searchings to good Bishop Grindal. But, as with William Byrd, organist of the Queen's Chapel, his talents were too valuable to be dispensed with, and the Queen herself intervened twice to protect him. In spite of all complaints Westcott held on till he died in 1582, was buried in the choir of the cathedral where he had served, and, having prospered, was able to leave legacies in various directions. During his career his boys performed almost every year at Court. At his death they joined up for performances with the Children of the Queen's Chapel in the theatre at Blackfriars. These had been playing there since 1576 – the signal date of the opening of the first public theatre, Burbage's 'Theatre' in Shoreditch. The theatre – men's as well as boys' companies – was becoming professionalised from its summit in London. Up to that date, out of 78 payments for performances at Court by a considerable majority the boys' troupes had it: 46 as against 32 performances by the men's. Of the boys, the children of Paul's were in the lead: 21 as against 15 from the combined Chapel children (based on Windsor and Greenwich), and ten from other schools.[16]

With the university drama we come closer to what the specific Elizabethan drama became. For one thing the leading dramatists who created it were either university men – Peele and Lyly from Oxford, Marlowe and Greene from Cambridge, or London wits who were as good as university men, Kyd, Shakespeare, Jonson, each of whom had had an education sufficient for the purpose and essentially shared their culture and approach. We should see this against the European background, for there was more of a cosmopolitan coming to-and-fro of entertainers, acrobats, jugglers, musicians, players, than we are aware of. The Renaissance impulse made for increasing secularisation of subject, and the revival of classical drama, but especially Roman: Plautus and Terence dominated comedy as Seneca tragedy. Because so much of the university drama was in Latin – a good deal of it lost – we tend to overlook its importance; but Latin was a spoken language at school and university, and all these dramatists were brought up in it. Latin tragedies were superior in structure and characterisation to the vernacular, until these same men got to work. Similarly the influence of Plautus and Terence was universal, and highly beneficial in raising standards in dramatic form and technique. In England tragedy developed late, and as in Spain the native instinct was opposed to formal classicism: these opponents each had a strongly developed character of its own, addicted to medieval romances and therefore more medieval and romantic. Besides this, 'in England there was an inexhaustible appetite for straight history', laced with comic interludes. Altogether, Renaissance drama was 'an expansive drama, suited to an age when the boundaries of knowledge and of the world's geography were being burst on all sides.'[17]

It is no wonder that our comedy is so dominated by Italy, for Renaissance romantic comedy was an Italian creation, with the new dimension it gave to sexual love, its characteristics of professionalism, improvisation and popular appeal.[18] We should have been better able to catch the migration on the wing if more of the plays of Grimald, besides Udall, had survived from mid-century. Grimald was of Italian blood (Grimaldi), and his plays mingled lyrical and comic elements with his classical models, as did Udall with his biblical themes.[19] Cambridge favoured comedy, both Plautine and Renaissance, in the first phase; Italianate and then vernacular comedies, topical and with a satirical inflexion, later on. At St. John's in 1579 there was a memorable play, *Hymenaeus* – which no English comedy yet could equal in construction or dexterous dialogue. The leading part of Ferdinandus was played by Abraham Fraunce, up from Shrewsbury. Next year Fraunce acted in Legge's *Ricardus Tertius*: a much admired play that set a new model for historical chronicle, subjecting it to form and classical restraint. Fraunce was a *protégé* of Sir Philip Sidney and went on to an admired literary and scholarly career, more difficult for us to admire since he was addicted to unfortunate English hexameters. Harington says that he and Essex saw the comedy *Pedantius*, in which Harvey was guyed, when they were at Cambridge.[20]

Oxford went in more for tragedies and spectacular productions. A group at Christ Church, Eedes, Hutten and William Gager, had come up from Westminster, where Latin plays were the rule for the school and English plays for the choirboys. Of these Gager was a dramatist whose importance has been obliterated by the fact that he insisted on writing, both plays and poems, in Latin: he thought English beneath the attention of a scholar – and died a frustrated and disappointed man.[21] His first play, *Meleager*, was a success and was later revived before Leicester, Pembroke and Sidney. For Count Laski's reception at Oxford two plays by Gager were produced, his comedy *Rivales*, interspersed with choral interludes and songs, and a *Dido* with huntsmen and hounds, and 'a tempest wherein it hailed small confects, rained rosewater, and snew an artificial kind of snow.'

He was hardly less famous for his controversy with a leading academic Puritan, Dr. Reynolds of Corpus, as to the morality of playing. In his youth Reynolds had played the part of a woman in Richard Edwardes' *Palamon and Arcite* at the Queen's first visit – Edwardes had come back to his old college from his job as Master of the Children of the Chapel to produce it. Now, having seen the light of middle age, the Doctor could not 'have fellowship with the unfruitful works of darkness'; he feared 'the danger which my example might be bred to others if I were present at them.' Gager riposted that he did not think it an abomination for a young man to put on his wife's petticoat for a good purpose. Reynolds called down from on high the authority of Calvin, 'as sound and learned an interpreter of the Scriptures as any since the Apostles' times'; once that fatal name was invoked reason flew out of the window. The arguments Gager adduced were excellent, but we have not the space for such exchanges here.[22] Suffice it to say that the majority of university people approved of plays and enjoyed them. We have a revealing list of the young men who acted before the Queen in 1566, Reynolds among them, and the leading places they rose to in the Church, deans, canons, Heads of Houses, a vice-chancellor and one archbishop.[23] The Queen herself gave Reynolds his answer on her later visit in 1592, schooling him in public 'for his obstinate preciseness, willing him to follow her laws, and not run before them.'[24] All in Latin – good for her! But what Puritan ever listened to an opponent's arguments?

For the plays at Count Laski's reception in 1583 we find those former Oxford men, Peele and Lyly, helping. Peele, who was a friend of Gager, came back to aid with the productions; Lyly, now head of the earl of Oxford's company of boy-players, lent several lots of apparel. The three chief colleges given to dramatics were Christ Church, principally, St. John's and Magdalen. Peele was ten years at Christ Church, 1571–81, before he carried his talents, well employed at the university, to develop in London; Lyly was four years at Magdalen, 1571–5, before he followed the same course. At Cambridge more colleges put on plays: at St. John's they became a regular feature of college life. Greene was there for some seven years, 1575–83, Nashe for five, 1582–8. Marlowe had had the chance of participating in Christmas plays at King's School, Canterbury, in addition to the frequent visits of the men's companies, Leicester's in the lead.[25] Then he was at Corpus Christi, off and on for the years 1581–7, where there were plays in addition to what was going on in other colleges, and the visits of the professionals to the town.

Is it not evident that all these – to become leading figures in the theatre in London – would carry over to it a considerable experience already of drama from school and university?

In the 1590's Cambridge produced a number of Latin comedies based on Italian models. *Laelia* was an adaptation from the famous play, *Gl'Ingannati (The Cheated)* which was imitated and adapted all over Europe – Shakespeare looked at both it and an imitation of it, *Gl'Inganni*, for his *Twelfth Night. Laelia* so much impressed Essex on his visit in February 1595 that he secured two of the actors for an Accession day performance before the Queen.[26] *Hispanus* was very topical, with an anti-Spanish and anti-papal strain. Two more plays were based on della Porta. At the turn of the century came a number of vernacular comedies, including the three *Parnassus* plays from lively St. John's. These offer a series of farcical skits on university and literary life in London, bringing them closer together than ever before. Student divisions and difficulties over logic are aired – Puritans prefer Ramus, conservatives traditional scholastics. These St. John's men reveal themselves as closely following contemporary writers, who are scored in up-to-date student fashion. *Venus and Adonis* is several times cited – it was naturally a favourite with students – but a 'graver' subject would be preferable: a laugh at its dedication. Marlowe's genius was recognised; his wit came from heaven, but his vices from hell. As for Ben Jonson: 'a mere empiric, one that gets what he hath by observation . . . so slow an inventor that he were better betake himself to his old trade of brick-laying: a bold whoreson, as confident now in making a book as he was in times past in laying of a brick.'[27]

The actors are brought on too: Burbage and Kemp have a scene, in which they look down on university plays and acting. The actors do not speak naturally in their walk but must stop, 'just as though in walking with a fellow we should never speak but at a stile, a gate, or a ditch, where a man can go no further.'[28] As for the plays: 'few of the university pen plays well: they smell too much of that writer Ovid, and that writer Metamorphoses.' Will Kemp is made to say, 'Why, here's our fellow Shakespeare puts them all down': the joke rebounds on them, for this is precisely what he had done by then. As the public theatre in London flourished and grew splendid so the university drama declined. But the latter was not the least of the contributories to the Elizabethan drama, which owed its strength and richness to its fusion of so many elements. Thus too its representativeness: it came to mirror the whole society. The actors who created it were receiving their reward: become respectable at last, they were moving up in the world:

> With mouthing words that better wits have framed
> They purchase lands, and now Esquires are named.

This was a palpable hit at William Shakespeare, who had taken out a coat-of-arms in 1596, though he never called himself more than 'gentleman'. Five other members of his company followed his example; they all purchased lands and properties. Edward Alleyn became a rich landowner, and founder of Dulwich.

The decisive step in making the Elizabethan drama what it became was taken in 1576, when James Burbage – a joiner, and himself a player in his youth – built the Theatre and the little Curtain within the precincts of the former priory of Holywell in Shoreditch: one more visible sign of the secularisation of society consequent upon the Reformation. ('Curtain' has nothing to do with theatre-curtain, but refers to the curtain-wall of the enclosure.) Hitherto the favoured places for acting had been innyards and great halls, and this is reflected in the construction of the early theatres: there was the space of the pit for the 'groundlings' open to the skies, surrounded by galleries running up two or three storeys, as we can still see in a few old innyards; but the back of the stage, with its entrances, embrasure and minstrels' gallery above, comes straight from the arrangement of the medieval hall, as we still see them in historic houses and colleges. A number of the early stage-people were connected with inns, the clowns Tarleton and Shanks, for example, and Alleyn himself. Several inns continued as regular playing places – good for custom – along the highway from London Bridge north to Bishopsgate. There were, besides, the private playing places of the boys of St. Paul's within the cathedral precincts, and of the Children of the Chapel at Blackfriars. But the inns were within the jurisdiction of the City, and the City authorities were consistently opposed to the professional players. These honest bourgeois regarded the theatres as schools of vice and lust. We have seen earlier, with Simon Forman, that they did operate in this direction:[29] what of it?

From the 1570's things had been moving towards the pro-fessionalisation of dramatic activities: one aspect, as we can see now, of the increasing efficiency of society. As against the strolling players, quasi-vagabonds, of whom nasty things could be said– even the friendly Harsnet says, 'it is the fashion of vagabond players that coast from town to town with a truss and a cast of fiddles to carry in their consort broken queans and Ganymedes, as well for their night pleasance as their day's pastime'[30] – an Act of Parliament of 1572 licensed troupes, but restricted their number, and confirmed the status of the lords' companies, wearing the badge of their lord. This was no empty formality in so hier-archical a society: it gave them social recognition, it was a measure of protection, the players could always appeal to their lord in case of trouble. From 1559 Lord Robert Dudley – a great patron of the arts and a lord who 'loved a play and players' – had his men. Now, in 1574, when faced with the interferences and restrictions, the real ill-will, of the City authorities, Leicester's men obtained Letters Patent under the great seal, with his backing, establishing their right to act in London and all towns throughout the country, 'any act, statute, proclamation . . . to the contrary notwithstanding', provided that their plays were allowed by the Queen's Master of the Revels.[31] This was a triumph indeed; there was no going back on this, the players could only go forward. Their names were James Burbage, John Perkyn, John Laneham, William Johnson, Robert Wilson – most of them to become well-known figures in connection with the stage. This not only set them on the way, but set the pattern for others.

We may observe that there is a certain class-significance in this. The enemies of the theatre were apt to be tradespeople of the mercantile middle-class, whose allies were the preachers with their emphasis on proper vocation and the doctrine of work, and of course the Puritans. The City authorities embarked on three determined attempts to put down plays; each time the theatre emerged stronger than before – until the City won, two generations later, with the Civil War. Plays appealed, like other entertainments, to the average sensual man; and in the conflict over them we observe, not for the last time, the natural alliance of aristocracy and people, as against the more repressed and repressive middle class. The trump-card the theatre-people could always call upon was the Queen, and the necessity to train players and produce plays for her 'solace'. So the appeal of the drama was very wide: Court, nobility and people; university, inns of court and schools; with fringes of tradespeople and townsfolk, so that even the middle class was represented, not least by young people and apprentices. If not quite a universal appeal – the religious were insufficiently represented – it was sufficiently representative of the nation.

Thus the players won for themselves a new status and stability for their profession. After the defeat of the City's attempt to put them down during the years 1576–80, they received their final imprimatur from the Queen herself with the organisation of her company in 1583. Twelve of the leading actors were selected from the lords' companies, Leicester surrendering his three best men, including his famous clown Tarleton, the first to become a national star. This company proceeded to dominate the 1580's, until the death of both Tarleton and his patron, Leicester, in Armada year. That opened up prospects for new men, new patrons, already on the scene: for the next few years the stage was dominated by the Admiral's men with Alleyn, and Marlowe to write for them. Having achieved something like the fellowship of a gild organisation the players could call the tune, attract to themselves the poets and wits, and command their talents. We find them living in convenient proximity in and around Shoreditch: the Burbages lived there all their lives, Tarleton was buried in the parish church, Marlowe and Watson haunted the neighbourhood, Shakespeare lived close by in the earlier years.

Following in the wake of James Burbage came Philip Henslowe (his name was pronounced Hensley as Marlowe's was Marley). As Burbage took the lead in Shoreditch so Henslowe was the pioneer of Bankside, where the Liberty of the Clink in Southwark gave freedom from City jurisdiction. Henslowe, a poor young fellow, became well-off by following the common prescription of the time and marrying his master's widow. He was a jack-of-all-trades, with his finger in many pies, from property to starch-making. Entertainments, the Bear-Baiting, the theatre, formed only one side of his investments. He was an entrepreneur: he had not the inside experience of the theatre that Burbage had. So he welcomed the alliance with the brilliant actor, Ned Alleyn, who married his stepdaughter in 1592. It was a love-match, and also very good business. Alleyn, too, had been born in Bishopsgate; in addition to his genius as an actor – he was best for tragedy – he was a musician. His rival, and supplanter, Richard Burbage was no singer, but had a wider range. Alleyn also had a head for business and made an able partner for Henslowe; in the end business claimed him, and he left the stage for Burbage to take first place, with Shakespeare to write his parts for him. That combination, with the Chamberlain's men, later King's, came to win the ascendancy.

It is a thousand pities that the papers of the Burbages do not remain, as we have those of Henslowe and Alleyn, for we should have had perhaps the theatre-correspondence of Shakespeare and invaluable information about his plays. Henslowe's papers then give us our most intimate close-up of the life of these theatre-folk. In 1585 Henslowe bought the Little Rose inn, on the South Bank, and there built the Rose Theatre, which abutted conveniently on the well-patronised brothels, the Barge, the Bell and the Cock.[32] (It seems that when Ben Jonson killed the quarrelsome actor, Gabriel Spencer – he, too, was buried in Shoreditch church – his widow became the landlady of these much-used establishments.) Alleyn's letters home to his wife and her stepfather, when touring the country in the plague-year 1593, give us a picture of domestic bliss and bourgeois respectability on its way to affluence. Alleyn writes to his 'good sweetheart and loving mouse' from Chelmsford in May – he was touring with Lord Strange's men.[33] Then from Bristol in August, when the plague was at its height, with instructions for cleansing and fumigating. His mouse had written to him by the actor, Cowley; Alleyn replies, 'I have sent you by this bearer, Thomas Pope's kinsman, my white waistcoat, because it is a trouble to me to carry it . . . lay it up for me till I come . . . And, Jug, I pray you let my orange tawny stockings of woollen be dyed a very good black against I come home to wear in the winter.' He directs that any more letters be sent by the carriers to Shrews-

bury or Chester or York 'to be kept till my Lord Strange's players
come . . . and thus, sweetheart, I cease, from Bristol this Wednes-
day after St. James's day, being ready to begin the play of *Harry
of Cornwall.*'

Henslowe writes back to Alleyn in similar terms of affection:
they made a close-knit family circle of mutual trust and confidence,
and on that basis went on to make a fortune. Five years later
Henslowe is relying on Alleyn's advice about his purchase of the
Bear Garden: 'and therefore I would willingly that you were at
the banquet, for then I should be the merrier. Therefore if you
think as I think, it were fit that we were both here to do what we
might, and not as two friends but as two joined in one . . . Therefore I desire rather to have your company and your wife's than
your letters.'[34] This is the letter that informs Alleyn of the heavy
loss Henslowe has had in the death of Gabriel, 'for he is slain in
Hogsden fields by the hands of Benjamin Jonson, bricklayer.' Ben
Jonson was already the author of *Every Man in his Humour*, a great
success of the rival Chamberlain's men, with William Shakespeare
acting in it. We need shed no tears for Gabriel Spencer: he too had
killed his man in the house of a barber in Shoreditch a couple of
years before.[35] This serves to call attention to an aspect of theatre-
life, also characteristic of the time, in which Alleyn and Shakespeare, who rose to recognised social position as 'gentlemen', were
rather exceptional.

The most effective enemy of the players was plague: it provided not only an argument for the City authorities, but a means
of closing the theatres. The fact that there was plague two years
running in 1592 and 1593 meant a severe crisis for them. With
the theatres closed most of the time, they took to the roads, as
Alleyn did, but many of them were not so fortunate. In London
the actor, Robert Browne's whole family and household were
wiped out; from touring the country Pembroke's men came back
bankrupt, having to sell their apparel and playbooks. We may
infer from several Sonnets that Shakespeare was touring in the
country in both 1592 and 1593:[36]

> Alas, 'tis true I have gone here and there,
> And made myself a motley to the view,
> Gored mine own thoughts, sold cheap what is
>   most dear . . .

from which we may conclude that he was acting in his own plays
– and several of his earliest plays belonged to Pembroke's men. In

that year 1592 he was singled out for personal attack by the dying Robert Greene, best known literary journalist in London, leading writer of *novelle* (rather than novels), who had also written for the players and now felt himself deserted by them in his necessity. For his attack has a general significance: he was speaking for the writers, the poets and playwrights, who, in spite of their being university men and Masters of Arts, were now at the beck and call of the players. He gave an urgent death-bed warning to Marlowe, Nashe and Peele, 'base-minded men all three of you, if by my misery ye be not warned; for unto none of you, like me, sought those burrs to cleave: those puppets, I mean, that speak from our mouth, those antics garnished in our colours. Is it not strange that I, to whom they all have been beholding, is it not like that you, to whom they all have been beholding, shall – were ye in that case that I am now – be both at once of them forsaken?'[37]

There follows Greene's insulting reference to Shakespeare as an upstart actor, who has taken to writing plays and supposes that he can write blank verse as well as the best of them – parodying a successful line in his recent *3 Henry VI* – a perfect Johannes Factotum who could turn his hand to anything. The gravamen of the charge is that this man is an outsider, a mere actor who presumes to write plays, not one of the university wits, i.e. intellectuals, like Greene himself, Marlowe, Nashe, Peele and Lyly. The wounding implication was that he had beautified himself with their feathers, i.e. was not above plagiarising from them. What was recognisable in this was that the outsider, in fact, did learn from these by imitating them, and then going one better. Ben Jonson, who knew the facts better than anyone, resumed the actor-dramatist's progress in the craft with great conciseness:

> Thou who didst our Lyly and Kyd outshine,
> And Marlowe's mighty line.

Greene went on to call a curse down on his fellow-writers 'if they persevere to maintain any more such peasants', i.e. countrymen.

All this is immediately recognisable; but no less so to contemporaries would be the earlier passage in Greene's book, in which Roberto falls in with a countryman who turns out to be a player, i.e. whose profession was 'to get by scholars their whole living.'[38] 'What is your profession?' said Roberto. 'Truly, sir, I am a player.' 'A player!', quoth Roberto, 'I took you rather for a gentleman of great living; for, if by outward habit men should

be censured, I tell you you would be taken for a substantial man.'
'So I am where I dwell,' quoth the player, 'reputed able at my
proper cost to build a windmill. What though the world once
went hard with me, when I was fain to carry my playing-fardel a
footback? *Tempora mutantur*: I know you know the meaning of it
better than I; but thus I construe it: it is otherwise now, for my
very share in playing apparel will not be sold for £200.' 'Truly,'
said Roberto, 'it is strange that you should so prosper in that vain
practice, for that it seems to me your voice is nothing gracious.'
The player insists that besides playing, 'I can serve to make a
pretty speech, for I was a country author, passing at a moral . . .
and for seven years was absolute interpreter of the puppets.'* It is
just seven years since we last hear of Shakespeare at Stratford,
the birth of his twins in 1585. Who was the countryman with the
uncouth voice, who was both player and playwright? It is likely
that Shakespeare would have spoken with a West Midlands accent,
even if his spellings – 'smoake' and 'woonder' and 'kuckow' – had
not registered it for us.[39]

That Shakespeare much resented this humiliating attack upon
him is witnessed by his protesting to Chettle, who had published it.
He made a handsome apology, since he had now had the opportunity of seeing the player for himself, 'his demeanor no less civil
than he excellent in the quality he professes' – Elizabethan English
for his bearing being as gentlemanly as his acting was admirable.[40]
'Besides, divers of worship have reported his uprightness of dealing, which argues his honesty, and his facetious grace in writing
that approves his art.' This was a testimonial indeed: it indicates
Shakespeare's preference for better society than that of literary
Bohemia – he had already been taken up by young Southampton
– apart from the tribute to his writing, which could speak for
itself. The player was a more honest citizen than the late Robert
Greene: 'ask the Queen's players if you sold them not *Orlando
Furioso* for twenty nobles, and when they were in the country
sold the same play to the Lord Admiral's men for as many more.'[41]
So an anonymous writer had charged Greene, who, 'I hear, when

---

* There is no doubt that Roberto's story is autobiographical. Notice, p. 25, 'the
shameful end of sundry his consorts . . . of which one, brother to a brothel he kept,
was trussed under a tree round as a Ball.' This is a reference to Greene's whore, sister
of Cutting Ball, a notorious cutpurse who was hanged at Tyburn. In the story the
player ends by inviting Roberto, poet and scholar, to pen plays, 'for which you shall
be well paid . . . Roberto, perceiving no remedy, thought best, in respect of his present
necessity, to try his wit and went with him willingly: who lodged him at the town's
end in a house of retail.' It may be that something happened between Greene and
Shakespeare to account for the former's personal animosity.

this was objected, made this excuse: that there was no more faith to be held with players than with them that valued faith at the price of a feather. For, as they were comedians to act, so the actions of their lives were chameleon-like; that they were uncertain, variable, time-pleasers, men that measured honesty by profit, and that regarded their authors not by desert but by necessity of time.'

This was the background to Greene's obvious jealousy of the players who were on their way up as he was on his way out, and now, to add insult to injury, had produced a playwright of their own, ready to challenge anyone.

Those years of confusion and stress owing to plague called only a brief halt in the progress of the drama. Already it was achieving maturity with the acting of Alleyn and the writing of Marlowe. A fresh appreciation of the drama in terms of theatre – as against bookishness – brings out its dependence on actual stage conditions. These literally *conditioned* the drama, as has not been fully appreciated before: the character of the stage and stage-production, the nature of the audience thus regularly attracted, the interaction between familiar actors and regular audience, achieving something like an integration as never since; the emergence of individual actors, stars in their Heavens; the integration of a company into a fellowship by their constant playing together in the same theatre; the necessity to write the plays according to the talent available, to double the parts to fit the cast; the influence of all this on the dramatic writing. We have for centuries seen it too much as literature: we should see it as theatre, first and foremost – as Shakespeare certainly did. It is not surprising that the writer who was most completely the man of the theatre eventually came out on top. But even with Marlowe, who was not an actor, we see how the players called the tune, the stage-conditions determined the play. All his great parts, Tamburlaine, the Jew of Malta, Dr. Faustus, were written for Alleyn and the Admiral's men; his last play, *Edward II*,* where the parts are more equally distributed, was performed by Pembroke's men, who had no star among them.

Elizabethan acting was declamatory, gestural and stylised – we must not think of it in modern naturalistic terms. The actor's delivery was that of the orator, addressed to the audience even more than to the stage. After all, at school they had been trained

* Since writing my *Christopher Marlowe: A Biography*, in which I considered *Dr Faustus* his last play, I incline to think *Edward II* later.

in rhetoric, and the emphasis here was on making boys pronounce, i.e. speak out. There was a whole language of signs, which the audience would understand, where we might not: a text-book gives a hundred ways of using the hands, each with its meaning – the left, for example, always for thieving. (So Autolycus's neat transfers should be left-handed.) 'To frisk the thighs together [we should not know how to perform that] is a sign of indignation and stirreth up the hearer.'[42] There was a great deal of stamping the foot: a stage direction for Reagan, reading her sister's letter in *The Chronicle History of King Leir*, reads, 'She reads the letter, frowns, and stamps', which the messenger reinforces with:

> See how she knits her brow and bites her lips,
> And stamps, and makes a dumb show of disdain,
> Mixed with revenge and violent extremes.

The drama was very sententious, as the whole of life was – even more so than medieval life, with which it was continuous; but now there was a new society to be educated. Wherever one looks at interiors of the time, in house or church, they are plastered with moralising sentences. (The same is true throughout Western Europe: one thinks of the inscriptions in public places, on gateways, monuments,[43] or in the privacy of Montaigne's chamber, where he could look up at the ceiling and renew wisdom from the pithy sentences of the ancients.) In the drama these sentences took the form of rhymed couplets punctuating the blank verse at intervals, bringing a section to a close. For the rest the play flowed on and on its two hours without the interruption of act- or scene-divisions, flowed up and over one, until one was submerged in the tide of rhetoric and action, words and gesture: moved to rapture or, if one was disappointed, to corresponding hisses and hoots of derision. We have plenty of evidence as to both, such was the double hazard of playing so closely to the audience, that the whole thing was knit together to a degree we can hardly conceive with the modern picture-stage.

Elizabethan psychology held that it was natural to express the emotions, they were not to be repressed (excepting always the Puritans, and they directed them elsewhere – with sometimes distasteful results).[44] Hence the expressive quality of life, going straight over into the theatre, and the immediate response of the audience. Stephen Gosson, a reformed penner of plays on his way into the Church – he would have been schooled in them at King's School, Canterbury, and tells us he was 'instructed' in them at the university – reports how the audience at a public play-house 'generally take up a wonderful laughter and shout all together with one voice when they see some notable cosenage practised, or some sly conveyance of bawdry brought out of Italy.'[45] Even he could not resist a comedy: 'comedies make our delight exceed, for at them many times we laugh so extremely that, striving to bridle ourselves, we cannot – delight being moved with variety of shows, of events, of music, the longer we gaze, the more we crave', and, remembering our delight, we go again.[46] Delight is the effective word. Despite all that preachers can urge against them, 'yet will not my countrymen leave their plays, because plays are the nourishers of delight.' With so naif and spontaneous an audience, the passions observed on the stage communicated themselves to the beholders, one might almost say, the partakers. A scene of love-making, with so suggestible an audience, had the effect that 'the beholders rose up, every man stood on tiptoe and seemed to hover over the prey; when they sware, the company sware; when they departed to bed, the company presently [i.e. immediately] was set on fire: they that were married posted home to their wives, they that were single vowed very solemnly to be wedded.'[47] For the rest, other resort was open: the theatres were a place to make assignations, and the brothels stood very convenient.

To this Heywood could reply that the theatre incited patriotism no less. 'To turn to our domestic histories: what English blood, seeing the person of any bold Englishmen presented, and doth not hug his fame and honey [delight] at his valour, pursuing him in his enterprise with his best wishes and, as being rapt in contemplation, offers to him in his heart all prosperous performance, as if the personator were the man personated? So bewitching a thing is lively and well-spirited action that it hath power to new-mould the hearts of the spectators. . . . What coward, to see his countryman valiant, would not be ashamed of his own cowardice?'[48] He goes on to cite the patriotic inspiration of the medieval English kings', especially Henry V's, descents upon France. Nashe cites the example of Talbot, doughty campaigner in France in the last stages of the Hundred Years War: 'how it would have joyed brave Talbot, the terror of the French, to think that, after he had lain two hundred years in his tomb, he should triumph again on the stage and have his bones embalmed with the tears of ten thousand spectators at least, at several times, who, in the tragedian that represents his person, imagine they behold him fresh bleeding.'[49] That was an element in the success of Shakespeare's *Henry VI* plays – as also that they were timed to coincide with Essex's campaign in Normandy in 1591. The Elizabethans, keyed up by the Armada years, the exploits of Drake and the voyagers, the renewed war on the Continent as in the days of Henry V and Henry VI, were addicts of history plays – much more noticeably than in any other country. They appealed not only to their sense of community, as it is fashionable to say, but to their patriotism – why not say it? Patriotism and the sense of the English past were an inspiration. William Shakespeare, who responded to both, made them an inspiration in his work and, a complete man of the theatre, gave the public more of what they wanted, and better, than anyone.

And the response of the audience? Leonard Digges tells us:

> So have I seen when Caesar would appear,
> And on the stage at half-sword parley were
> Brutus and Cassius – O, how the audience
> Were ravished! With what wonder they went thence!
> When some new day they would not brook a line
> Of tedious, though well-laboured, *Catiline*.
> *Sejanus* too was irksome, they prized more
> 'Honest' Iago, or the jealous Moor.[50]

Or Dekker, that honest craftsman of the public theatres, exclaims,

> Give me that man . . .
> Can draw, with adamantine pen, even creatures
> Forged out of the hammer, on tip-toe to reach up
> And, from rare silence, clap their brawny hands
> To applaud what their charmed soul scarce understands.[51]

Well, understanding is on different levels: a good many people understand emotionally, or intuitively, what they cannot express intellectually. That is what the players and playwrights were for: to express it for them.

The drama was the most social of all the arts, depending upon player, playwright, audience – in that order – and even upon entrepreneur, manager, hired men, scrivener, doorkeeper (James Burbage, in early days, collected the cash himself). We have been apt to think of it too much, if not solely, in terms of writing. Even the building itself reflected the social structure, with its grading of seats: 'The relation of one part of the audience to the rest also imposes a social relation which moulds the total dramatic response.'[52] We know that the audience was acutely aware of itself;

there was the vibrant reaction of the sexes to each other, described by Gosson; some sections went to be seen as well as to see – the lords above the stage, in their room or box, and in the private theatres they sat on the stage. Then there was the symbolism of the throne itself, not only apex of the society but the linch-pin without which it could not hold together. (Over now – as everything is over, save only art.) 'For centuries kings had been presented to the public, whether real kings in public ceremonies or actor-kings in plays and pageants, in a throne backed by a symbol of the realm . . . The Elizabethan stage had absorbed all these medieval symbols. Its background structure resembled a castle, a throne, a city gate, a tomb or an altar: it was a symbol of social order and of divine order.'[53]

Similarly 'the players were ideal instruments with which to portray the spiritual qualities which went with the different ranks and occupations of the "persons of the drama".'[54] In their society a lord was expected to behave, as well as dress, like a lord; a commoner like a commoner. The drama reflected the society. In 1563 an observer of the social structure, in a book on the nobility, says 'how hiss we out a well-apparelled player if, counterfeiting a king on the stage, he fail of his gesture, speak yawning, have a sour and harsh voice . . . or use unseemly gesture for so stately a personage!' Kings behaved like kings: when King John despaired in a sea of troubles, he is admonished by Faulconbridge:

> Let not the world see fear and sad distrust
> Govern the motion of a kingly eye:
> Be stirring as the time, be fire with fire,
> Threaten the threatener, and outface the brow
> Of bragging horror: so shall inferior eyes,
> That borrow their behaviours from the great,
> Grow great by your example, and put on
> The dauntless spirit of resolution.

We may conceive how much greater was the dramatic effect of the fall of kings, when people really believed

> There's such divinity doth hedge a king:

'the shock to Elizabethan sensibilities provided by the spectacle of the gentle, saintly Henry VI bending his anointed head submissively in surrender to his own misguided subjects'; the bitterness of Hamlet's 'That it should come to this', but two months after his father, the king, was in his grave, the corruption that ran through the whole state of Denmark with the usurpation of the throne.[55] Perhaps we should remember here the old tradition that Shakespeare himself played kingly parts:

> Some say, good Will, which I in sport do sing,
> Had thou not played some kingly parts in sport
> Thou hadst been a companion for a king,
> And lived a king among the meaner sort.[56]

Similarly, comic behaviour was for commoners. 'Just as the nobility of the superiors was shown in speech with facility of gesture, so the commonness of commoners is expressed in the lack of these accomplishments . . . The ordinary commoner was not "exercised in speaking" . . . Conversely to bring grand personages into comedy shatters the familiar style, unless the nobles are treated in such a way that they are no longer in bearing; and that to the Renaissance mind would have been a contradiction in terms . . . The nobles of popular drama, like those of classical tragedy, are not perfect; but, except in the case of specialised satire striking at individuals, not a class, their imperfections are not portrayed in such a style as to make the nobleman seem a commoner. Nor is the commoner shown as grand.'[57] Such an articulated society, with its greater variety and interest, gave far more scope for dramatic effects than the kitchen-sink theatre of today or the trash-bins of Samuel Beckett – really no more than an interior monologue: not drama at all. (What should we think of Elizabethan drama if it consisted only of soliloquy?) A one-class society naturally expresses itself in a less subtle and complex, a callow, literature – compare the literature of Soviet Russia with that of nineteenth-century Russia, or, for that matter, the world of Henry James with that of Saul Bellow. When we know how the social structure and outlook are expressed in the theatre, then we perhaps appreciate how wrongly we interpret without a proper knowledge of it. For example, the usual literary misconception of Prince Hal's relation to Falstaff and his dismissal of him: it is not only anachronistic and a-political, but it understands neither the purpose of the Prince's disguising nor his conversion on coming to the kingship.[58]

The audience itself reflected the integration of the society – during those blissful decades that constitute the Elizabethan age, before things began to fall apart with the Stuarts: with the end of the unifying effect of the war upon the nation and increasing internal strains, particularly the conflict for power. 'Shakespeare's audience was literally popular, ascending from each gradation from potboy to prince. It was the one to which he had been conditioned early and for which he never ceased to write. It thrived for a time, it passed quickly, and its like has never existed since ... The drama reached its peak when the audience formed a great amalgam, and it began its decline when the amalgam was split in two.'[59] We appreciate now what Shakespeare owed to his reciprocity with that audience, as of course he would with his 'fabulously acute sense of the theatre.' We must not, however, fall over backwards – though democratically – as if the audience wrote the plays![60] Only genius does that – and that is even more important. The theatre gave it its chance, provided the conditions, and shaped its expression.

Along with the development of the public theatres there was the intermittent accompaniment of the boys' companies, their sweet or piping trebles counterpointing the heavier fa-burden of the men. Until the formation of the Queen's men in 1583, the boys' companies, those of St. Paul's and those of the Chapel, had the lead in performances at Court, and when we read the plays of Lyly we can see why. After neglecting his studies at Magdalen (in spite of being Burghley's scholar), he went down and was taken up by Burghley's scapegrace son-in-law, Oxford, who was interested in boys and their acting. Lyly's, *Euphues* had taken the sophisticated and courtly public by storm in 1579–80 ; then, as assistant-master (or, as Harvey unkindly said, Vice-master) of Paul's boys, he directed more performances of theirs at Court than any adult company.

The language of the Court was the language of love, but it was the discourse of fantasy, artificial, with scholarly and romantic overtones, like the courtly entertainments: a similar idiom attuned to the presence of the Queen and often similarly addressed to her. Take a characteristic play of Lyly's, *Endimion*, played before her at Greenwich one Candlemas night. (We have a contemporary reference to the boys coming back one such winter's night up-river, cold and sick, and the payment for coals to warm them up by the fire.) Endimion pines for the love of regal and inaccessible Cynthia, for whom he has deserted his former love. The latter employs a witch to charm him into a forty-year spell upon a moon-bank, from which only a kiss from Cynthia can recover him. The plot is complicated by Endimion's former love being imprisoned and ultimately paired-off with her gaoler. In the end Cynthia's chaste kiss awakens Endimion and her gracious allowance of his faithful love restores his youth.

Several attempts have been made to construct a rigid allegory, making a close parallel between actual events and the play.[61] A subtler knowledge of history should enable us to appreciate that no such precise an allegory could be enacted before the Queen. All that can be said is that it portrays in allowable fashion a suspension of Leicester's favour, and a permissible plea for its restoration. This was quite regular form, with Leicester, Hatton, Ralegh, Essex, one after the other. The situation was familiar, all expressed with profound deference, addressed to the Queen directly throughout the play: she was present, she was also Cynthia. Beyond that one cannot go: there are only flecks of reality. Endimion's former lover is imprisoned; there is the slightest suggestion of the supposed relation between Mary Stuart and her gaoler, the Earl of Shrewsbury. But there is really nothing beyond the fact that Cynthia and Endimion are Elizabeth and Leicester. To suppose that there is any rigid allegory is to misconceive how a creative writer works.

For Lyly was a creative writer, and it is his literary qualities and effects that matter. He was all elegance and refinement, as befitted one whose writings were directed to the Court, his plays for representation before Cynthia: no bawdy, nothing coarse, nothing beyond the remotely suggestive. Yet the language is always that of love – as Ralegh said, the Queen kept it up too long (but he said it after she was dead). Lyly's plays have a moony, silvery atmosphere, with their emphasis on the element of dream: 'Remember, all is but a poet's dream.' It is a world of escape from the harsh realities and strains of politics, that occupied the inner mind of a ruling Queen. Lyly's function was to provide relaxation, not high drama; his intention to move inward delight, soft smiling not loud laughing. His easy dialogue, with quip and repartee, his word-play catechising for meanings, with proverbs from common use to catch the ear – from this Shakespeare learned attentively and, picking up something from everywhere (as Greene had charged), from this very play he picked up the name of Sir Tophas, as the name Dromio from *Mother Bombie*.

During the 1590's the boys' companies lapsed, and with them Lyly's career was extinguished. But he had made his contribution to the greater things now coming into existence. Though without force or passion, he was a man of taste with many talents and with a particular appeal for women, much to the fore at Court. After the resolution of the theatre crisis of 1597, the boys started up again at the private theatre in Blackfriars. Here, as before, they appealed to a more select and refined audience, with their combination of fantasy and satire, turned out with music, in which they excelled. Entrance to a private, indoor theatre was more expensive, so were the tastes for which they catered – the tastes of a cultivated minority. Marlowe had written his *Dido*, with its suggestive episode between Jupiter and Ganymede, for the Children of the Chapel. Now in 1598 Ben Jonson wrote his first comedy, *The Case is Altered*, for the boys at Blackfriars; this is the beginning of his long connection with them. For the boys of the Chapel he wrote *Cynthia's Revels* and the *Poetaster*, and for those of the Revels his *Epicoene or The Silent Woman*.

Altogether, the boys' companies had a distinguished run of playwrights to serve them, from Richard Edwardes to Lyly and Marlowe, then Ben Jonson, Middleton and Jonson's pupil and boy-actor, Nathan Field, whom he trained and educated. Nathan, who became a star in Shakespeare's company, was the son of the indefatigable Puritan organiser, John Field, castigator of the stage, who had reproached his (political, not moral) leader, Leicester, for originally yielding to the players, 'to the great grief of all the godly.'[62] For the rest, we may recall Jonson's touching epitaph on one of his boy-actors, 'Solomon Pavy, a Child of Queen Elizabeth's Chapel':[63]

> Years he numbered scarce thirteen
> When fates turned cruel,
> Yet three filled zodiacs had he been
> The stage's jewel;
> And did act, what now we moan,
> Old men so duly
> As, sooth, the Parcae thought him one,
> He played so truly.

A turning point in the history of the public theatres was reached after the stress of the plague years with the formation of the Lord Chamberlain's company in 1594, 'destined to become the most famous and most successful in the history of the English theatre.'[64] Once more the initiative was taken by James Burbage, but now his son Richard was a star-actor, so was Will Kemp, the comedian; no less important was Will Shakespeare, the player who was also playwright. It was a promising combination, and that these three players were co-sharers from the start appears from their taking payment for the new company's performance at Court their first Christmas. This element of co-partnership, further extended in 1598, helped forward the company's swift rise to first place. Another was the withdrawal from acting of the foremost rival, Alleyn, while the Henslowe-Alleyn combination, so far from having the advantage of co-partnership, became further removed from the immediate running of its theatre. A third factor was the more than fulfilment of the hopes in the new company's dramatist.

Shakespeare's patron during the plague years, the young Southampton, had rewarded his poet by enabling him to purchase a share in the company at its foundation. To it he also brought a number of his earlier plays, notably the *Henry VI* trilogy. But we must not forget the persistent popularity of Marlowe's plays, which always provided a draw for the Admiral's men. This offered a challenge that his junior proceeded to meet with his first masterpiece, *Richard III*, with Burbage's creation of the part remembered long after he was dead. Those years of stress left more important marks. In 1592 Greene and Thomas Watson, Marlowe's friend, died; in 1593 Marlowe was killed in a brawl over the reckoning in the tavern at Deptford; towards the end of 1594 Thomas Kyd died; George Peele, after long sickness, died of the pox a couple of years later. Lyly's talent was unsuited to the public stage and, discouraged of his hope of ever becoming Master of the Revels, he was silent. The way was thus clear for the actor-dramatist to make the most of his unchallenged opportunity; after a long, hard-working apprenticeship luck was at last with him as with no one else. For the next few years, until the emergence of Ben Jonson and Chapman among the younger generation, he had things very much to himself.

This was confirmed after the theatre troubles of 1597, provoked by a topical play at the Swan by Nashe and Ben Jonson, *The Isle of Dogs*, reflecting on government – a mistake that the prudent, conformist countryman never made. A Privy Council order commanded the plucking down of the theatres – even if it was only a threat held in reserve.[65] The Burbages plucked down their ancient playhouse, the Theatre, in Shoreditch, and used the materials to build an up-to-date new house, to meet the requirements of their company: the Globe, on the South Bank. A couple of years previously they had bought the Blackfriars for eventual use as an indoor theatre; but, not obtaining licence to play, were fain to lease it out to the boys of Paul's. To raise money to build and furnish the fine new theatre, Cuthbert Burbage parted with a half-share in its ownership to six of the actors, of whom Shakespeare was one. These were now not only co-sharers but part-owners: this gave still further incentive to the company, as never before or since, a close cohesion as one functioning unit. With the exception of Kemp, who left after a couple of years, the fellows of the Company remained in good fellowship the rest of their days, prospered together, remembered each other in their wills and, after their fellow Shakespeare's death, brought out what they could collect of his plays, without which the bulk of his work would have been lost for ever.

As has been said, 'he was a member of a kind of theatrical enterprise, which had the best actors (Burbage and his colleagues), the best theatres (the Globe and the Blackfriars), the best official patronage (the Lord Chamberlain and, later, the King), and, as one of the company, the best dramatist. It seems a certain recipe for success.'[66] The company was able to open with a new masterpiece by its actor-dramatist, *Henry V*. It needs no stretch of imagination to see that he himself probably played the part of the Chorus, with its very personal inflexion and references to the new theatre:

> But pardon, gentles all,
> The flat unraised spirits that hath dared
> On this unworthy scaffold to bring forth
> So great an object. Can this cockpit hold
> The vasty fields of France? Or may we cram
> Within this wooden O the very casques
> That did affright the air at Agincourt?

And again, at the end, with his usual tactful courting of the audience – so unlike Ben Jonson:

> Thus far, with rough and all-unable pen,
> Our bending author hath pursued the story,
> In little room confining mighty men,
> Mangling by starts the full course of their glory.
> Small time – but in that small most greatly lived
> This star of England.

The author concludes by knitting this play with the *Henry VI* plays, 'which oft our stage hath shown', and with which he had first won notice.

The so-called War of the Theatres, which raised so much dust in 1600–1, began as a quarrel between Ben Jonson and his admirer, John Marston, who – Ben thought – had caricatured him. Its importance for us is that it was in part a quarrel between the public and the private theatre: it portended the growing split within the public, the end of Elizabethan integration and national unity. We are observing the transition to the Jacobean age: from the Shakespearean to the Jonsonian.

Shakespeare had given his burly, rumbustious junior by eight years – ugly, pock-marked face with fine eyes – his big chance by putting on his *Every Man in his Humour* and himself acting in it. At one step Shakespeare brought forward his younger rival, whose play opened up a new vein of satirical comedy, and who was shortly to surpass his senior in critical esteem, though not in the devotion of the public. Jonson, with his quarrelsomeness, his dominating personality, his self-will and self-esteem, along with his genuine intellectual superiority, always made trouble for himself and had a much more troubled life than his elder – for one thing, he always took risks. He had had a hard and difficult beginning: in the course of the quarrel this arrogant would-be literary dictator (in the end he achieved something of this position) was reminded, 'thou hast forgot how thou ambledst in a leather pilch [overcoat] by a play-wagon in the highway and tookst mad Jeromino's part to get service among the mimics.'[67] At least he had taken the leading part in Kyd's famous tragedy; but Jonson was not a good actor.

Taking umbrage easily, as he always did, he moved his pitch to the boys of the Chapel, now playing again at Blackfriars, for whom he wrote *Cynthia's Revels* and the *Poetaster* and proceeded to attack the public theatres. Marston and Dekker replied on their behalf with *Satiromastix*. The truth is that, in spite of Jonson's disclaimer in the Prologue to *Epicoene*, he despised the public: he respected the judgment only of the few, and even then only when they agreed with him. He was essentially a man of the private theatre (and of Court masques) with its specialised appeal. This point has been rather overlooked by people emphasising that his masterpieces were performed by Shakespeare's company – *Volpone* and *The Alchemist* – but they were written for the Blackfriars audience, after the company had taken it over in 1608. Even so, when Jonson published the new version of *Every Man in his Humour* in his *Works* in 1616, he could not refrain from reflecting on the public stage and its most popular dramatist – who had been willing to purchase delight

> with three rusty swords,
> And help of some few foot and half-foot words,
> Fight over York and Lancaster's long jars . . .

He himself wrote plays,

> such as other plays should be,
> Where neither Chorus wafts you o'er the seas,
> Nor creaking throne come down the boys to please –

– as in *Henry V*, *Henry VI*, *Richard II* and *Richard III*.

The fact was that Shakespeare (and his constant and continued success) bothered Jonson, as H. G. Wells confessed himself to have been 'bothered' by Henry James – though the writing rôles were reversed. It riled Jonson that the older man could proceed serenely on without attending to the critical rules of 'art' – it is fair to say not only Jonson's rules, but the rules laid down for Renaissance drama, as much by Sidney as by Jonson, and exemplified by Jonson as, say, by Garnier. Again and again Jonson comes back to it, not exactly in an ill-natured way: he is just bothered. He could not approve of *Julius Caesar*: it was not written according to the rules of classical tragedy. His own *Sejanus* and *Catiline* were – but the public could not abide them. In fact, both *Julius Caesar* and *Coriolanus* have a definite classic quality, but it is Shakespeare's version of the classic, following his own genius – and the public responded as ever. Still less could Jonson approve the romantic fantasies with which Shakespeare could appeal to all audiences, Globe, Blackfriars and the Court. 'If there be never a servant-monster [i.e. a Caliban] in the Fair', wrote Jonson in introducing *Bartholomew Fair*, 'who can help it? – nor a nest of antics . . . like those that beget *Tales*, *Tempests*, and suchlike drolleries.' Of *Pericles*, a fascinating experiment with which Shakespeare tried his hand with the Blackfriars audience, of which we get only a muffled idea from the ruined state of the text that has come down to us, Jonson says grumpily:

> No doubt some mouldy tale
> Like *Pericles* . . .
> May keep up the Play-club.

It did: it was immensely popular.

No doubt it was vexing that success came so easily to Shakespeare by following his infallible instinct for (as well as life-long experience of) the theatre, without blotting a line; while Jonson had to work hard, and according to the book, for his grudging

and limited successes. When one reads his plays one is often surprised that they should succeed on the boards at all, and one is
frankly bored by the constant tone of self-assertion and self-
justification that runs all through his many Prologues and Prefaces. Yet some of his plays do come off on the stage – usually
when he gives full scope to his intellectual high spirits and suspends the rules. All the same, they are written by intellect and
industry, rather than with heart and soul, though these make
occasional brief appearance, particularly in his comedy.

Jonson may not have known that Shakespeare's opposite-
number in Spain as popular dramatist, Lope de Vega, expounded
a similar practice. He knew very well that Aristotle had laid down
the rules, and that Terence and Plautus were the models to follow
for comedy. 'But what can a playwright do? The people, the whole
nation, demands that things be otherwise. The audience stays
away when he composes in accordance with all these excellent
principles . . . The audience pays for plays, and so the taste of the
audience must be followed.'[68] Lope confessed, with something of
Shakespeare's modesty, that of over four hundred of his plays all
but six were wanting in regard to correct principles of dramatic
art. But Lope's plays were alive – and so much the worse for
principles, we might add.

Shakespeare himself had something to say both with regard to
the nature of acting and to the row between the public and private
theatres. Blackfriars for the moment was all the fashion, and no
doubt the fashionable elements were preferring it to the Globe.
Blackfriars offered pointed, satirical comment, sometimes personal
and topical – perhaps all the more shrill in boys' voices – music
in more sophisticated surroundings with an upper-class *clientèle*,
the inside pleasure of intimate revue, sometimes the scandalous
suggestiveness of *Beyond the Fringe*. Shakespeare has his comment
on them in *Hamlet*: 'an aery of children, little eyases, that cry out
on the top of the question and are most tyrannically clapped for
it.' No one has noticed the characteristically bawdy suggestion of
'little eyases'.* Why does he call them that? To raise a laugh.
Everyone then would know the suggestion frequently made –
against Ben Jonson among others – as to the relation between the
actors and their boys. 'These are now the fashion, and so berattle
the common stages – *so they call them* – that many wearing rapiers
are afraid of goose-quills and dare scarce come thither.' Hamlet
says: 'Will they pursue the quality no longer than they can sing?

* The literal meaning is young hawks just out of the nest.

Will they not say afterwards, if they should themselves grow to *common players* . . . their writers do them wrong to make them exclaim against their own succession?' This was just what happened to Jonson's favourite, Nathan Field, one of the Chapel boys, who graduated to becoming a King's Man. Nevertheless, for the moment the boys were carrying it away . . . 'Hercules and his load, too,' which meant the Globe itself.

The remedy became obvious in time: to take over the Blackfriars.

This was accomplished in 1608. It was a new development of great significance for Shakespeare's company and for the future of the English theatre. The Globe had been the most attractive playhouse in London, from the players' and playwrights' point of view, designed to meet their requirements and for the company's exclusive use. The annexation of the Blackfriars increased the spread of their appeal, but involved a change of policy. Here was a more select and financially rewarding audience, here were different demands and conditions to be catered for, a new challenge for the master. A few years later Shakespeare bought himself a convenient lodging over the gatehouse into Blackfriars: it registers the fact that he had transferred his main interest there. Still more so do the plays of his last period – the experimental nature of *Pericles* and *Cymbeline*, capped by the mastery in a new genre of *The Winter's Tale* and *The Tempest*. (The news-letter from Virginia that suggested *The Tempest* was written by a former Blackfriars resident.)

Shakespeare continued to write for the public theatre and its popular audience. It was as the result of a couple of cannon being shot off during a performance of *Henry VIII* that the Globe burned down in 1613. Though it was immediately rebuilt with ease, from the resources of this rich company, the destruction was in a way prophetic. The future was with the private theatre – from which our modern stage has developed. The Elizabethan age was going over: Shakespeare sang its farewell, with a personal note of nostalgia, in Cranmer's speech at the baptism of Elizabeth in this same play, his last, *Henry VIII*.

The most complete man of the theatre of them all had been characterised from the first by his ability to turn his hand to anything, by the flexibility of his response to theatre-conditions, by the way the challenge of the theatre expanded his genius – how much superior the poetry of the plays is to that of the undramatic poems! Just as he had responded to the recruiting of the curiously gifted actor, Armin, by creating for him the idiosyncratic parts of Touchstone, Feste, the gravedigger in *Hamlet*, the Fool in *King Lear*, so now he catered for more select tastes with the psychotic character of Leontes, the fantasy world of these last plays. They may not have been wholly approved by Ben Jonson, but they were to the taste of the Blackfriars audience, for whom Beaumont and Fletcher continued the genre. And Ben himself was recruited for the less popular and more intellectual tastes to which he appealed.

Tastes were becoming categorised, the audience splitting, class-differences accentuated, like the society which it mirrored. What was characteristic of the greatest of Elizabethans in the theatre of which he was the most complete representative was the width and spread of his appeal. Shakespeare's tastes were aristocratic and popular, not *bourgeois*. He was himself a middle-class man bent on becoming a gentleman; but at a royal command, he was as capable of writing a *bourgeois* comedy as Dekker's *A Shoemaker's Holiday*: the characters of *The Merry Wives of Windsor* are recognisably good citizens of Stratford, the environment that of his home-town. The earlier Elizabethan audience had been naively keen on history, they could not have enough of the chronicles of England – all very natural in the years before and after the Armada, with their redoubled sense of national solidarity in time of danger, the excitement and the inspiration. Shakespeare gave them more of what they wanted in this kind than any other playwright.

The attitude of mind expressed, the outlook on life and society, their conflicts and problems, were in keeping with all this. It is only to be expected that the taste of the more sophisticated and upper-class audience of the private theatres would be less common and demotic, less rounded and whole, perhaps even less wholesome, than the great heart of the people. A select public would want something new and less platitudinous, more piquant – we do not have to be moralistic about it.[69] Christopher Marlowe had written for the public theatres and he was not much of a moralist, still less of a democrat. William Shakespeare was a more sensitive man, with an acute dislike of cruelty. With his nature he would have been bound to be a proponent of social order, since he knew too well that, when it is undermined and a country is plunged into confusion and civil conflict, individual human beings suffer all the more – and more of them suffer. The ice of civilisation is very thin, and there are deep waters beneath: it is important to keep the crust intact. In the way nature has of imitating art, this was brought home to people in the generation after: if Shakespeare had lived to be eighty he would have seen Charles I's Queen in his own house at Stratford, in the distress of an odious Civil War, the ruin wrought by a recapitulation of the conditions of the time of Henry VI and the Wars of the Roses.

In any case, William Shakespeare was a conservative and a conformist. Like Montaigne he had too wise and profoundly sceptical a view of human nature to think it sense to upset the natural arrangements of society for hypothetical gain and evident illusions. He was never the one to get into trouble with government for religious 'convictions' on either side, or for criticising government or reflecting on its beasts of burden. So many other playwrights did, one after the other, and got into trouble – Marlowe, Kyd, Nashe, Jonson, Middleton – but William Shakespeare never. He certainly knew as well as Marlowe or Ben Jonson, as well as anybody ever did, what fools people are. That being so – and no one ever knew better the truth about human nature – he drew the proper conclusions, naturally, with complete consistency, with no difficulty or sense of strain. (Unlike Milton, whose low view of ordinary human beings is in complete contradiction to his expectations of them: he was the very type of a doctrinaire.)

With far better knowledge of men, Shakespeare knew that society needed order and people direction; that society was best organised hierarchically, according to their function and calling and natural aptitudes; that some few must govern, the rest obey – indeed most people are incapable of self-government (as Communist countries know very well – no liberal illusions in those quarters). Therefore he believed in order and degree, authority and obedience, with monarchy at the apex, and everybody's duty to take his part according to his sphere. If a ruler is no good at his job then he goes, his fall all the more resounding and bloodier than that of a commoner, the ineptitude of ordinary mortals a matter for comedy throughout the plays. There is a sense in which the comic spirit is profoundly conservative – doctrinaires have not much sense of humour. (Did John Milton ever make a joke?)

The assumptions and character of Elizabethan society were borne out in the rise of the players. Half a dozen fellows of Shakespeare's company took out coats of arms. Heming and Condell became property-owners in the parish of St. Mary Aldermanbury, where they lie buried. Edward Alleyn was disappointed of a knighthood just at the end – which he should have had for the scale of his public benefactions. His father-in-law Henslowe had been made a Groom of the Chamber. At James's coming-in he took the Chamberlain's men under his patronage: as such all the partners in the company became Grooms of the Chamber, officially members of the Household. The Stuarts, opting as cultivated persons for the theatre as against the Puritans, improved the status of the players, doubled the number of performances and their remuneration compared with the Queen's time. 'The Crown aligned itself unmistakably with the theatre', we are told, and – somewhat summarily – 'prompted all those who were its enemies to align themselves against the monarchy.'[70] It fell to Shakespeare's daughter to entertain Henrietta Maria at New Place in 1643; his granddaughter, last of his stock, died in 1670 as Lady Barnard.

By then the Elizabethan theatre had passed into history. Aware as we are of the myopia of mere criticism *in vacuo*, we are the less surprised that, where contemporary critics hardly noticed the popular theatres or the players, foreigners regarded them as the glory of their country and almost the only one. All visitors to the little country on the fringe of European civilisation noticed the splendour of the London playhouses. Ambassadors were entertained with performances of plays, or sought them out themselves. At a time when no one thought it worth while to learn the language or translate an English book, the Elizabethan drama and its performers were, along with the musicians, the country's only cultural exports. English players were all over Northern Europe – especially Germany: an interesting return for the import of Lutheranism, theology, and German mining technicians.[71] Robert Browne spent most of his acting career in Germany, between 1590 and 1620; he had many associates with him at different times, setting going a group of companies. John Spencer's operations, beginning in 1604, were independent. A large number of German princes and cities extended their hospitality and patronage to the English actors. In the Netherlands we hear of 'the wonderful concourse' to them and of the young virgins – if that is what they were – falling in love with them and following them from city to city. Leicester took his troupe there with him in 1585, and thence recommended another company to Frederick II of Denmark. English actors were familiar with Elsinore: they often acted there – once in 1585 a wall gave way in the courtyard of the town hall, there was such a press of people.

Robert Browne toured the Netherlands as well as Germany, but it is in the latter that English cultural influence abroad is to be seen. The German theatre had been slow to develop on professional lines; it came to do so by imitating English methods and taking

English plays as models. The Duke of Brunswick and Jacob Ayrer of Nuremberg were among those who wrote plays under the influence. Prince Maurice of Hesse-Cassel wrote an 'English' comedy in Latin. In 1592 English players were performing Marlowe at the Frankfort fair; adaptations were made of *Dr. Faustus*, which had had after all a German origin, thus keeping going the long affiliation that led from the *Faustbuch* to Goethe's *Faust*.

We even hear of English players in France – in spite of her cultural superiority; but they are more likely to have been dancers and performers of jigs.

By the year of Shakespeare's death, which was also, significantly, that of Ben Jonson's offering to the public of his plays as *Works*, we are observing the transition to literature. While Shakespeare had been content to create plays, Jonson was intent on creating literature – in the French sense of *faire la littérature*.

LANGUAGE, LITERATURE
AND SOCIETY

I

LET us look away from England for a moment to illustrate how the cultural movements of the time were similarly affecting others: in the matter of language, for example, our neighbour France. From the glorious mish-mash of Rabelais to the chaste severity of Malherbe one observes a process of selection and refinement so rigorous as almost to amount to a linguistic revolution. Malherbe, who came just at the right moment when needed, achieved regularity and clarity: his aim was to impose the uniform language of the Court and educated society of Paris upon a country more diverse, and much larger, than England.[1] A certain linguistic nationalism is evident: Francis I imposed French upon the law-courts, while in England a Norman-French law-jargon continued ridiculously into the eighteenth century. The Reformers were in the lead in using the vernacular, as the Protestants were in England and gained much thereby. But French and English alike were lacking in the technical terms of art to keep pace with the intellectual gains. Expansion in the realm of the mind brought new needs and refinements: to express them both French and English imported terms galore from Latin, Greek, Italian. To these English added a further enrichment from French, with more loan-words from Spanish and Dutch.

Anyone who wishes to view at a glance the comparable change that was effected in England should look at a couple of paragraphs from correspondence of the reign of Henry VIII, and spellings like 'byschoppynge' and 'manne' for 'bishoping' and 'man', with the letters of Essex or Robert Cecil. Or, from Skelton to Sidney, one sees the revolution in prosody even more striking than the linguistic change. Something like an avalanche had overtaken the language in the fifteenth century: the loss of the final e in pronunciation let loose other changes. So that, so far as metre was concerned, all was yet to do before the Elizabethan poets could get going – they did not really get going until the 1580's. As C. S. Lewis observes, the achievement of the inferior mid-sixteenth-century poets was 'to build a firm metrical highway out of the late medieval swamp.'[2] They did not achieve this without much forethought and experimentation, with many failures – experimenters are usually not the best artists, others reap the rewards of their experiments. And though the Elizabethans unanimously regarded Chaucer as the greatest of English poets, they still could not scan him.

The subject has many aspects, which cannot be dealt with here as ends in themselves: we have to relate them to general cultural trends and to the developments of society. We must follow Bacon's advice to study phenomena over a wider field than that in which they occur, across the boundaries of religion and society, of literature, language and ideas, of art and literature, music and words. Up to the Elizabethans there was a marked inferiority-complex about the language as about so much else. English was 'uneloquent', eloquence could only come from the classics; it was wanting in style, which only words from the ancient tongues could give. Even a nationalist like Andrew Borde considered that 'the speech of English is a base speech to other notable speeches, as Italian, Castilian, French. Howbeit, the speech of England of late days was amended.'[3] We should say, amending. Ascham was a Protestant patriot (and a very good writer of English), who disapproved of the naughty sophistications of Italy, but 'next to the Greek and Latin tongue, I like and love Italian above all others.'

Some idea of the diversity of speech then may be gathered from the fact that even today so small an area as Cornwall enjoys two distinct dialects of English, East and West. The grand movement of the time was towards establishing a standard English, the speech of the Court and the educated classes of London and about sixty miles round, thus including the universities. A potent factor advancing this must have been the growth in the preponderance of London. And perhaps – less obvious – the crowding in of so many superior immigrants with their natural desire to learn good English. Certainly the spelling reformers make a point of the utility of reform in teaching foreigners the language and to advance trade. Spelling reform is one aspect of the complex subject; as such it goes back to the impulse of Erasmus, the schoolmaster of Europe, and his influence upon the Cambridge Edwardians, Sir John Cheke, Sir Thomas Smith and Ascham. Ultimately it was to be the marvellous achievement of Elizabethan literature itself that was the culminating factor in the maturing of the language and the fixing of its usages and forms for the future. This was part cause, part consequence; many factors converge together, one must not enforce a harsh separation.

Among these was the conscious and deliberate work for reform of the Edwardians: we see in how many respects the Elizabethans fulfilled or refined upon what the Edwardians began. The earlier Elizabethans were Edwardians in their *Bildung*. In language, as in religion, the Edwardians were too radical for their work to hold; the sense of the country imposed a *via media*. But their work set things going. Smith and Cheke were too doctrinaire, especially the latter with his Teutonising tendencies, his craze to confine the language to its Saxon roots; this went along with his extreme Protestantism, a concatenation which the Puritans carried well into the seventeenth century. Actually, the development of the language took precisely the opposite turn, with its vast increase of vocabulary from classical, Italian and French sources. Even the more moderate Ascham, with his dominantly Saxon diction, realised the necessity of importing technical terms, those of art and science, of logic and mathematics, from those more sophisticated tongues. Without them one simply could not go forward. Already by 1562 Richard Eden was writing to Cecil that English has hitherto 'been accounted barbarous much more than it now is – before it was enriched and amplified by sundry books, in manner of all arts, translated out of Latin and other tongues.'[4]

The work of the Edwardians was refined upon and carried to perfection by John Hart, 'one of the greatest of English phoneticians and authorities on pronunciation.'[5] He was close to Smith, and was well known to Cecil; with an excellent knowledge of modern language, he had studied the work of the French spelling reformers. He started from the standpoint that 'few of any nation do come to the perfect speech of their mother tongue in all their life: which few are the lettered, much using the writing and reading thereof.' He cited Quintilian: 'the vices which may be used of the multitude shall be no custom.' The ideal of English speech must be that of the educated, who know other tongues. 'Others there are of far West or North countries [i.e. counties] which use differing English terms from those of the Court and London, where the flower of the English tongue is used.'[6] Hart looked forward to a proper reduction of both English grammar and spelling on a settled basis like the classical languages.

To this end he put forward, in his works on Orthography and Pronunciation, 'the first attempt at a really systematic description of the sounds of English.'[7] We cannot go in detail into his phonetic work, but his analyses of differences in vowel-sounds and his solutions of problems 'evoke admiration' today. He provided 'the earliest discussion of intonation in the history of the English language': it was not for two centuries that the study of this subject caught up with him. His was the first discussion of word-stress in English. But his main interest was in the much-needed reform of English spelling. As early as 1551 his first book, *The Opening of the Unreasonable Writing of our English Tongue*, advocated a system of spelling on a purely phonetic basis, 'by the law of reason, which is in our head.' Reform, in religion, in law, music, was in the air in Edward's brief reign. With Hart's two later books, the *Orthography* of 1569 and the *Method* of 1570, works of systematic clarity and logical precision, he provided 'the first truly scientific discussion of English spelling, and Hart's arguments are still valid.' Jespersen considered that Hart's alphabet of twenty-six symbols was more consistently phonetic than some twentieth-century phoneticians'. Hart realised, however, that a more consistent system, accents and all, would not gain consent as being too radical. By then progress was being made, empirically by writers and printers, even in spelling; and he was being urged 'not to speak of any misuse in our English writing, which is of late brought to such a perfection as never the like was seen.'[8] The future was to be with the moderates and the empirical, and in the event was largely determined by the creators of a new literature.

Mulcaster, finest of schoolmasters – a gallant crew if somewhat too free with the rod – was characteristic of the middle way.[9] He was a North Countryman, from Cumberland, and his interest may have been sharpened by the criticism made at the first visitation of Merchant Taylors' school that the ushers, 'being Northern men born, had not taught the children to speak distinctly, or to pronounce their words as well as they ought.'[10] Such a schoolmaster perceived the need of an established spelling, consistent so far as might be. But he was not in favour of a radical, doctrinaire reformation – the inconvenience would be far greater than the benefits. Custom was king, and those who went clean against it would not prevail; in fact, by 1582 when Mulcaster wrote, the 'use' of the country had already rejected the notion. Adherents of good custom did not object to particular reforms; his own spelling approximates more to modern English than most books of the time, which shows that he was in keeping with the trend of the language, as well as expressing the consensus of opinion.

By now it was possible to be proud of it, and this was the inspiration of his work. He regarded languages as having their ideal periods, the Greek of Demosthenes, the Latin of Cicero, and contemporary English 'to be the very height thereof.' He was in favour of enriching the language by adopting foreign words; he foresaw its extension by means of foreign trade and overseas expansion – though he can hardly have dreamed that English would become a world-language. Above all, he was in favour of teaching in English: 'and why not, I pray you, as well in English as either in Latin or any tongue else?'[11] In time English would displace Latin, as Latin had others. Here he was a revolutionary modernist: it was not until the nineteenth century that education loosened its bondage to the classical tongues.

Suddenly the change was there – though it had been long prepared – in the 1580's, as with so much else: a complete change of attitude with regard to the language. Of course the country was going up in the world: so was the language. Where previously people had apologised for it or been at least defensive about it, the tone abruptly changed. Even the pedestrian Holinshed spoke up to the effect that no speech had more variety or copiousness. This became the main theme of commentators – the burgeoning enrichment from foreign sources, though they do not emphasise the initial potentialities of a mixed language, Teutonic at root but with a larger Romance vocabulary. It was the Elizabethan expansion of vocabulary – ransacking other languages as their ships ransacked on the high seas – that made all the difference. Florio noted the 'yearly increase' of words: himself alone added a good many. Everybody took part in the pillage.

Scientists like Thomas Digges were not 'shamed to borrow of the Grecians these and many other terms of art' they needed – diagonal, pentagonal, etc.[12] His son emphasised his father's decision to write his mathematical works in English, wishing rather 'to *store* his native language and benefit his countrymen than by publishing in the Latin to purchase fame among strangers.' Nashe particularises the increase of technical terms in the mechanical arts: 'how eloquent our gowned age is grown of late, so that every mechanical mate abhors the English he was born to and plucks with a solemn periphrasis his *ut vales* from the ink-horn.'[13] This represents the condescension of a university wit to the banausic arts, but it affords evidence, from another angle, of the advance towards a standard English, 'of the process whereby lower class people, whose natural speech was dialectal or vulgar, gave up that speech in favour of another form which they regarded as better.'[14] By 1619, we learn from Milton's old master at St. Paul's that 'this standard speech is recognised as such all over the country,' though in the North even the upper classes still spoke Northern. No doubt the planting of grammar schools throughout the country had something to do with it.

Of all prose-writers Nashe himself was the most spontaneously creative of vocabulary; in this respect he has more than a touch of Shakespeare. One of the prime elements in the genius of Shakespeare, as well as of his lasting influence upon the language and its literature, is his proliferating creativeness in words: there never has been anyone else equal to it. Part of it comes from the instinct of genius; but he also owed much to the multifarious challenges of the theatre and again to the inspiration of the time. Even a conservative, in matters of language, such as Sidney introduced compound adjectives from French. While Spenser stretched his net backwards and outwards, fishing up archaic words, medievalisms, provincialisms, dialect words, to fashion that extraordinary vocabulary that made Ben Jonson say he 'writ no language'. Yet everyone agrees that Spenser's unique variant of Elizabethan English exactly expresses his aesthetic intentions, his mood and atmosphere. The contemporary judgment of Francis Meres paid tribute above all to the poets, by whom 'the English tongue is mightily enriched and gorgeously invested in rare ornaments and resplendent habiliments.'[15] When Guarini said to the poet Daniel in Italy that English was too barbarous a language for poetry to be written in it, he was already out of date. The poets had made him so.

II

The sudden flowering of a new literature began, with Sidney and Spenser, in the 1580's after the long hiatus since Wyatt and Surrey: after the black years of mid-century, the burnings and executions, the uncertainties and hazardous changes of course, and the country's need to recuperate with the stability and sense of Elizabeth's first two decades. The significant thing is that Sidney and Spenser were at once recognised for what they were, harbingers of a new literature, the new voices people had been waiting for. We now know that these two poets were not so close as was once thought, and indeed their backgrounds were very different. Spenser was a middle-class man with the academic ambience of Cambridge, and to the encouragement of his friends there he owed much. From the first they believed in him; when *The Shepherd's Calendar* appeared (1579), with its wide range of new measures, still more when they could appreciate the design and intentions of the projected *Faerie Queene*, they hailed him without hesitation as the successor of Chaucer they had been waiting for.

Sidney's historical significance is even greater. It is important to realise with imagination that his position was quasi-princely: he stood at the top of European Protestant society, this is why, as a young man, he was received everywhere as the equal of princes. Except during the brief life of Leicester's little son, Philip Sidney was the heir of his uncle, whom all Europe recognised as closest to the Queen; Philip was also heir to the Earl of Warwick, as well as to his father, who ruled both Ireland and Wales. The world knows that, when the news of his death reached the Escorial, Philip II minuted in the margin, 'He was my godson.' He had outstanding qualities of character and intellect, so that the age saw in him its ideal incarnation. In addition to all this he possessed literary genius.

We are not concerned with his career here, but we must realise that his exalted position no less than his genius gave him immense influence and, more subtly, that it conditioned the character of his work. He was a European figure, who moved naturally in the milieu of Court life, to which he belonged; he provided the English embodiment of Castiglione's ideal Courtier. What more perfect a figure for the fulfilment of the Renaissance impulse in creating a literature in English that could hold its own with Italian, French and Spanish? (Sidney knew all three languages, in addition to the classics; he knew Germany – and refused to learn German.) This was his deliberate intention; no one else could so powerfully advance it: on two fronts, as a writer himself, and as a patron of others.

In him the Renaissance took a very English form, for he was an ardent Protestant, with a profoundly ethical nature. This is the keynote of the Sidney-Pembroke circle – his sister, the Countess of Pembroke, who herself had literary talent, carried on his patronage after his death. (It is an inflexion and has a tone in complete contrast with that of the Catholic Southampton, the circle to which Shakespeare for a few years belonged.) Sidney's numerous contacts in France were all Protestant; he never went there again after the massacre of St. Bartholomew, but even his literary contacts were not with Ronsard and the Catholics: they were with Marot and Duplessis-Mornay, Du Bartas and Beza. Though young, he won the admiration of William the Silent, as of Hubert Languet, Jacob Sturm and the German Reformers. It was partly due to his princely position and his death as a Protestant hero, besides the quality of his writings – all achieved and over before he was thirty-two – that they were translated into European languages long before other Elizabethan works. In England he continued to be the most admired and the most read writer of his generation for a century after his death.

He was above all an aristocrat and a courtier. Even in his most personal poetry, the sonnets of *Astrophil and Stella*, he maintains an aristocratic reserve – and those which make clear his love for Penelope Rich were withheld from even manuscript circulation. His was a controlled emotion: he was always conscious

> that to my birth I owe
> Nobler desires, lest else that friendly foe,
> Great expectation, wear a train of shame.

Even his love

> would not let me whom she loved decline
> From nobler course fit for my birth and mind.

This dedicated him to a life of action, and for some time before he left for his last journey to the Netherlands he laid aside secular poetry for religious, his translation of the Psalms into verse, and left his extensive revision of *Arcadia* unfinished. But what beautiful poetry he left behind! while the *Arcadia* proved the most influential literary work of the age. His only close literary friend, apart from his sister, was another courtier, Sir Edward Dyer, much his senior; Fulke Greville was more of a disciple. He specifically said, 'I have found in divers smally learned courtiers more sound style than in some professors of learning.'[16] (No doubt!) He would mean Sackville, Dyer, Oxford, Greville, Ralegh. All his work would naturally have a Court audience in view. So, too, did Spenser's, for all his difference of background; and this brings him closer to Sidney in the upshot. It is said that he encouraged the *Faerie Queene*. Shakespeare was no aristocrat (except in his tastes): hence the much wider front he exposed to life, redoubled by his experience of the theatre, with no inhibition upon his expression of it. Yet even his poems, with which he challenged fame as a poet, were aimed at a similar audience.

We must remember that a general reading public hardly existed; there were different audiences, with some overlapping. Most important culturally, socially, artistically was the Court, in literature as in the other arts, painting and music. This had its effect in the country, among nobles and the grander gentry to whom the Court was open. We are reminded of the English preference for country life as against the city-life of Italy, and that many country houses were creative centres of culture. Not only Penshurst and Wilton of the Sidneys and Herberts, but Polesworth and Clifford Chambers of Drayton's patrons and friends, Hengrave of the Kitsons and Cornwallises with their love of painting and music, of George Gower and Wilby, Stondon and Ingatestone of the Petres and William Byrd, the houses that received Ben Jonson for years on end. There was the London public of the theatres, of broadsides and news-ballads, as well as a middle-class public for the moralising tracts of such as Greene and Chettle, the novels of Deloney. There was the intellectual, argumentative public of the universities, merging into the much wider audience for theology and religious writing of every kind. It is characteristic of the age – to judge from booklists, diaries and notes of people's reading – that the nearest to a general public was that for religion, theology, morals, much of it controversial and disputatious.

When Sidney and Spenser began, there was no poetic tradition for them to latch on to: all was yet to do. With the rapid changes in the language, early sixteenth-century prosody was in deliquescence. Both Sidney and Spenser, to begin with, experimented with a wide variety of new verse-forms, and succeeded in establishing a number of them, permanently expanding the capacity of the language for poetic expression. Sidney's initial preoccupation was with structure, the creation of artistic forms. In this he was immensely successful; with his work and Spenser's, 'at one bound English was established among the great literatures of Europe.'[17] It is not our business here to go in detail into the works of literature or art as ends in themselves, but to relate them to the movements of the time. But the historian may conclude that these works would not have had the resounding success they had, or established themselves as classics, if they had not given aesthetic satisfaction to their readers from the first. And what Sidney taught his countrymen in the 1580's they practised and developed in the 1590's. To take only one example: the surreptitious publication of

Astrophil and Stella after his death started all the sonnet-sequences that followed, and – so strong was its impact – the omission of the lovely songs that originally accompanied the sonnets fixed the restriction of these sequences to sonnets only. Sidney was a more scrupulous artist than most professional writers, constantly revising his work. On the other hand he composed easily, with a natural disciplined facility, and he wrote rapidly: he had that in common with Shakespeare. It is astonishing how much he accomplished in his brief life.

Along with his creative work, providing models in every kind of verse, there went a critical clearance of the ground, which reminds one of Eliot in our time (with whom there are marked points of resemblance: the ethical perfectionism, the cool intellectual discipline, the personal aloofness, the absence of passion, the concern with religion). In the realm of criticism Sidney's influence was decisive: he introduced or gave authority to basic critical terms, lyrical, madrigal, stanza and octave, couplet, masculine rhyme and so on.[18] He wrote his *Defence of Poesy* early on, along with his poems and the first version of *Arcadia*. Extraordinary for so young a man, he proceeds with the complete assurance of a master: in the event justified, for he writes like a cultivated European, which he was, not a nationalistic provincial, as so many Elizabethans did.

To read Sidney's work afresh – it was twice published in 1595 as *The Defence of Poesy* and also as *An Apology for Poetry* – makes a surprising impression. We are so much accustomed to think of the age as pre-eminently that of poetry, and rightly – apart from quality, in sheer quantity, it has been calculated that there were well over two hundred writers of verse (what other age could show so many?) – that we do not expect the evident necessity to defend poetry as such or Sidney's own very low opinion of English poetry to date. One publisher referred in his Preface to 'the stormy winter which hath so long held back the glorious sunshine of divine poesy'; and Sidney describes his tract as 'a pitiful [i.e. pitying] defence of poor poetry, which from almost the highest estimation of learning is fallen to be the laughing stock of children.'[19] He repeats this several times. The same line is taken by Puttenham in his much fuller *The Art of English Poesy*, with which Sidney's *Defence* is closely connected. They come out of the same Court background and exemplify an approach so close that one work must have been available to the other, one can hardly say which was the debtor – though I should hazard a guess that it was the younger man.* They both seem dominated by the necessity to defend poetry in so Protestant a society, especially against its downgrading by Puritans.

In that atmosphere Sidney's ethical bias was the most effective line of defence, all the more so because it represented his deepest convictions. With him the whole end of poetry – and by that he means imaginative literature, whether in verse or prose – is ethical, as with Spenser. Not so with Marlowe and Shakespeare, those lower-class men – nor do moderns accept this ethical pre-eminence over art. Art has its own autonomy, where Sidney denominates 'the moral doctrine the chief of all knowledges.'[20] We are reminded that the English Renaissance was more moral than the Italian.[21]

We are liable to forget, the book had such authority, that it was a young man's book – as practically the whole of Elizabethan literature was a young men's literature. Lyly, Kyd, Greene, Nashe; Marlowe, Spenser, Shakespeare; the earlier Drayton, Daniel, Jonson, Donne, Bacon – all of it the work of men in their twenties, thirties, forties. This may partly account for Sidney's spirited, humorous writing down of philosophy and history; he despised philosophical disputation, while he regarded the historian as 'captived to the truth of a foolish world.'[22] Young as he was, he realised that most men are children in regard to 'the best things, till they be cradled in their graves.' It is not the only time that Sidney insists what fools humans are: all Elizabethans had a more realistic attitude to the facts of human nature and the human condition than the humbug of today. Nor was this simply a patrician attitude: it was realised to be the truth from the top to the bottom of society, or at least by all who were literate and could express it.

Sidney's account of English poetry to date is very sparse, there was so little to approve of. He asks, 'why England, the mother of excellent minds, should be grown so hard a step-mother to poets?'[23] There was only Chaucer to look up to as a great poet on a European level. Sidney had a low opinion of the earlier Elizabethan versifiers, except, for want of better, of *The Mirror for Magistrates*, where I expect he was thinking of his fellow courtier, Sackville's contributions, the only good poetry in the book. He approved of *The Shepherd's Calendar*, though not the archaic, rustic

---

* The authorship of *The Art of English Poesy* has been disputed between George Puttenham and Lord Lumley. But both these were Cambridge men, while the author says 'when I was a scholar at Oxford.' This is not necessarily decisive; a number of people studied at both. I use 'Puttenham' for convenience.

diction. He found nothing to approve in drama except Sackville and Norton's *Gorboduc*; even so he objected to its departure from the classical rules of unity of time and place. His admiration was directed to the classical tragedies of Buchanan. Sidney was writing before the Elizabethan drama burst upon the world. He held up for imitation the 'ordinary players in Italy'; in the event Italian drama was far surpassed. If Sidney had survived into the 1590's he might have revised his views, for he was not a doctrinaire; though he objected to the mingling of tragic and comic in the drama, he allowed for mixed genres in poetry. He was critical of much love-poetry, and wrote it down as insincere. If he could have witnessed the fantastic mushroom-expansion of heterosexual love-poetry in the 1590's he might have been as bored in bulk as the modern reader, and welcomed Shakespeare's sonnets to his young patron, if only for a change!

There are all kinds of things in Sidney's high-spirited tract – like one of his tourneys at Whitehall – to reward the reader. Its whole foundation, its citation of authorities and examples, are almost all from the Greek. This is very exceptional in that age; but there was something of ancient Greece in Sidney's nature. Above all, in the end, there is his absolute confidence in the future of the language. Some pointed at it as 'a mingled language'; but Sidney saw that that doubled its capacity – he could not have foreseen that the writer to exploit that good fortune to its fullest would be a man of the despised theatre. He realised that the loss of inflexions was an immense gain in flexibility; that the variety of vowel-sounds offered remarkable scope for rhyme. It is refreshing, after Sidney's supercilious dismissal of earlier English writing (he was a very young man), to find him concluding that, for poetic effects, English was better than Italian, French or Spanish, let alone German.

The Art of English Poesy, which goes under the name of Puttenham, has wider scope and wider sympathies. An older man, he is more generous in his estimate of English writers; he has a remarkable appreciation of the medievals – he saw in the author of *Piers Plowman* a precursor of Protestantism – and of the romances. One would suppose that Sidney took his historical account of poetry, pre-dating civilisation, from him. This author too has an exceptional knowledge of Greek literature. He also defends poetry against moralists like Ascham, and Philistine Puritans, but he does not subordinate poetry to ethics: he regards poetry as the expression of the whole range of human needs and interests, the artistic outlet of human instincts. Nature and common reason are the best authorities, common sense a better guide than authority or accepted opinion, custom always has its rationale and is to be respected. The book, which was intended for the Queen herself, offers its own *via media*, in keeping with the norms of men and society. Published by Shakespeare's schoolfellow, Richard Field, it was read with close attention by the budding dramatist, with whose point of view it remarkably agrees: it clearly helped in his formation.

The thesis of the book is 'that there may be an art of English poesy as well as there is of the Latin and Greek'; it carries out this programme in full, in detail with which we are not here concerned.[24] More to our purpose is to observe its social affiliations and attitudes. Its author was an aristocrat and courtier, more expressive than most as to the class-bases of literature. He regards heroic poems, the celebrations of the deeds of princes and noble personages, the relation of affairs of state, war and peace, along with divine subjects, epics and such, as the highest literature, the proper province of aristocratic taste. 'The mean matters be those that concern mean [i.e. middle-class] men, their life and business as lawyers, gentlemen, and merchants, good householders and honest citizens . . . the common conversation of the civiler and better sort of men.'[25] Here is the province of middle-class literature, not concerned with those higher themes. 'The base and low matters be the doings of the common artificer, serving man, yeoman, groom, husbandman, day-labourer, shepherd, swineherd and such like of homely calling, degree and bringing up.' The values current in different classes are not the same, nor are the virtues and vices to be equally rated since they are not equipollent; nor are the themes and styles of their respective literatures required to be the same – all is according to degree, and decorum. 'The actions of mean and base personages tend in very few cases to any great good example; for who passeth [cares] to follow the steps and manner of life of a craftsman, shepherd, or sailor . . . How almost is it possible that such manner of men should be of any virtue other than their profession requireth?'[26] This refreshing candour offers a useful approach to the understanding of Elizabethan literature, reflecting an hierarchical order, besides a salutary comment on that of our own confused and disordered society.

He was confident as they all were in the future, both of language and literature – critics and creative writers alike. Standard English, he too says, was to be that of London and the

Court and sixty miles around. 'Faith in the latent capacities of the language and in the native genius, rather than respect for past literary achievements' was what inspired people.[27] From scholars, critics, writers alike unremitting attention had been paid to the language – there has been nothing like it since. Nor was it confined to them: Lyly tells us, 'it is a world to see how Englishmen desire to hear finer speech than the language allows.'[28] From which we see that larger circles were awakening and aware, society at large involved. The language might be described as 'in a certain condition', pregnant with possibilities: 'a national consciousness enormously extended, enriched and disciplined the language itself.' How full Shakespeare's mind was of it we see from *Love's Labour's Lost*, or no less remarkably in the prose of Nashe. Harvey wrote, 'England, since it was England, never bred more honourable minds, more adventurous hearts, more valorous hands, or more excellent wits than of late.'[29] They were aware that they were living in great days for their country, and were inspired to create a literature that was worthy of it. But it no more came into existence in a fit of absence of mind than the British Empire itself did.

The modern reader has much more difficulty in appreciating the *Arcadia* than Sidney's poetry, the latter as notable for its ease and clarity as for its splendour. Yet the Elizabethans found gathered in it 'what a whole generation wanted to say.'[30] There is everything in it: prose and verse, both alike exquisite, pastoral and romance, stories, some of them sensational, ethical discussion and moral guidance. Overriding everything is the book's message: discipline of mind and heart, control of passion and desire: only a right rule of conduct can carry one through the evils and storms of life. In one sense the main story of the book is a parable. Arcadia is no remote, romantic kingdom; in a way, it is an idealised England, with moral and political implications for it. Arcadia was of good repute for 'the moderate and well-tempered minds of the people'; Greville, Sidney's closest follower, tells us that the book embodied a political allegory.[31] The adventures of the princely friends, Pyrocles and Musidorus, formed their education in life: their surrender to desire against the rule of reason is paralleled by a breakdown of order in the state, with hideous consequences.[32] Order and natural justice are restored by a surprising *dénouement* at the end, with the arrival of a just monarch, like the *deus ex machina* in a Greek romance. The disorder in Laconia reveals the evils of democracy; out of disorder and decline come despotism

and tyranny. Pyrocles and Musidorus, sentenced to death, are released only by the subjugation of the passions to chaste love, with
its fulfilment in marriage and increase prefigured at the beginning.
(Philip Sidney said of his own love: 'which I did with so much
covering hide that I was thought void of it'.[33])

Since there is everything of its generation in it, no wonder it
was the most influential work of fiction for a century. Other
writers rifled it, notably Shakespeare, not only shipwrecks, the
blind Paphlagonian king, touches in *The Winter's Tale*, *The
Tempest*, but verbally; two centuries later Richardson got his
Pamela from it. C. S. Lewis, always so reluctant to admit historical
elements in the shaping of a work of art, sees in it 'the first fruits
of returning civilisation and an earnest that this civilisation will
rise high and last long'.[34] (We are now at the end of it.) Elizabethan ideals and values are given their proper expression: not
only the highest conceptions of love and friendship, duty and conduct, a refined aristocratic notion of women (as against the Puritan
view of them simply as housewives), but their ideas of countryside,
architecture, the usual English inexpertness at the beginning of
wars, premonitions of the war in the Netherlands. In an aside, we
are let into Sidney's most intimate religious belief, 'I would then
have said, the heavenly powers to be reverenced and not searched
into, and their mercies rather by prayers to be sought than their
hidden counsels by curiosity.'[35]

For a modern generation, to whom the religious and ethical
concern of the book has not much meaning, there is always the
aesthetic appeal, and the human. The book has an overwhelming
sense of visual beauty: sometimes one sees the flowery meadows of
Wilton or the woodland of Penshurst, where it was written, or
pictures are conjured up with all the clarity and purity of Botti-
celli, or again the scene moves like a tapestry moved by the wind.
Or there is the sheer music of the prose, like the evocation of silver
trumpets echoing against castle-walls. There is complete harmony
of atmosphere throughout the book, the harmony of Sidney's
achieved nature, along with delightful touches of humour, and a
graceful irony, an aristocratic quality. He was satirical about
goddesses – remember that he had not been afraid to address a
personal remonstrance to the Queen against her marrying Anjou.
The Queen of Laconia is described as seeming born only on the
boundaries of beauty's kingdom, 'for all her lineaments were
neither perfect possessions thereof, nor absent strangers thereto.
But she was a queen, and therefore beautiful.'[36] Philip Sidney was

no sycophant. Early on in the book occurs the phrase, 'if I die, love my memory.'[37] These last were the words he uttered on his death-bed. How they all cherished his memory!

For our purposes Spenser is the poet of the *Faerie Queene*, though other works of his have social and historical significance, in addition to their literary value, notably the satirical *Mother Hubberd's Tale*, the autobiographical *Colin Clout's Come Home Again* and his prose *View of the Present State of Ireland*. The *Faerie Queene* is the great poem of the age, the poem in which it is *mirrored* – in the precise sense of the word: it is a reflection, from an eminence, not the direct rendering of the Elizabethan world, on one significant side, of its prose-epic, Hakluyt's *Principal Navigations*. It is all there, but refracted as in glass or clear water; the eminence is ethical as in the *Arcadia*, with which it is comparable, and with its own euphonious atmosphere as unmistakable as that. Though a fusion of medieval romance with Italian epic, the poem derives more from English roots and is closer to Chaucer and Malory. Spenser was indeed a backward-looking man, as was Shakespeare – the greatest art springs out of the inspiration of the past, never the future. Nevertheless his imagination was much enriched by the contemporary arts of pageant and masque, tournament and emblem, woodcut and tapestry. In his quieter way he was as ambitious as Sidney to make English a European literature: he deliberately set himself to rival Ariosto, and provide a comparable work in English. From an historian's point of view the *Faerie Queene* is more original and curious, very English in being of a mixed genre, ambivalent and various – and more richly rewarding. 'Among those who shared, or still share, the culture for which he wrote, and which he helped to create, there is no dispute about his greatness.'[38]

More narrowly to the point, the age itself regarded him as its great poet. Nothing is more remarkable than the confidence from the beginning that their expectation of him would be fulfilled in the grand poem; Spenser prepared himself for his vocation quite as consciously and deliberately as Milton in his generation. The aim of the poem as a whole was to portray the Elizabethan ideal of a gentleman, an English version of Castiglione's Courtier (like Philip Sidney's life). Each book was to exemplify a quality, holiness, temperance, chastity, friendship, justice, courtesy, and so on, culminating in the magnificence – or true greatness – to be described in the person of King Arthur. Dying at forty-six, Spenser completed only half of his immense project. Elizabethans were so ambitious – and died so young – that many of their vast projects were left uncompleted. As it is, the *Faerie Queene* is one of the longest poems in the language, and again everything is in it.

For these ethical values were embodied in stories to seduce the reader: 'which I conceived should be most plausible and pleasing, being coloured with an historical fiction, the which the most part of men delight to read, rather for variety of matter than for profit of the example.' (A gentle irony is one of Spenser's pervasive characteristics.) He was really interested in states of the heart and mind; but Elizabethans demanded action, excitement, plot, comic relief, and Spenser gave them all these. There has been much discussion as to the historical allegory in the poem. There is, of course, an immense deal of ethical allegorising in it; but the historical element is both more direct and more subtle. Persons really familiar with the age can recognise Spenser's allusions to people and events: they are direct, though under a name of fable. Duessa is Mary Queen of Scots and her execution is directly alluded to. Artegall is Lord Grey of Wilton, Lord Deputy of Ireland, Spenser's patron, whose soldierly and Puritan qualities Spenser much admired (as he did his swimming, a rare accomplishment then among commanders). Irena is Ireland, about which there is a great deal: Spenser wrote the first three books beside the literary Liffey, enjoying the friendship of Sidney's friend, Ludovic Bryskett. The later books were written in southern Ireland, whose landscapes, mountains and streams Spenser appreciated as few Elizabethans did: they are celebrated in the poem.

It includes personal advocacy for Ralegh and his point of view, propaganda for Guiana, the ups and downs of his relations with the Queen, under the transparent disguise of Timias and Belphoebe or again Cynthia. Spenser makes all this clear in his Prefatory Letter: 'in that Fairy Queen I mean glory in my general intention, but in my particular I conceive the most excellent and glorious person of our sovereign the Queen.' As such she is Cynthia; as a person, in her individual relationship with Ralegh, she is Belphoebe; as the exemplar of chastity, and in relation to Grey, she is Britomart. One can usually tell; contemporaries can have had no difficulty. In dedicating the whole six books to the 'Empress' in 1596 he added to her styles, 'Queen of England, France, and Ireland', that of Virginia – emphasising the imperial point of view, that of his friend Ralegh. Throughout the book the addresses to the Queen, descriptions of her, adjurations, apostrophes, incantations, run a thread through the long poem helping to pull it together; or, to vary the metaphor, they provide the dominant motif in its music.

The *Faerie Queene* was intended as a celebration of the age; it was received and recognised as such, not only by the grant of an official pension to the poet (which he did not live long to enjoy), but by contemporaries. One sees the historic claim set forth in the accepted dedication and in the prefatory sonnets to all the leading figures of the Court. There they all are – except for Leicester, Spenser's earlier patron, who had died after the passing of the Armada. But there is Essex, who had succeeded to something of Sidney's position as the pattern of chivalry: Spenser promises to sing his heroic parts in the last books yet to come. There is Lord Admiral Howard:

> those huge castles of Castilian King,
> That vainly threatened kingdoms to displace,
> Like flying doves ye did before you chase.

Lord Grey is hailed as 'the pillar of my life, And patron of my Muse's pupillage'; Ralegh as 'the summer's nightingale, Thy sovereign goddess's most dear delight'; Walsingham as 'the great Maecenas of the age'. There is Buckhurst, formerly the poet Sackville, 'whose learned Muse hath writ her own record'; Burghley, on whose shoulders rests the burden of the treasury – he is said to have halved the pension of £100 that the Queen had allowed. Hatton, the studious Northumberland, the privateering Cumberland, Lord Chamberlain Hunsdon (responsible for the theatre), the famous soldier Sir John Norris, the poetising Oxford of such ancient ancestry: they are all passed in review, to end with the ladies, Lady Carew and the sister of Sidney,

> Who first my Muse did lift out of the floor.

He concludes gallantly – his idealised addiction to women is evident all through his work – with a sonnet 'To all the gracious and beautiful ladies in the Court.'

The poem offers the chief poetic expression of the English Renaissance and, with its Protestant view of the events of contemporary Europe, is a deeply patriotic work. Inspired as Spenser was by the romance of the past, by the legendary pre-history of Britain, by Brutus and the Trojans and Leir, by Arthur and

Merlin and Gorlois, he takes pleasure in the thought that the fame of the land was now known

> From th' utmost brink of the Armerick shore
> Unto the margent of the Moluccas:

Drake's achievement in the voyage round the world. Ralegh's exploration of the Orinoco is referred to, 'though but known late' . . .

> And shame on you, O men! which boast your strong
> And valiant hearts, in thoughts less hard and bold,
> Yet quail in conquest of that land of gold.

Spenser took pride in Elizabeth's rôle in aiding the Protestants under oppression abroad:

> Whose glory is to aid all suppliants poor,
> And of weak Princes to be Patroness.

The intervention in the Netherlands is described figuratively, with Prince Arthur to the rescue, i.e. Leicester in 1585. Sir Burbon in trouble, who is similarly aided, is of course Henry of Navarre; but his change of faith, which much distressed Elizabeth, caused him to be written down as 'faithless and unsound' – and that is reflected contemporaneously in *Love's Labour's Lost*. Spenser prophesies, as in duty bound, the future greatness of Britain equal to that of Troy. In fact his sensitive mind, given to melancholy, was more affected by the hideous events of the religious conflicts of his time, as well it might be:

> O sacred [i.e. cursèd] hunger of ambitious minds,
> And impotent desire of men to reign!
> Whom neither dread of God, that devils binds,
> Nor laws of men, that commonweals contain,
> Nor bands of nature, that wild beasts restrain,
> Can keep from outrage and from doing wrong,
> Where they may hope a kingdom to obtain . . .

He might be writing about the twentieth century! – some indication of the permanent relevance of a great writer.

As to the contents of the poem, stuffed with every kind of richness, like the contents of an Elizabethan house with all its galleries and pictured tapestries, it has been well said that it creates a world, 'a world which exists in some fashion even in the minds of people who have not read the poem.'[39] Spenser's literary impact was prodigious: all the poets of the 1590's reflected it in some way or

other. But, then, the nineties were filled with the delayed publication of his works, to which he had dedicated himself even
from his schooldays. Regarded as their head by all the poets, a
position which he naturally assumed without affectation, he
devoted a part of *Colin Clout* to a survey of the poets who were the
ornaments of the reign, mostly recognisable under their fanciful
names: Sackville was Harpalus, Dyer Corydon, Gorges Alcyon,
Drayton was probably Aetion; William Alabaster's unfinished
Latin poem in twelve books, *Eliseis*, receives a tribute, and of
course Ralegh as poet:

> Full sweetly tempered is that Muse of his
> That can empierce a prince's mighty heart.

Daniel, who confessed his own self-distrust, is encouraged to speak
up: in the end he did. When, as Camden says, 'our principal
poet' died and was buried in Westminster abbey, his hearse was
'attended by poets, and mournful elegies and poems, with the
pens that wrote them, thrown into his tomb.'[40]

After the highminded ethics of Sidney and Spenser it is a relief
to turn to the world of the senses, the passions, the pleasures of the
flesh, especially sex, with Marlowe and Shakespeare. This is one
reason why they are so much more alive to the modern reader,
still living presences, where so many others are but shadows. For
one thing, William Shakespeare is the sexiest writer in the
language: to anyone who knows Elizabethan English his work
proliferates plain bawdy, salacious puns, innuendoes, double meanings, sly suggestions, naughty puns – but it is all normal heterosexual bawdy of the natural man.* It is the salt that is an element
in preserving the life in his work. In Marlowe the situation is very
different, for an obvious psychological reason: as usual with homo-
sexuals there is hardly any of the bawdy of the normal man. His
sexual deviation and – more dangerous in that age – his religious
heterodoxy make him more of a modern writer, more real and
living to us.

Marlowe's signal importance in the history of literature is in
the drama: he was the first to marry splendid verse to the stage,
he was the creator of the 'mighty line', the blank verse that was
to be its chief vehicle of expression. He was the originator, the
pioneer: we are only now appreciating once more how original his
contribution was, in plot-structure, characterisation, speed and

---

* In my *William Shakespeare: A Biography* I did not sufficiently emphasise this:
my chief criticism of the book now.

impact. His plays again hold the stage, and his authentic voice comes through, with all the passion, conflict, anguish, the intellectual and spiritual torment in his mind. The plays contain many passages of pure poetry. Where Shakespeare's genius was essentially dramatic, Marlowe's was less so, and not exclusively. He might have written anything if he had lived, satire, or even epic; Shakespeare not, in those genres. The theatre was incredibly fortunate to recruit to it the two finest, most richly gifted, poets.

Splendour is the only word for Marlowe's poetry, a brilliant jewelled quality, infused with intellectual light, of finished artistry. He had the passion and the ecstasy that Sidney and Spenser lacked; everybody recognised his genius, even those who disapproved of his morals and his irreligion. (What a Renaissance figure he was! the Italy of Alexander VI and Leo X would have been a more appropriate background for him than Protestant England: he scorned Protestantism and preferred Catholicism, without believing in it, of course – another recognisably modern inflexion.) Everyone is agreed as to the quality of *Hero and Leander*: Bush calls it 'the most beautiful short narrative poem of its age.'[41] Besides its scintillating brilliance, it is a smiling ironical poem: ironical because Marlowe could not really be expected to take its heterosexual situation seriously, while the smile is that of sexual desire expected and gratified. It was obviously written for fun. Bush sees, from *Venus and Adonis*, that Shakespeare had knowledge of *Hero and Leander* in manuscript from the first. But of course: the two poems were written concurrently in friendly rivalry for the favour of the young Adonis, Southampton.[42] Marlowe's poem, left unfinished at his death in 1593, was published five years later with a much longer continuation by Chapman, a fine poem in itself. But Chapman, with his own genius, moralises Marlowe's tale:

> Joy, graven in sense, like snow in water wastes:
> Without preserve of virtue nothing lasts.

For Marlowe there was no need of a moral: joy is an end in itself.

Even the chaste Lewis sees how superior Marlowe's poem is to *Venus and Adonis* artistically, as Shakespeare himself seems to have been aware – and promised a graver labour on a more serious theme, fulfilled in *The Rape of Lucrece*. *Venus and Adonis* was also ironical, smiling and naughty, befitting the circle of young men for whom it was written. Lewis is enthusiastic over Marlowe's qualities, regarding him as 'the poet of the material imagination.'[43]

This is true, but wholly inadequate: Marlowe was even more that rare thing in English, an intellectual poet, passionately interested in ideas. He was concerned about philosophical and political issues, agonised by the insoluble dilemmas posed by religion. He could make poetry out of abstractions, as no one else except Donne:

> Nature that framed us of four elements,
> Warring within our breasts for regiment,
> Doth teach us all to have aspiring minds:
> Our souls, whose faculties can comprehend
> The wondrous architecture of the world,
> And measuring every wandering planet's course,
> Still climbing after knowledge infinite,
> And always moving as the restless spheres,
> Wills us to wear ourselves and never rest . . .

That speaks for Marlowe. The inspiration of the very idea of writing poetry in that age thrills him:

> If all the pens that ever poets held
> Had fed the feeling of their masters' thoughts,
> And every sweetness that inspired their hearts,
> Their minds and muses on admirèd themes:
> If all the heavenly quintessence they still
> From their immortal flowers of poesy,
> Wherein as in a mirror we perceive
> The highest reaches of a human wit:
> If these had made one poem's period,
> And all combined in beauty's worthiness,
> Yet should there hover in their restless heads
> One thought, one grace, one wonder at the least,
> Which into words no virtue can digest!

That may stand as epigraph for all that age of poetry. When Drayton came to sum up the qualities of his fellows, he wrote:

> Neat [i.e. perfect] Marlowe, bathed in Thespian springs,
> Had in him those brave translunary things
> That the first poets had: his raptures were
> All air and fire, which made his verses clear;
> For that fine madness still he did retain,
> Which rightly should possess a poet's brain.

And that is the answer to C. S. Lewis.

We take Shakespeare so much for granted, like a mountain-range dominating the landscape, that our chief need is to see him anew, if we can. There is no doubt about his dominance in the literature of our language, at home and overseas – where he bulks quite as largely in the study of it (and, creatively: William Faulkner is as Shakespearean a writer as Walter Scott or Thomas Hardy). It is an American scholar who brings home to us imaginatively by what an extraordinary accident, by what a narrow shave, Shakespeare's Plays have come down to us at all[44] – almost as unique a chance as the coming into existence of the Tudor dynasty.* Of Shakespeare's thirty-seven plays eighteen were given to the world, in a variety of texts – some more, some less, satisfactory – by his fellow-actors, Heming and Condell, in the First Folio seven years after their author's death. *What* we owe to those two! – we might so easily never have had eighteen plays at all, including some of the masterpieces, *Antony and Cleopatra*, *Othello*, *The Tempest*, *Macbeth* (of which we have not the full version). Think of what the world might so easily have lost! The remaining nineteen plays appeared in quarto in his life-time, some of them 'in such a mangled form as to be only partially intelligible.'[45] The Folio provided better versions of the worst texts later, but since *Pericles* did not appear in it, we have only a mutilated text. And there *may* be plays lost, the mysterious *Love's Labour's Won* and *Cardenio*. The establishment of the text of the plays of our greatest writer has been the work of generations of helpers and scholars ever since his death, for he did not provide it for us.

In his lifetime he took no trouble, or very little, to give the reading public a decent text of his plays; some nineteen of them he can never have seen in print at all. He certainly was too busy, all his time pre-empted for the theatre; and he seems to have been carried off by death somewhat unexpectedly, at fifty-two. If he had lived longer, would he have taken the trouble to give us a Folio volume of his plays, a text corrected by himself, as his junior Ben Jonson did with his? Jonson treated himself like the classic he was; that was not like William Shakespeare's sense of humour. Yet, on the other hand, there can be no doubt about the inner inspiration and belief of the artist in his art, nor about his self-aware literary ambition; and he was always regarded by his contemporaries as one of their best poets as well as their foremost writer for the stage.

His neglect to produce a literary text for his plays, as also the unsatisfactory text of his Sonnets, for the publication of which

---

* Henry VII was born when his mother was hardly fourteen, two months after his father's death.

(1609) he was not responsible, stands in marked contrast to the text of *Venus and Adonis* (1593), *The Rape of Lucrece* (1594), and *The Phoenix and the Turtle* (1601), for which he was responsible. These are the poems with which he challenged fame as a poet, and with which he took the trouble to provide an admirable text, carefully proof-read. We need say little about them here: better to see what contemporaries thought of them. Though *Venus and Adonis* is inferior in art to *Hero and Leander*, yet one can already see the promise of wider capabilities foreshadowed in it, the writer of the comedies to come. And one can see in *The Rape of Lucrece* the writer of the tragedies, heavy with foreboding, the guilt-laden atmosphere. There is something of *Titus Andronicus* in it, as there are touches of it remembered before the end, in *Cymbeline*. As for *The Phoenix and the Turtle*, it is beyond criticism: if anyone wants to know what pure poetry is – Valéry's ideal of *la poésie pure* – there it is in its essence.

We confine ourselves to what was new, unique about Shakespeare, and the impression he made in his time – we know what he has been in our literature. 'His comedy now seems so normal that it is difficult to realise how novel it was to the audience of his day.'[46] He was the effective perpetuator of the history-play, and the initiator of our long tradition of literary traffic with fairies in his wholly original *Midsummer Night's Dream*. To judge from Ben Jonson, his early tragedy *Titus Andronicus* made as much sensation as Kyd's *The Spanish Tragedy*. 'To be popular and successful, yet not to be at the mercy of the lowest part of the audience, was a task which none but Shakespeare accomplished.'[47] For sheer originality again, no one else writes a poem in which the woman is the pursuer; while, in a general outpouring of sonnets about romantic idealised love of women, he writes his to a male friend, the ups and downs, the ecstasies and deceptions, of friendship, with uncommonly plain speaking about the woman in question. They are different from everybody else's, and they live.

There is no mystery about the Sonnets, though we should like to know more about the circumstances of their publication, and we do not know the name – and are never likely to – of Shakespeare's mistress, the dark woman. Much unnecessary confusion has been caused, by people who should know better, simply by failing to notice that the dedication to 'Mr. W. H.' is the publisher's, and not Shakespeare's. So that 'Mr. W. H.' is not the 'lord' of the Sonnets, who is the obvious person, Shakespeare's

youthful patron – to whom the long poems were dedicated contemporaneously – whose personality and circumstances are perfectly clearly delineated in the Sonnets. Southampton was born
and reared a Catholic, though he was not a strong one or particularly religious; a beautiful, ambivalent youth, in these years
he was averse to marriage – the Sonnets were undertaken to persuade him to it. But they developed into something else – an
arresting and entangled story of friendship crossed by lust after a
woman, which, as a perceptive critic sees, is much too odd and
too closely linked with the plays (in particular, *Love's Labour's Lost*)
to be anything but true.[48] The whole tone of the Southampton
circle is in striking contrast to that of Penshurst and Wilton: it was
altogether more lax and sensual, and Shakespeare was for a time
its poet. All we need observe here is that the Sonnets are filled with
the poignant Renaissance sense of the beauty of youth and its soon
passing, that they contain some of the best poetry of the age, and
that they are intimately autobiographical. To that they owe their
vitality and permanence – as no doubt also that they were not
published at the time of writing, but by another odd chance so
much later: too intimate and revealing.

Ovid was above all, the poet of the Renaissance, with his un-
inhibited response to the senses, his love of a story, sensation,
rhetoric.[49] To his contemporaries Shakespeare, as a poet, was the
English Ovid. Already in 1598 Meres was writing, 'the sweet witty
soul of Ovid lives in mellifluous and honey-tongued Shakespeare,
witness his *Venus and Adonis*, his *Lucrece*, his sugared sonnets among
his private friends, etc.'[50] Sweetness and honey recur more than
once in references to his poetry. As early as this, in Meres' brief
survey of contemporary writers, Shakespeare is cited more than
anyone else, nine times. For comedy he is the English Plautus,
for tragedy Seneca, whom the early Elizabethans rated highest;
and just as it was held of old that the Muses would speak Plautus'
tongue, if they spoke Latin, so 'the Muses would speak with
Shakespeare's fine-filed phrase, if they would speak English.' He
is also estimated with the best for both lyric and love-poetry.
Gabriel Harvey reports by 1601, 'the younger sort takes much
delight in Shakespeare's *Venus and Adonis*, but his *Lucrece* and his
tragedy of *Hamlet, Prince of Denmark* have it in them to please the
wiser sort.' When his life was over, not yet old, Ben Jonson
summed up his work as having surpassed Lyly, Kyd and Marlowe,
and placed him with Aeschylus, Sophocles and Euripides. The
contemporary estimate of him did not differ much from ours.

We have noticed the immense popularity of history on the stage – more than a third of Shakespeare's plays were historical. It was not less so with the poets: the age demanded it. A large proportion of Daniel's work, and a considerable section of Drayton's, were concerned with history. And we may consider these two as representative professional men of letters: a new type of author who makes his living out of various kinds of writing, aided by patronage. C. S. Lewis describes Daniel as 'the most interesting man of letters whom that century produced in England'; *ipse dixit*, but Drayton was hardly less so.[51]

The Countess of Pembroke, carrying on Sidney's campaign against 'this tyrant of the North: Gross Barbarism', recruited Daniel and to her encouragement he owed the flowering of his literary career.[52] She herself, in touch with the French Renaissance, approved the classicism of Garnier and translated his *Mark Antony* into excellent blank verse. This was followed by Kyd's translation of his *Cornelia* and, groomed by her, Daniel's *Cleopatra*. His sonnets to Delia were much influenced by, and sometimes versions of, Desportes. Daniel, who married Florio's sister, was also a good Italian scholar, and tells us that he derived his ideas of writing history abroad: he considered it 'some blemish to the honour of our country to come behind other nations in this kind.'[53] He did his best to remedy this defect, in verse with his long poem *The Civil Wars*, and in prose with *The Collection of the History of England*. Drayton thought that he was 'too much historian in verse'; but in truth he was a good poet as well as a good historian. This is a very rare combination. It may be that Daniel's cool and balanced judgment, the total absence of illusion, depressed his ardour as a poet. But he was a true historian, a much rarer thing in that age, striving always to fuse the claims of historical truth with literary art. Perhaps no one else achieved both.

He responded to the inspiration of patriotism like (almost) everyone else:

> Why do you seek for feignèd palladins
> Out of the smoke of idle vanity
> Who may give glory to the true designs
> Of Bourchier, Talbot, Neville, Willoughby?
> Why should not you strive to fill up your lines
> With wonders of your own, with verity?

As Philip Sidney had answered himself, 'Look in thy heart, and write', so Daniel looked into his country's past, from the tragedy that overwhelmed Richard II onwards to the Wars of the Roses.

In the upshot his depiction came close to Shakespeare's. But he wrote not so much an heroic poem as history with moral reflections: he was a very reflective, and a moral, man. Nor did he care for the alarums and heroics of war, he saw too well the other side; so he reduced the element of battles, to depict characters, and states of mind, where he was just and perceptive.

He wrote a distinguished work of criticism with his *Defence of Rhyme* against Thomas Campion's biased attack upon it in his *Observations in the Art of English Poesy* (1602). It must be said that Daniel got the better of the argument, when Campion urged the 'inaptness of rhyme for poesy': he should have contented himself with supplementing rhyme, not substituting for it, and extending the variety of measures, where his case was good. Daniel was more closely in keeping with the nature of the language: he was in favour of reform and improvement, while adhering to what was natural and customary in its usage. Like Puttenham, he was much better informed about, and sympathetic to, medieval poetry. 'All our understandings are not to be built by the square of Italy . . . We are the children of nature as well as they.'[54] He took a far broader view: China was not to be subjected to Greek and Roman rules, regarding others as barbarians. And he foresaw, more clearly than anyone, the future place of English in the world.

Clarity, perspicacity, foresight were the rewards of absolute candour of mind and no illusions. He realised that he was living in a great age, but saw the cracks and abysses under the surface, and prophesied the confusion ahead. His remarkable poem, *Musophilus*, is very relevant to our day. He was aware, as few writers are, how small a part literature and intellectual pursuits play in human affairs, which anyway require other talents. In the midst of the inspired outpouring of Elizabethan literature, he faces a question of pointed cultural concern today: how if few read any books at all?

> How many thousands never heard the name
> Of Sidney, or of Spenser, or their books?
> And yet brave fellows, and presume of fame
> And seem to bear down all the world with looks.

A creative writer himself, he well understood the corrosive effect of much supposed 'criticism' by people who achieve nothing themselves:

> Presumption, ever fullest of defects,
> Fails in the doing to perform her part;

64

> And I have known proud words, and poor effects,
> Of such indeed as do condemn this art.
> But let them rest – it ever hath been known
> They others' virtues scorn that doubt their own.

A man who chose to live much to himself, he watched the literary game, and despised it. A writer of utter sincerity, communing with himself, he was thus neglected by those inferior to him in talent and accomplishment. He fell back on the artist's consolation, that art is an end in itself, even if no one listens or is capable of comprehending.

Art is its own reward – though it promises also reverberations in posterity: 'who in time knows whither we may vent the treasure of our tongue?'

> Or who can tell for what great works in hand
> The greatness of our style is now ordained?
> What powers it shall bring in, what spirits command,
> What thoughts let out, what humours keep restrained?

And in these lines we find him expressing confidence in the achievement of the English Renaissance that was already being borne out:

> Or should we careless come behind the rest
> In power of words that go before in worth,
> Whenas our accents equal to the best
> Is able greater wonders to bring forth,
> When all that ever hotter spirits expressed
> Comes bettered by the patience of the North?

Drayton's long, immensely productive career (1563–1631) 'mirrors the poetic history of a whole period', not only the Elizabethan but the Jacobean, though he was out of sympathy with the latter.[55] He began very early, as 'a proper goodly page, scarce ten years of age' at Polesworth, in his native Warwickshire:

> 'O my dear master, cannot you,' quoth I,
> 'Make me a poet?'

Later on, when he succeeded best with his Odes, 'Agincourt' and 'To the Virginia Voyage', he said:

> They may become John Hughes's lyre
> Which oft at Polesworth by the fire
> Hath made us gravely merry.

In those long empty nights there was leisure for poetry and such things, for a Welsh harper to sing ballads – we find Philip Sidney inquiring after the services of one, and we know how his heart was stirred by Border ballads. From first to last Drayton had no other ambition but to be a poet, and the best possible; he worked at his craft all his life, was wholly professional and very versatile, trying out every form with the artistic determination to make a good job of it.[56] Though he has not the intellectual interest of Daniel, he reaped the reward of virtue in his art: one watches him improving all the time. The final version of his sonnet-sequence, *Idea*, makes it one of the noblest of them all; and his very last poem, *The Muses' Elizium*, written when an old man, is one of his best.

His most successful poem in his day, *England's Heroical Epistles*, had no less than thirteen editions: one more indication of the thirst for history, and Drayton's feeling for it. He was widely read in, and inspired by, the chronicles of the past, which he loved calling up and reflecting on, with a strong leaning towards the antiquarian.[57] This is evident in what he considered his chief work, *Polyolbion* – surely one of the longest poems ever written. It is a complete description of England, county by county, really a versified Camden's *Britain*. In spite of its *longueurs* it has always had its admirers, even its enthusiasts; for what keeps it fresh and living still is Drayton's evident love of the countryside and all country pursuits. And how beautiful England must have been then, with woodland and forest still unspoiled, the country unravaged, room for the imagination to move about in! Drayton's especial love was for his native, wooded Warwickshire, to which he usually retired – as Shakespeare did – for the summers. He resorted to Clifford Chambers, a pretty half-timbered country house on the Stour, a couple of miles across the meadows from Stratford:

> dear Clifford's seat, the place of health and sport,
> Which many a time hath been the Muses' quiet port.

(The house was burnt down in 1918, but one still sees his friends, the Rainsfords, on their monuments in the church.)

His inspiration was no less the love of his country, the patriotism all these poets felt, 'the excitement of living (as they knew they lived) in England's golden age', 'that new awareness of what it felt like to be mere English which is so characteristic of the Elizabethans.'[58] But the golden age was soon over, and with the ineptitude of the Stuarts the country was on the way to the confusion that culminated in the Civil War. Drayton was as disillusioned as Daniel by the new face of things – James I was no inspiration to anybody, not even his boy-friends – and Drayton felt nothing but contempt for his Court. He also resented it that no mark of reward or honour was paid him for his life of dedicated achievement – though when one thinks of the hundreds of thousands of pounds the fool of a king poured out on Hay, Carr and Villiers, a very little would have sufficed to spare Drayton his years of poverty.

No wonder he turned to satire and bitterness. This is not evident, however, in his summing up of the poets of the age in his verse-letter 'To Henry Reynolds', with its tributes to his colleagues – far more generous and just than contemporaries usually are to each other (but Drayton was a noble spirit). Here is his 'countryman':

> Shakespeare, thou hadst as smooth a comic vein,
> Fitting the sock, and in thy natural brain,
> As strong conception and as clear a rage
> As anyone that trafficked with the stage.

(Drayton's own traffic with the stage had been a failure.) Again, at the end of his life, he achieved one of his best poems out of turning back to contemplate a vanished world:

> Decay nor age there nothing knows,
> There is continual youth,
> As time on plant or creatures grows
> So still their strength reneweth.

> The poets' paradise this is
> To which but few can come:
> The Muses' only bower of bliss,
> Their dear Elizium.

It was indeed a paradise for poets; happy were they whose work fell within it: they were borne up by its inspiration.

III

From the point of view of literature, in that age prose was distinctly secondary: its real voice was expressed in poetry and drama, to both of which prose-fiction was much inferior. With regard to prose in general we must at the outset correct, with Bush, a 'vulgar error' – though it was the error of Lytton Strachey and Virginia Woolf, who never understood the Elizabethans –

namely that prose was artificial, fantastic, over-elaborate, removed from reality.[59] This applies only to a restricted area: the Euphuism of Lyly, early Greene and the prose romances; while the prose of Hooker is elaborate and unwieldy (not so much so as Milton's, however), for all its nobility. But histories of literature are apt to omit the straight and perfectly satisfactory prose of chroniclers and historians, Hakluyt, Holinshed, Stow, though they are aware of the splendour of Ralegh or North, without any difficulty as they are. Then there is the direct and adequate prose of broadsides, tracts, pamphlets, of such lower-class writers as Dekker and Deloney, Chettle and Munday, or the universe of correspondence, the letters by which people conversed, of which the historian is constantly aware. In this last field alone there is much diversity, according to temperament: the pride and obsessive egoism of Ralegh, the poetry and pathos of Essex, the politic courtesy and insinuation of Robert Cecil. All are lucid, with very few exceptions: Lord Henry Howard, devious, convoluted because un-candid, always covering up; and the Queen, who thought it due to herself that she should write like nobody else, and did.

Fiction in prose, of Renaissance inspiration, was transmitted by the usual channels, translation from Italian and French, and to a much lesser extent from Spanish.[60] The first, largest and richest collection of stories in translation appeared early in the reign, William Painter's *Palace of Pleasure* (1566–7). Painter's aim was to make an impressive collection to rival the Italian and French; but even the ancient stories came through Bandello, Cinthio, Belleforest. Bandello's Tales, translated in the same year by Fenton, were stories of violence and horror which much appealed to the Elizabethans. But they were toned down and shortened for the English public; Painter gave them a moral flavouring, since this was a Protestant country. Later, the dramatists drew upon them for their plots, and as time went on, with Webster, Tourneur, Ford, they burst forth in their full horror and beauty. An Italianate flavour was as much the fashion in fiction as in the drama.

With Pettie's *Petite Palace of Pleasure* ten years later (1576) all the tricks of Euphuism are already anticipated. He wanted to show that an enriched (and fantasticated) English was as good as Italian or French for prose-fiction. Actually such writers adopted this elaborated prose to make up for the deficiency they felt in writing without verse: hence the balanced antitheses, the repeated rhythms, the proliferating alliteration. In consequence, their con-sciously artistic prose was more artificial than contemporary verse, particularly the blank verse of the drama. For formal speech in English is apt to fall naturally into blank verse pentameter – witness, for example, the speeches of Abraham Lincoln. These collections, and others such as Whetstone's, were aimed at a Court audience, where women were much to the fore: another reason for refining their sentiment and improving their moral tone. The naughty *Decameron* was not translated till James was on the throne; even then Mabbe toned down in translation the unflinching realism of the wonderful Spanish picaresque novel, *Celestina*.

Out of these influences the English produced their first original example of the new fiction, the poet Gascoigne's *The Adventure of Master F. J.* (1572): a good story, it is given an Italian colouring, but is probably autobiographical in essence. Lyly's *Euphues, the Anatomy of Wit* and its sequel *Euphues and his England* made not only a sensation but literary history. People have been apt to be hard on it ever since, partly under a misapprehension; a very young man's book, it must not be judged too severely, or taken too seriously. The tale is merely an excuse for ethical discourse – 'anatomy' means a dissection or inquiry; the book appealed to the widespread taste for such and perhaps especially to women readers. Society was not yet ripe for the discursive art of the mature novel, which implied a common readership that did not exist; it was the common audience there was for drama that gave that its depth and force. Gabriel Harvey applied the name 'Euphuism' to the catching tricks of style that captivated these young writers. We can see in them the similarities of ornamentation in Elizabethan architecture, furniture, dress.

The stylistic influence is observable, in lessening degree with each, in Greene, Lodge and Nashe. Robert Greene was one o the first to wrest a precarious livelihood from journalism – he would have been in his element today, when all is journalism. As Nashe describes him, 'in a night and a day would he have yarked up a pamphlet as well as in seven years, and glad was that printer that might be so blessed to pay him dear for the very dregs of his wit' [i.e. brain].[61] So in his early romances he exploited the fashionable Euphuism – anything to sell. It makes them unreadable to us. *Pandosto* is said to be the best of them, and was frequently reprinted down to the mid-eighteenth century. Considering the ambiguity of the relationship between Greene and Shakespeare, it is piquant that the player should have used Greene's novel for the plot of *The Winter's Tale*; characteristically, he removed the element of incest between father and daughter for *his* public. Greene turned to a simple and graceful prose with his autobiographical and cony-catching pamphlets for a lower-class audience. They gave freer rein to his talent for stories and for squalor: they are the beginning of realistic fiction, the precursor of the modern cult of shady life, making heroes of thieves and cut-throats. There is something Dickensian about Greene's depiction of the low life of London.

Lodge's romance, *Rosalind*, provided Shakespeare with a story for *As You Like It*. His best work, *A Margarite of America*, was in turn based upon parts of *Arcadia*. There was a free, if one-way, traffic between novelists and dramatists, and with these latter among themselves. Nashe's chief interest lies in his portrayal of professional literary life in London, and in his extraordinary linguistic originality and virtuosity. From the point of view of language, he is the most inventive of prose-writers, coining words as he went along, words, images, abuse, bubbling up with that 'happy extravagance and triumphant impudence of tone, which the Elizabethans have, perhaps, bequeathed rather to their American than to their English descendants.'[62] (There is something that reminds one of Dylan Thomas in him.) His satirical talent was much stronger than his creative; so he must have been grateful for the embittered literary quarrel that brewed up with the Harveys, for Nashe is inspired to his heights of abuse whenever he thinks of them. Many Elizabethans had a talent for describing personal appearance, as we know from their police and spy reports. But Nashe was a small-scale Rabelais: he piles up ludicrous detail to achieve a toppling caricature. Elizabethan humour was often cruel: even the sainted Sidney allows that people laughed then at deformity (which makes Bacon's covert reference to Robert Cecil, in his essay, the more envenomed). Gabriel Harvey was proud of his swarthy complexion, because it made him look like an Italian. Nashe describes it: 'It is of an adust [scorched] swart choleric dye, like rusty bacon or a dried skate-fish. So lean and so meagre that you would think (like the Turks) he observed four Lents in a year, or take him for the gentleman's man in the *Courtier*, who was so thin-cheeked and gaunt and starved that, as he was blowing the fire with his mouth, the smoke took him up like a light straw and carried him to the top or funnel of the chimney, where he had flown out God knows whither, if there had not been crossbars overthwart that stayed him . . . His skin riddled and crumpled like a piece of burnt parchment, and more channels and creases he hath in his face than there be fairy-circles on Salisbury Plain . . . For his stature, he is such a pretty Jack-a-Lent [scarecrow] as boys throw at in the street, and looks, in his black suit of velvet, like one of these jet drops which divers wear at their ears instead of a jewel.'[63]

Harvey – in return he gave almost as good as he got – was a poor scholar who pinched himself to cut a fine figure; he was a moral man, and not the one to go drinking with the lads. Now Greene – 'a good fellow he was, and would have drunk with thee for more angels than the Lord thou libeldst on gave thee in Christ's College; and in one year he pissed as much against the walls as thou and thy two brothers spent in three.'[64] (No doubt; but does that recommend him? It did to the denizens of literary Bohemia, who lived fast and died young.) Nashe would go to outrageous lengths for a laugh; his pornographic poem, 'The Choice of Valentines', which describes a visit to a brothel, is one of the naughtier poems of the age. Naturally such a young man would not love Puritans; in fact, he detested them and his first entrance into literary life was on the side of the bishops in the Marprelate controversy. Martin Marprelate, whoever he was, is considered by some to be one of the best prose-writers: he has a talent for comic abuse, a down-to-earth, racy style, with homely images, a rude bouncing vigour. But I find his incessant abuse of the bishops – those much overworked donkeys of administration – tiresome, and his complete indifference to truth in flinging mud at them (much of it stuck and did untold damage into the next century) rather shocking. The Puritans deserved everything they got at the hands of the Church, and a great deal more. Nashe was genuinely orthodox in his convictions, as often happens with humorists: humour is a saving, conservative element.

Each of these men wrote verse even better in quality than their prose: that is significant. Even Nashe, whose prose has a touch of genius, wrote what Yeats thought the most beautiful lines in English:

> Beauty is but a flower
> Which wrinkles will devour;
> Brightness falls from the air,
> Queens have died young and fair,
> Dust hath closed Helen's eye.
> I am sick, I must die.
> Lord, have mercy on us!

He was still young when he died, 'tender young Juvenal'.

These men, being university wits, looked down upon plebeian writers like Deloney and Dekker. They were the best of a class which nevertheless had solid virtues. For one thing, they displayed common sense as against aristocratic fantasy, they have more sense of life, besides a hard-headed realism which the romancers never descended to. They have a solider, if rougher, characterisation, and a good idea of a story – though often the stories are quite separate interludes detachable from the work as a whole, which is not a work of art. They give us depictions of a new sphere of life, which literature had not hitherto included. Deloney renders the country-town life of Newbury, with which he was familiar, as also the city-life of Westminster; Dekker that of London. Deloney's best novel, *Jack of Newbury* (1597), is a tale of the industrious apprentice who makes good, marries the mistress of the business, and becomes a rich and famous man. This was much to the taste of middle and lower class readers: Deloney was the Elizabethan Defoe, his utilitarian values those of Benjamin Franklin.

These works exemplified a democratic spirit, exceptionally for the age – as against its greatest writer, for example, and all the others. Deloney, especially, put forward in Jack of Newbury, Simon Eyre, Thomas Cole, the rich clothier of Reading, plebeian heroes with whom lower-class readers could identify. He was no social critic; he had a popular idea of monarchy – the monarch righting wrongs and restoring rights: a concept which the Queen tried to uphold and now and again exemplified in her actions. Dekker took over the story of Simon Eyre for his best play, *The Shoemaker's Holiday*. His most original tract, *The Gull's Hornbook*, was an attempt to adapt a German contribution to the Renaissance, Grobianism, though it failed to reach the depths of German grossness and brutality.

All these writers wrote too fast and too much, there was such a greatly increased demand for reading matter in the classes they catered for. The interesting thing is – and this would have surprised the grander Elizabethans – that they are more readable today, for they have the salt of life in them, immature and in-artistic as they are. And, an ironical conclusion, theirs was the prose that pointed the way to the future, direct and realist as against the artificiality, regarded as a commendation then, of the upper-class romances and ethical tales.

In those earlier writers the essay was not yet differentiated from the novel; by the end of the century it was. Francis Bacon provided the most famous example with his *Essays* (1597), though shortly after Sir William Cornwallis produced more complete specimens of the genre patented by Montaigne. Cornwallis belonged to that East Anglian Catholic family that patronised the arts, and was a friend of Donne, who was at this time writing his Paradoxes and his very un-Elizabethan verse. Both lived extravagant and raffish lives. Cornwallis's father lamented to his friend Wotton 'mine unthrifty and unfortunate son. He hath spent me in that Court [Spain] above £5000. And now having given him £200 a year more wherewith to live, he turns his back to his fortunes. Of all sorts of people I most despair of those of this sort, that are philosophers in their words and fools in their works.'[65]

Perhaps the dichotomy was useful to the reflective essayist: one observes the weakness of will to follow out what he knows and thinks. 'I wrote thus; I think thus; and I hope to do thus. But that blessed time is not yet come.' A devoted reader of Montaigne in Florio's translation, to whom he pays a tribute, he was a true essayist. In 1601–2 he was in Scotland, where he became acquainted with the brilliant young Overbury, who won fame for his *Characters* – still more for being poisoned by the wicked Countess of Essex. It was in Scotland that Overbury became an intimate friend of Robin Carr, then page to the Earl of Dunbar, but to be promoted to the Bedchamber of James I. Cornwallis was a protagonist of male friendship: 'I hope I shall not offend divinity if I say the conjunction of man and wife is not love . . . That which comes nearest to love is this: man with man agreeing with sex. I cannot think it is so between man and woman, for it gives opportunity to lust, which the pureness of love will not endure.'[66] His friend, Jack Donne, could inform him about that. 'After that celebration [the coupling of friends in pairs] it is irreligious to divorce a friend, though guilty of many deformities.' 'Mine are but essays, who am but newly bound prentice to the inquisition of knowledge.' A good fellow, Cornwallis was dead at thirty-five; one already sees the tendencies and colours of the Jacobean Age in him.

Bacon was thirty-six when he published the first version of his *Essays*, along with *The Colours of Good and Evil*. This last work is extremely interesting intellectually. Literary scholars seem to find it difficult to appreciate the *Essays* at their true worth, their tone is so worldly and without any illusions: they give one an insight into the political mind at the top of Elizabethan society, the necessary craft, the uses and the unveiling of dissimulation, complete awareness of what men are – 'there is little friendship in the world,

and least of all between equals' – and they do not like it. To C. S.
Lewis *The Colours of Good and Evil* would be exceedingly uncongenial. 'Colours' meant pretences; 'to colour a thing' meant to
give it a twist, a favourable guise, a false colouring. Bacon's sharp
eyes, with their adder-like glitter, had evidently noticed people
constantly at it, especially in the law and in politics. His tract,
unfinished, is an attempt to expose methodically the false arguments people will use to cover up, to deflect attention from the
personal interest they have in an issue; to show up the way in
which circumstances make people think what they think, and
that to discover what makes them think as they do is often more
important than *what* they think. And this obtains all through man's
'thinking', quite obviously in politics, economics, and religion. But
no less in all other matters. For example: suppose a man teaches
English Literature at Cambridge: he is apt to think that the Cambridge English school, his version of it, is the be-all and end-all of
a university education (even if the only foreign language he knows
is English). To be able to spot the ways in which people are influenced, consciously or unconsciously, by their motives is a short
cut to truth, besides an immense economy of time and intellectual
energy – one simply does not have to take seriously most of what
most people think about anything. The historian knows this in-
stinctively, or by experience; the penetrating Pareto based his
whole system of sociology upon it. Bacon prefigured it in the work
that accompanied his *Essays*; it is no less a revelation of his inner
mind than they are.

Bacon's essays were originally aphorisms, into which he dis-
tilled his observations, and which he subsequently expanded and
added to; with their final version (1625), we see fully portrayed
the most magnificent intellect of his time. But its character is
already clear in the earliest essays. 'Reading maketh a full, con-
ference a ready, and writing an exact man.' Different subjects are
apt to have different values and effects as intellectual discipline:
'Histories make men wise; poets, witty [i.e. clever]; the mathematics, subtle; natural philosophy, deep; moral, grave; logic and
rhetoric, able to contend.' In conversation he favoured asking
questions; for it flattered people's self-esteem, their prevailing
quality, and perhaps one may at least learn something. He had no
high opinion of the average man: 'if you would work any man,
you must either know his nature and fashions, and so lead him;
or his ends, and so win him; or his weaknesses or disadvantages,
and so awe him; or those that have interest in him, and so govern

him.' No illusions anywhere: it is a very mature state of mind, but antithetical to poetry.

We may take Bacon to represent the very spirit of prose, and it is evident that it has already achieved a mature modernity – what English was to become. As Lewis says, 'somehow or other during the latter part of the 16th century Englishmen learned to write.' The historian may add – as they learned everything else.[67]

IV

The reaction against the dominant Elizabethanism in poetry may be seen in three writers of genius, George Chapman, Ben Jonson, Donne, in each of whom it took a different form.

Chapman reacted into an obscure intellectualism, which he justified by regarding himself as a superior spirit with a hatred of the common man, and this he expresses obsessively. 'The profane multitude I hate, and only consecrate my strange poems to these searching spirits whom learning hath made noble.'[68] The public responded by never demanding a second edition of his books. In an unexampled moment of truth, he confessed to his friend Hariot that he had not the divine afflatus to achieve poetry:

> O that my strange Muse
> Without this body's nourishment could use
> Her zealous faculties, only t'aspire
> Instructive light from your whole sphere of fire.

He speaks pathetically of

> that chaos whence this stifled verse
> By violence breaks, where glowworm-like doth shine
> In nights of sorrow this hid soul of mine.

On such small indications has been built up a 'School of Night' now recognised for a mare's nest, or, perhaps one should say, a mares' nest.[69] Others have seen in this strangulated poet the rival poet of Shakespeare's sonnets. Such people have no sense of literature, and should get out of the field.

Chapman was an intensely serious solitary spirit, with no sense of humour but an aspiring intellectual energy true to the age. He had genius of a kind: Lewis calls it a 'sultry genius', and regards his poetry as transitional. Most of his best work falls in the Jacobean age, and even what does not is on the way to it – if one diagnoses what is Jacobean, with F. P. Wilson, as more complex, more burdened with thought, more laboured and often more tortuous.[70]

This applies in part to Ben Jonson, though his reaction in poetry was towards a classic simplicity, in the drama to classical tragedy with *Sejanus* and *Catiline* and to topical satirical comedy with his masterpieces, *Volpone* and *The Alchemist*. The whole cast of his mind was unromantic, unlike the characteristic Elizabethans, and towards satire. Above all, it was intellectual: he was a brain. One does not think of him as having much other than the more intellectual emotions: it was a woman who said, very shrewdly, that Ben Jonson 'never writes of love, or, if he does, does it not naturally.'[71] What a world of difference from Shakespeare! – no wonder Ben could never quite come to terms with him, though he admired his genius this side of idolatry.

With Jonson we are passing out of the region of the Renaissance: his inspiration rather was classical, Latin verse and prose, in especial Horace. He evidently thought of himself as an English Horace, laying down the law. 'Reacting against Elizabethan vagaries of matter, form and style, Jonson demanded, and unceasingly strove for, the ageless classical virtues of clarity, unity, symmetry, and proportion; in short, the control of the rational intelligence.'[72] What the intellectual will could achieve at its best he could achieve: models of precision, clarity, classic severity, as in his songs. He also popularised the 'epigram' – a flexible form, which might be long or short, but is again dominantly intellectual, reflecting on person or subject. With all this, it is the less surprising that Jonson wrote his poems the way that Camden had taught him at Westminster, first in prose, then turning them into verse. It is hardly the way to gain inspiration, nevertheless Jonson often achieved a classic perfection in his songs and shorter pieces. He cared everything for 'art'. We are on the way to the metaphysical school, the cult of cleverness, intellectualism, the far-fetched conceit: the poets of the next generation were happy to inscribe themselves of 'the tribe of Ben'.

A Catholic, a member of a persecuted minority, with martyrs in his family, John Donne did not appreciate the Elizabethan Age – though he went on one of its grand exploits, the capture of Cadiz – nor did he think much of its literature. He is a singular, isolated phenomenon, with no obvious affiliations; of extraordinary originality, emotional intensity, intellectual vitality, he is already on his way to the next age, a forerunner, a precursor.

How different a spirit from Sidney, Spenser, Shakespeare! We could already tell from his images, even if we did not know, that his was a Catholic background. In one poem we hear of those whose state

> Is poor, disarmed like Papists, not worth hate.

The winds 'in our ruined abbeys roar', and he knows about

> Simony and sodomy in churchmen's lives;

about the ways of monks and friars, with their beads and paternosters; fasts are not Puritan, but Carthusian; wasting candle-droppings are kept like relics.

For, an exceedingly erotic spirit, there is a thin line between religion and sex in Donne: even his devotion is erotic. And he was obsessed with sex. Take, again, one poem only: 'On his Mistress Going to Bed.'

> Come, madam, come, all rest my powers defy:
> Until I labour, I in labour lie.
> The foe oft-times, having the foe in sight,
> Is tired with standing though he never fight . . .
> Full nakedness! All joys are due to thee,
> As souls unbodied, bodies must unclothèd be
> To taste whole joys . . .
> To teach thee, I am naked first: why then,
> What needst thou have more covering than a man?

The next poem is more specific in its imagery from war:

> Other men war that they their rest may gain,
> But we will rest that we may fight again . . .
> Near thrusts, pikes, stabs, yea bullets, hurt not here.

How different from those chaste Protestants, Spenser and Sidney!

And again we see how different from the age in that, in his most ambitious poem, *The Progress of the Soul*, in the end the soul of heresy, after a sojourn with Calvin, was to come to rest in the body of Queen Elizabeth! The poem was, appropriately, abortive and was never finished; but to it Donne added a coda that expresses a cynical distrust about ever finding the truth intellectually. This is a Catholic inflexion, not a Protestant one.

> Who'ere thou beest that readst this sullen writ,
> Which just so much courts thee as thou dost it,
> Let me arrest thy thoughts. Wonder with me

77

> Why ploughing, building, ruling and the rest,
> Or most of those arts whence our lives are blest,
> By cursèd Cain's race invented be,
> And blest Seth vexed us with astronomy.

And the conclusion? –

> There's nothing simply good or ill alone:
> Of every quality comparison,
> The only measure is, and judge, opinion.

Scepticism, cynicism, relativism: with that he was finding his way out of Catholicism.

It is an unattractive mixture; but what wins respect is his tormented search to find truth somehow, somewhere. It took him a long time.

Meanwhile his poetry made a sensation among the young and intelligent. His method was that of paradox, in verse as in prose; of conceits as unexpected as might be in order to shock, of analogies so far-fetched as sometimes to be ridiculous; to twist the accentuation of words and the rhythms of lines to get away from smoothness, often achieving surprisingly fine effects; to phrase with telescoped conciseness, and then produce a catalogue of words, nouns or verbs, one after another. Everything was done to make verse as different as possible from Elizabethan facility and ease and regularity. But there is no doubt that this was genuine and corresponded with Donne's genius: the irregularity of his life is reflected in the irregularity of his poetry, along with the intellectual restlessness, the torment of mind and spirit – in a word, the *Angst* – that gives him a living appeal to us moderns.

Brilliantly gifted, fascinating to women and men-friends alike, he was not a nice man.

Donne's deformation of conventional metrics – for which Ben Jonson said he should have been hanged – was deliberate and conscious. But there takes place a comparable breakdown of the famous blank verse line in the drama, so regular and formal at the beginning. Verse-forms undergo a certain evolution according to an inner logic, but also in response to the demands upon them of thought, of content – thus indirectly even reflecting the conditions of society. Blank verse becomes more flexible, less endstopped; with so much pressure of imagination, images, thought, as Shakespeare grew older his blank verse became verse-paragraphs. With others too. A contemporary noticed that blank verse was really too facile – for poor poets. In the Caroline drama the deliquescence goes so far, it often ceases to be recognisable as verse. In Shakespeare difference of function between verse and prose still exists, in accordance with aesthetic decorum. Later on, it might often as well be written, as with later Auden, in the form of prose.

V

We may conclude that where, before the Elizabethans, there was no continuous English literature, after them it flourished, rich, mature and full. They started it. Sidney and Spenser achieved their aim, perhaps beyond their dreams.

CHAPTER III

WORDS AND MUSIC

WITH music we reach, as with poetry and drama, the height of English achievement in art; though with music, sad to say, after the 'Golden Age'* there was a descent from the heights never to be recovered. The Civil War did some irreparable damage to the most sensitive of the arts, or to the ligaments and fibres – perhaps to the very nature – of the society most propitious to it. Circumstances and accidents, such as the untimely death of Purcell, played their part. The most splendid age of music reflected an integrated society, along with the favouring circumstances, the inspiration of Renaissance Italy. Since music is the most international of the arts, the contacts and interchanges were more direct, the cross-fertilisation more fruitful and prolific than ever. Outside Italy, only England produced an independent school of madrigal – the characteristic musical form of the Renaissance; though much smaller, it reached comparable quality. In keyboard music England led Europe; indeed English keyboard technique became the basis of Western keyboard music. Never again was such a thing to happen. What England received from Italy she more than handed on to the music of Northern Europe, especially to the Netherlands, Germany and Denmark, and in keyboard and lute-music to France. Much of this has been the rediscovery of scholarship in our time, and one of its most rewarding chapters.

Henry VIII's Court had been under French influence musically, as in other ways;[1] Elizabeth's was more responsive to Italy. Until the disaster of the Wars of the Roses English music, with Dunstable, had been a major influence in Northern Europe.[2] That deplorable time of anarchy left its effect in the cultural lag evident until the rise of the new humanism. Then the promise of this was bitten off by the bitter blasts of the Reformation – and all was to do again. In music, as with poetry and the drama, the full flowering of the Renaissance does not show itself until the

* This was Sir Donald Tovey's phrase.

1580's; it continued until about the death of its greatest jewel, William Byrd, in 1623.

The impact of the Renaissance was to be seen in the bursting out from the cocoon of medieval faith, hitherto the centre of man's experience, to the discovery of man as an end in himself. More and more secular forms gain importance; in vocal music the movement is towards the madrigal; in Italy away from polyphony towards monody and, with the domination of the words, to the invention of opera. Secular keyboard music developed a world of its own, where English masters were supreme (and this was not even realised a brief generation ago). The essence of humanist belief is necessarily the dominance of the Word, and the movement of Renaissance culture is towards its realisation, in music only less than in literature.[3] Musical developments become increasingly coordinated with poetry; never was there such close contact between poets and musicians. Nevertheless, as often happens in the arts, the finest achievements were made in the art on its way out: the last flowering of polyphony, before modern music took first place with monody and tonality (the major and minor scales), was its noblest.

For this divine interval a balance was achieved, which may correspond with some balance of forces in society, too subtle to break down in analysis, though it may be illustrated. The movement was increasingly away from the horizontal line of melody in different parts (polyphony) towards the vertical (harmony). But the former still dominated in 'the consummate merging of melodic and harmonic elements which characterises the second half of the sixteenth century.'[4] The very ambivalence in itself, exploring the borders between two worlds of feeling and thought – as we have noticed with Shakespeare and his contemporaries – doubled the possibilities of imagination and expression open to them. Behind them the medieval world of faith; before them the voyage into the modern unknown. In music 'these two aspects of melody and harmony were then more interdependent than they have ever been before or since in musical history.'[5] And we must add: more flexible. Of all nineteenth-century writers, only the poet Gerard Manley Hopkins understood this – because of his intense musicality and his abnormal sensibility.

This ambivalence between two worlds of experience extended itself more subtly still to rhythm. Underneath the long and flexible rhythms of the earlier melodic line there is the encroaching, if still latent, sense of accent. There is, underneath the beautiful balance, an inner tension that is indescribably affecting: to anyone responsive to it there is no music (except occasionally in Bach and Mozart) that makes such an impact on heart and soul. What is the reason for it? Perhaps it is beyond analysis: one is in a region of experience that lies beyond words. The Elizabethans themselves knew this, though even they could not give it verbal expression. Music is a world in itself; those who cannot enter it do not know what it is about: it reflects, but it also transcends, experience.

An historian of the art tells us that 'there was a collective rhythm with regularly recurring accents between which and the individual rhythm of each part there was a continual tension. This tension was the real core of sixteenth-century style.'[6] He suggests that it is no accident that 'in England this supreme development of musical rhythm coincides with the development of mature Shakespearean blank verse, which achieves its effect from a delicate tension between speech rhythm and metrical accent.' Anyone can see that this flexible situation would multiply the possibilities of expression. He concludes: 'the second half of the sixteenth century seems to me the most *fundamentally* musical period in European civilisation . . . The general level of taste, among artists and folk, has never been so universally creative. Some of the music has a poignancy almost too great for the human heart to bear.'

He adds, 'if today we cannot listen to the music with precisely the exaltation and radiance with which we presume contemporary audiences heard it, we cannot but listen to it with an intensity no less sharp for being different, and with a reverence born of nostalgia.'[7] It is evident that explanations carry us beyond the merely social; perhaps the historian may be allowed a personal confession. The music of the sixteenth century grips me as no other music, lays a finger on the pulses of the heart, steals into the crevices of the mind, from a world inexplicably close to tears. On the other side of the experience is the sense that in listening to their music we hear the beating of their hearts. And that this is no mere sentimentality is borne home by the fact that musical rhythms are intimately connected with physical responses – at bottom the musical beat refers to the pulse, the beat of the heart. So it is not strange that one should feel in their music still the implications of the world of medieval faith, the tenuous hold of its vanishing consolation, the poignancy of their sense of the briefness of life and beauty and joy. It may be because modal music expresses the timeless spirit of another world that one is overwhelmed

by its haunting poignancy and, when one hears it, for a moment
time is suspended and the heart stands still.

I

Late medieval Church music stood in need of reform, like the
Church itself. Some of the later pre-Reformation Masses lost sense
of time and place with their over-elaboration, complexity and
length; as with the chantries, piling up thousands of obits and
masses, a cutting out of dead wood was necessary. In music this
came with Cranmer's directive that singing in church should be
'for every syllable a note', with the sensible qualification 'as near
as may be.' (Not long after, the Council of Trent directed a
similar simplification in the Roman Church.) 'The effect of the
adoption of this principle has profoundly influenced English
Church-music from that day to this. At the moment it was revolutionary . . . A new beginning had to be made, and few there were
that made it.'[8]

The Reformation at large gave a resounding blow, in its first
impact, to music. The Dissolution of the monasteries meant the
destruction of a number of organs, the dispersal of some choirs and
music-books. With the first Prayer Book of 1549 the destruction
of all old service-books was ordered. 'Latin church music had
been attainted and proscribed', though perhaps its development
could have gone no further on the old lines; 'musicians who had
grown up in the tradition of the old free writing may well have
wondered what future there was for the idiom they had learnt.'[9]
The finest composer among these, Taverner, who wrote such
splendid works as his 'In all devotion',* 'O Michael' and 'Western
Wind' Masses, became a Protestant fanatic, ceased to write and
acted as an agent for the Dissolution in Lincolnshire. Marbeck
provided the new English liturgy with a complete set of services,
the *Book of Common Prayer Noted*, adapting the ancient plainchant
to the words, with all excrescences removed – in its way a nice
epitome of the English Church. After that he declined into writing Protestant tracts. A finer composer, Christopher Tye, found
the struggle too much for him and, defeated, resigned from being
organist at Ely to retire to a country living. But a composer of
genius, Tallis, held on to effect the transition, continuing to compose Latin motets while providing the English rite with services,

---

* *Not* 'Small Devotion', as it is often mis-read.

chants, hymn-tunes, anthems, the litany which we still sing in our churches today. Brought up and trained in the Latin rite, reared as a Catholic, in the end both he and his wife died as Anglicans. Not only had he successfully made the transition, but the English Church owed him everything for continuing and refining the tradition: good reason for the veneration in which he was held as the 'Father of Music'.

For what eventually happened was more rich and rewarding than might have been feared in Edward VI's reign, when the Calvinists were in the ascendant, or than the later Puritans hoped. Calvin restricted Church music to the congregational singing of metrical psalms, a simple art. This took on in Protestant London at the beginning of Elizabeth's reign. The Church authorities proceeded to meet this demand by prescribing, in 1559, 'a modest and distinct song . . . that the same might be as plainly understanded as if it were read without singing.'[10] Next year John Day – in the first piece of music-printing – provided three full services with hymns and anthems. We are already on the way to a new efflorescence of Church music. It is frequently to be observed in a society that the nature of the institutions will in the end determine their ideological and cultural expressions. The English Church, whatever doctrinal accretions were removed, retained its Catholic structure; it was not long before it was producing a reformed Catholic music.

The life and work of Tallis are symptomatic of the process. Shortly after the suppression of Waltham abbey, where he had been organist, Henry VIII appointed him to the Chapel Royal, whither he brought his service-books. There he remained for the rest of his life, through all the changes of ritual. Such unbroken devotion to music enabled him to carry forward the best of the old tradition into the new. And in fact the polyphonic development continued in both Latin and English Church music, reinvigorated for the shaking up it had received. The tradition of the past flowed powerfully in the new direction, with 'increased articulation of the melodic phrase and a growing feeling for conciseness and economy of means.'[11] It also flowed into new channels: 'the lesser forms were there waiting to be given richer content and deeper significance.' There is the even stronger inspiration of writing new music for the English language, with its very different character, its lighter, more accentual rhythms. It is like the transition from Skelton to Sidney; as in poetry, the Elizabethans ended by writing far finer music than there had been before.

This, again, did not come about until the threshold of the
1580's, and then not without a struggle. Again the Court held and
manned the inner fortress. The Chapel Royal maintained the
standards, supported the musicians, encouraged the composers.
It was in close touch with the cathedrals, the collegiate churches
and college chapels, which carried Church music on and forward.
One finds a regular interchange of personnel between these and
the Chapel Royal, to which musicians looked for preferment and
where standards were highest. The Master of the Children of the
Chapel had the right to tour the country and recruit boys with
likely voices into its service. Meanwhile the Court had need of
every kind of music for its activities, its ceremonies and pleasures,
dancing, theatre, song. Even the large Accession Day tilts included music – Sir Henry Lee's farewell as Champion in 1590
was graced by his song being performed by Robert Hales, the
Queen's favourite singer.[12] An early Elizabethan play like *Gorboduc* reads rather bleakly, but one must think of it more favourably with the music with which it was accompanied. For all the
varied Court purposes a considerable establishment of instrumentalists, many of them foreign, was maintained: some ninety
men and twelve boys altogether.[13]

The Puritans found it impossible to carry this fortress, though
they tried hard enough: it was not until the monarchy fell that
they had their way. Then, in 1645, they ordered the destruction
of the organs in the churches, they dispersed the choirs and the
service-books, while the most original genius among composers,
William Lawes, was killed this same year, quite young. Here
was the target the Puritans had aimed at all along. In 1563 they
petitioned that 'all curious singing and playing of the organs may
be removed.'[14] In 1572 they were at it again with their Admoni-
tion to Parliament against the church services, 'where there is no
edification according to the rule of the Apostles, but confusion:
they toss the Psalms in most places like tennis-balls.'[15] This is their
way of describing the affecting alternation between the *decani* and
cantoris sides of the choir. For good measure, the odious Cartwright added, 'As for organs and curious [i.e. elaborate] singing,
though they be proper to Popish dens – I mean to cathedral
churches – yet some others also must have them. The Queen's
Chapel and these churches, which should be spectacles of Christian
reformation, are rather patterns and precedents to the people of
all superstition.'[16] As if a cultivated Queen would listen to these
detestable people, as foolish as they were Philistine!

It seems absurd that such fanatics should have to be answered. But it brings home an important historical point: these people were in fact a small minority in an age when all the world made music. Revolutions, however, are made by small, relentless minorities; and these people were relentless. In 1586 a distinguished Oxford scholar took up the defence of music, just as Sidney and Puttenham were doing for poetry. This was Dr. John Case of St. John's; his book, *The Praise of Music*, was the first to come from the newly founded University printing press.[17] He followed it up two years later with a Latin tract, *Apologia Musices*, for the learned. Musicians were grateful: Thomas Watson and William Byrd published a *Gratification* to him, verses and music; years after, Ravenscroft recalled his service to the cause in his *Brief Discourse*.

Dr. Case had been a chorister at New College and Christ Church, so he knew what he was talking about. He was a successful doctor, who published a series of works on Aristotle, ethics and medicine. More rare, he was a philanthropic connoisseur, who encouraged and wrote prefaces for Haydock's translation of Lomazzo's treatise on painting, and Nicholas Breton's *Pilgrimage to Paradise*. Case's two treatises are not unlike Sidney's and Puttenham's in method, grounding himself on the antiquity of music, the good opinion of received authorities (such as the early Fathers), its necessary uses in society, for celebrations, weddings, feasts, funerals, as in war to encourage martial spirit. There is also its benefit to health. Several musicians refer to this in their prefaces: singing opens the pipes, expands the chest, helps stammering, cures nervousness. All agree as to its psychological benefit in helping to cure melancholy. Philip Sidney advised young Robert, 'now, sweet brother, take a delight to keep and increase your music: you will not believe what a want I find of it in my melancholy times.'[18] On his death-bed he had sung to him 'La Cuisse rompue', the song he had himself made on the death-wound he had received. So, too, Essex's father, the first Earl, dying of dysentery in Ireland, had the song he had composed sung to him by his musician, William Hales. Music is a great consolation.

That profoundly religious spirit, William Byrd, went further. Music was for the service of God: *omnis spiritus laudet dominum*. He was a Catholic, as Case's sympathies were also. Indeed we shall notice how splendid the contribution of Catholics and quasi-Catholics was to Elizabethan music. The Anglican position was stated for good and all by Hooker. Music 'delighteth all ages and beseemeth all states, a thing as seasonable in grief as in joy . . .

The reason hereof is an admirable facility which music hath to express and represent to the mind more inwardly than any other sensible means [i.e. through any other sense] the very steps and inflexions every way, the turns and varieties of all passions whereunto the mind is subject . . . There is one [kind] that draweth to a marvellous grave and sober mediocrity [i.e. even frame of mind]. There is also that carrieth as it were into ecstasies, filling the mind with an heavenly joy, and for the time in a manner severing it from the body.'[19] It is clear that Hooker *understood*. Here in music was ground upon which Catholics could co-operate with the English Church, in spite of all the religious and political hatreds of the time – as they proceeded to do.

Of course the real reply to the fanatics was something they would never understand, the created works of art themselves. Such people were the enemies of culture, of the enjoyment of life, of human fulfilment, of civilisation. But they are dead and gone; the works of genius of Tallis and Byrd, Wilby, Weelkes and Morley, Dowland and Bull and Gibbons, are alive and with us still. For only art redeems human experience from the sentence of time.

The fruits of co-operation, the continuity of the tradition and its further development, were made evident to the cultivated world by the joint publication, by Tallis and Byrd, of their *Cantiones Sacrae* in 1575. It was a quasi-official publication, dedicated to the Queen with a tribute to her musical skill, 'vel vocis elegantia, vel digitorum agilitate', by the two organists of her Chapel Royal, the Anglican ritual of which impressed foreigners and was so offensive to Puritans. This was the seventeenth year of the Queen's reign, so there are seventeen compositions by each composer, in compliment to her.[20] The Latin poems prefixed to it by dear Mulcaster and a talented amateur of the Queen's Household, Sir Ferdinando Heybourne – whom we can still see today on his tomb in Tottenham parish church[21] – make it clear that this was a manifesto to the musical world of Europe. Its spirit was comparable to the intention of Sidney and Spenser in literature: a declaration that a new power had arrived in music. The printing press enabled English music, hitherto hidden, to be brought to light. Heybourne, Tallis's pupil along with Byrd, specifically states the claim of these leaders of English music to take their place along with those abroad, Lassus, Gombert and Ferrabosco.

All was naturally in Latin, though the words of the motets eschewed the controversial (excrescences in honour of the Virgin Mary, for example – one Virgin was enough). Tallis revealed himself the master of the older traditional style; Byrd, with his *Emendemus in melius*, the greater genius that he was so richly to fulfil. The relationship of master and pupil was close and affectionate; Tallis became godfather of Byrd's son, Thomas. The two musicians, in addition to their appointments, the various leases they enjoyed which gave them a modest prosperity, were now rewarded by the grant of a monopoly of music-printing for twenty-one years. Though Byrd was the greater composer, Tallis has always been the household name, because of the familiar place his music has held in the regular liturgy of the Church. In hundreds of churches all over the country we sing his Preces and Responses at matins and evensong, his chants and hymns, his litany.

Both composers were more inspired by the Latin rite and continued to compose for it, in addition to their Latin motets and English work for the national Church. Tallis wrote at least three Masses – most of a 7-part Mass has only recently been recovered. Two very fine Lamentations we owe to the religious change – the pre-Reformation Church did not set Lenten texts. His gigantic 40-part motet *Spem in alium* – really for five choirs of eight voices – is a *tour de force*. One is struck by the statuesque effect of this mountain of a work, not much inner movement is possible in such a lay-out; but the whole gives the effect of a sea of sound, a surge of prayer and propitiation. Tallis was as deeply religious a spirit as Byrd, in such works more austere, though he was capable of tenderness. There is a certain majesty in his work; one hears it in a motet like *Loquebantur variis linguis*, with its symbolism: 7-part, seven-tongued, it is written for vespers at Pentecost, with wave upon wave of Alleluias, the waves reaching up out of the sea of faith, surging and withdrawing until the last whisper upon that unrecapturable shore. Without their music we cannot feel what those people felt about life; with it we can.

In his settings of the Psalms in free and elaborate chant-form Tallis carried over from the Latin to the English use. He adapted some of his Latin motets into English anthems of sober beauty. His were the finest tunes contributed to Archbishop Parker's Psalter; that they are still a source of inspiration is clear from Vaughan Williams' *Fantasia* upon one of them. Tallis's prime work was vocal, but he was an all-round musician, composing in other genres, though much of it is lost. There survive various secular part-songs in English, crisper like the language. For stringed instruments there are only two 'In nomines'; two 'Felix namques' – organ-interludes often played during the offertory at Communion – attest his virtuosity as composer for the keyboard, with their coruscating flourishes and runs. Since these two forms are peculiarly English their derivation may be explained. The 'In nomine' plainsong tune is that to the words *In nomine Domini* in Taverner's *Gloria Tibi Trinitas* Mass. It became a tradition among English composers to use this as a theme upon which to write variations, a test of virtuosity, ingenuity and imagination. No less than 150 sets of such variations survive; even a composer as late as Purcell wrote one. Milton's father composed an 'In nomine' of 40 parts, to show off his amateur expertise, for which Count Laski awarded him a gold chain. The 'Felix namque' tune came from the offertory for the Vigil of the Assumption, and was only less popular for variations. Variations for keyboard music later became a strongly marked feature of the English school.

Tallis died, an old man, in 1585 having done his work for which the Church of England has always held him in honour: he had piloted her music safely through the transition and laid the foundations of English Church music. He is buried in the church of St. Alphege at Greenwich, near the palace where he had so often performed. In his will he left £3.6.8 to 'my company the gentlemen of Her Majesty's Chapel towards their feast.'[22] Anthony Roper was to have his gilt bowl, William Byrd his large gilt cup. Richard Cranwell of the Chapel took loving care of Tallis's widow; when she came to die, specifically reciting the Protestant doctrine of salvation through the merits of Christ, she left Cranwell most of her quite comfortable possessions. The moiety of the music-printing monopoly was left to the godson, Thomas Byrd. Everything shows the entire confidence and good feeling within this devoted circle.

Byrd succeeded to Tallis's primacy among English musicians, and to become the greatest composer they have ever produced. This claim is solidly based upon the absolute mastery he displayed over so many fields, the breadth and grandeur of his conceptions, the variety and originality of his invention, the utter integrity and loftiness of his spirit, which also included a gay, blithe side along with tenderness and charm. He was a very catholic composer, who – like Shakespeare – could put his hand to anything; but he was also an uncompromising Counter-Reformation

Catholic, who, though organist of the Queen's Chapel, ceased to communicate with the Church for which he wrote its finest music. From the intensity of his devotion to Catholicism, and his closeness to some of the Jesuits, it looks as if he underwent a conversion, or a renewal of faith around 1580[23] – and this was the time of the mission of Campion and Parsons, which reconciled a number of important persons and alarmed the government. He was always protected, however; though both he and his wife were presented often enough for recusancy – i.e. for refusing to attend their parish church where they lived, at Stondon in Essex – nothing ever happened to them. Byrd received special licence excusing him, as if he were a peer.[24] Indeed, he was without a peer among his fellow-musicians: they all accepted his primacy, without any envy, they all looked up to him and honoured him. There was some quality of personality in him that commanded universal respect. Besides that, all had a patriotic pride in him, the unquestioned master of English music, taking his place alongside Lassus and Palestrina.

It was probably Byrd's close relationship with Alfonso Ferrabosco, senior, that helped to bring him (and his country with him) into the main stream of European music. Ferrabosco was one of a considerable number of Italian musicians in the Queen's service – there was a whole family of Bassanos – but a distinguished composer, in touch with the latest developments in Italy. He was not a composer of genius like Byrd, but must have stimulated his colleague's work – perhaps something like that which Coleridge did for Wordsworth. Thomas Morley has a story of a 'contention in love' between the two in making canons upon the *Miserere* and halting at forty, when each could have gone on. The English prized Ferrabosco, as an Italian; and when he left the country in 1578, after some fracas in which a fellow Italian was killed, the Queen held on to his family in order to force him to come back. He never did – and the country was the richer for a second Alfonso, who became an excellent composer of madrigals and a friend of Ben Jonson, for several of whose masques he wrote the music. There was even a third generation of Ferraboscos in royal service.

It is impossible to do justice to Byrd's immense output here – it would be like trying to sum up Shakespeare's in a few pages.[25] For he was very prolific and lived to be eighty; no less than 250 motets survive, even so some of his music is lost, and we are only now establishing the canon and chronology of much of it.[26] In his

twenties he was composing mainly instrumental music – not surprising considering the liturgical changes of the 1550's. In 1563,
at about twenty he was made organist of Lincoln Cathedral, and
when promoted to the Chapel Royal in 1572 he was favoured
with a further annuity on the revenues at Lincoln.[27] Coming to
London, in Chapel and at Court 'his musical and intellectual
horizons were at once widened' – as with Shakespeare on entering
the Southampton circle – and Byrd grew deeply interested in the
composition of motets.[28] As Morley tells us, these were the most
highly regarded and profound form of vocal composition. By 1575
Byrd had assembled enough to vie with his master, Tallis, and 'in
these works the mood of experiment and discovery is everywhere
evident.' The 1570's were a time of powerful development on all
sides, showing 'the kind of astonishing growth that is the characteristic mark of artistic genius.' In the 1580's he is composing
motets radically new in musical style, of marked expressive power
and individuality. As against the smooth perfection of Palestrina
there is an English vigour and more rugged vitality. (Instead of
eschewing false relations and dissonance, the English school made
a point of them – we must remember that the tuning of sixteenth-
century instruments softened the effect, must have made it more
plangent.)

   In 1588 Byrd was at length ready to publish his first collection
in English, *Psalms, Sonnets, and Songs of Sadness and Piety*, dedicated
to Lord Chancellor Hatton whose love of music and dancing was
well known. Once more the publication is something of a manifesto: in a Preface Byrd makes propaganda for everyone to learn
to sing. He states his conviction that no instrumental music is
comparable to the best vocal, and 'the better the voice is the
meeter it is to honour and serve God therewith, and the voice of
man is chiefly to be employed to that end.'

> Since singing is so good a thing,
> I wish all men would learn to sing.

To this end he has provided music of all kinds: 'if thou be disposed
to pray, here are Psalms. If to be merry, here are Sonnets. If to
lament for thy sins, here are songs of sadness and piety.' We
cannot go into technical questions, but some of the songs had
originally been made for solo voice accompanied by four instruments; all had now been transposed into 5-part songs for voices.

   As a composer, Byrd lets us into his inner mind with his words:
'to sacred words, as I have learned by trial, there is such a

profound and hidden power that, to one thinking upon things divine and diligently and earnestly pondering them, all the fittest numbers occur and freely offer themselves to the mind.' It is very much what Elgar said about composing, whose attitude about music for all was much in keeping with Byrd's. The collection had a wide spread of appeal.

The success of this publication encouraged Byrd to bring out another collection in 1589. He had certainly started something, this kind of music had evidently caught on – he told the reader it had 'exceedingly increased' in that year. Henceforth there is a spate of publications till the end of the Golden Age. Byrd must have been hard at work to have written the whole collection in the interval: '*Songs of Sundry Natures*, some of gravity and others of mirth, fit for all companies and voices.' There was wider diversity, in that the songs were for 3, 4, 5 and 6 parts. The book was dedicated to Lord Chamberlain Hunsdon, who had the oversight of the Queen's musicians, as well as the theatre. Byrd assures him that in the past year (Armada year!) 'divers persons of great honour and worship have more esteemed and delighted in the exercise of that art than before.' Once more he exercises his persuasions upon the public: the songs are 'for all companies and voices: whereof some are easy and plain to sing, others more hard and difficult, but all such as any young practitioners in singing, with a little foresight, may easily perform.'

Meanwhile Byrd's friends had been urging him to publish the Latin motets piling up over the years, and in 1589 and 1591 he printed two collections of *Cantiones Sacrae*, containing just over sixty motets altogether. From the dedications one sees who the encouraging (and generous) friends were, the Earl of Worcester and Lord Lumley, both Catholics. And from the works themselves one can read his inner heart. These had been ill years for Catholicism in England: the old faith proscribed and persecuted, its professors fined and imprisoned, priests hunted down; then the arrival of the Jesuits and seminarists; conspiracies, tortures, martyrdoms. All this is expressed again and again in Byrd's music, the anguish, the sorrow, faith the only consolation. This is especially so of the First Book, the setting of the Psalms calling upon God to deliver his people from the yoke of their captivity: *ut cito venias et dissolvas iugum captivitatis nostrae*, with prolonged grieving, cadences on *nos*. '*Tristitia et anxietas*', '*Memento, domine, congregationis tuae*', '*Vide, domine, afflictionem nostram*', '*Jerusalem desolata est*', repeated over and over – these are the themes of the first volume.

'*Vigilate, nescitis enim quando dominus domus veniat.*' Nobody, and nothing, came to their help, for all their calling; however, the desire itself, as Kierkegaard well understood, is sufficient inspiration.

The Second Book has a more varied note, songs of joy and praise prevailing. It begins with the magnificent motet, one of the most justly famous, '*Laudibus in sanctis*', with wreaths of joy praising the Almighty, with all the blithe gaiety of praise, the certainty of faith. There is the usual extraordinary tenderness of the passages referring to the Cross; and then, a continuous garland of Alleluias.[29] The book ends with '*Haec dies*' – This is the day that the Lord hath made, Alleluia, with its overwhelming effect of joyfulness, the upper and lower parts echoing each other, like peals of bells. (There is the impossibility of describing music in words – the music *is* the experience, in its most intense and purest form.)

We know now that Byrd was composing his three Masses in the 1590's – the 4-part and 3-part Masses in the years when Shakespeare was writing the Sonnets, 1592–5.[30] We also know that there were occasions when a full choral Mass was surreptitiously celebrated. For one thing the religious devotions of peers were not open to public inspection – and Byrd numbered Catholic peers among his friends. There were other occasions, too, and he was a neighbour of the Catholic Petres at Thorndon – we hear of him spending a musical Christmas, i.e. the whole holidays till Twelfth Night, with them.[31] The first two works are less elaborate than the great 5-part Mass, now familiar to us again – we have frequent opportunities of hearing it. They have a more cheerful swing with their simpler rhythms. They have all the unsullied purity of Byrd's mind, with the utter innocence of vulgarity that all Elizabethan polyphony possesses. They have too the intense expressiveness he can give to a word or a phrase – in the 4-part Mass the falling cadences on '*descendit*', with the wonderful bass-burden of the *Agnus Dei*', with a figured pattern upon which the upper parts rest: '*Miserere nobis.*' Then the long drawn out propitiation of '*da nobis pacem*' – which means even more to those of us today who know all that is involved.

This is intensified and deepened, if possible, in the later Mass. The addition of a fifth part enriches the polyphony and broadens the effect. And everywhere there are marvellous effects: this is one of those divine works of art of which, as Hazlitt said of *King Lear*, 'all that we can say must fall far short of the subject, or even what we ourselves conceive of it.' We confine ourselves to what Byrd reveals of himself. He never fails to assert, what gave all the meaning to his life and work, his absolute assurance in the Faith: one hears in the defiant assertion '*et unam sanctam catholicam et apostolicam ecclesiam.*' One never comes to the end of the subtlety and mastery of this mind – as with Shakespeare: Byrd is full of thematic cross-references only an artist can detect. When *he* comes to the words '*in nomine domini*' he goes right back to Taverner's simple plainsong – if that isn't an assertion of the continuity of the Faith! Then after the expressive characterisation of '*descendit de caelis*', there is the sudden simplicity, the mystery, '*et incarnatus est*'. The historian was quite right in saying that there are moments that have 'a poignancy almost too great for the human heart to bear.'[32] He goes on to add, 'but the human heart, the music tells us, rests secure in the love of God.' Altogether, Byrd was the noblest religious spirit of the age in England – as perhaps Palestrina was in Italy.

Nothing brings home more clearly the essential difference of character – certainly not all the volumes of ulcerated religious disputation – between the Elizabethan and the Catholic Church. Catholicism depends upon an inner mystery. The English Church had much to offer – reason and moderation, decency and decorum, a sufficient code of life, scope for poetry, art and devotion; but it had lost the element of mystery, coming one knows not whither.

These Masses could not be published in England in Byrd's lifetime; but he was not one to give up, or give way. In 1605 and 1607 he brought out his *magnum opus* in two parts, the *Gradualia*, containing well over a hundred motets.[33] His aim was to provide settings for all the offices for the festivals of his defeated Church throughout the year. We only now appreciate that all this represents a completely articulated liturgical system, ready for use. He must have hoped that some of this music would be found useful abroad, apart from its restricted use at home; that this happened may be indicated by the fact that a second edition was soon called for. Byrd's name was well known abroad. As early as 1583–4 Philippo de Monte and he had exchanged compositions: an 8-part setting of the Psalm '*Super flumina Babylonis*' of which de Monte set the first half, and Byrd completed it. The first book was dedicated to Henry Howard, now Earl of Northampton, and a leading minister of James I, in spite of his Catholicism, with a tribute to the tribulations of his family, whose glory was now revived in him. (This was before his inculpation in the murder of

Sir Thomas Overbury.) In the dedication of the second book to the more respectable Lord Petre, Byrd grieves at the recent deaths of his pupils, musicians of exceptional skill. This refers especially to Morley, and reminds us that – like Bach – Byrd's influence continued through these, as well as through his music.

His last publication was another collection of *Psalms, Songs, and Sonnets* in 1611, the finest of the three. As before it mixed secular with sacred, and now added fantasies for strings. It was dedicated to Francis, Earl of Cumberland, another aristocratic devotee of music, to whom Byrd was beholden for many favours. It is interesting that he never had to complain of any detractors – almost the only one in that age. Once more he addresses the reader with a direct persuasion – 'that you will be but as careful to hear them well expressed as I have been both in the composing and correcting of them.' He was a most careful proof-reader. 'Otherwise the best song that ever was made will seem harsh and unpleasant; for that the well expressing of them is the life of our labours . . . Besides, a song that is well and artificially [i.e. artistically] made cannot be well perceived nor understood at the first hearing, but the oftener you shall hear it the better cause of liking you will discover.'

Actually Byrd went on writing for many years after this, but we must sum up his contribution to English Church music. It represents another, equally authentic side to his enormously rich musical personality. Where his Latin music is intense and *innerlich*, his writing for the English rite is more extrovert, altogether more blithe and cheerful. The rhythms that arise from the spoken language are liable to prompt a more sinewy and invigorated outline. (After all Byrd, though a Catholic, was an entire Englishman: was it not Queen Elizabeth who said, 'a strong Papist, but a good subject'?) But much more of his work for the English Church is missing; this sounds paradoxical, but it is understandable. For in the churches, the liturgical music was sung from manuscript: hence the fearful losses from the destruction of choirs and their service-books with the Civil War and Commonwealth. Weelkes wrote ten complete services, and he was a master; little of them has survived, of his forty anthems only a fraction.

Byrd's Great Service is one of his grandest works; indeed, it is on such a splendid scale that one rarely hears it – elaborate polyphony for a double choir of five voices each, passages written in 6, 7 and 8 parts, one even for 10 parts.[34] It ceased to be performed with the Civil War, and has been recovered only in our time. The Glorias with their wonderful repeated Amens are among the finest ever written for the English use – which, incidentally, preferred Amens to the Latin Allcluias.[35] There is a complete, more usable Short Service, two more fairly entire, a 4-part Litany, three sets of Preces and Responses for Matins and Evensong, besides many anthems and Psalm-settings. Some have wished that his Preces and Responses had come into general use instead of the more austere Tallis's; but the old master came first and has never been displaced in the English Church.

It has only recently been realised that Morley, famous as a madrigalist, wrote a number of Latin motets, beautiful in themselves and in marked contrast with his secular work.[36] His earlier sympathies were probably Catholic, though he conformed; the texts of his motets are penitential. When organist of St. Paul's Morley was used on a visit to the Netherlands to report on the exiles there. To Charles Paget he seemed a good Catholic; then intercepted letters 'discovered enough to have hanged him, but as he with tears asked forgiveness on his knees', Paget let him go home.[37] Next year Morley was recruited to the Chapel Royal – his relations with Byrd do not seem to have suffered – and his career went forward to sickness and an early death. He, too, as an organist made his contribution to English Church music, services, anthems, and so on. It has been observed that he re-modelled his Latin style after 1588: a good date to do so.

A more original genius, Weelkes wrote more services than other leading composers: he has left us ten as against Tomkins' seven, Byrd's four, and Gibbons' two.[38] Fragmentary as they are, it is clear from them that English composers of the time found the Service an exciting form with potentialities comparable to those of the anthem. The language itself was proving a challenge and an inspiration, in particular the translation of the Bible – as we see in so secular a writer as Shakespeare. The consequence is that by now the music of the Reformed Church has achieved first-rate quality: the best anthems and Services of composers like Byrd, Weelkes, Gibbons and Tomkins could equal the achievements of pre-Reformation polyphony. 'English Church music was now worthy of the attention of any musician in Europe.'[39]

Weelkes' numerous services and anthems are due to the fact that he was all his life a practising organist, first at Winchester College, then at Chichester cathedral. Such organists and choir-masters were expected to provide music for their choirs – hence the quantities of manuscript music lost or destroyed. Most of it would be by lesser composers, whose work we can only take for granted here, though it is part of the perspective for the greater. Weelkes' Church music is much more restrained than his splendid and original madrigals; though some of his finest sacred works, 'O Jonathan' and 'When David heard, O my son Absalom', approximate to those in style. Weelkes, like Bull, had 'personality difficulties': he married and took to drink. Elizabethan choirmen were given to tippling: it was considered good for their voices to wet their whistle.

With our last great composers of Church music, Thomas Tomkins and Orlando Gibbons, we are passing out of the Elizabethan age, though both received their training in it and their inspiration from it: men of original genius as they both were, they are deeply grounded in the polyphonic school. Indeed Gibbons is the true successor of Byrd; he had a similar depth of spirit, conservative in inspiration though forward-looking musically, his work may be regarded as the culmination of English Church music as such. When Byrd was long forgotten, one of Gibbons' Services never lost its place in the cathedrals and 'places where they sing'. And so his name went forward in the tradition along with Tallis. He was named after Lassus (Orlando to the Elizabethans), since he came from a family of musicians: his father was one of the town-waits of Oxford, where the boy was born in 1583.[40] He was not yet forty-two when he died in 1625, at Canterbury for Charles I's reception of the ill-omened Henrietta Maria.

Thomas Tomkins was some ten years older, having been born in 1572 at St. David's, where his father was organist of the cathedral. The family came from Cornwall – the Cornish form of the name is Tonkin – and produced a whole dynasty of musicians, of whom some half a dozen had talent. Only one had genius, and Byrd was his master. Young Tomkins was appointed organist at Worcester, at twenty-three, in 1595 and there in the service of the cathedral he spent most of his long life. Some twenty years later he became an organist of the Chapel Royal along with Gibbons; since this post was held in rotation, he could combine it with Worcester, as Weelkes did with Chichester. No sooner was he appointed than he began composing music for the Church, 'and for the next forty-five years the stream of anthems and services flowed on steadily, increasing in quality though not necessarily in complexity.'[41] After his death his son was able to collect most of it for publication, *Musica Deo Sacra*, with the result that Tomkins has continued a living figure in the cathedral repertory.

The work contained five Services, the Preces and various psalms, with ninety-four anthems. This was not the whole of his Church music, and it was only a portion of his contribution to music in every kind. In 1613–14 he had a fine organ built. In Edward VI's reign and again in the early years of Elizabeth there had been a monstrous destruction of organs; it was only at the very end of her reign that organs began to be built again in England.[42] Culture was recovering from the blows it had received. But Tomkins lived on too long. He witnessed the destruction of his organ and choir, and even of his house in Worcester. Undeterred, he turned over to keyboard music: one of his last works, on the king's execution in 1649, was his 'Sad Pavan: for these distracted times.'

However, the music of the English Church had been safely launched, the transition from medieval Catholicism effected, its own tradition established, and many imperishable works of art created.

II

The most characteristic Renaissance development was, however, the madrigal, in Italy closely married to words, dominantly Petrarchan. Indeed the nature of the Italian madrigal was defined by the closeness with which it expressed the words – one sees that it is on the way to declamatory solo-singing and so to opera. The English madrigal, though giving expression to the words and often going in for word-painting, remained musically determined. Though it is impossible to give precise explanations of these subtle inflexions, this is probably due to the strong element of the native part-song, with its gift for melody (which everybody noticed to be an English characteristic), continuing into and through the dominance of the Italian madrigal, to emerge again with the English Air, melodic solo-song with instrumental accompaniment. For we recognise now that the English madrigal was neither wholly English, nor wholly Italian.[43] Once more, it was the result of fruitful cross-fertilisation. To vary the image, it covered a spectrum from the English part-songs of Byrd, who refused to write in the Italian style (though he could), to the madrigals of Morley at the other extreme which were wholly Italianate.

In any case, in this field the influence of Italy was at its highest; there were signs of its being prepared before the madrigal burst into fashion at Court and with cultivated musical circles – for, as a sophisticated art, its vogue was essentially aristocratic. The curious figure of Thomas Whythorne is that of an individual, isolated precursor – though, like John Shute and William Thomas, he had had contacts with the Dudleys from Edward VI's time. In Mary's he travelled on the Continent studying music, especially during six months in Italy.[44] (Later, we find Arthur Throckmorton learning the lute while there, as no doubt other young Englishmen were doing.[45]) In 1571 this bore fruit with Whythorne's publication of his Songs for three, four and five voices: one hardly knows whether to call them madrigals or part-songs. One thing merges into another.

Italian madrigals had been coming in from the 1560's, but it was not until Armada year that Nicholas Yonge published the first and most important collection of them in translation, *Musica Transalpina*. Yonge had been stimulated by the output of the Netherlands music-publisher, Phalèse; in the ten years, 1588–98, five anthologies of Italian madrigals were published in London, along with the first crops from English soil.[46] Yonge was a lay-clerk of St. Paul's who mentions 'a great number of gentlemen and merchants of good account, as well of this realm as of foreign nations . . . by the exercise of music daily used in my house, and by furnishing them with books of that kind yearly sent me out of Italy and other places.'[47] Here now was a middle-class public for the art, though five years earlier Yonge had come across Neapolitan madrigals Englished not long before 'by a very honourable personage and now a Councillor of state.' Ferrabosco's compositions were drawn on more than anyone else's: another indication of his importance as a link with Italy. They were in a conservative style: the book represented the taste of English music-lovers for the serious-minded, the earlier style of Marenzio, not the later, more extreme.

Marenzio was the greatest composer of madrigals, his vast output covering the whole range of the genre. In 1590 Thomas Watson came out with his *First Set of Italian Madrigals Englished*, which was mainly devoted to Marenzio. Watson made free versions of the Italian directly under the music, sometimes according to the meaning, sometimes according to the note: a compromise, so that one must not judge his versions *in vacuo* as poetry. He prevailed on his friend Byrd to contribute two settings of 'This sweet and merry month of May' 'after the Italian vein', though he wrote no more in it. The work was dedicated to Essex:

> *Inclyte Mavortis, Musarum dulcis alumne,*
> *Accipe iuncta Italis Anglica verba notis . . .*

Here was propaganda for Italian culture from Marlowe's friend. One must not overlook Watson's significance because much of his work was in Latin – it was well appreciated by the Elizabethans. He translated Petrarch's Canzoniere into Latin, as also Tasso's *Aminta*. His *Hekatompathia* (1582) was the first sonnet-sequence in effect, his posthumous *Tears of Fancy* (1593) the first actual one. Watson may not have had his friend's genius, but we do not know what he might have accomplished: he died, aged only thirty-six, some months before Marlowe.

The leadership of the campaign for the Italian madrigal was immediately taken over by Morley; himself a gifted composer, he carried it forward by example as well as precept. He wrote the classic *Plain and Easy Introduction to Practical Music* (1597), the best manual of instruction for singing, vocal music and composition, of the time; and from it we learn much about the condition of contemporary music. The book was dedicated to Byrd, 'in all love and affection to you, your most addicted Thomas Morley.'[48] Behind it was Morley's long experience with cathedral choirs, now infused with his addiction to everything Italian. His first *Canzonets* for three voices of 1593, dedicated to the Countess of Pembroke, were direct imitations of the light-hearted type of brief Italian madrigal. Its fresh, bright, somewhat brittle, style took on at once, and the book went into several editions. He was extraordinarily energetic and prolific; volume after volume followed in quick succession: a *First Book of Madrigals* for four voices, the first in which the Italian name was used, next year.

In 1595 Morley produced two volumes. The *First Book of Ballets* introduced a gay new type of composition straight from Italy, modelled mainly on Gastoldi, with both English and Italian words. It was dedicated to Sir Robert Cecil, himself a connoisseur of music. A German edition of this was published at Nuremberg in 1609. The *First Book of Canzonets* for two voices also contained a number of instrumental fantasies. His expressive gifts and effective variations of rhythm endeared him to a wide public, and that he was an original creator is witnessed by the fact that such pieces from these books as 'Now is the month of maying' and 'Sweet nymph, come to thy lover' are still favourites with us. The *Canzonets* for five and six voices, of 1597, contain Morley's maturest work and reveal him well in sad and affecting moods as well as cheerful: he was clearly of a mercurial temperament. A noble elegiac madrigal is in memory of Henry Noel, a gentleman pensioner of the Queen, skilled in music and beloved of the musicians.

Dowland composed seven hymns for his funeral and later published a galliard after his name. Weelkes wrote an elegy:

> Noel, adieu, adieu, thou Court's delight,
> Upon whose locks the graces sweetly played . . .

Not content with this, in these years Morley made two collections of Italian madrigals, adapting the words to English. The second of these is dedicated to Sir Gervase Clifton: 'Good sir, I ever held this sentence of the poet as a canon of my creed: that whom God loveth not, they love not music . . . For your part, I cannot easily tell whether I may more commend in you Art itself or the love of art . . . It is not with you as with many others which for form affect it much.' In addition to the Italians Morley included two Italianate madrigals by the gifted Catholic exile, Peter Phillips, who became organist to Philip II's daughter and son-in-law at their Court in Brussels. Nine volumes in seven years! – with his important manual on music, and a volume of consort lessons for instrumental ensemble. The flood of musical publications made 1597 an *annus mirabilis*; it was the year after the expiry of the Byrd-East printing monopoly. Thomas East was the man who changed the face of music-printing, partly by his adoption of Italian standards, his introduction of Italian compositions, and by more prolific publishing: he was keen. Tallis and Byrd had not made their monopoly very profitable, probably because they were not business men – their minds were elsewhere.[49]

Morley crowned his career by editing the famous *Triumphs of Oriana* in 1601. This was the culmination of the cult of the Queen in music, celebrating her victories over all her enemies (the last of them being Essex). The idea was derived from the Venetian *Il Trionfo di Dori* of some years before. Over twenty leading composers and amateurs joined together to do honour to the famous old lady (who had been such a good friend to music). Verses were set, each ending with the refrain:

> Then sang the shepherds and nymphs of Diana:
> 'Long live fair Oriana.'

Some composers were late with their contributions, which appear elsewhere; Morley and Ellis Gibbons filled in with two each. Among those who appear are Weelkes, Wilby, Tomkins, John Mundy, Robert Jones; among cultivated amateurs, Michael Cavendish, William Cobbold and Milton's father. The book was dedicated to Lord Admiral Howard, who had triumphed over the

Armada. Two of the most eminent composers were missing: Byrd, in spite of all that he owed to the Queen, and Dowland, already at Elsinore in the service of the King of Denmark. (This was also the year of *Hamlet*.)

During these years Morley lived in the parish of St. Helen's, Bishopsgate, where Shakespeare also was living in 1598. They were rated at the same assessment for the subsidy, and apparently both appealed.[50] It seems probable that they knew each other, since Morley composed the music for 'It was a lover and his lass' and may have done also for 'O mistress mine'. Morley's health, however, was reducing him to 'a solitary life ... being compelled to keep at home', and in 1602 he resigned from the Chapel Royal. Next year he was dead, only forty-six. His feverish energy may indicate that he was a consumptive; apparently everybody fell for his charm, and he certainly was the most popular composer of madrigals, with a catchiness in his melodies that made them easy to remember. Though an *aficionado* of the Italian school, he had played a significant part in the formation of the English. Weelkes paid tribute to him in a noble madrigal, to the words of John Davies of Hereford, with plangent grieving cadences on the word 'dearest':

> Death hath deprived me of my dearest friend:
> My dearest friend is dead and laid in grave ...

The English school reached its peak with Weelkes, the most original madrigalist, and Wilby, the most polished; both were deeply indebted to Morley, both surpassed him. Weelkes had the most restless, exploring musical imagination of any, achieving greater extremes of expression within the compass of one madrigal, as well as width of human experience, from care-free drinking or tobacco songs to care-laden masterpieces, like 'O care, thou wilt dispatch me.'[51] With him one is relieved from the Petrarchan obsession with the love of women (the women themselves must often have been bored!). There is a whole spectrum instead, from the Cries of London, 'New Walfleet oysters', or 'The ape, the monkey and baboon', through the bell-like gaiety of 'On the plains', to the most astonishing of madrigals, 'Thule, the period of cosmography', and 'The Andalusian merchant'. These last, with their fantastic descriptiveness, the musical leaps from Hecla's fire to 'frozen climes', the references to cochineal and china dishes and 'how strangely Fogo burns', throw the mind back to the world of the *Madre de Dios* with its cargo of cochineal, the Chinese Ming porcelain that came into Burlegh's possession and, tricked out in Elizabethan silver garnishing, is to be seen now in the Metropolitan Museum in New York. It is not fanciful to see the physical expansion of their world reflected in the explorations and discoveries of their minds.

Weelkes was familiar with the chromatic expressionism of the Italians, but it corresponded with his own emotional needs and trials. In his finest madrigals in this vein, 'Hence, care, thou art too cruel', and 'Cease sorrows now', one hears the autobiographical inspiration. He wrote more madrigals than any, except Morley, but, with his intensity of temperament, crammed the bulk of his work into four early years. He was about twenty-two when he produced his first set in 1597: 'unripe in regard of time', he said in dedicating 'the first fruits of my barren ground' to a Hampshire gentleman who had been good to him. From the time of the severe Bishop Horne there had been no organ in Winchester College. Not until Weelkes' appointment in 1598–9 was the organ restored to chapel services.[52] In 1598 Weelkes followed Morley with a set of Ballets – these delightful compositions are always distinguished by Fa-la refrains. He displayed a wider range than most in his choice of words, in this volume drawing upon Barnabe Barnes as in the former from Barnfield's poems in *The Passionate Pilgrim*. In his dedication to Edward Darcy, who became Groom of the Privy Chamber, Weelkes says pathetically, 'although poverty hath debarred them [musicians] their fellow arts-men's company, yet nature hath set their better part at liberty to delight them that love music.'

Weelkes' masterpiece came in two volumes he published in 1600, the first with a dedication to Lord Windsor. Once more there is the defensive note: the impoverished musician could hardly expect a lord to 'descend to the notice of a quality lying single in so low a personage as myself.' Weelkes' one and only talent was music: 'I confess my conscience is untouched with any other arts . . . many of us musicians think it as much praise to be somewhat more than musicians . . . and if Jack Cade were alive yet some of us might live.' It seems sad that, 'without the assistance of other more confident sciences', discouragement should often have weighed down the spirit of one capable of such a joyful masterpiece as –

> Why are you ladies staying,
> And your lords gone a-maying?
> Run, run apace and meet them,
> And with your garlands greet them . . .

Hark! hark! I hear some dancing
And a nimble morris prancing,
The bagpipe and the morris bells . . .

As one reads the score five thousand miles away in California, the Maytime meads of Winchester are brought before one's eyes.

The second set of 1600, all composed for six voices, was dedicated to George Brooke, who fetched up on the scaffold three years later for conspiring with the Catholic Father Watson against James I ('the fox and his cubs'). This set opens with the bellicose and descriptive, 'Like two proud armies marching in the field', and includes the wonderful 'Thule'. This virtually closed Weelkes' marvellous madrigal output, seventy compositions, some of them more contrapuntally elaborate than any other. He moved on to Chichester and Church music. In 1608 there came a kind of coda, *Airs or Fantastic Spirits* for three voices. These are on a smaller scale, in a quite different vein: they reveal the humours and quirks of Weelkes and his drinking and smoking companions:

> I swear that this tobacco
> It's perfect Trinidado . . .
> Fill the pipe once more,
> My brains dance trenchmore.
> > It is heady,
> > I am giddy,
> > Head and brains,
> > Back and reins,
> > Joints and veins:
> > From all pains
> It doth well purge and make clean.

Or, for a familiar theme in social life:

> Some men desire spouses
> That come of noble houses.
> And some would have in marriage
> Ladies of courtly carriage.
> > But few desire, as I do
> > The maidenhead of a widow.

John Wilby,* who never married, writes of nothing but love; he is the most perfect artist of the school. Kerman pays tribute to

---

* There is no point in spelling him Wilbye: it misleads people into pronouncing the name to rhyme with Lullaby – as I have heard a well-known composer do. The name is clearly a shortened form of Willoughby.

'the seriousness of his approach, the sensitivity of his grasp of poetry and language, the polish of his style and the subtlety of his musical ideas and their treatment', and compares him to Marenzio.[53] Born at Diss in Norfolk in 1574, his father, a well-to-do tanner, left the boy his lute; when the Cornwallis daughter of neighbouring Brome Hall married Sir Thomas Kitson of Hengrave, she took young Wilby with her to provide music and he spent the rest of his life doing so. Up to our own destructive time Hengrave still possessed the collections of the Kitsons, portraits, manuscripts, inventories, which tell us what a part music played in their lives: payments for kersey for the musicians, seven cornets, a treble viol, a pair of virginals, for 'stringing, tuning and fretting my mistress' lute', for 'the musicians of Swan Alley for many times playing with their instruments before my master and mistress.'[54] A few miles away across the fields was Rushbrooke of the Jermyns – a fine Elizabethan house pulled down by Lord Rothschild after the war. There resided George Kirby, another composer and friend of Wilby: they both set the words 'Alas, what hope of speeding' in friendly rivalry.[55]

Though the musicians' gallery in the hall had gone, at Hengrave one could still see Wilby's chamber, looking east towards the church. In 1603 he had hangings of green say, a plain corded bedstead. When older, he was treated more grandly: a tester of blue and yellow say, bed-curtains of green and white striped mocado, window curtains of blue and yellow say, a trestle-table (on which he wrote those madrigals), 'a staff to beat the bed with.' There was a chamber for the musicians, with many instruments and books: a chest with six viols, another six violins, a case with seven recorders, four cornets, sackbuts, hautbois, lutes, flutes, a bandora, cithern, virginals, and a great pair of double virginals in the parlour. Among the large number of music-books was a large red-leather and gilt book that came from the sack of Cadiz in 1596. The church had a pair of organs. Lady Kitson left all the instruments and books as heirlooms to Hengrave – so she must have brought them from Brome, where nothing of the house remains; but the tombs of the Cornwallises are in the church.

A late letter of Wilby's tells us that little Henry – evidently a singing boy – 'has been dealt with again to go to my Lord Arundel, but he hath no will that way': he prefers to serve the Countess Rivers. So did Wilby, after her mother's death. The steward thought that Wilby 'had enough and would marry'; this annoyed Lady Rivers, a dominating female who had separated from her

husband. Wilby knew better, and followed Lady Rivers to Colchester, where he had a room of his own in the 'great brick house' –
still there – opposite the west end of Holy Trinity church. Here
Wilby ended his successful, well-conducted life, a rich bachelor:
a contrast with Weelkes. The eldest Cornwallis girl had married
Bess of Hardwick's third son, Sir Charles Cavendish, to whom
Wilby dedicated his first set of madrigals in 1598, for his 'excellent
skill in music, and great love and favour of music.' Sir Charles was
a cousin of Michael Cavendish, who remained at the old family
house in Suffolk; as an amateur madrigalist, a good follower of
Morley. Sir Charles's niece was Lady Arabella Stuart, to whom
Wilby dedicated his second Set in 1609. Thomas Greaves, composer of lute-songs, was lutenist to Sir Henry Pierrepoint in Not-
tinghamshire, who had married another of Bess's daughters. We
see what a widespread musical circle this was in its generation –
quite unlike the old lady herself!

Wilby published no more than these two volumes, but they
contained sixty-four madrigals. He was a perfectionist: it was impossible for the genre to go further in style, in delicacy of imagination and unerring touch – and in fact its vogue was passing.
Wilby has never failed to evoke response, and such masterpieces
as 'Sweet honey-sucking bees' and 'Flora gave me fairest flowers' –
he seems to have written or adapted his own words – have never
been forgotten. When one hears the lovely 'Draw on, sweet night',
it still evokes those green spaces under the cedars of Hengrave,
summer or autumn night drawing down over the distances of the
park, the shadows growing round the house while the vanished
voices murmur those cadences of evocation and longing.

Of the other leading composers of the time Gibbons published
only one *First Set of Madrigals and Motets of 5 parts* in 1612. The
title draws attention to the fact that the two genres were not far
apart in Gibbons' mind. Motet meant grave, intellectual music,
usually of a religious character, vocal polyphony; Gibbons' madrigals hardly differed from that, still completely polyphonic, aus-
terely beautiful, set to texts of a highly ethical character from
Spenser and Sylvester. Gibbons' lofty music is of a complex
character with subtle rhythms, but the splendid 'The Silver Swan'
keeps his work in this kind alive to us. His setting of Ralegh's
'What is our life' has the lines

> Our graves that hide us from the searching sun
> Are like drawn curtains when the play is done,

which serve to show us that on some stages at least curtains were in use. The songs were dedicated to Hatton's nephew and heir, the younger Sir Christopher, musical and extravagant: 'they were most of them composed in your own home . . . they are like young scholars newly entered that at first sing very fearfully.'[56]

Tomkins did not publish his madrigals until 1622, when they were on the way out and the lute-song had already taken first place in favour; in consequence they have always been neglected, though among the finest in their kind. The volume was appropriately dedicated to Pembroke, Lord Warden of the Stannaries of Devon and Cornwall, and is singular for each number being separately dedicated. From this we can reconstruct Tomkins' musical circle; no less than five musical brothers and his own son Nathaniel; Gibbons, Dowland, John Cooper (called Coprario from long residence in Italy), John Daniel, Phineas Fletcher the poet, Dr. Heather who made the splendid collection of music at Oxford and founded the professorship there.[57]

In addition to these men of genius, others of talent and many amateurs of distinction contributed to the vogue in its brief glory; we can note only a few for the light they throw on society. Giles Farnaby, who published his one volume in 1598, was a composer of real originality, with a love of bold chromaticism and ingenious rhythms.* 'Construe my meaning' is one of the finest madrigals; he did not fear to set 'Susanna and the elders' already set twice by Byrd and Lassus. The book was dedicated to Ferdinando Heybourne, 'for your manifold courtesies and loving kindness at all times', with Latin verses by Anthony Holborne, a personal servant of the Queen, who had published *The Cithern School* the year before, jaunty verses by Dowland, others by Hugh Holland, a Cambridge don, and Richard Alison.[58]

Next year Alison published his *Psalms*, and in 1606 a volume of madrigals dedicated to Sir John Scudamore, gentleman usher to the Queen and standard-bearer to her Pensioners. He was the son of the Sir Scudamore of the *Faerie Queene*, whom we see in armour, or rather his carapace, in the Metropolitan Museum. Alison was a serious soul, who chose his words from Thomas Campion and Chideock Tichborne. He was grateful for 'those quiet days which by your goodness I have enjoyed' – evidently at Holme Lacy in Herefordshire, where he provided the music.[59] The

---

* Several works describe the Farnabys as Cornish; they were not. The father had come to Truro as master of the grammar school, but they originated in the Eastern counties.

talented Michael East, at one time organist of Lichfield, was very prolific, publishing no less than five Sets, well over a hundred madrigals.[60] He dedicated his first to another Herefordshire gentleman with Court connections, Sir John Croft; his second to Sir Thomas Gerard, of the Catholic branch of the family, with a tribute to his 'indefatigable assiduity in the private exercise [of music], which hath gained you such a perfection that way as is rare in a gentleman of your rank.' One of the madrigals was in praise of tobacco – several such were devoted to the craze, as were a number of the riotous songs of the gifted but eccentric Tobias Hume.

The composers were sometimes professionals, connected with cathedrals, sometimes stewards or tutors in the house, or gentlemen amateurs. Thomas Bateson was organist at Chester; he sent his madrigals to his friend, the soldier Sir William Norris, as they were composed in loose papers.[61] Francis Pilkington was precentor of Chester, and a gifted lutenist. He dedicated a first Set of madrigals, 'from my mansion in the monastery of Chester', to Sir Thomas Smith of Hough; his second to Sir Peter Legh of Lyme.[62] It included a pavan for olpharion made by William, Earl of Derby (we remember, from Aubrey, that Ralegh's brother, Carew, had a delicate clear voice and played skilfully on the olpharion). Various verses paid tribute to 'Thine and the Muses' friends of Chester'; so there was a musical circle there, around the cathedral. Not far away, in Lancashire, Ralph Assheton was the patron of a gifted madrigalist in John Bennet.[63]

In East Anglia we find another group. Richard Carlton was master of the choristers at Norwich cathedral and wrote mostly in a serious vein, several settings to words from the *Faerie Queene*. He dedicated his book to Thomas Fermor of Norfolk; it included an elegy for a Norfolk knight, Sir John Shelton, slain in a duel.[64] Henry Youll was tutor to the sons of Edmund Bacon in Suffolk; apparently all four brothers were at Cambridge together, and Youll recalls 'what a solace their company was once to you when I nursed them amongst you.'[65] He writes as an amateur, whose main employments are otherwise; but his Canzonets have charm and individuality, while his choice of words – from Sidney, Ben Jonson, Sir John Davies – indicated a man of taste.

John Ward, an accomplished madrigalist, also had good taste in verse, setting poems from Sidney and Drayton. He served in the household of Sir Henry Fanshawe, the Exchequer official who owned a fine collection of musical instruments at his house in

Warwick Lane.[66] Henry Lichfield was steward to Lady Cheney at her splendid 'Court-like' house at Toddington, near Luton: 'so I, bestowing the day in your ladyship's necessary businesses, borrowed some hours of the night to bestow upon these my compositions . . . yet it pleased your honour with gentle ear to receive them, being presented by the instruments and voices of your own family.'[67] The lady is saluted with charming verses by Christopher Brooke:

> Unto that vale-like place of lowly height,
> Where joy, peace, love make an harmonious chime,
> Where civil sports, music and Court delight
> Do run divisions on the hours of time,
> Where reigns a lady crowned with highest merits
> On whom the muses and the graces wait . . .

Leicestershire had another group, which included the cultivated Beaumonts and Villierses – the Duke of Buckingham's mother was a Beaumont; their madrigalist was an accomplished professional, Thomas Vautor, who published an excellent volume in 1619.[68] With them we come back to the Court, upon which the whole musical movement pivoted.

Closely associated with the Court was John Mundy, organist at Windsor and Eton, whose father had been a notable composer of Church music. Mundy sought Essex's patronage 'as under privilege of a religious sanctuary'.[69] He set English verses by Lupo, one of the Queen's Italian musicians, Tichborne (again), and Oxford's poem, so revealing of the edge on his temper, the insatisfaction, the aristocratic disdain:

> Were I king I might command content,
> Were I obscure unknown should be my cares,
> And were I dead no thoughts should me torment,
> Nor words, nor wrongs, nor loves, nor hopes,
> nor fears.
> A doubtful choice, of three things one to crave:
> A kingdom, or a cottage, or a grave.

Robert Jones was the most famous lutenist, after Dowland, and an exquisite and prolific composer of songs. He offered his madrigals to Salisbury, for the encouragement 'you have given to many professors of music', hoping that 'your spirits, which are encumbered with many cares, may a little be delighted in the hearing of these songs.'

III

We are so apt to think of Robert Cecil as the professional politician he was and the statesman he became, that we forget his cultural interests. He claimed that he loved books more than gold, but he loved music no less. He kept a choir for his chapel, and one way to the great little Secretary's favour was to recruit the best voices for him. Richard Champernowne of Modbury Castle near Plymouth also kept a choir: 'being naturally and often oppressed with melancholy more than he could wish, he has – though to his own charge – bought such as he has found whose voices contented him.'[70] His neighbour, Sir Francis Drake, told him that the rumour at Court was that Champernowne was a gelder of boys to preserve their voices. This he strenuously denied; it would not do in England, though it might – and did – in Italy. However, Cecil wanted a particular boy of his with a fine voice. Champernowne pleaded that the report of his voice was beyond his deserts; then, that if he lacked this youth he knew not where to get another, 'his whole consort of music, which most delights him, were overthrown.' Finally, 'if, for his private contentment, Cecil would like to have the youth attend him sometimes for a month or two, and so to return again, that that comfort of music wherewith he is delighted be not utterly overthrown, the youth shall be at his command.' This was in October 1595.

During that winter Cecil was inquiring after a musician of the soldierly Lord Burgh, another devotee, who was more ready to oblige. 'Daniel you shall have; three other boys with him are mishappened to me: one of them both plays and sings an excellent treble, but his conditions are not stayed, and one other hath a voice for a very high mean. The last is Jack, of whom I think you have taken best notice. The four, with all his instruments, were all by my worthy companion bequeathed me.'[71] Burgh himself loved music; when he died in 1597 Weelkes wrote a fine madrigal in remembrance of him.

In 1598 Morley was granted a monopoly of printing songbooks and music-paper; he tried to enlist Cecil's favour to extend it to 'all, every and any music', against the Attorney-General's wishes.[72] Morley pleaded that the reward Cecil had given him for his dedication was worth more than any benefit he had received from his publications. He made the rather obvious bid to go half-shares on the profits with Cecil's servant, brother to

Ferdinando Heybourne. That December there turned up from the Netherlands one of Cecil's singing boys, who had absconded; by name Henry Phillips – one wonders if he were a relation of the celebrated expatriate composer.[73] The boy had offered to serve Sir Percival Hart in Kent, who reported that he was sick: it would be better for Cecil to send down a servant to persuade him to return rather than to enforce him up. Next year we learn of a boy brought up to play the lute and other instruments being used as a trusty messenger by the exiled Westmorland family to keep in touch with Catholic friends in the North.

A few months before the Queen's death there was a characteristic episode at Court. Young Lady Derby was wearing in her bosom a fine jewel with a miniature. The Queen was determined to know whose picture it was, and snatched it away, to find it was Cecil's, the young lady's uncle. Whereupon the old lady 'tied it upon her shoe and walked along with it there. Then she took it thence and pinned it on her elbow . . . which Mr. Secretary, being told of, made these verses and had Hales to sing them in his chamber. It was told her Majesty that Mr. Secretary had rare music and songs: she would needs hear them, and so this ditty was sung which you see first written . . . Some of the verses argue that he repines not, though her Majesty please to grace others, contents himself with the favour he hath.'[74] Clever man, so to turn what might have been an awkward incident to good use! He had instrumental musicians as well as singers in his household. Altogether, what with music, plays, learning Italian, gambling, hawking, horse-racing – he presents a very different picture from his father. Where Burghley was a man of the Reformation, Robert Cecil was a Renaissance man.

In September 1602 Worcester writes, 'we are frolic here in Court: much dancing in the Privy Chamber of country dances before the Queen's Majesty, who is exceedingly pleased therewith. Irish tunes are at this time most pleasing, but in winter "Lullaby", an old song of Mr. Byrd's will be more in request, as I think.'[75] Dancing was a ritual of a Renaissance Court. Its formal nature shows up in the masquing at Lord Cobham's in Blackfriars in June 1600. 'After supper the masque came in . . . Mrs. Fitton led . . . and after went to the Queen and wooed her to dance. Her Majesty asked what she was. "Affection," she said. "Affection!", said the Queen, "affection is false." Yet her Majesty rose and danced.'[76] She was getting old, her mind full of

forebodings at Essex's disloyal course, yet it was difficult to refuse
to take part in the ritual.

Sir John Davies devoted his poem 'Orchestra' to its significance. He had a special facility for philosophic argument in verse;
he began with the cosmic dance of the planets, the dance that
incites to love, and goes on to describe the various dances that
were such a fruitful new source of inspiration to music:

> Who doth not see the measure of the moon,
> Which thirteen times she danceth every year,
> And ends her pavan thirteen times as soon
> As doth her brother . . .

evidently Elizabethans pronounced the word pávan. Each planet

> doth itself advance,
> And by itself each doth a galliard dance.

The pavan was a slow and stately dance, usually followed by a
galliard, in quicker tripping measure – both from Italy: scores of
them survive in English keyboard music, and many of the best
composers were inspired to write them, Byrd's 'Earl of Salisbury's
Pavan' being familiar still. Davies cites 'winding hays' and rounds
(we still dance 'Sellinger's Round') – these were country dances –
and 'brawls', i.e. 'bransles' of French origin. Davies gives us a
clue to the nature of the brawl:

> Upward and downward, forth and back again,
> To this side and to that, and turning round;

it was a dance for the populace,

> And ever with a turn they must conclude.

One of the significant features of Renaissance music all over
Europe was its impregnation by the music of the people in song
and dance. Even before the Reformation Taverner's finest Mass
had used the folksong, 'O western wind', for its *cantus firmus*.
We are reminded 'how closely associated with music was the
literature of the ordinary people. Poetry to them meant song
almost exclusively.'[77] And 'ballad' to them meant something *sung*,
not the modern meaning of ballad, the archaic narrative poems
that have been so much collected by professors – though those
too must have been sung originally. 'Ballade' originally meant a
dancing-song; the musical genre, Ballet, is cognate with it. 'There
was constant interchange between folk tradition and the art of the
educated classes. Conditions were favourable for folk arts and

crafts, and communication between different levels of artistic taste was assisted by the simplicity of the social structure,' we are told. But we have seen that the social structure was by no means simple: it was its articulation into an integrated whole that was so effective, and so stimulating.

Autolycus in *The Winter's Tale* is a familiar figure of the ballad-monger to us. 'He hath songs for man or woman of all sizes; no milliner can so fit his customers with gloves. He has the prettiest love-songs for maids – so without bawdry, which is strange; with such delicate burdens of "dildos" and "fadings", "jump her" and "thump her". And where some stretch-mouthed rascal would, as it were, mean mischief and break a foul gap into the matter, he makes the maid to answer, "Whoop! do me no harm, good man" – puts him off, slights him, with "Whoop! do me no harm, good man".' Notice that – so like Shakespeare – every phrase is suggestive (a dildo is an artificial phallus, one can imagine what 'fadings' means), and the passage should be performed with appropriate gestures. For the censorship of the time was very tolerant of the obscene, recognised it for the social safety-valve it is; and cracked down severely only on what was seditious, politically dangerous, socially disruptive – and that included religious disputation.

In the popular ballad the tune was the important thing; everybody recognised the tune, and new sets of words were set over and over again to well-loved melodies. There was only the roughest recognition of propriety: one tune would do for serious events, a murder, a hanging or a monstrous birth, another for jollity, a wedding or a victory. This was in contrast with sophisticated art-songs, where the music was expressive of the words, and the words were usually worth expressing in music. But it is art alone that transcends time, and thus it is that the melodies are still alive where the often fatuous words are forgotten. Take the lovely tune of 'Greensleeves', so spacious and haunting: it apparently came down from the North in 1580, and immediately caught on.[78] Several ballads were at once made to it; so many that Elderton, the most celebrated ballad-monger, sought profit with 'A Reprehension against Greensleeves'. Some eighty ballads, at least, were set to the tune; until with over-use 'greensleeves' came to mean a whore. This is the point of Mrs. Ford's comment, in the *Merry Wives*, on the gap between Falstaff's professions and his actions: 'they do no more adhere and keep place together than the Hundredth Psalm to the tune of "Greensleeves".'

'Fortune, my foe', a stately, solemn tune, was no less popular for lugubrious accounts of murders, natural disasters, confessions of criminals – the kind of thing the people at all times like to hear about. A ballad 'of the life and death of Dr. Faustus, the great conjurer' was set to it[79] – it was quite usual to follow up a successful play with a ballad upon it, much as our populace takes to a paper-back 'book of the film', rather than the book itself. This tune was given a lute setting by Dowland, and was used by William Corkine for viol variations. It became equally popular – as so many English melodies did – in the Netherlands, where it appears in a dozen Dutch song-books and was used as a theme for variations by the great Sweelinck and by Scheidt. Corkine has a tune for 'Come live with me and be my love' among his lyra-viol Lessons.[80] He had particular reason to remember Marlowe: only seven months before his death there had been a *fracas* between these two at the Chequers Inn at Canterbury. 'Whoop! do me no harm, good man', a catchy jigging tune, appears in a later book of Corkine's Airs. How these things connect up, so that the life of the time is brought before our eyes.

The plays were full of references to ballads and catches, quotations from them, in addition to their direct employment of music. More in touch and sympathy with folk-life, Shakespeare uses more than any. Deloney employed the tune 'Light o' Love' for a ballad.[81] It is cited in *The Two Gentlemen of Verona* and in *A Midsummer Night's Dream* with the usual suggestiveness. The term entered into popular phraseology, the tune taken up in Holland as *Engelsche Volte*, i.e. the leaping dance known as the volta, from its Italian origin. Thus flourished cosmopolitan interchange. A popular Italian melody 'Chi Passa' had a number of English settings.[82] Elderton used it for a ballad, Byrd made arrangements of it for keyboard in 'My Lady Nevill's Book' – there could be no nicer example of the spectrum from the red-nosed balladmonger to the lofty, but humane, spirit of Byrd. The latter made two arrangements of the dance-tune 'Monsieur's Almain', named for Elizabeth's hopeful young suitor, Anjou. This in turn was used by Deloney for a ballad on the capture of the Great Galleass from the Armada.

Even Ben Jonson condescended to write several ballads, one of them for *Bartholomew Fair*. 'Oh, I love a ballad but even too well. Heaven forgive me for being so given to the love of poetry.' Such was the people's idea of poetry, as we see from the doggerel epitaphs all over the country – a contrast with the inspired poetry of the poets. Chettle gives us a vivid description of a ballad-monger: 'an odd old fellow, low of stature, his head was covered with a round cap, his body with a side-skirted tawny coat, his legs and feet trussed up in leather buskins; his grey hairs and furrowed face witnessed his age, his treble viol . . . in his hand . . . on which, by his continual sawing, (having left but one string) after his best manner he gave me a "Hunts-up".'[83] Once more Byrd uses this popular melody for a fine set of keyboard variations – as he used others: 'The woods so wild' (the words are lost), 'Gipsies Round', 'Malt's come down', 'The carman's whistle', 'Peascod time'. He is 'of all virginalists the one who most frequently evokes these impressions of nature.'

Ballads sold for a penny, where the quarto of a play cost sixpence: most people could afford neither, they listened to the ballads sung in the streets. The demand for them never failed. There were some forty publishers of ballads in the first ten years of the reign, while up to 1580 another thirty printed without registering. They throw the kind of lurid light on the life of the age that popular journalism does on ours. There never lacked 'a subject to write of: one hangs himself today, another drowns himself tomorrow, a serjeant stabbed next day. Here a pettifogger o' the pillory, a bawd in the cart's nose, and a pander in the tail; *hic mulier, haec vir*, fashions, fictions, felonies, fooleries.'[84] Most ballads were written down to the level of the least intelligent, like the popular press today: they have a more accurate estimate of average intelligence than most intellectuals. The difference was that, in that singing age, the news was sung. The best ballads were scooped up by the anthologists into their *Handful of Pleasant Delights*, *A Paradise of Dainty Devices*, *A Gorgeous Gallery of Gallant Inventions*, and these provided subject-matter for the poets and dramatists. The speciality of the English Jig was really a development: they were farces in ballad measure sung and danced on the stage to ballad-tunes, often at the conclusion of a play. These were very popular in Northern Europe, and the performers carried the ballads abroad in hundreds – over forty of them still survive in translation: a humble form of cultural export.

IV

In the full flowering of the age two more notable cultural exports made their appearance, lute-songs and lute music, and music for keyboard, particularly for virginals. In these two forms England took the lead for a brief and brilliant period – some return for all that she had received. (Just as at the beginning the country depended on imports for gunpowder and ammunition, by the end she became the chief exporter of cannon.) There is a vast mass of lute-music still unpublished – some two thousand pieces in England alone. But many of the songs written for lute-accompaniment have come back into circulation in our time: particularly those of Dowland, the greatest song-writer English-speaking people have ever produced (he may have been an Irish Dolan from Dublin). The first manual of instruction in lute-playing was translated from French in 1568; and shortly after Whythorne was composing his airs, or solo-songs, which Peter Warlock considered worthy of ranking with the later.[85] Poor Whythorne had no luck – he was premature in everything, including his system of orthography which he took over from Hart: it puts off moderns from reading his autobiography.

No one equalled Dowland as lutenist or composer and singer, at home or abroad. But he was given no place among the royal musicians until 1612, in his decline. The reason was that he became a Catholic in France, as a young man in the service of the English ambassador; when there was a vacancy in the Queen's Music, this prevented him from succeeding. So he went abroad again, with the intention of studying in Rome with Luca Marenzio, where he would certainly have had to do as Rome did. This was the sticking-point: he had become a Papist abroad (Byrd never went abroad). We have a fascinating letter from Dowland to Robert Cecil describing his journey and his troubles,[86] while his prefaces have autobiographical touches complaining of exile, his non-appreciation at home, his sense of being a pilgrim. All this comes through in his exquisite, most moving songs, in which one can often hear the accents of pathos transformed into perfect art.

Actually, his songs were much appreciated, and his 'Lachrimae', the melody of his 'Flow, my tears', was famous all over Northern Europe. Other composers, notably Byrd, paid him the compliment of writing variations on the theme; it is more frequently referred to on the stage than any other. Barnfield addressed a sonnet to a friend:

> If music and sweet poetry agree,
> As they must needs, the sister and the brother,
> Then must the love be great 'twixt thee and me,
> Because thou lov'st the one, and I the other.

> Dowland to thee is dear, whose heavenly touch
> Upon the lute doth ravish human sense . . .
> Thou lov'st to hear the sweet melodious sound
> That Phoebus' lute, the queen of music, makes;
> And I in deep delight am chiefly drowned
> Whenas himself to singing he betakes.

In 1597 he published his *First Book of Songs*, with the accompaniments arranged for lute, olpharion or viol da gamba, though he considered the lute as 'the most musical instrument.' The book was dedicated to Hunsdon, and ends with the 'Lord Chamberlain's Galliard' for two players on one lute; there is a Latin tribute from Thomas Campion. Dowland submitted his songs to 'Courtly judgment' and that of the universities, the cultivated public at home and abroad. 'The better to attain to so excellent a science', he had travelled widely in France, 'a nation furnished with great variety of music', then in Germany where he had found favour with the musical rulers of Brunswick and Hesse. Finally he had made the acquaintance of Marenzio, Giovanni Croce and Alessandro Horologio, and studied in Italy. No English musician was so widely known abroad or more admired, for as a lutenist he was unsurpassed.

Finding it impossible to surmount the Queen's objection, he took service with Christian IV of Denmark in 1598, who treated him generously. There Dowland remained, but for two absences in England, until 1606, writing his incomparable songs, complaining of exile, then – after complaints on the other side – he was dismissed. He seems to have suffered from too much artistic temperament. The purpose of his leave in 1601 was to purchase musical instruments for the Court of Denmark. On his dismissal Christian applied to his sister, Queen Anne, for another English lutenist: Lady Arabella Stuart's Thomas Cutting, excellent as performer and composer, was sent. When one looks at the royal palaces in Denmark, particularly Rosenborg, one has an ocular demonstration of the later ripples outward of the Renaissance impulse. It was significant that in music it was coming from England, but even in France the English lute-school contributed considerably to the subsequent native development.

This volume* – it was usual for a song-book to contain twenty-one songs – was reprinted several times; Dowland claimed that music of his had been printed in eight foreign cities. His *Second*

---

* The Huntington Library copy of the original edition is inscribed, 'This Booke is Mr John Alystagon 1602', evidently a foreigner in London.

Book of Songs was dedicated to Lucy Countess of Bedford from Elsinore, 'the Court of a foreign prince', in 1600.* With his exquisite taste Dowland sought words from the best sources: from Fulke Greville's thoughtful poems, and Sidney's

> O sweet woods, the delight of solitariness –

dedicated to that cultivated don, Hugh Holland. Still popular with us are 'I saw my lady weep' (dedicated to Anthony Holborne), and 'Shall I sue? shall I seek for grace?' 'Dowland's Adieu', a lesson for lute and bass-viol, was inscribed to Master Oliver Cromwell, the later Protector's extravagantly hospitable uncle.

A *Third Book* appeared in 1603, the first two having sped so well and fetched these 'far from home and brought even through the most perilous seas.' This contained songs still famous, 'Weep you no more, sad fountains', and 'Flow not so fast, ye fountains'; 'What if I never speed?' has the personal reference so frequent with Dowland, which inspired so much of his art. In 1605 he produced his *Lachrimae, or Seven Tears Figured in Seven Passionate Pavans* – instrumental music in 5 parts for dances, based on his most famous melody. From his house in Fetter Lane he dedicated it to Queen Anne, having been 'twice under sail for Denmark . . . to your most princely brother, the only patron and sunshine of my else unhappy fortunes . . . but by contrary winds and frost I was forced back again and of necessity compelled to winter here in your most happy kingdom.' Evidently he had overstayed his leave again, and went back to be dismissed.

Six years later Dowland published his finest work, *A Pilgrim's Solace*. It contains one of the masterpieces of the time, 'From silent night', and ends with magnificent sacred songs, that are more like madrigals. There is one maritime piece,

> Up, merry mates! To Neptune's praise
> Your voices high advance . . .
> Steersman, how stands the wind?
> Full north-north-east . . .

that describes his reluctant journeys across the North Sea. He dedicated these 'poor man's prayers' to Suffolk's son and heir: he was holding him up who had been 'long obscured from the sight of his countrymen . . . which could not attain to any (though never

---

* The publisher promises 'shortly to set at liberty for your service a prisoner taken at Cales, who, if he discovers not something in matter of music . . . let the reputation of my judgment in music answer it.' This reference puzzled Warlock, but it clearly refers to a music-book looted from Cadiz. It might possibly refer to Ornithoparcus' large treatise on music, *Micrologus*, which Dowland translated.

so mean) place at home.' Since his return he had found himself unwelcome to other singers who say 'what I do is after the old manner . . . though the proudest cantor of them all dares not oppose himself face to face against me.' No doubt, with such people. A younger generation had grown up who 'vaunt that there was never the like of them', but he had not yet seen work to bear out their words. We recognise that type too – though no one now knows who they were. At just this moment his reiterated pleas were answered; he got his post in the King's Music. Having got it, he wrote no more.

Perhaps he had aged prematurely, or his intensely personal art had exhausted him – as with other song-writers. Peacham addressed him with affectionate sympathy:

> So since, old friend, thy years have made thee white,
> And thou for others hast consumed thy spring,
> How few regard thee whom thou didst delight
> And far and near came once to hear thee sing:
> Ungrateful times and worthless age of ours
> That lets us pine when it hath cropped our flowers.

This was now the Jacobean age, which Drayton and Daniel had also reason to resent. Let these lines stand for epitaph on the greatest of British song-writers.

Campion has the unique interest of being equally eminent as poet and composer; for that matter, he earned his living as a doctor. That age did not make specialisation, though necessary, its ideal; its ideal was the well-rounded man of Castiglione, *l'uomo universale* of Sidney or Ralegh, Harington or Dyer. Campion began as a disciple of Sidney, as we can see from the variety of his measures, some of them of a quantitative character. He has been described as the poet of the auditory imagination and, exquisitely sensitive to the sound-values of words, his constant aim was to achieve a perfect balance between words and music.[87] To have achieved it is his uniqueness. Naturally, he paid a certain price for the perfection of his ambivalence: his music does not have the poignancy of Dowland, nor his words the power of Donne. But his lyrics have, what is rare, organic structure, and he commands words and music to one aesthetic effect.

Campion published five books of songs – some 120 in all. From the first he had the classic aims of precision and conciseness; as he went on he became more terse. 'What epigrams are in poetry, the same are Airs in music, then in their chief perfection when

they are short and well-seasoned.'[88] He yielded first place in music,
as everyone did, to 'the grave and well-invented [i.e. developed]
motet.' Solo-songs, with instrumental accompaniment, were a
later invention, and Campion indited a persuasive manifesto for
them, as against those who 'will admit no music but that which
is long, intricate, bated [filled out] with fugue, chained with
syncopation, and where the nature of every word is precisely expressed in the note.' In his second book he made a concession.
The Airs – many of them 'long since composed' – had been
framed for solo-voice with accompaniment. 'Yet do we daily
observe, that when any shall sing a treble to an instrument, the
standers-by will be offering at an inward part out of their own
nature, and – true or false – out it must, though to the perverting
of the whole harmony.'[89] So he had filled in more parts, 'which
who so please may use, who like not may leave.' Campion was
a highly educated man, who wrote good Latin verse, and had
studied on the Continent. He said, with authority, 'some there are
who admit only French or Italian Airs, as if every country had
not its proper Air, which the people thereof naturally usurp in
their music.' He was conscious of the chief musical defect of the
language – its proliferation of consonants, which in his practice
he tried to reduce.

Campion divided this collection into two Books, one grave
and pious, the other amorous and light. And in fact his work has
a wider range of mood and variety of subject than is usually suspected from the popularity of the love-songs. Still the most
familiar of his songs is

> Shall I come, sweet love, to thee
>> When the evening beams are set?
> Shall I not excluded be?
>> Will you find no feignèd let?
> Let me not, for pity, more
> Tell the long hours at your door.

Et cetera. Or,

> There is a garden in her face,
>> Where roses and white lilies grow . . .

When we tire of the plaints and pinings – or the signs and satis-
factions – of Petrarchan love, there are humorous moods to turn
to or ever-fresh transcripts from nature:

> Now winter nights enlarge
> The number of their hours,

And clouds their storms discharge
Upon the airy towers –

one sees the towers of Hardwick, where Thomas Hobbes used to
sing in his room on the roof, if only (he was a utilitarian) to exercise
his lungs.

In his day Campion's most famous song was

What if a day, or a month, or a year
Crown thy delights with a thousand sweet contentings?
Cannot a chance of a night or an hour
Cross thy desires with as many sad tormentings?

This crossed the seas, to be copied into Dutch song-books.
Campion ended his career with an admirable little treatise on
Counterpoint, which, Peter Warlock comments, 'might well be
used today by students of composition in preference to many a
modern textbook.'[90] More to the point historically: it registered
the change to modern music. Campion's life and work were so
closely associated with Rosseter's that in some places it is hard to
disentangle them, and they seem to have lived together. For
Warlock Rosseter's songs have 'a curious fascination . . . so slight,
yet so insinuating . . . they are a little remote, they trouble the
mind like half-remembered things.' He was one of the lute-
musicians to King James, and was besides in charge of the
Children of the Revels, so that almost all his work was for the
stage. Campion too provided songs and music for Court-masques.
When he died in 1620, he left all his worldly wealth to his friend;
it amounted to £22. It does not seem much for so many exquisite
contributions to cultural life. However, in death he was not parted
from his friend: they lie together, not far from where they lived in
Fleet Street, in St. Dunstan's-in-the-West.

Though John Daniel* published hardly a score of songs, Warlock places him second only to Dowland for their quality, the
spaciousness of his style, the originality of his harmonic sense.
Warlock was taken with 'the quaintly entitled "Mrs. Anne Green
her leaves be green".'[91] But this means a 'Browning', a set of
variations on that melody, which was another English speciality –
there are many of them. Daniel produced his song-book for the
daughter of a Somerset knight –

Which, having been but yours and mine before
(Or but of few besides), is made hereby
To be the world's, and yours and mine no more.

* There is no point in spelling him 'Danyel'.

The world took no notice of it:

> Though I might have been warned by him, who is
> Both near and dear to me, that what we give
> Unto these times, we give t'unthankfulness,
> And so without unconstant censures live.

This refers to his brother the poet – remarkable that a Somerset yeoman family should have produced two such sons.

Robert Jones was a more professional figure, a leading lutenist who published no less than five books of Airs. He had a gift for simple, light-hearted songs, and says disarmingly in his First Book that the words were the work of certain gentlemen 'who were earnest to have me apparel these ditties for them.' This gives us an important clue to the way the immense body of anonymous verse in the song-books and madrigals came into being: nothing could indicate more clearly the place of music and poetry, song and dance, in that society that created its own recreations. A. H. Bullen was able to make an admirable anthology of such lyrics from the song-books. In his prefaces Jones gives the critics what they ask for – something in his tone, in addition to his name, indicate a Celtic temperament. The Sidneys were his patrons: his first book was dedicated to Sir Robert, his last to the daughter, Lady Mary Wroth, of whom we have a well-known portrait standing up with her arch-lute.

Where the elder Ferrabosco wrote madrigals, the younger wrote songs and music for Ben Jonson's masques: we witness the change of taste. Jonson paid eloquent tributes to his colleague in prose and verse; one of them describes the power of music on the mind:

> To urge, my loved Alfonso, that bold fame
> Of building towns and making wild beasts tame
> Which Music had, or speak her known effects,
> That she removeth cares, sadness ejects,
> Declineth anger, persuades clemency,
> Doth sweeten mirth and heighten piety,
> And is to a body often ill inclined
> No less a sovereign cure than to the mind . . .

Such was the doctrine of the age with regard to music. Many more amateurs and composers – some of these more famous for their madrigals – contributed lute-songs and lute-music before the golden vogue faded.[92]

V

The greatest composers contributed more to keyboard music, the most remarkable development to take place, one which had continuing effects on European music. This art reflected above all the triumph of the dance, which meant regular rhythms, according to the dance-form. The establishment of instrumental music independent of voices is a creation of the Renaissance.[93] Again the fact that the themes thus treated had their origin in the voice and words, in the plainchant of the Church or in folksong, added emotional undertones never more haunting than in the keyboard music of Byrd.[94] It is like the way the subconscious images in Shakespeare's poetry connect up, as if underwater, beneath the surface of what is being consciously said.

English keyboard music considerably antedated the madrigal. The variation form came in about mid-century; by the end of the century the variations being written here surpassed anything. Variations were a means of extending the development of the theme, and led to patterned figurations which much increased the brilliancy of the effect. These were a speciality of the English school. An improvement of the instruments went along with this: it would have been impossible to play the difficult and sophisticated works of Byrd, Bull and Gibbons on earlier ones. These wrote mainly for the virginals, a kind of spinet, but the strings were plucked; the keys were called jacks. Shakespeare describes his far from virginal mistress playing on the instrument, like the lady engraved as frontispiece for *Parthenia*, the first printed collection of such music:

> How oft when thou, my music, music play'st
> Upon that blessèd wood whose motions sounds
> With thy sweet fingers, when thou gently sway'st
> The wiry concord that mine ear confounds,
> Do I envy those jacks that nimble leap
> To kiss the tender inward of thy hand . . .
> O'er whom thy fingers walk with gentle gait,
> Making dead wood more blest than living lips.

In this strictly musical development the key-figure was again Byrd, with his immense versatility, his complete command of form, his catholicity of spirit, in the secular sense of the phrase. For the social historian must notice how this music draws up into itself and expresses the life of the time. Not only are numerous folksongs and dances made use of, there are dirges and 'domps' (another English speciality, a thumping kind of dance, used more in instrumental ensembles or consorts). There were several sets of variations by different composers on 'The carman's whistle', on town and country cries. Gibbons, Weelkes and Richard Dering (who became a Catholic and wrote much of his music abroad) all treated these themes; with voices they became almost comic cantatas.[95] There was a good deal of programme-music: 'Mr. Byrd's Battle', with 'The March to the Fight', 'The Retreat', 'The Burying of the Dead', 'The Soldiers' Delight' and 'The Morris'.

Altogether there is an immense corpus of this music; up to forty years ago over 600 pieces were known – much more has come to light since – and of these 120 are by Byrd.[96] We owe the survival of perhaps most of them to the industry and accomplishment of the younger Francis Tregian, who copied them into the vast manuscript, the Fitzwilliam Virginal Book, without which the bulk of them would have been lost.[97] It should, of course, be known as the Tregian Virginal Book. He left two other immense volumes of madrigals, mostly from printed collections – one in the British Museum, the other in the New York Public Library. But it is from Tregian's Virginal Book that we derive the essentials of the school. The Tregians – the name is pronounced Trudgian – were obstinate recusants, both father and son.[98] The father had been rich and, with an Arundell for his mother, rather stuck-up; for their long-continued obstinacy they eventually lost all their estates. They both spent many years, comfortably enough, in the Fleet prison – at least the parents, having little else to do, had eighteen children. The more interesting son and heir was educated in France and became a gentleman of the chamber to Cardinal Allen in Rome; extremely cultivated musically, he used his opportunity over the years to collect Italian and Italianate madrigals, many of Peter Phillips, John Cooper, Dering and friends abroad, for example. Coming back to the Fleet, for the last fourteen years of his life – rather than go to Church – he was well occupied with his monumental work of copying. Never can an imprisonment have so justified itself.

Nothing could exceed the importance of Tregian's Virginal Book in the literature of the subject.[99] The pieces range over the whole period from 1550 to his death about 1619, so that all the resources of the golden age and its varied styles are fully illustrated. Moreover, Tregian was able to transpose all the pieces, some 600, from the archaic systems of notation to the new: a crucial document therefore in the history of musical notation. He was more than a copyist: he was the anthologist, it represents his musical taste, he could also compose. He was not exclusive: there are pieces all the way from Sweelinck, greatest of Dutch composers, to the talented amateur Heybourne. The end of the collection is dominated by Giles Farnaby, as the bulk of it is by Byrd and Bull. One collects together this cultivated Catholic circle in the names: Byrd's 'Tregian's Ground', and 'Mrs. Katherine Tregian's Pavan'; Sybil and Philip Tregian appear, the latter with a pavan. Peter Phillips wrote a 'Pavana dolorosa, Tregian', and a 'Pavana Paget' – another exile. Phillips's compositions are on Continental themes, from Lassus or Marenzio. The home-grown composers are faithful to homely themes.

The book begins with Bull's Walsingham Variations, thirty of them, the high peak of sophisticated virtuosity in the art. When we listen to them, with their astonishing range, power and complexity, yet always maintaining the emotional intensity of the obsessive theme, we realise that within their own terms they are on a level with the Goldberg or Diabelli Variations. Bull was an incomparable performer and his forceful personality comes through, with the figuration passing from one hand to another, two hands in parallel or contrary movement, or counterpoised rhythms of two beats against three – there was a perverseness about his temperament in conflict with itself. Some prefer Byrd's Walsingham Variations, twenty-two in number, less brilliant and virtuosic, more in keeping with the inner spirit of the theme; or the melody and evocation of atmosphere of Farnaby, with 'The King's Hunt' and an original piece for two virginals. Both Byrd and Gibbons have variations on the favourite 'The woods so wild'. In this field too Gibbons is the real successor of Byrd, with his perfect balance between past and future, his mixture of grave and gay, his nobility of spirit. His Fantasia a 4 is one of the masterpieces; Morley had pointed out that the development of the Fantasy offered a new challenge, for the composer was set free from the restrictions of set theme. From the irregular grouping towards the end one can watch Tregian copying pieces into his book as a particular work came to hand.

Dr. Bull is a spirit apart, a legend in his own time: such virtuosity, such *fougue* of temperament, were thought demonic. His portrait at Oxford has the inscription, 'The Bull by force doth reign'. Mellers has well described the almost El Greco-like elongation of the face, 'the nose long and straight, the mouth at once severe and hypersensitive, the eyes blackly penetrating, but wistful. The vitality of the eyes and the resplendent decoration of the collar are sharply opposed, with an effect as of metaphysical wit, to the skull and hour-glass in the background. His virtuosity itself reveals the exhibitionism and egoism of the Renaissance. Virtuosity was said to imply demonic possession: there are legends about his sorcery at the keyboard. There is indeed a distinctly Marlovian, Faustian flavour about Bull's personality: the same conflict between traditional pieties and a courageous yearning to allow the human will to control its own destiny.'[100] Above all there is tension. If Byrd was the Shakespeare among composers, Bull was the Marlowe – or perhaps the Donne.

He was, exceptionally, newsworthy: his presence was noted, when no other composer's was. When the Queen went to St. James's to communicate at Easter 1593, it was noted that Dr. Bull played at the offertory.[101] Or again at a City feast, entertaining the King, Dr. Bull was at the organ. When Gresham College was founded, he was made its first professor of music; because he could not lecture in Latin (as Byrd could have done) he was given a special dispensation to lecture in English. He was always well treated; extravagant as he was, the State Papers record his requests for special grants, in addition to his appointments. A dark West Countryman by origin, from Somerset, he began as a chorister in the Chapel Royal, and was a pupil of Blitheman (also an original composer), with whom he had a father-son relationship. Appointed organist of Hereford cathedral at nineteen, in 1585 Blitheman got him back to the Chapel Royal, where Bull succeeded him as an organist in 1591. His career was made, his fame grew; during 1601–2 he was allowed to travel on the Continent, but was recalled by the Queen. He gave up his professorship to marry, and was made musician to Prince Henry.

Suddenly, in 1613, at the height of his *réclame*, he fled the country, and never came back. The tensions within him broke. The absconding of the best publicised of English musicians made a sensation, and James protested against the Archduke Albert taking him into his service in Brussels.[102] The English envoy reported that he had not absconded for religion, but 'for incontinence, fornication, adultery'. Very likely, with his temperament; but it is also likely that religion was an element in the crisis, for there is no further evidence of trouble, once he settled down abroad. The Archduke could not keep him against James's protest, but he maintained him till 1617, when he became organist

of Antwerp cathedral. In the Netherlands he had the company of
the English exiles, the musical companionship of Phillips and the
acquaintance of Sweelinck, in whose memory he composed a
noble elegy. His influence on music in the Netherlands was considerable; he was held in honour and regard, and seems to have
found serenity in his last works. Dying in 1628, he is buried in the
little graveyard on the south side of the cathedral.

Altogether, he was as astonishing an apparition as Marlowe.
His early organ-music was naturally influenced by Blitheman,
who had already emerged from medieval limitations into a freer
field of richer harmony, expressive figuration and contrasted
rhythms. But Bull could play whirlwind figurations faster than
any contemporaries and was fascinated by his own virtuosity. He
was evidently out for excitement. His finest organ-works were
probably written in exile, fusing his experiments with traditional
polyphony, as in the A minor 'In Nomine', with its mystical
sensuousness and fluctuation of key. Hardly any of his later
fantasias are even yet published. He became more disciplined,
with a kind of radiant simplicity, in the 'Alma mater redemptoris'
fantasy and the masterly variations on 'Laet ons met Herten
Reijne', at the last.

Hardly any of his vocal church music survives, and none of
his string music is published. His genius is at its height in that for
virginals. It has been diagnosed as exhibiting a split personality:
on one side, the exuberant zest for life and adventure (possibly
adventures); on the other, introvert and melancholy, with the
consciousness of time and death. He does not possess the inner
serenity and outer charm of Byrd; there is a passionate modernity,
along with the assertion of the will and the ego. There is a glitter
upon his personality that comes through in the music, passion
and audacity in the novel effects. One notices for oneself the
beautiful bone-structure in the sensitive, questing face, the slightly
demonic ears. Yet he was capable of simplicity: his 'Goodnight'
being one of the loveliest in that way: perhaps the simplicity of
sophistication, the tormented spirit finding peace, as Marlowe
never did.

English chamber music was an art of the home: it meant
private music for the chamber, as against the orchestral concerts
which the urban civilisation of Italy was already developing. It
was then called consort music, which meant an ensemble of instruments of the same kind – for which purpose were the chests of

viols we find in inventories of musical homes. A 'broken consort' meant an ensemble of instruments of different kinds: viols, which produced a softer tone from the curved bow, along with the piercing violin; the nostalgic, nasal tone of lutes of various sorts; recorders, which produced an organ-pipe sound. By 1600 the English school had reached its zenith; by 1620 it was making history on the Continent.[103] It is not too much to say that it was the foundation of modern chamber-music.

Some thousands of pieces attest the fertility of the school, all the chief composers contributed to it. Hundreds of these that remain are instrumental arrangements of vocal works, and again 'the old choral polyphony determined the form as well as the style' of this music.[104] The English school remained attached to polyphony and did not go over to the showy effects, the harmonics, of public performance; it remained an individual activity, and retained its individuality. The dominant forms were the 'In Nomines', the dance and dance-song, reflecting their respective origins, religious and secular. But now came to the fore another English speciality, the string fantasy. Morley defined it: 'the most principal and chiefest kind of music which is made without a ditty [poem or words] is the Fantasy, that is, when a musician taketh a point at his pleasure and wresteth it and turneth it as he list . . . In this may more art be shown than in any other music, because the composer is tied to nothing, but that he may add, diminish, and alter at his pleasure.'[105] Meyer tells us: 'the whole period of polyphonic string fantasias belongs to the musical history of this country much more than to that of any other', it is one of its 'most important contributions to the great musical achievements of recent centuries.'

The public demand for music increased beyond all bounds. Bookshops sold tutors for lute and cithern and viol, printed music paper, collections of published music as well as in manuscript, imported music, quantities of fantasies. After the Restoration, with the change of musical taste, Roger North says that 'of these fancies whole volumes are left, scarce ever to be made use of but either in the air for kites or in the fire for singeing pullets.'[106] From John Cooper alone – what is the point of calling him Coprario because he spent a few years in Italy? – 96 fantasies survive. From Tomkins, a much more original spirit, with exceptional technical skill, over twenty. The younger Ferrabosco made numerous contributions in this field, rather more dramatic in style, though still of the English school. One of the last works of the master, Byrd, is a superb fantasia a 6, quite as elaborate as any of the younger generation. Of these the foremost master was Gibbons, whose 'advance in the field of form as in other fields shows him as an independent personality gifted with greater courage and deeper understanding than most of his contemporaries.'[107] His early death coincided with the decline of the school; new tendencies and forms took shape. The turn-over between England and the Continent was extraordinarily quick, the contacts, as we have seen, close and very varied. Anthony Holborne produced his lesson-book of dance-tunes in 1599; it was republished in Hamburg in 1607. All over Northern Europe England was making its contribution: modern music was taking shape.

VI

We may conclude, with Mellers, that the Golden Age produced 'a school of vocal composers whose work can stand with the greatest achievements of European music at any time or place', while contemporary opinion held that the English shone even more brilliantly in instrumental music.[108] Alas, never again! In its way it was as splendid as the contemporary drama, though this is much less generally realised. The means with which it was accomplished were simple and even humble; but the finest achievements of the human spirit are a question of quality, never of mass, size and quantity. The circumstances of the time must have been uniquely propitious, and the time itself offered inspiration.

Woodfill points out that circumstances affect musical composition even more closely than literary: composers are more dependent on performers.[109] If choirs are available they will write choral music – what a merciful blessing that the English Church took the turn it did, instead of following Geneva! Apart from the voice, the instruments at hand were comparatively few, though they underwent a notable development. More important is the fact that the whole society was enthusiastically engaged in musical activity: it was infused with music from top to bottom.

London was the dynamic centre. There were not only the Court, with attendant Chapel Royal, but St. Paul's, Westminster Abbey and other churches and private chapels with choirs. We have seen how closely connected the leading composers were with these establishments, even when they earned their living as organists in the cathedrals in the provinces. London also had its civic establishment: the London Waits, a dozen skilled musicians with a score of apprentices.[110] There was hot competition for the posts – Nicholas Yonge, strange to say, was turned down: obviously he was a vocalist, not an instrumentalist. One year three Bassanos, of the Queen's Music, examined the candidates. Three of the London Waits (one of them, an Ives) published their works. In spring and summer, from Lady day to Michaelmas, they gave a concert every Sunday and holiday, from the balcony of the Royal Exchange. On City festivals they played before the houses of the Mayor and sheriffs, and for the aldermen when requested. Private persons could also engage them: we find Lord Willoughby and Sir Thomas Kitson doing so, while they were called in on special occasions, such as to entertain the Queen when she was staying at Gorhambury in 1587. These London musicians were organised in a small impoverished 'Worshipful Company of Musicians', which received its charter in 1604, though it went back to an earlier gild.[111] Its affairs – regulation of numbers, conduct, apprenticeship – were just like any other company, except that its resources were minimal.

There were waits in towns across the country, from Barnstaple to Beverley: over seventy towns altogether, and York had a Gild of Musicians. At Nottingham, as elsewhere, the waits brought in the May, with morris-dancing and shooting off of guns. It was regular custom for them to play at the mayor's dinner, at quarter-sessions dinners and such hospitable occasions. The waits of Norwich, second town in the kingdom, were highly thought of, and they also gave concerts. Drake and Norris took them to make music on the Lisbon expedition in 1589. They were frequently called upon to provide music at neighbouring houses: the Carlisle Waits at Naworth Castle, the Newark Waits at Belvoir, the Grantham or Nottingham Waits at Hardwick when the great Bess was in residence. When Sir Arthur Throckmorton entertained Lord Wotton for seventeen days at Paulerspury in the summer of 1613, he employed musicians who cost him £5, a goodly sum.[112] Inventories show a considerable variety of instruments: cornets, flutes, recorders, sackbuts (trombones), shawms (rather like oboes) indicate that wind-instruments prevailed, but they sometimes had bassoons and viols. As for country people at large, they had pipes and tabors (drums). The self-righteous Presbyterian Baxter said of his youth, 'we could not, on the Lord's day, either read a chapter or pray, or sing a psalm or catechise or instruct a servant, but with the noise of pipe and tabor continually in our ears.'[113]

Loud-mouthed Perkins added to his list of detestable popish practices, 'consort music in divine service, feeding the ears, not edifying the mind.'[114]

The universities made no provision for teaching music, as some schools did.[115] James Whitelocke was taught singing and playing on instruments at admirable Merchant Taylors' under Mulcaster. But university courses were purely theoretical. We need not bother with theory, Pythagorean or Platonic; it is the art that counts. Practical music went on in the college chapels, where there were choirs: at Oxford in Christ Church, Magdalen, New College (as today), at Cambridge in King's. A number of noted musicians started as choirboys, so also did some bishops: Cooper of Winchester, whose wife was such a liability, and Bickley of Chichester, both at Magdalen; Milton's father, that admirable musician, had been a choirboy at Christ Church.

We now realise, as never before, how musical the Elizabethan stage was, and many actors were musicians, as we know from their wills. Augustine Phillips, who left to 'my fellow, William Shakespeare, a 30 s piece in gold', bequeathed to his apprentice a cithern, a bandora and a lute.[116] There were also the professional instrumentalists, besides those men and boys who were singers, like Robert Armin, who sang the songs of Feste in *Twelfth Night*. In transferring the life of society to the heightened, rhetorical conditions of the stage, it recapitulated formally the regular code that would be recognised by the audience.[117] A flourish of trumpets heralded the entrance of a king, or the beginning of a battle; 'loud music' meant wind and brass, appropriate to a banquet; discordant music for surprise, or contrast, or a reverse. The dramatists used music to enforce a point or underline an emotional state: soft music is directed to help Lear back to sanity, to restore Marina to life from her trance. There is harmonious music as Prince Hal places the crown on his head as the rightful successor of his father; but Ferdinand uses singing madmen to attack the Duchess of Malfi's sanity, Marston's *Malcontent* opens with discordant music from within his chamber, to depict Malevole. *The Old Wives' Tale* suggests its rural atmosphere by opening with a three-men song. That means singing in canon, like 'Three Blind Mice', which goes back to then. Country people were much addicted to these catches, or rounds, and of course they are caught up on the stage, as we remember from Sir Toby Belch. For, stage music precisely reflected the music of society at large.[118]

From the first Shakespeare made good use of music; but Long

has noticed that this greatly increased in the comedies beginning with *A Midsummer Night's Dream*. An unusually large number of musicians are necessary, and he makes the percipient suggestion that they were probably drawn from a noble household, the play written for a sophisticated audience.[119] But, of course: I have shown that it was written for Southampton's mother's marriage to the elderly Sir Thomas Heneage, and there would be the resources of both their great households to draw upon.[120] Subsequent comedies like *Much Ado* and *Twelfth Night*, and romances like *The Tempest* are permeated by music; the tragedies less so.[121] The development of the private theatre immensely increased the musical possibilities, being indoors and with a more cultivated audience. In fact, it was demanded: there was consort music before and after the plays, and between the acts, as well as in the plays, where, with Beaumont and Fletcher, music became an integral part. The situation is reflected upon in *Ratsey's Ghost*: 'I have often gone to plays more for music's sake than for action.'[122] This registers a change indeed. Yet, to sum up the picture as a whole, 'the Elizabethan drama occupies a unique position in the history of both drama and music in that it is an art-form which has firmly integrated the sister arts – poetry, drama, the dance and music.'[123]

CHAPTER IV

ARCHITECTURE AND SCULPTURE

I

ARCHITECTURE may be described as frozen history. No other art so visibly, so obtrusively, or so fully and exactly, expresses the society that creates it. All over England – we must except the backward Northern counties and Wales – there was a vast rebuilding that affected all classes of society from the top to the bottom. All educated people have long been aware of the palaces built by the most conspicuous members of that society – though they are less aware that for every palace that remains there is one that has disappeared. We still have Longleat, Longford and Wollaton, Burghley, Hatfield and Hardwick, Bramshill, Blickling and Montacute; but Holdenby and Theobalds – grandest of all – Wanstead, Wimbledon and Basing, Worksop, Caversham and Copt Hall, have all gone; Kirby is a ruin, and Audley End a fragment, the main side of what was once two large courts. Many are aware of the large number of Elizabethan country houses of the gentry that remain, in varying proportions and character in different counties. Others can recognise the admirable examples of prosperous yeomen's houses, particularly in areas like East Anglia, southern counties from Kent to Somerset, rich Midland counties like Northamptonshire and Lincolnshire, and along the Severn border. But few people know that scores of towns and hundreds of villages were largely rebuilt in this period – with many new quarries opened up[1] – for much of the evidence has perished in subsequent rebuilding. What it all goes to show is the widespread increase of wealth, prosperity and population: one does not need dubious statistics to demonstrate the visible and obvious.

However, that 'the Great Rebuilding' affected middle-class townspeople, farmers and peasantry as well as the nobility and gentry has not been realised until recent years. 'Few major events in English social history have so completely escaped the notice of historians as the revolution in the housing of the generality of people that occurred between about 1570 and the outbreak of the Civil War.'² This could be said only a few years ago, by Professor W. G. Hoskins; we know better now, largely as the result of his own work. He tells us that 'many English towns were substantially rebuilt or enlarged in these two generations'; and cites examples such as Shrewsbury, where many of these fine houses survived until recently; Exeter, Oxford, Norwich, Bristol and such towns, where they were mostly swept away in the Victorian age. At Plymouth the population 'about doubled between 1580 and 1610, and we hear of at least half a dozen new streets', several of them named after leading merchants who became mayors. Building activity in the countryside is no less striking. 'In Devon one finds overwhelming testimony to rebuilding and enlargement from about 1560 onwards in many hundreds of scattered farmhouses'; while, at the other end of the country, 'at Chiddingstone, in Kent, there survives a virtually complete Elizabethan street.' At other places, too, in Warwickshire towns such as Alcester, if one looks with discerning eye. It was no less true of peasant cottages – modernisation, insertion of a floor and partitions, chimney and glazing, or rebuilding. 'There is a good deal of documentary evidence that large numbers of new cottages were being erected from the last quarter of the sixteenth century onwards', but few of these have survived. In any case, they are of no interest architecturally, and here we are concerned with architecture as an art.

Art is a matter of the higher levels of culture, not the lower, whatever the society. We find complex movements, ebbs and flows and again recessions of cultural influence from abroad, in accordance with conscious attractions and rejections. The earlier Renaissance in England left as its grandest monument the Torrigiani tomb of Henry VII in Westminster Abbey. But this was an Italian work, and no English artists were capable of carrying on its inspiration. Even in France, so much closer to the source and more advanced culturally, the Renaissance influence in architecture was for long confined to decoration, detailed design, externals: it was by way of externals, working from outside appearance to inner integration, that it ultimately triumphed.³ This was still more the case in England. The Gothic spirit of Northern Europe – instinctive preference expressing itself in conscious taste – was too strong. And this in spite of the fact that the native Perpendicular style in its last manifestation was moving towards a certain classicism of its own, in its leaning towards the flat, the shallow, and the square, as one sees in the late chapel of Trinity College, Cambridge, or a church like Saffron Walden.[4]

The earlier, Italian Renaissance idiom could not gain favour: it was too exotic, too remote from the English medieval tradition, still overwhelmingly strong. The austere purity of Bramante's classicism could simply not be appreciated in this forested, turreted, pinnacled country, let alone reproduced. When the Renaissance influence gathered strength later in the century, it took a Mannerist form[5] – significantly and with reason, for Mannerism is the Gothic of classicism. It must have appealed to the deeper instincts of Northern Europeans, of the Netherlands and France as well as of England: hence the fantastic roofscapes of Chambord and Burghley, the gables and dormers of Fontainebleau and Villandry as of Nonsuch or Gresham's Royal Exchange, the decorations and coruscations upon Anglo-Netherlandish monuments in our churches.

We see an object-lesson in the whole movement of taste, a demonstration of English preferences, in the monuments of the Dormers in Wing church in Buckinghamshire. The family's prosperity was increased by the grant to them by Henry VIII of this fat manor of St. Albans' abbey: they remained devoted to Catholicism, a daughter, as Duchess of Feria, the chief patroness of the religious exiles in Spain. The recipient of the grant, Sir Robert Dormer, has a completely classical tomb of 1552: more like a Roman portico than a tomb, wide-spaced Corinthian columns, pilasters at the back, the simple tomb-chest decorated with ox-skulls and swags of flowers and fruit: the whole utterly secular, not a reference to religion. This Edwardian work of art is so purely Italian, it can never have been made by an Englishman. In the chancel there are two more tombs, one of 1590, the other of 1616, to the son and grandson and their wives. These are straight out of a Southwark workshop, probably Gerard Johnson's, of the type of which we have hundreds of examples all over the country. They, too, are Renaissance in detail: marble columns, pediment, ribbon-decoration, nulling. But the point is that they are hybrids: they effect a compromise with the traditional, with their medieval-style effigies, in the first recumbent, in the second kneeling. It is evident that the severity of pure Renaissance style, exemplified in the Edwardian monument, did not appeal to the Elizabethans. This was not successfully implanted in England until Inigo Jones imported it from Italy – and he was a Welshman.

In the second half of the century we see the English experimenting, trying out new designs, applying bits of Renaissance decoration often in a rather *gauche* manner, varying the traditional forms – the placing of and approach to the hall, for example – sometimes achieving external symmetry quite early, as at Sutton Place in Surrey or Barrington Court in Somerset. They are feeling their way to what best suits their convenience and their taste. They must not be condemned for not understanding the classical, when they clearly did not like it in its purity and rigour – any more than contemporary French architecture opted for it. It was not congenial to the spirit or the conditions of Northern Europe. Consider: pure Italian Renaissance architecture (i.e. that of Florence and Rome, not Venice) was a wall-architecture, quite rightly for the climate, needing to mitigate sun and utilise shadow. The Elizabethans favoured a window-architecture, letting in light and looking out at the prospect on every side – sometimes with a 'prospect-room' as at Wollaton and Worksop – and ending up with the shimmering walls of glass of Worksop and Hardwick. This was more appropriate to the English climate. Let us add, too, that it reflected the emergence from medieval insecurity to a prosperously expanding and secure society.

The finest Elizabethan architecture, then, represented a fertilisation of native vigour with foreign sophistication, as in music and literature. We can watch the evolution most notably, from the earlier impulse to its full fruition, at Longleat where a succession of three, if not four, houses has been traced on the site in as many decades. In the end, in the 1580's, a wonderful palace was achieved, a veritable fusion of classic with native inspiration, as indeed both English and foreign craftsmen worked at it. To the eye the splendid pile achieves classic symmetry, with its regular fronts: 'it is a work of art, noble, delicate and intelligent.'[6] Sir John Summerson expresses a doubt whether there is such a thing as an Elizabethan style of architecture – and yet every cultivated person can recognise an Elizabethan house when he sees one.[7] Pevsner has no such doubt as he observes the progress made in the interior planning of these houses, and he specifically compares what was 'a process of ordering' to the parallel ordering taking place in poetry: from Skelton to Surrey, from Surrey to Spenser.[8] Still more, it reflects the progressive ordering and articulation of society. In architecture, as in the drama, it produced something unique at its height. It exhibited, and exhibits to us still, 'a true synthesis, a style in its own right. It could not last: too many external influences were hammering at the door. But for twenty

supreme years houses were being built all over England of which
we can justly be proud, for not only were they of the greatest
daring and beauty but they were, as no house has been since,
unique to England.'⁹ Of all our authorities Mark Girouard has
had the imagination to see this clearly. 'The aberrations and provincialisms of Elizabethan detail are unimportant in comparison
to the novelty, daring and unity of the architecture as a whole
that emerged in the last twenty years of the reign and ran on well
into the 17th century: an architecture which would have been
impossible if England had been exposed to the full blast of the
Renaissance, and which was one of the curiosities and the triumphs
of European art.'

But, then, what would not that fortunate, insular society,
calculatingly, dare?

The effective new impulse came from the Edwardian circle.
Where full Italianate classicism did not catch on, the Northern
French version of it did – as could be seen from Protector Somerset's house in the Strand (using stone from the cloister of St.
Paul's), with its coupling of windows under a classic pediment.
The façade of Old Somerset House was not really satisfactory,
for all its seminal importance; it was a clumsy adaptation: the full
fruition is to be seen in the beautiful fenestration of Longleat
thirty years later. We owe this to Sir John Thynne, who was one
of the Protector's circle, went out of politics with his fall, and
devoted himself to his estates and to building. Three houses, each
bigger than the last, took shape on the monastic site, until the
last burned down. Undeterred, and with the aid of his English
and French devisers and craftsmen, Robert Smythson and Alain
Ménart (Maynard), Thynne erected the palace we see today. It
was unfinished at his death in 1580; he can never have lived in it,
and hardly in any of its predecessors, for the house was always a-
building. The same was roughly true of Burghley with Burghley
House, Hatton with Holdenby, Leicester at Kenilworth, for they
were always at Court or in their London or suburban houses,
Theobalds or Wanstead.

Then what were they building for? For magnificence, for their
families, for posterity.

Many of the leading figures of the time, at the centre or in
the localities, had an absolute passion for building – as indeed
had their opposite numbers abroad. (The spirit of the age and
the nature of the society offer as good an explanation as any

other.) We see this in so symptomatic a figure as Sir Thomas Smith, one of Somerset's 'new men', Secretary of State under Edward VI, ambassador to France under the more conservative Elizabeth. Smith was a brilliant poor boy, son of a small sheep-farmer at Saffron Walden, who became a Cambridge intellectual (with some of the disadvantages); he was as keen on the new architecture as he was on the new pronunciation of Greek and spelling reform. In his library he had a dozen books on architecture, unprocurable in England, including six editions of Vitruvius, on which all Renaissance architectural thought was based.[10] Burghley later on wrote to an English envoy in Paris to get him a foreign book on architecture which he had seen at Smith's. Marrying a rich wife (whom he could not make happy), Smith was at least able to indulge his architectural tastes by building two houses on her estate at Theydon Mount in Essex. Smith was at it – building – for years; and the classic front of Hill Hall, with its giant order of columns at either end (now, appropriately, a women's prison) remains to testify to his advanced taste and knowledge. There was hardly such a thing as an architect in our sense of the word in those days. Smith had Richard Kirby for his 'chief architect and master of works', but it was Smith who gave *him* the plan of what he wanted. Smith did take Kirby's advice over his tomb, upon which we see a rather original effigy, the old balding knight holding hand to head as if he has a headache. His chief headache, however, concerned the finishing of his house, about which he expresses anxiety in his will. And we note this with several others – Thynne and Bess of Hardwick, for example: it was natural enough with people whose real passion was for building.

Burghley was another Edwardian, whose passion for building was almost a mania, the only activity that approached scandal in that so well-considered, well-ordered life. It was the Lord Treasurer that Spenser had in mind, when he wrote in 'Mother Hubberd's Tale':

> But his own treasure he increasèd more
> And lifted up his lofty towers thereby
> That they began to threat the neighbour sky,
> The while the Prince's palaces fell fast
> To ruin – for what thing can ever last? –
> And whilst the other peers for poverty
> Were forced their ancient houses to let lie
> And their old castles to the ground to fall . . .

Unfair, but Spenser here was the satirist, and anyway was Leicester's man, not Burghley's. It was the only one of his activities for which he thought it necessary to apologise, and he did so in suspiciously uncandid terms. His vast palace at Burghley was erected, he said, only upon the foundations left him by his father, and it was his mother's inheritance, of which he was but a tenant.

He had more excuse, if he needed any, with the equally splendid palace he erected at Theobalds. He had not originally intended such an enormous house for his younger son, but said 'it was begun by me with a mean [moderate] measure, but increased by occasion of her Majesty's often coming.'[11] And this was true. The Queen liked staying there at his expense, and this necessitated accommodating all the train that came with her. Moreover, she was apt to encourage her principal officers of state to bigger efforts – we have seen her hinting as much to Lord Keeper Bacon whose house at Gorhambury she thought too small. (Part of the sophisticated Renaissance façade remains in ruin.) Burghley received another hint: 'upon fault with the small measure of her chamber, which was in good measure for me, I was forced to enlarge a room for a larger chamber.' (Chamber meant a grand room.) In the end Burghley finished up with a vast fabric, which, with its four square towers and turrets, its loggias and courts, gardens and canals, must have been one of the grandest, as it was one of the most influential, in the country. So, too, with Hatton's enormous Holdenby: its purpose was to entertain the Queen on her summer progresses, 'for whom we both mean to exceed our purses in these.' For this purpose Leicester rushed up his new wing at Kenilworth, and Hertford added a whole range of apartments at Elvetham.

The Queen considered herself sufficiently well housed with the palaces she had inherited from her father, in particular Whitehall, Richmond and Greenwich, though she bought back Nonsuch which Mary had granted to Lord Lumley. Moreover, she well understood the need there was to economise and husband the small country's resources; so the money went on the fleet that fought the Armada. The result was a suspension of royal patronage for architecture, in marked contrast to her contemporaries abroad. Philip II, in addition to building three unsuccessful Armadas, built the Escorial: no wonder he twice went bankrupt, in spite of the treasure of the Indies. But he was at least the patron of a great architect in Herrera. Even Catherine de Médicis, amid all her distractions, built the Tuileries and Henri IV started work on the Louvre. Elizabeth contented herself with a gallery at Windsor, a fountain or two, and her ships.

Thus in England effective architectural patronage, though still radiating from the Court, was left to the ruling courtiers, not exercised by the Crown. They were all Edwardians – Smith, Cecil, Bacon, Sir Anthony Cooke with Gidea Hall, Sir Thomas Heneage with Copt Hall – and they began operations from the early 1560's, when the Edwardian march was resumed under surer conditions and sunnier prospects.

We must above all observe, what has not been brought out by the authorities, English eclecticism and empiricism at work, and the astonishing variety achieved in consequence. There is much wider variety of appearance and design in Elizabethan, than in Georgian, houses. The owner-connoisseur will select what he wants, from his knowledge, his experience and his books. The books that Burghley so much wanted to consult were Philibert de l'Orme's; Serlio and du Cerceau were available, with their practical illustrations to draw upon, for chimney-pieces, door-cases, friezes, gateways. Burghley inspected Holdenby with thoroughness and approbation; what he liked about it was the 'great magnificence in the front or front pieces of the house, and so every part answerable to other, to allure liking. I found no one thing of greater grace than your stately ascent from your hall to your great chamber, and your chamber answerable with large-ness and lightsomeness.'[12] What he meant by 'answerable' was balance and proportion. His own Theobalds exerted its influence upon Audley End and Hatfield, Castle Ashby, Rushton and Mildmay's Apethorpe. Before Bess of Hardwick built her second house there she went out of her way to inspect Wollaton, Holdenby, Worksop – and then improved on them in the finest work of them all.

Naturally, then, the earlier work is hesitant, feeling its way, sometimes awkward and sometimes dull – though this is not true of an exquisite house like Kirby, which Hatton started on before he had finished with Holdenby. There is the craze for building again, which Thynne's enemy, 'Wild' Darrell of Littlecote (a big traditional house) satirised in Longleat: 'But now see him that by these thirty years almost, with such turmoil of mind, hath been thinking of me, framing and erecting me, musing many a time with great care; and now and then pulling down this or that part of me to enlarge sometimes a foot, or some few inches, upon a conceit or this or that man's speech; and bye and bye beat down windows for this or that fault here or there.'[13] It brings Thynne vividly before us. Burghley, too, was hardly 'out of mortar' for thirty years, from beginning to end his own director and master of the works, using experts but to please himself.

As the result of all this experiment, the splendour of Elizabethan architecture burst forth at full, like literature, the drama and music, in the 1580's. There is then a new departure: they had found their style. They no longer express subservience to the classical; they use it only in so far as it suits them. 'There is a striking contrast between the grand buildings of the 1570's and early 1580's, which are elaborately and classically decorated, and the grand buildings of the late 1580's and 1590's, which obtain their effects of magnificence in a quite different way, through height, huge windows, distinctive plans and vivid skylines.'[14] Some of these contrasts, not all, are observable between Wollaton, say, and Hardwick. Girouard concludes: 'the style came to maturity with the suddenness and drama of an explosion. The truth is, I think, that the native Perpendicular Gothic tradition was too strong to succumb to the new style.' Any more, we might add, than that the Gothic tragedies of *Macbeth* and *King Lear* would give way to the classicism of *Sejanus* and *Catiline*. Girouard, with a perspicacious inflexion from outside, sees the continuity of the medieval Perpendicular, with the squareness of shape, the use of recession, the walls of glass in late Elizabethan. 'For fifteen or twenty years, in every part of England, it seemed as though the Elizabethans could do no wrong, as with wonderful fertility and resourcefulness they experimented with endless and exciting combinations of window, gable and tower. Yet, if one surveys the whole galaxy of buildings of this date, the impression that remains is one of gravity and restraint, of quiet outlines and broad expanses of wall: an impression quite at variance with the accepted notion of Elizabethan architecture, but surely a true one.'

In the end they certainly achieved a style.

It is remarkable that the man who did so much, in forty years of office, to build up the real, material resources of the nation, should also have been a leading figure in its architectural ornamentation, in the development of gardening, the introduction of new plants and flowers. The nation has reason to be grateful to him for Burghley House alone, a magnificent heritage. When we look up at the palatial pile, rising above the level Northamptonshire pastures and water-meadows, we realise its common source of inspiration with Longleat, its external four-squareness, the eclectic fusion of English tradition with French detail. It is raised up on a basement – something new that had come in from France; but the dominating feature of the west front is a traditional gate-house, as part of the front. (There was a similar medieval feature at Old Chatsworth, which Bess and her husband were then building.) The long interior court at Burghley gives a French impression, with its loggias leading up to a clock-tower with superimposed orders, derived from de l'Orme. The latest feature, of 1587, is the elaborate and subtly beautiful porch with its corona that provides the entrance on the north front. Within are chimney-pieces straight out of Serlio, as at Wollaton and Hardwick. Mr. Hussey can suggest no derivation for the stone staircase with its barrel-vaulting;[15] to my eye it is de l'Orme again, as at the Château d'Uzès. Altogether the house is more exuberant and less delicate than Longleat, but it imposes itself no less on the imagination; and for all the influences that have been absorbed into it, from home and abroad, it is as English in its impact, in its power and fantasy, as the work of Elgar.

Burghley's second palace, Theobalds – at Waltham Cross, conveniently near to London – was, astonishingly, being built along with Burghley House, if at a slightly different rhythm: work upon it proceeded mainly in the 1570's. It was more regular in plan and may have been more strictly beautiful, with a low entrance front – an idea derived from France – enabling one to see the four-towered central mass dominating the whole. It had a long straight approach – such as Burghley had admired at Holdenby – a 'walk for length, pleasantness and delight rare to be seen in England.'[16] Burghley used his friend Sir Thomas Gresham not only to supply slate from Flanders but architectural features, such as the loggia in front of the hall, sent over entire ready to be set up. We hear of a Dutch master-mason being employed, Hendryk, who at one point lost the pattern of the pillars – either for Theobalds or Burghley. Henry Hawthorne, Purveyor of the Queen's Works, drew the plan for the Inner Court. The Great Gallery had a painted frieze with landscapes of the principal cities of Europe, the Green Gallery with all the English shires represented as trees hung with the coats of arms of the chief families.*
– So like Burghley, with his passion for heraldry, to combine decoration with information.

* A similar feature survives in the contemporary dining-room at Gilling Castle, of the Fairfaxes, in Yorkshire.

It is hardly surprising that when James I set eyes on Theobalds and Holdenby, he wanted to annex them to the monarchy, and did. And so they perished, as victims ultimately of the Civil War, like Nonsuch.

Wollaton, near Nottingham, is even more original for all its eclecticism and has the significance that it is the work of one man who can at last be recognised as the leading Elizabethan architect, Robert Smythson. Three generations in that family produced names in the craft: the profession of architect was just beginning to establish itself as distinct from surveyor or master-mason.[17] On his tomb at Wollaton he is described as 'architector and surveyor unto the most worthy house of Wollaton with divers others of great account.' The house makes an extraordinary flamboyant impression, with four towers at the corners, a skyscraper of a hall in the middle and a prospect-room corbelled out above that. Much of the decorative detail comes from Vredeman de Vries's book; but this decoration is 'wrapped round a building of a shape and plan far more exciting than any in the Low Countries. The whole upper portion, being only one room thick, is transparent; and in the evening sunshine the combination of this transparency with the spread of window down below makes the house, rearing its extraordinary skyline on the hilltop, an unbelievably fantastic sight.'[18] When I first saw it, emerging out of the autumn mist across its park, I thought of the *Faerie Queene*.

Worksop Manor – built for the Earl of Shrewsbury while Bess was his Countess – was probably Smythson's next house: even more dramatic, if possible, a very tall building on a high hill, looking out all over the country, a more integrated composition. We know what it looked like, with its walls of glass and luminous gathered turrets – plans, and Renaissance designs for screen and decoration within survive. The plan exerted its influence upon neighbouring fine houses, still happily with us, Doddington near Lincoln, and Barlborough in Derbyshire – though Heath Old Hall in Yorkshire, with its fine Jezebel chimney-piece, is passing into ruin. So, too, with the Old Hall at Hardwick, the two large wings Bess added on, with the tall plasterwork figures and the friezes, now mouldering in decay, a stone's throw away from the new palace she all but completed.

The Countess must have been dissatisfied with the irregularity of her ancestral house, even as improved with balancing wings. Her architectural ambition, her perfectionism, urged her on to demand a design, regular and symmetrical, no less daring and dramatic, facing westward on its escarpment looking over the park. 'She knew what she wanted, and she got it: Hardwick remains today the supreme triumph of Elizabethan architecture.'[19] Here, again, the house expresses the personality of its creator: as Burghley and Theobalds bore witness to the weight and magnificence of the Lord Treasurer, Wollaton to the restless, fantastic personality of Sir Francis Willoughby, so Hardwick expresses the soaring ambition, but outward sobriety and restraint that clothed its owner's fabulous career. Girouard perceives that Hardwick 'in a wonderful way, gets the best of both worlds' – as Bess did: 'a house of great and romantic beauty, of a ruthless and uncompromising design . . . As one walks round and watches the masses group and regroup, contract and spread out, advance and fall away, shifting from the full weight and splendour of the elevations to the view from the side, when the house shuts up narrow and bears down with the race and speed of a ship in full sail.'

Hardwick is no less marvellous within, with the dramatic ascent to the grand rooms on the top floor, the Long Gallery going the whole length of the house, the Presence Chamber that Sacheverell Sitwell describes as 'the most beautiful room, not in England alone, but in the whole of Europe', with its romantic painted frieze of a stag-hunt, the Court of Diana and the story of Orpheus.[20] Hardwick, on the edge of those forests, had a cult of the stag which is taken up by the coat of arms, the three stags' heads with upreared stag-supporters in coloured plasterwork in the hall, and again in the marquetry of a beautiful Renaissance table in the Great Chamber:

> The redolent smelle of eglantine
> We stagges exalt to the Divine.

From the Building Accounts it appears that James Rowarth did the decorative painting, John Mercer was head of the *corps* of plasterers, Abraham Smith the designer of the plasterwork.[21] Some of the pedimented and obelisked doorcases, and the chimney-pieces with their sculpted figures, or alabaster bas-reliefs, carved apparently by Thomas Accres, come out of Serlio. The whole interior still speaks of Bess: the tapestries she acquired after Sir Christopher Hatton's death, 1200 ells in all, are still in the house. She was an accomplished needlewoman: there are the embroidered hoods of copes from Lilleshall worked into secular uses, coverlets or counterpanes. We know what her own rooms looked like: her bed of black velvet with gold fringe, curtains of black damask trimmed with gold lace, chairs of crimson velvet. When all was new, the marbles bright and coloured, black touch and white alabaster, the tapestries fresh and figured, the rooms in primitive colours, crimson and blue, green and gold, the effect must have been incomparably rich and splendid, with all the brilliance and vulgarity of the Renaissance. Now all has faded with the centuries into muted half-colour; just as the music of the age has gained the dimension of nostalgia in place of directness and brilliance, so this house that hummed with activity – for its creator was a capitalist on the grand scale – and a household a hundred strong is all the more affecting in its withdrawal from life, the memoried silences of gallery and corridor, the reflected lights of morning and evening, moonlight and shadow in the deserted chambers, the fires of sunset in that towering wall of glass.

There is no point in calling these palaces 'prodigy-houses', for they do not differ in essence from the houses of the gentry, except in size and splendour. Some hundreds of manor-houses were built all over the country, making a spectrum from quasi-palaces, like Drayton, Castle Ashby or Wimbledon (another Cecil creation, built for Burghley's elder son), down through every variety of size and aspect, to the small specimens hidden away on starveling Yorkshire moors or Lancashire fells, or Cornish upland, like the little hall-house of Methrose in Luxulyan, to which the family added parlour and great chamber, with carved chimney-piece (now lost somewhere in America) and plaster coats-of-arms. It is the immense variety that is so eloquent, speaks of the different kinds of materials according to the district, the local traditions and idioms of craftsmanship and design.

We learn that nine-tenths of our stone buildings are of sandstone or limestone, but within these fields there is room for every variation, and beyond them are such outliers as the granite of Cornwall, the millstone grit of Yorkshire.[22] To this the Elizabethans added an immense expansion of brick-building, particularly in the eastern counties, and of timber-building, notably in western counties from the Severn estuary northwards, and in all towns. The materials offered various combinations; for example, the chequer-patterning of flint and stone in beautiful Lake House, Wiltshire, begun in 1580, or in the house that was till recently part of Chard School, as elsewhere in Dorset and East Anglia. Actually oak is more durable than most English stone; so there are whole areas of timber-framed houses, those of the South-East being more sophisticated than North-West.

Not much space can be devoted to such symbolic architecture as Sir Thomas Tresham's curious buildings in Northamptonshire – they represent a too individual, an eccentric, fantasy. Tresham was an obstinate Recusant who, to raise money for his buildings and his fines, forced unpopular enclosures upon his unfortunate tenantry.[23] At Rothwell he built a small Renaissance *palazzo* for market-house, characteristically garnished with ninety coats-of-arms.[24] At Rushton there is his Triangular Lodge, in honour of the Trinity, plastered with Latin sayings and esoteric symbols. Away on its ridge is Lyveden New Building, designed by Stickells, but never completed: it was to have been the centre-piece of an elaborate scheme of gardens and walks. The building was to represent the Passion, with its seven emblems, the end of each wing presenting seven faces of five feet, five being the number of salvation, and so on. Fifteen years in prison and the involvement of his son in Gunpowder Plot rather hampered Tresham's operations, though they did not prevent the Jesuits from denouncing him as an 'atheist', for his loyalty. Very proud of his family, in a quarrel with the newly-created Lord Spencer, he wrote: 'I commend to your memory whether the Treshams or the family of your Spencers have been in this county of longest continuance, both in honourablest and worshipful calling.' The good sense of the Spencers kept them there, where the Treshams evaporated in fantasies.

More to the point, penetrating to the realities of society, was the inscription that John Talbot put up over the window of the great chamber of Grafton manor near Bromsgrove, which he began to build in 1567, with classical porch, pediment, Doric columns (built by Stephen Merryman, the mason):

> Plenty and grace
> Be in this place:
> While every man is placed in his degree
> There is both peace and unity.
> Solomon saith there's none accord
> When every man would be a lord.[25]

It is the message of Ulysses' speech in *Troilus and Cressida*; it has not lost its point today.

Urban building was dominantly of timber-framed houses, even of London, which could easily import stone and slate by sea.[26] But timber had considerable advantages: it was not only more durable – as we see from timber-framed houses that have lasted to today – but the beams of each storey could overhang the one beneath, gaining space, heading off rain, and giving some shelter below. Moreover, maximum window-space could be provided along the front, and surfaces carved or pargetted with decoration. The patterning varied locally; it was apt to be rather coarser and more ornate in Lancashire and Cheshire. The street-fronts of the richer streets were highly variegated with their gables and decoration, their glittering panes and shadowed recesses, their array of signboards – altogether a Gothic effect. The chief danger was fire – injunctions were laid down to roof with tile or slate; it must have been the thatched roofs that accounted for the fires that consumed so many country towns – Tiverton, Cullompton, Stratford, Nantwich. All the same, it was a wonder that London was not burned long before 1666.

Some more important town-houses had a different plan from the familiar sandwiching of tall fronts along the street. There were those built around a small court, like that by Sir Nicholas Bacon in Aldersgate.[27] It had a long gallery over a walk, alongside the garden – just like the little gallery built on to the Warden's Lodgings at All Souls, now vanished. Sir Nicholas shot up so far in the world after 1558 that he did not occupy this house long; it was subsequently occupied by Fleetwood, the City Recorder whose vivid letters make good reading, and after 1580 by Christopher Barker, the Queen's Printer.

Perhaps it is old inns that have most effectively conserved these types for us – and it was with the internal peace of the time that the historic inns entered on their great days.[28] 'The Feathers' at Ludlow preserves such a richly decorative front, along with panelling from the ruined Castle within. 'The Peacock' at Rowsley is a fine composition in stone, gables and porch, just after the turn of the century; 'The Dolphin' at Heigham in Norfolk another example of chequer-work. Numerous are, or till recently were, such half-timbered inns in the wooded regions westward, the 'Angel' at Ludlow, the 'King's Arms' at Ombersley, the 'Swan' at Bridgnorth, the 'Crown' at Nantwich, or the 'White Swan' at Stratford with its contemporary frescoes of Tobias and the angel.

II

Elizabethan church-building has hardly been studied at all,[29] but, when all has been said, it does not amount to much: it was largely a question of maintenance and repair. It is true that people did more in this direction than has been realised, but even after the havoc of the Reformation the country had more churches than it could fully utilise. Occasionally, when a church fell down or a part of it was in serious disrepair, rebuilding was undertaken. The most notable instance is that of Standish, in the suburbs of Wigan, which was completely rebuilt on medieval lines, though with Renaissance pepper-pot turrets at the junction of chancel and nave. Professor Simmons has shown that Lancashire provides more instances than any other county; coupled with the drive for founding grammar-schools there, it probably bears witness to the effort to reclaim this backward area from its Catholicism. At Ormskirk, however, a mortuary chapel was built on for the Earls of Derby, as at Kirtling in Cambridgeshire a chapel was added to the church to house the monuments of the Norths.

When one looks at the rebuilt nave of the church at Great Dalby in Leicestershire, one sees at once how secular it is: it is the hall of a manor-house with tall transomed windows, a square room divided by a couple of arches, outside the royal arms, shields with E.R. and gryphon. A few church-towers were built: Hartlebury in Worcestershire, East Lockinge in Berkshire, Brooke in Rutland and Hulcote in Bedfordshire, along with their churches, the upper part of Great St. Mary's at Cambridge. At Haseley in Warwickshire, the Protestant Clement Throckmorton, succeeding his Catholic uncle Michael in the manor, modernised his church with plain Elizabethan windows in the little nave, and building out a small bay for his tomb, on which he lies in full armour.

One may legitimately conclude that church-architecture as such went by the board, and that, when it was necessary to effect repairs or make a small addition, the builders knew only now the idiom of secular building – evidences of secular expansion were rising in hundreds and thousands all over the country. By far the chief activity in masonry in the churches was the putting up of monuments, mainly to the gentry, and to a smaller extent to prosperous, if less armigerous, merchants and yeomen. Few were the monuments to clerics, except for bishops in their puffed sleeves and black chimeres in their cathedrals. In these facts the character of the society is laid bare before our eyes.

The interiors of the churches revealed that there had been a religious revolution: they had been stripped of altars, shrines, roods and roodlofts, images and much else. Though painted glass and carved benches remained, the frescoes and wall paintings were whitewashed over, stencilled patterns and scriptural texts took their place, the Ten Commandments where had been reredos and retable. The ugly marks of idiotic iconoclasm were left visible; when the Queen visited Worcester cathedral and saw the open gashes round the tomb of King John she ordered them to be plastered over. But whatever was done to maintain or repair, church interiors were on the whole at a standstill, until the Jacobean and Laudian revival. There are not really very many Elizabethan pulpits – two or three in a county; they were mostly put up in the early seventeenth century, the golden age (if that is the word for it) of preaching.[30] Preaching was not a frequent activity in churches – that was one of the complaints of the Puritans – nor did the Queen wish to encourage it. When a pulpit was put up, it was of decent workmanship, usually with simple rectangular panelling. They became more elaborate, like the sermons, under James, achieving the splendid late Renaissance woodwork of Croscombe in Somerset, Littleham in Devon, or St. John's Briggate at Leeds.

New fittings are few and far between: they reflect the needs of the parish community, of the new religious rite, or the private whim of a benefactor. Christopher Barker the printer was a Yorkshireman; at Marr near Doncaster, where he was born, he 'made the best pews in the church, paved the alleys, and builded the pulpit.'[31] Pews are thus the more frequent addition to comfort in church – as at St. James, Garlickhythe, where Edmund Chapman, Joiner to the Queen, appropriately

> Fine pews within this church he made and with
> his arms support,
> The table and the seats in choir he set
> in comely sort.[32]

Elizabethan communion tables are rare; there is a fine one at Blyford, Suffolk, with bulbous legs – just like a refectory table for secular use.[33] A number of alms-boxes indicate the concern for the poor, the subject of so much legislation. At Rycote near Oxford there is a splendid canopied pew, occupied by the Queen on her visits to the Norrises, and opposite it a later one for the family. This leads to a general consideration of some significance: the medieval chantry chapel of the squire's family, to pray for the souls of his ancestors, often became the manor-pew.

The arts of incised slabs and brasses reflect the rhythms of the time. Brasses were artistically at their height in the fourteenth and early fifteenth century – one thinks of the splendour of Sir Simon Felbrigg and his wife, lady-in-waiting to Richard II's Bohemian Queen, at Felbrigg in Norfolk. During the black decade, 1547 to 1558, they fall off markedly in number.[34] After 1558 they increase again, but with a lowering of quality, and with new patterns and designs. Their historical and social interest is considerable; even artistically they have a certain attraction as portraiture. Sometimes a traditional brass, like that of Avice Tyndall, 1571, at Thornbury, Gloucestershire, has elegance and charm. There is a group of emblematic brasses with figures and symbols by the connoisseur, Richard Haydock, Fellow of New College: one in the ante-chapel there (another was destroyed in the Civil War); that in Wells Cathedral shows Humphrey Willis equipped with hat, sword and violin, looking up with 'Da me Domine' issuing from his mouth, cherubs answering equally in Latin.[35] Two more are in Queen's College Chapel, and two at Tingewick and Bletchley. Or there is the unique design at All Saints, Maidstone of Thomas Neale and his ancestors, six tiers all told. Everything speaks of family pride, become an end in itself, with the removal of purgatory and praying for the dead. Another development is the memorial to women who died in childbirth being portrayed in bed with their baby, Elizabethan four-poster, curtains, valences and all, as with Anne Savage at Wormington, Gloucestershire, or Joan Mellow at Talland, in Cornwall. Haydock has left one of these, to the wife of the innkeeper of the 'King's Arms' in Holywell, in St. Cross church at Oxford. Merchants appear with the tools of their trade, scissors, shears or compasses. Sometimes the effect is comic, as with Thomas Inwood with three wives, 1586, at Weybridge, Surrey, or parents encumbered with an appalling number of children. Small heraldic brasses, often with crests and plumes, touched with traces of colouring, are often beautiful.

Brasses developed out of incised slabs, but the latter have survived in far fewer number.[36] In the late medieval period the best monumental work of this kind centred upon Burton-on-Trent. After 1550 the firm of Royley gained ascendancy there, and for two or three decades turned out good work. Their fine slab at Aston Flamville, Leicestershire, to Sir William Turville and his wife, shows admirably firm linear pattern in the figures and the folds of their dress. A slab at Peatling Magna, also by the Royleys, but half a century later, 1597, shows the deterioration that has taken place. There were other local centres: a good tradition in Cornwall continued up to 1640, though the best monuments were those in slate, of figures sculpted in relief, coloured and ornamental – a provincial art of which the most notable exponent was Peter Crocker of Plymouth.[37]

III

The first and most important book on the aesthetics of architecture was Sir Henry Wotton's, *The Elements of Architecture*, published in 1624, after his return from his Venetian embassy.[38] He had been long in Italy, and so his book represents years of observation and reflection. Yet it was as much in advance of English thought as Inigo Jones was, whose late-Renaissance outlook it entirely shared. Wotton was a distinguished connoisseur, one of the virtuosi who shaped the taste of the Caroline age. He had no sympathy whatever for the Gothic past: pointed arches 'ought to be exiled from judicious eyes and left to their first inventors, the Goths or Lombards amongst other relics of that barbarous age.'[39] He considered the colouring of statues, even of regal statues, 'an English barbarism'. It is revealing that the Gothic spirit of John Aubrey, though a generation younger than Wotton, preferred Elizabethan architecture to Caroline. Not so Wotton, the Elizabethan – born only four years after Shakespeare; but his taste, his standards and aesthetic principles were based on Italy.

He shows himself very well-read and well-founded in his book; better still, he had used his eyes, his experience and his acquaintance in Italy to good purpose. The authority to him was Palladio, whose writings and buildings he had admired. Behind him was Vitruvius, of whom Wotton is discerningly critical, Alberti whose penetrating observations are cited, Dürer from whose geometry the Italians had learned, and the practical genius of de l'Orme, always quoted with respect. Wotton's is the first English aesthetic treatise on architecture; in spite of the generalised approach he hopes to do justice to 'divers modern men that have written out of mere practice', for one, de l'Orme.[40] The foundation principles of architecture are 'commodity, firmness, and delight.' Nevertheless we recognise an English strain of practicality in the importance he gives to siting – 'builders should be as circumspect as wooers' – and the old client of Dr. Forman in his allowance of astrological influences in regard to the site: 'the consideration is peradventure not altogether vain.'

We have an example of the way people of taste discussed the siting of houses in a letter Bess of Hardwick's son, Sir Charles Cavendish, wrote to her in 1606: 'I think a house whose square stands upon the eight-division is better than upon the four points of the compass, as your coming in to be south-west and not full south or west. So shall all sides of your house have the sun, and yet not in a direct line and therefore not so violent, partaking of two points.'[41] He goes on to say that high windows send away noise and smell, and that the kitchen should be out of the house. A few years later Sir Charles began the building of romantic and beautiful Bolsover, on its high ridge looking across to Hardwick – Robert Smythson's son, John, was his architect.[42]

For all Wotton's being an *inglese italianato* we recognise English characteristics in his moderation, empiricism and the overriding importance he gives to the natural principle in art. 'Art is in truest perfection when it might be reduced to some natural principle.'[43] He disapproved of classical columns being given a fashionable bulge in the middle, as clean contrary to the growth of trees from which their model came. He did not care for designs that aimed at rarity rather than commodity, pentagons, triangles, and what not – thus excluding Tresham's fantasies from the ground of art. On the other hand, it was possible to be too natural: he agreed with those Italians who thought that Dürer came too close to the real, and Michelangelo for being too extreme in his adherence to an ideal. This is very far-sighted of Wotton and shows him much ahead of his time: he is here on the same ground as Reynolds in his *Discourses on Art*, the generalised classicism of the eighteenth century, avoiding the extremes of realism and Mannerism. Wotton was a precursor of English Palladianism.

Practicality prevails in his view that every part of a building should be determined by use. But the superior spirit of the aesthete comes out in his realisation that the inner tension that makes architecture an art comes from the conflict between uniformity and variety, and their reconciliation in form. The effect aimed at is to 'ravish the beholder – and he knows not how – by a secret harmony in the proportions.'[44] There is the mystery that makes an art of it, hardly explicable, though Wotton gives the classical rules for just proportion. He comes back to this again and again, though we may observe that he is too exclusively classical; when he specifies 'that agreable harmony between the breadth, length, and height of all the rooms of the fabric, which suddenly, where it is, taketh every beholder by the secret power of proportion', does this not apply equally to Hardwick, which he never saw?

He much approved of the Italian hipping up of buildings on a basement, raising the ascent – as we see in Palladian villas; he regarded windows, particularly approaching the angles of a building, as 'weakenings' – which excluded the Elizabethan passion for light. He thought that building should proceed from a model of the whole – surely a correct principle, as against the haphazard joining up of parts. Ornament should be used with moderation, made subject to the overall design; there should be decorum in everything, in the placing of pictures within, and the design of fountains without. In this we see how much before his time he was. Even in his principles of criticism he is much more intelligent than many critics today: he tells us that to condemn the good for not being the best is too sour an attitude – we might add that it is usually a sign of the inferior.

He is unexpected on the subject of garden-design: 'I must note a certain contrariety between building and gardening; for, as fabrics should be regular, so gardens should be irregular, or at least cast into a very wild regularity.'[45] This again looks forward to the eighteenth century, for Elizabethans regarded gardens as an extension of the house, with their green rooms, their alleys and straight walks like corridors, all making with the house one unified design – as we can see in the 'plats' of Smythson or Thorpe.[46] We are apt to overlook the subtlety of Elizabethan garden-design; Wotton commends Sir Henry Fanshawe's at Ware: 'he did so precisely examine the tinctures and seasons of his flowers that in their settings, the inwardest of which that were to come up at the same time should be always a little darker than the outermost, and so serve them for a kind of gentle shadow – like a piece not of nature but of art.'

He treats the arts briefly, in so far as they are accessory to architecture: sculpture, 'as being indeed of nearer affinity to architecture itself, and consequently the more natural and suitable ornament'; painting, about which he is more enthusiastic, regarding it as an 'artificial [i.e. artistic] miracle' – and perhaps this is an English preference.[47] The miracle to him consisted in the painter giving the illusion of three dimensions to the two-dimensional. He proceeds to give us the principles by which to judge of these arts and their dependents: plaster-work being the subordinate of sculpture, mosaic considered as that of painting. We ask of painting whether it is well designed – if so it must exhibit truth and grace; if well coloured, then it should display force and affection. Affection is defined as 'the lively represent-ment of any passion whatsoever, as if the figures stood not upon a cloth or board, but as if they were acting upon a stage.' All other values were consequent upon these.

In the end Wotton discloses a proper modesty on the part of critic towards artist. 'Let no man hope by such a speculative erudition to discern the masterly and mysterious touches of art, but an artisan [artist] himself. To whom therefore we must leave the prerogative to censure the manner and handling, as he him-self must likewise leave some points, perchance of no less value, to others; as, for example, whether the story be rightly repre-sented, the figures in true action, the persons suited to their several qualities, the affections proper and strong, and suchlike observations.'[48]

It is a discriminating distinction between the rôles of artist and critic, leaving plenty of scope to the latter without trenching on the proper sphere of the artist; and it gives us a revealing in-sight into the contemporary principles of aesthetic judgment.

IV

Of all the arts, that most deleteriously affected by the Reforma-tion was sculpture. In the first place there was the immense destruction of statues, images, shrines, sculpture of every kind with the monasteries, and subsequently in the churches.[49] This brought to an end the workshops in cathedral yards – no wonder that, by the 1570's, English sculptors were dying out.[50] Then there was the direct prohibition upon religious sculpture in Protestant churches – which had been the chief source of inspiration through-out the Middle Ages. All this meant cutting off contacts with the Continent, particularly Italy and France, where sculpture was best, but whose religious themes were prohibited in England. When contacts were effectively resumed, English sculpture came to be dominated by Dutch craftsmen who were prepared to work on English assumptions and, being Protestants, raised no problems. Thus an Anglo-Netherlandish school of monumental sculpture came to the fore.

For, overwhelmingly, this took the form of monuments, with effigies, busts, decoration, in the churches. Thousands of monu-ments filled the place of the thousands of altars and shrines destroyed. The amount of work executed was enormous: a mass-output came about to meet the massive demand. In these circumstances most of the work cannot rate highly as art – though there are exceptions. On the other hand, it may be mistaken to subscribe to too derogatory a view[51] – such work was certainly better than anything of the sort to be seen today or, with some exceptions, in the Victorian age. If we study it for what it is, on its own assumptions, we shall find that it is at least authentically revealing of the society; that, artistically, it has a good deal to offer, in design, proportion, decoration and, not infrequently, impressiveness or charm as portraiture. One must discriminate: a great deal, as with any mass-production, is dull and monotonous in design, coarse in detail. On the other hand, there is much of decent, good craftsmanship, some that is masterly, and an individual artist, such as Epiphanius Evesham, who stands out at the end of the period. The art is recovering.

First, for what it reveals as to society. The progressive secularisation is evident. Increasingly the figures on the tombs are represented not as in death, to be prayed for, but to be remembered as they were in life. Earlier, the portraiture is representative. At Somerton in Oxfordshire, Thomas Fermor was to have 'a very fair, decent and well proportioned picture or portraiture of a gentleman, representing the said Thomas Fermor with furniture and ornaments in armour', his wife to appear 'a fair gentlewoman with a French hood, edge and habiliment, with all other apparel, furniture, jewels, ornaments, and things in all respects usual, decent, and seemly for a gentlewoman.'[52] As time went on these representations became individual portraits, parallel with the vast increase in painted portraits contemporaneously. For all that has been said against the bust of Shakespeare in Stratford church, there is no doubt that it is a portrait, and agrees with the Droeshout engraving of him.

We notice that the main point of the Fermor stipulations is to render accurately their social rank. There is nothing new in this,[53] it is quite traditional; increased prosperity enabled more variety in class and calling to be represented. Social rank is registered as in life: a noble, if his heirs did their duty and could afford it, received a monument on the grand scale. Sir Christopher Hatton, who died Lord Chancellor, got a colossal monument in Old St. Paul's, which elbowed others out of the way; at the end of the south aisle of Salisbury cathedral we can still see the megalomaniac structure built right up to the roof, which the insufferable family-pride of the Seymours thought due to a Protectoral line. Few went to quite such lengths, or heights, but there are many instances where a chapel is practically occupied by an outsize monument: the Tanfield monument at Burford, the Southampton at Titchfield, by the same hand as the Montagu monument at Easebourne in Sussex which was largely dismantled by the Victorians for taking up so much room. (The obelisks at Titchfield were derived from du Cerceau.) In several places there are whole chapels given up to a succession of family monuments, from which we can observe the development of tomb design and sculpture: the Spencers at Brington, Russells at Chenies, Rutlands at Bottesford, as with the tombs at Framlingham or Wing.

The family comes into its own – though that also is not new merely accentuated and made obvious. In place of medieval, weepers, the children are portrayed. The ancestry is brought into the foreground; again that is now new, merely emphasised. What is new is the increasing variety of the postures: in place of recumbent effigies, lifeless and timeless, man and wife are kneeling at a prayer-desk, children lined up behind them; or they are reclining, as Webster expressed it,

> with their hands under their cheeks
> As if they died of the toothache; they are not carved
> With their eyes fixed upon the stars, but as
> Their minds were wholly bent upon the world.

Often the children are portrayed with a sober, affecting charm, like Southampton as a boy on his father and grandfather's pyramid of a monument; or there are the busted academics, one hand on book, the other pointing to themselves, like Sir Henry Savile in Merton College chapel. The sculpted figures at the top, Chrysostom, turbaned Ptolemy, Euclid with compasses, Tacitus, are expressively and elegantly carved.[54] (They are by Nicholas Stone.) This reminds us that such figures may well be by a more sophisticated hand than the rest of the monument. Dr. John Caius' classical sarcophagus, panelled and pedimented, is known to have been carved by Theodore Haveus of Cleves 'and others'.[55] Or the departed may be rendered as having fallen asleep in his chair, like Francis Bacon in his Renaissance niche at Gorhambury. With a really expressive sculptor possessing a touch of genius, like Epiphanius Evesham, the children are grouped more naturally, in attitudes of grief as on the Teynham and Hawkins monuments, both in Kent. The daughters on the latter, at

Boughton-under-Blean, almost persuade one to think of him as a precursor of Flaxman. The art is on the way, after 1600, to realistic portraiture.

The revolution, when it came, had been prepared by a long evolution at home.[56] As with architecture, we notice that the dominant type of Elizabethan altar-tomb is an adaptation from the medieval, and that it was ultimately the native types, or compromises based on them, not the purely classical, that prevailed. Large sums were spent on painting and gilding and to make the figures life-like – of which we have seen Wotton disapprove, for aesthetic reasons: he wanted the full impact to be made by the sculpture in itself, as in Italy. We learn that by 1580 the formulas that were to gain acceptance had been worked out, the experimentation over. There is no doubt that it appealed to the taste of the time; orders poured in to the Southwark workshops by the hundred, and the demands were met by a close-knit group of Dutch or Flemish immigrants, who were specialists in meeting the expanded demand. They provided tombs and tomb-sculpture from one end of the country to the other, from their recognisable Robartes monument at Truro to the painted Maddison monument at Newcastle. Their standards and forms were widely imitated.

The English were elbowed out, at any rate of the foreground, by the newcomers. They were not so specialised. Walter Hancock, who built beautiful Condover Hall in Shropshire, was described as 'a very skiful man in the art of masonry, in setting of plots [plans] for building and performing the same, ingraining in alabaster in other stone or plaster', who had made 'most sumptuous buildings, most stately tombs, most curious pictures.'[57] Evidently a perfect Johannes Factotum. But Robert Smythson, who designed Hardwick for Bess, also designed her tomb, with the life-like figure, in Derby cathedral. With the Rutland tombs at Bottesford, Leicestershire, we can see the foreigners taking over. Richard Parker, of the Burton school, made that of the first Earl in 1543–4 for £20 – and a very good piece of work it is: grave and noble traditional effigies on top, lively little up-to-date figures for weepers around the chest below. Garret Johnson (Gherardt Jannsen) received a final instalment of no less than £200 in 1591 for the tombs of the third and fourth Earls: massive affairs with Corinthian columns, entablature, coats-of-arms, arcading kneeling children. Even more to the point, the foreigner Hollemans settled at Burton-on-Trent itself, headquarters of the old English school, and executed the work for the Spencers at Brington and other families in the neighbourhood.

'By the end of the century the Southwark men had completely taken over the native form of the tomb. They then proceeded to use their superior technical skill and greater acquaintance with Continental motifs to exploit the market they had moved into in a number of ways . . . They were able to carve, in a manner that outclasses the native craftsmen, the figures of parents, children, and "virtues" that the social and intellectual ideas of the time demanded.'[58] Nor was there much difference between turning out these rather secular works, with their standard designs and columns, motifs and tricks, and the domestic work in demand, hall-screens, chimney-pieces, roundels with their busts. When Sir Arthur Throckmorton built his fine new house at Paulerspury, now under the grass, 'I must pay Garret [Johnson], the marble-carver of Southwark, £60 for making me a chimney-piece of Sussex marble, alabaster, touch and rance [black and reddish marbles], according to a pattern left with him . . . He to be at all the charges and gilding whatsoever, but only the carriage.'[59]

The Cure workshop was older and lasted longer than the Johnsons, three generations as against their two – but Garret Johnson had two sons and they turned out more work. William Cure was 'sent for hither when the King did build Nonsuch.'[60] He maintained his contact with the Court, and must have been responsible for a number of things not identifiable now, for he did not die until 1579, when he left all his books, patterns and tools to his son.[61] Cornelius Cure made the enormous monument to Mary Queen of Scots in Westminster Abbey, for which he received immense sums. The Cures and Johnsons were Dutch. Maximilian Colt, a more imaginative sculptor, was a Huguenot from Arras. He was the choice of connoisseur Salisbury for Queen Elizabeth's tomb and for his own, a very different affair. Salisbury's at Hatfield and Sir Francis Vere's in Westminster Abbey derive from the famous tomb of Engelbert of Nassau at Breda, by a Bolognese sculptor. Entirely Italianate, the effigy recumbent upon a table supported by four half-kneeling figures, the model was too foreign for English taste and was not followed. Salisbury, like Bess of Hardwick, had himself selected the design for his tomb, as did others, too, before their demise. Richard Stevens, who made Hatton's vast tomb, was a Brabanter; he had for pupils Isaac James, another foreigner, and Evesham. But James' pupil was Nicholas Stone, and with Evesham and Stone English sculpture returns to the fold of art, for these two were artists.

Epiphanius Evesham is a rediscovery of our time, though the eighteenth century knew him as an 'exquisite artist'. This is true, and it particularises his difference from other sculptors: there is a refinement about his work, a released naturalness that sharply expresses the sentiment behind it. There is grief and weeping portrayed in the daughters of Lord Teynham; a grave masculine awareness in the two sons, with the affecting touch of hound and hawk on perch behind them; there is the soldierly bearing of the soldier-sons of Lord Norris in Westminster Abbey. Evesham was born in Hereford, where there was a distinct school of local men who did good work in that area.[62] Of these the oddest is John Gildon, the rustic Italianate character of whose tombs at Bosbury gives one a thrill of surprise when one comes upon them in that remote country church. He must have got it from some Continental pattern-book, as Evesham derived inspiration from the emblem-books that were so much to the taste of that leisured age – not to ours – when people had time on their hands, time to play with. Evesham is a singular apparition, with his touch of genius: he is not really like anybody else. His work comes very late: from 1600 to 1614 he was in France, where he executed a tomb for the Archbishop of Sens in Notre-Dame.[63] It is probable therefore that he was a Catholic, and there was more complicity with Catholicism at James I's Court than Elizabeth's.

It is difficult to appreciate the emblem-cult that swept Europe in the later sixteenth century and became a perfect mania in Italy. Fortunately for us, though it began in the 1580's with Geoffrey Whitney's *Choice of Emblems* – straight from abroad – it did not reach its height in England till beyond our period, with the later, rather than the earlier, Donne. The craze left its marks in the arts, in *imprese* and tapestry, even in literature and painting; sometimes the figures it left upon monuments are not without charm, particularly when indicating the occupation of the deceased – the beautifully sculpted anchor upon John Gildon's tomb of Dr. Lewis at Abergavenny, to show he was Judge of the Court of Admiralty – but more often they have the tedious appeal of a crossword puzzle. Even the authority on the subject admits that the English made no new contributions to the cult.[64] One finds more entrancing the sculpted crests, the heraldic beasts or simply animals – a porcupine beneath a knight's feet, an angry coroneted hawk above a countess, a rhinoceros or a mermaid or a faithful hound. These are more in keeping with the English nature and are continuous with their medieval fancy for beasts, wild men and gargoyles.

Mrs. Esdaile, a pioneer in these studies, considers that eclecticism succeeded in welding the various elements into an artistic whole and that in the end English sculpture worked out forms more 'coherent than its Low Country originals.'[65] Certainly the Elizabethans were proud of their monuments. Those in the Abbey were already part of the regular tour of London, shown by a guide:

> the man that keeps the Abbey tombs
> And, for his price, doth with whoever comes
> Of all our Harrys and our Edwards talk.

Shakespeare shows himself very conscious of monuments, not only in the Sonnets:

> Not marble, nor the gilded monuments
> Of princes . . . ;

of 'unswept stone, besmeared with sluttish time'; of overturned statues and ripped-up brasses. When the Duc de Biron came over in 1601, Ralegh, to whom it fell to entertain the party, took them 'to Westminster to see the monuments': they seem to have enjoyed the Bear Garden more – but then Saint-Denis could show finer Renaissance monuments.[66]

There was much more garden sculpture than we realise – so much has disappeared since. 'At Whitehall the Queen's garden had thirty-four columns with heraldic beasts upon them; at Hampton Court, apart from innumerable heraldic figures, there were thirty-eight stone statues of kings and queens . . . At Nonsuch in the Grove of Diana was a fountain with Actaeon turned into a stag.'[67] Greenwich was embellished with a fountain, another was put up at Hampton Court in 1591–2. What these Renaissance pieces were like we can see from that which was removed from Cowdray, after the fire, to Woolbeding. In mortuary chapels in churches where the patrons were connoisseurs, as at Bisham in Surrey and Chilham in Kent, there are Renaissance funerary monuments clearly based on Roman imperial garden sculpture. Roman emperors decorated the vanished summer-house at Theobalds – what reason we have to deplore the destruction of that monument raised by the master-mind of the reign, architect of its triumph!

Of secular sculpture as such there is little to detain us: the four portrait busts of Tudor sovereigns at Lumley Castle, those of Sir Nicholas Bacon, wife, and son Francis as an engaging little boy at Gorhambury. These are 'not at all typical; on the contrary, they probably represent the very highest achievement of the period.'[68] Since Bacon, and still more Lumley, were connoisseurs it is possible that they were commissioned from foreign artists. We are back in a field that appealed strongly to the English, that of individual portraiture.

V

There is no decorative ironwork to equal the incomparable masterpiece of the late fifteenth century, Master John Tresillian's screen and gates in St. George's Chapel at Windsor.[69] Only in this late Gothic *chef-d'œuvre* does English ironwork reach the highest standard; the new impulses of the sixteenth century produced confusion, as in other arts and crafts: work sank to a low ebb, to pick up again later.[70] The domestic range was far more limited than on the Continent. Keys remained simple up to 1600 – though the subject of an extraordinary proliferation of folklore, as amulets, preventatives of impotence, kidnapping by fairies, what not. Hinges developed elaborate outline, like butterflies or dolphins, lighter and perforated. Wrought-iron font-cranes were introduced from the Netherlands. The Elizabethans were to the fore in developing cast-iron, and this enabled them to nourish the export of cannon. Pevensey possesses a beautiful Elizabethan gun, like a Venetian mooring-post, shapely and ringed, with ER and a Tudor rose.[71] With the development of wall-fireplaces there was a large demand for decorative firebacks, of which many remain, like the fine specimen decorated with Tudor rose and fleur-de-lis (made for J. and M. F. in 1588) that happily ornaments Mr. John Diebold's apartment in Park Avenue, New York.

Even so humble a subject as leadwork for rain-water pipes bears out the themes of this book. They are an English speciality, they do not floriate until the 1580's and, when they do, they exemplify the fusion of Gothic design with Renaissance decoration. Haddon Hall, where the lucky Mannerses added a fine Elizabethan gallery with a frieze of peacocks in pride, has a grand series of pipe-heads dating from about 1580.[72] They exhibit a wealth of design over a long space of time, while Knole Park 'certainly gives us the finest series of heads of one period. Dating from 1604 to 1607 there are forty-seven in all, including some thirty different types. These heads not only touch the highest point of decorative charm, but from their wealth of treatment reach the limit of dexterous craftsmanship.' These works of long-dead craftsmen, made to last, are with us still, unlike the works of yesterday. At Gothic Haddon one can see their descent from medieval gargoyles; at Hardwick they are puffed out and slit, like an Elizabethan lady's sleeve. How appropriate!

A rich quantity of admirable plasterwork remains in spite of constant, and continued, destruction. It was very much a thing of the time, at its height artistically in the decoration of ceilings and friezes. Wotton regards the chief of the plastic art as 'the graceful fretting of roofs'. With the immense architectural expansion at various levels craftsmen developed a comparable variety of design: geometrical, ranging from the simplest to the most elaborate shapes, or freer, with interlacing strapwork or floral patterns from the books.[73] At the intersections pendants were developed with ever more elaboration – at once we recognise them as characteristically Elizabethan. Friezes offered freer scope for figures and scenes. Abraham Smith executed the rather clumsy work in the Forest Great Chamber (now exposed to the elements) in Old Hardwick. For the New Hall Bess begged the use of the 'cunning plasterer', Charles Williams, who had made 'divers pendants and other pretty things and had flowered the hall at Longleat.'[74] King James's plasterer, Richard Dungan, did the work at Knole; in 1601 John Cobbe was employed in 'frettishing' the fine long gallery at St. John's college, Cambridge.

Many figure-subjects and panel-scenes came from the Low Countries pattern-books: their ornate richness appealed to the *art-nouveau* taste of the Elizabethans. Overpieces to fireplaces at Hardwick Old Hall came from Martin de Vos, a favourite source: the four elements, Fire, Air, Earth, Water.[75] The Nine Worthies came from Nicholas de Brouyn, from whom came prefabricated medallion heads for roundels in several places. Other Elements were derived from Marcus Gheeraerts, through engravings, as they mostly did. At Little Moreton Hall in Cheshire, the half-timbered house that looks like a top-heavy galleon moored in the meadows, the gallery has the Wheel of Fortune from the title-page of Robert Recorde's *The Castle of Knowledge*, with the sententiousness that raged all over Europe: 'The Wheel of Fortune whose Rule is Ignorance', 'The Spear of Destiny whose Ruler is Knowledge.'[76] By the end of the age the English were providing their own designs.

Henry Peacham's *Minerva Britanna* (1612) suggested the symbols of the senses in the splendid gallery at Blickling, with side-rows of emblems and virtues.

As for the craftsmen, 'contrary to the usual opinion, plaster in England was, with the exception of a certain number of Italian artists in the rococo style, the work of Englishmen; and both in the early and late Renaissance a distinctively national style was evolved, though naturally influenced by Continental sources.'[77] We must add that it varied very much in quality, and also locally. English plasterwork did not come up to Italian in refinement, though it has its own masculine vigour. Peacham describes the liking for 'the Antique: an unnatural or disorderly composition for delight sake, of men, birds, fishes, flowers, without rhyme or reason, for the greater vanity you show in your invention the more you please'.[78] The Italian influence of Henry's reign disappeared by Elizabeth's, and its place was taken by Netherlandish taste, of a lower aesthetic level, but more congenial to Elizabethans. Particularly, of course, for mass-consumption, and this is what it came to, with work on such a scale all over the country. Often local craftsmen imperfectly grasped the new style with its allegorical figures, and made them too big or out of proportion – as on the extraordinary plaster-relief in remote Bacton in Herefordshire, of Blanche Parry on her knees before her royal mistress, crowned, orbed and sceptred. Nevertheless, there were good local schools of craftsmen: notably in Devon, where there still remains a large amount of work in town houses at Barnstaple, Exeter, Newton Abbot, Dartmouth, as well as in country houses. For the prosperity of the age meant the extension of plasterwork to middle-class houses. The merchants of Bideford and Barnstaple, like those of London, hang up their coats-of-arms as well, if not so high, as the gentry.

CHAPTER V

PAINTING

DECORATIVE painting has been described as the 'complement to architecture in the adornment of ceilings, walls and woodwork.'[1] We now know that there was a much larger number of foreign artists working in this country than was previously realised. So the Renaissance influence, radiating from the Court, and evident first in details – classic arches, pilasters, medallions, roundels – was direct from Henry's time onward. With native craftsmen this led to an awkward hybrid with the Gothic vernacular, which one sees in numerous examples, and later to indirect imitation from foreign patternbooks for their decorative schemes. One cannot say that the English reached any high accomplishment in this field,[2] though there was an enormous amount of it, for the Elizabethans disliked blank spaces. In this they were medieval: they liked surfaces covered with colour, with paint and gilding (if they could afford it), with imitation draperies and *trompe-l'œil* work, brilliant, coruscating and rich. In spite of widespread erosion, from climate, iconoclasm, ignorance and fashion, it is surprising what remains. The pity of it is that, owing to the destruction or refurbishing of royal palaces, little of the best work remains; but in our time over three hundred examples have come to light, in country or, still more, town houses.[3] Of these some eighty are from Essex, an area much resided in by Court officials and important Londoners, and therefore particularly open to sophisticated metropolitan influences.

Let us consider the Court first. The Queen's first Serjeant Painter was Nicholas Lizard, a Frenchman, who had four little Lizards, of whom Lewis also did a good deal of work on the royal palaces.[4] We appreciate now that Renaissance painters were called on to paint not only portraits – that was a comparatively small portion of their work – but to do decorative work for festivities and revels, paint the interiors of palaces, banqueting houses, tents, cloths, barges, ships. They too were factotums, jacks-of-all-trades: specialisation was rather alien to the Renaissance mind. Holbein was used for all kinds of artistic activities, designing jewels, cups, besides decoration as above: less portrait-painting than is popularly supposed. Artistic activities all worked in together, neither so specialised nor so divided as today.

So we find all the Lizards engaged in painting for the Revels, and one for the Navy; Lewis Lizard painting the heraldic borders in the new (wooden) banqueting house at Whitehall, and the embrasures and shutters in the Long Gallery at Richmond, in imitation of cloth-of-gold draperies.[5] We can imagine the richness of the effect from the comparable gilding on the leaves of the books, all turned outward, in the Library at the Escorial. The canvas ceiling of the banqueting-house was rendered in water-colours. Leonard Fryer, Serjeant Painter, painted a gallery at Oatlands, the wainscot grained, with arabesques in gold and silver, the frieze with texts. Serjeant Painter George Gower executed the first architectural deception in England, a columned order in the hall with perspectives and a fountain; at Eltham, *trompe-l'œil* windows. Exteriors were painted as well as interiors. Serjeant Painter Herne painted the whole outside of the gallery at Whitehall with black and white antique-work, i.e. Renaissance grotesque. As Peacham wrote, 'you may, if you list, draw naked boys riding and playing with their paper-mills or bubble-shells upon goats, eagles, dolphins, etc.' All part of the fantasy of the age expressed no less in Marlowe's *Dido*.

We have some idea of the better work of this kind, from the Court circle, in what survives from Sir Thomas Smith's Hill Hall: almost life-size figures from engravings in a book of Agostino Veneziano, treated as counterfeit hangings of Brussels tapestry, rich with fruit and foliage. At ruined Cowdray there existed in the dining parlour a series of five episodes in the life of Sir Anthony Browne, creator of that fine house based on monastic spoil (the family continued devoutly Catholic). A good deal of antique-work in monochrome exists still, as in the earliest grand staircase at Knole. Allegorical subjects from the prints of Martin de Vos were popular and exerted a diffused influence, not only in great houses. This was a form of decoration that appealed widely to the middle-class, and many quite modest dwellings were richly, if often crudely, decorated with painting, 'carrying the ornament not only over the walls, but also over the timbers and ceilings', as one sees still in one or two houses in Cornmarket Street at Oxford.[6] Examples are constantly coming to light, beneath later decoration in farm-houses: attractive painted figures of contemporary gentle-men in ruffs from Huckster's End are now in the museum at St. Albans. At Amersham at least eight houses were revealed between the wars to possess Tudor wall-paintings: 'a distinct craft of the people of the middle and trading classes – the farmer, the artisan, and all those who shared the growth of prosperity of the period.'[7] For those who could not afford expensive painting there was the extensive use of stencil – much disapproved of by the Painter-Stainers' Company: 'a false and deceitful work and destructive of the art of painting, being a great hinderer of ingenuity and a cherisher of idleness and laziness in all beginners in the said art.'[8] With the decline of mural and cloth-painting at the end of the century the Painter-Stainers Company fell on evil days.

Medieval painting had the closest association with religion, and so it was to be expected that the breach with medieval religion would have as profound an effect as on sculpture. If England could – *per impossibile* – have remained a part of Catholic Europe its art would have been very different. But it became a Protestant country, and that inhibited most religious painting, or reduced it to insignificance. However, it remained open to Renaissance influence, and the Renaissance itself was virtually the creator of the art of portraiture. 'Portraiture is the depiction of the individual in his own character.'[9] The Humanist aim was the study of man in and for himself, abjuring the metaphysical and the mystical for whatever concerned man as man. Humanism did not lose influence in England by the Reformation: it took a Protestant form, extend-ing its sway and increasing its ethical concern and moral fervour.

So it is hardly surprising that here the cult of portraiture was redoubled in force: it came to include almost the whole of the significant painting of the time. To it was added the characteristic, the inquisitive and searching, English interest in personality and character, which has made their portrait-painting, on the whole, their richest contribution to painting. We hardly realise how new a thing it was. Before the sixteenth century there were hardly any portraits of persons other than the kings: and 'it was not until Elizabeth came to the throne that it became fashionable for the heads of any but the noblest families to have their portraits painted.'[10] In her reign the fashion gathered extraordinary im-petus: hundreds of people, not only of the nobility and gentry but middle-class folk – merchants, lawyers, doctors, academics, clerics, writers, musicians, even actors and dramatists – thought it proper to leave a record of what they looked like to their families and friends, and to posterity. It is in itself astonishing evidence of the spreading self-consciousness of the age. Since there was an enormous demand for portraits the mass-output in response meant low standards in general, as with the monuments, or anything else – even the general level of plays was not high.

But, at the top, in the best portraits of the time – not only with the miniatures, as has always been appreciated – but with large-scale portraits, the age made an individual contribution, with a character of its own. We must understand it in its own terms, consider the effects it was aiming at, its principles and its own aesthetic intentions: we must not condemn it for not achieving aims the Elizabethans neither intended nor valued. The process of understanding must be historical as well as visual, social as well as aesthetic. It is usual to hold up the painting of Henry's Court to abash that of Elizabeth's; and it is true that Holbein and his circle rendered Henry's in remorseless truth and power and realism as hardly any Court before or since. But before making any aesthetic judgment we should mark the contrast between its brutality and naked power-struggle and the civilised refinement, the fantasy and poetry of the feminine Court whose tutelary deity was a Virgin Queen. That, as a matter of plain fact, enters largely into the matter.

There is a subtler, and less decipherable, consideration. Holbein gave his character to the earlier period, and he was a German; the characteristic painter of the Elizabethan age, who impressed his artistic personality upon it, was Hilliard, and he was an Englishman. Criticism has tended to compare the linear emphasis of Hilliard's work unfavourably with the solidity and volume of Continental painting. No doubt it is inferior to that; but it is deeply English, and it goes back through the long medieval line of manuscript illumination perhaps to the earlier mingling of Anglo-Saxon and Celtic strains, the fusion of peoples out of which we come. Hilliard was rooted in the West Country: he came out of Exeter, that ancient border-city between Saxon and Celt. Art is as much a matter of the unconscious and instinctive affinities as of reason and training.

Wölfflin draws our attention to a further general consideration. Renaissance art is essentially aristocratic – though there are marked exceptions, particularly with the *bourgeois* Dutch. But in countries culturally dominated by a Court, 'all the distinctive criteria of manner and feeling prevailing in the higher classes were adopted

. . . A number of gestures and movements disappeared from pictures: they were felt to be too commonplace.'[11] We must always remember this in looking at Elizabethan portraiture: if the state-portraits have a statuesque quality, keeping their distance and reserve, before concluding that they are wanting in life and move-ment, we should consider the overriding intention and that to this we owe their dignity and calm, the sense of time standing still – as in their music (though that vibrates with emotion).

The age made a marked distinction between public and private portraiture, between pictures 'in great' and miniatures. That being so, it must very much influence our conception of the former – the latter have always been appreciated at their proper worth. What did the Elizabethans expect of their large-scale pictures? Since they were public in character, it was natural that they should display the rank and status of the subject, along with his appearance and personality, and record his place in his family by his coat-of-arms. The dominance of the family is evident over most of the field, as with the monuments. Nothing wrong with that, is there?* – the family is the basic human grouping, whether portray-ing nobles, gentry or middle-class folk. With grandees at the top of society there will be more variety: some of their simpler portraits record them in their family relationships, or as they appeared in daily life, like Burghley ambling round his garden on a mule (at the Bodleian). It is equally natural that high officials should be recorded in state-portraits in the panoply of their office: Burghley in Garter robes and with his wand of office as Lord Treasurer, as he again is rendered for posterity on his tomb; Nottingham as Lord Admiral, with ships in the background, as in Mytens' portrait at Greenwich; Hunsdon as Lord Chamberlain, or Hatton as Lord Chancellor in Hilliard's miniature of him. The lesser portraits were for the family or to exchange among friends; the state-portraits to preside in the galleries of the grandees' houses, or be awarded a place in the palaces of the sovereign they had served.

The most important artistic question was the portrayal of the sovereign herself, for the image presented sent its rays all through society, would be copied many times over, would affect her people's conception of her – in short, have much social and even some anthropological significance. Two objectives, if not three, had to be achieved in the official portrait: it had to be recognisable,

* As Mr Eric Mercer seems to imply in his book, *English Art, 1553–1625*, domin-ated by a crude Marxism. (*The Oxford History of English Art.*)

a likeness not too far removed from fact; it should be somewhat idealised – all English aesthetic theory was opposed to brute naturalness of the kind we see in German portraiture of the time. To this there should be added the dignity, if possible the aura, of majesty. This was the special need in royal portraiture – decorum, apart from anything else, demanded it and decorum was no less important in painting than in literature, if anything more so. For some years Elizabeth hesitated. She does not seem to have been willing to make much use of the best painter available, Hans Eworth, a foreigner – though he did paint the well known composition of the Queen discomfiting Juno, Pallas and Venus. Flattering as this is, it did not suit the purpose.

Her impatient subjects jumped the gun and produced daubs of her – probably signboards among them – which gave displeasure. Many years later Ralegh wrote that he had seen many portraits of her broken up and burned by order because they did not come up to what she required. In 1563 Cecil drafted an order prohibiting such portraits, until 'some special cunning painter might be permitted by access to take the natural representation of her Majesty, whereof she hath been always of her own royal disposition very unwilling.'[12] Polite and tactful Cecil! – in fact she knew very well what she wanted; about 1572 the 'special cunning painter' appeared: Nicholas Hilliard. A miniaturist, he produced the image the Queen approved; he possessed the refined and flattering sensibility, the grace and fantasy, that appealed to her and was in keeping with the idiom of her Court – in which the language was of love, like the poetry and music, but love held in leash and idealised. The image that Hilliard created in miniature was the starting point for her official portraiture, expanded in great, becoming ever more fanciful, symbolic, hieratic, removed from reality – until reality overtook her in Isaac Oliver's pathetic, unfinished miniature, of an ageing, toothless woman.[13]

But by then the work had been accomplished: she had imposed her image, as she wished it, upon her people and upon posterity. In the 1580's Hilliard seems to have been awarded a monopoly of portraying her in miniature, and Serjeant-Painter George Gower 'in great'. This may not have been carried into effect, but it offers at any rate a pointer: they were both Englishmen. Dr. Auerbach has no doubt that 'her patronage led to the emergence of a native school of portrait painting'; that it was due to her taste that, in particular, 'the typically English portrait miniature emerged, the essential characteristics of which remained unchanged for three centuries'; and that altogether this was 'the beginning of a new era in English portraiture.'[14]

Hilliard himself bore evidence that she knew what she wanted and that the choices were well within her field of competence; Mr. Buxton has properly interpreted the well known discussion between them, which has usually been misrepresented. She had observed 'great difference of shadowing in the works and diversity of drawers of sundry nations, and that the Italians – who had the name to be cunningest and to draw best – shadowed not.'[15] Now this was in keeping with contemporary Italian Mannerism – one would suppose she had a Court-painter like Bronzino in mind. Hilliard explained how the greater or lesser degree of shadowing was affected by where the painter was working. Since both Queen and painter had the native preference for linear design, and Hilliard was about to do a miniature, she at once met his desire by choosing to sit for him 'in the open alley of a goodly garden, where no tree was, nor any shadow at all.' It was not a question of concealing her age, but suiting the style; naturally, realistic naturalism was not even in question: it would have been contrary to decorum, contrary to taste.

And so the image was created that was reproduced a hundred times (with different costumes), refined upon, varied, enriched, inflated; but always there remained, what Hilliard had coined, the impression of regality. We know how given to symbolism the age was – often the portrait embodied a symbol, conveyed a message. The simpler ones we can interpret, but sometimes they are too esoteric, especially in the miniatures – which were private in their nature (like the sonnets) – and we have lost the key. The Phoenix portrait in the National Gallery is probably a large-scale by Hilliard, since we know that he painted such: it is an expansion from his miniature technique, with the characteristic attention to jewels for which he was famous. As the Catholic poet, Constable, wrote:

> But if in secret I his judgment shrive,
> It would confess that no man knew aright
> To give to stones and pearls true dye and light
> Till first your art with orient nature strive.

Very proper for a goldsmith-limner, to whom miniatures were jewels to be worn, and descried privately in intimacy, almost secretly.

In the *Faerie Queene* different aspects of Elizabeth's personality were expressed under different names; so with the portraits: the Ermine portrait at Hatfield – the ermine signifies spotless chastity; the Rainbow portrait there – the dispenser of power and promise of good things to the earth (she certainly had been to the Cecils), *Non sine sole iris*. The Ditchley portrait, the monumental white farthingale pyramiding up from the feet on Oxfordshire, speaks of patriotism, love of country, in storm and sheen. The Woburn portrait celebrates the defeat of the Armada, its wrecked ships in one inset, her fleet in the other, her hand on the globe, the imperial crown above; it is her reply to Philip's *Non sufficit orbis*: the Empress of Spenser's dedication.

These last are state-portraits, studded with jewelry, flamboyant, improbable ruffs, puffed-out lawn or cambric sleeves, the face a mask, pale, expressionless, timeless: an icon. Even so, beneath many of the portrayals, a sensitive eye can detect the real woman. There is sometimes an inexpressible sadness, a lonely isolation one catches sight of beneath the magnificence: in the beautiful Darnley portrait, for example, the long tapering fingers holding a plume of feathers, the shapely oval of the sad, controlled face, the hooded eyes. In the splendid picture at Sienna, which may be by Zuccaro, in which she is holding the sieve of virginity, there is an indefinable weariness in the watchful eyes. In the Portland portrait, standing by her throne with the sword of state at her feet and holding an olive-branch – arbiter of war and peace – and in William Roger's resplendent engraving with crown, orb and sceptre, she is even at length old.

What of the artist to whom we chiefly owe this impress upon the age? through whose eyes, and in whose idiom, we see, more than in any others', its representative characters?

Hilliard was precocious – we have three miniatures from his hand at thirteen – and he lived to be seventy-two; so that there is a large body of his work, not all of it now identifiable. We know him securely by his numerous miniatures; but since he did paint large-scale pictures, there can be no doubt that he had a hand in some of those that reproduce in large his miniature style. In addition, he designed the second Great Seal, executed medallions, the elaborate frames and lockets for his portraits, and no doubt some of the famous pendants that remain. This mass of minute and exquisite work went forward with the help of apprentices: one of them, Isaac Oliver, became Hilliard's chief rival and surpassed him in favour under James; Rowland Lockey became a competent painter whom Hilliard introduced to Bess of Hardwick and the Cavendishes, for whom he painted a number of pictures. John Davies of Hereford appreciated Lockey:

> As nature made, so thou dost make my face
> Yet with a better, and a worser, grace:
> With better, since thy work hath glory got,
> With worse, since thou giv'st life that moves it not.
> Yet, when cross-fortune makes me move the brow,
> Thine, without motion, better far doth show.
> But by ill fortune oft though marred it be
> It had good fortune to be made by thee;
> For thou dost Fortune's furrows quite out-strike
> And maks't it in all fortunes look alike.

This tells us what Elizabethans looked for in a portrait: lifelikeness, not with brute realism but grace. Hilliard was admired by a greater poet, Donne – whose miniature, however, is by Oliver (1616):

> A hand or eye
> By Hilliard drawn is worth an history
> By a worse painter made.

Hilliard's father was an Exeter goldsmith, of whom a couple of fine pieces have been identified: a simple but graceful communion-cup, and a rich, embossed Renaissance standing-dish. The clever boy was apprenticed to a London goldsmith, whose daughter he married at twenty-nine, when she was twenty. We have a miniature of her, very pretty and beguiling, dressed in the height of French fashion; Hilliard himself, with recognisably Devon oval face, fine intelligent eyes, sensibility in every line, curly dark hair, cap raffishly on the back of his head. We might call him, anachronistically, a dandy; he was extravagant, improvident about money (a mortgagor of his house in Gutter Lane, off Fleet Street, was Dean Wood, Mrs. Blague's lover).[16] His tastes were almost superciliously aristocratic, as we should expect of an aesthete.

After his acceptance as official miniaturist, or 'limner', to the Queen he was allowed to go to France in the service of Alençon, and was there for two years, 1576–8, overstaying his leave. There were no miniaturists to equal him in France – where the taste was for portrait drawings – and Hilliard won favour in Court circles, painting Alençon, and the Duke and Duchess of Nivernois among others. He met Ronsard, with whom he had a vein of Renaissance romanticism in common. We may say that romantic grace is the mood of his work – the mood of Shakespeare's earlier comedy; the technique combines the linearity of manuscript illumination with the precision and detail of the goldsmith's art. Harington said, 'myself have seen him, in white and black in four lines only, set down the feature of the Queen's Majesty's countenance . . . and he is so perfect therein that he can set it down by the Idea he hath, without any pattern.'[17]

Thus, with uncompromising dedication to his art, Hilliard accomplished a great body of work. Apart from any large-scale portraits, if we could identify all the subjects of his miniatures we should find that he had portrayed practically the whole Court. It is an essentially aristocratic art: 'he is, as it were, the sonneteer among painters, perfecting a work of art in a formally controlled pattern, in little, and in the tradition of compliment that Elizabethan lovers inherited from Petrarch.'[18] Within his chosen bounds there are both variety and development. He is responsive not only to feminine beauty, as we should expect, but to masculine looks as well. We have not only the pride of youthful male beauty in John Croker (in a double locket with his less good-looking wife), but the sober truth of middle-age in the portrait of his father Richard Hilliard, the blunt thrustfulness of Sir Francis Drake and some other men. Then we have the large rectangular miniatures like the famous one of Sir Anthony Mildmay at Cleveland, Ohio, in his tent with all his equipment, including a dog, or the privateering Cumberland dressed for the tilt with the Queen's glove in his plumed hat. There is another class of portraits of exquisite beauty, that are emblematic: the black-hatted man clasping a hand reaching down from a cloud; a dark-visaged man in cambric shirt open to the chest, against a background of flames, the flames of love; the youth leaning against a tree, a network of briar roses growing up over his long white-clad limbs – which is now thought to be a testimonial to friendship rather than to love. In the last phase, perhaps under the influence of his rival, Oliver, Hilliard developed a more psychological approach and more sentiment, though he had always exhibited sympathy for the sitter.

We know a good deal about what he thought of his art, for Richard Haydock persuaded him to write his *Art of Limning*, which he never finished and of which only one copy survives.[19] It was written in the latter part of his career, when he was no longer quite such an *arbiter elegantiarum*, and there is a slightly disappointed note, as with Drayton and Daniel (though with less reason), as to the new generation. His chief admiration was for Holbein, whose impulse had started the art on its way in England, and whose designs for jewelry continued to be an inspiration. Hilliard expressed a generous appreciation for Lucas van Leyden and Goltzius, and was well acquainted with Dürer, whose rules of proportion he thought too absolute. His own followed an English empiricism. Sir Christopher Hatton was accounted a very handsome man, yet he had a low forehead: one should draw, not according to theory, but as the eye sees, following the effect of illusion the perspective gives the onlooker. It may well be, as Bacon said, 'there is no excellent beauty that hath not some strangeness in the proportion.'

Others, too, thought limning the height of portraiture – and certainly it is a wonder to think what Hilliard and Oliver managed to achieve and convey in so small a space. All painting, to contemporary minds, imitated nature or life, but the hardest thing was to portray the face. Colour or complexion was least important (we must remember that something of the flesh-colours of Hilliard's work have paled in four centuries, and also that some colour-mixtures have been lost, as the scent of musk has been). More important was proportion, or 'favour', i.e. cast of countenance. Most of all is grace or expression, 'which can neither be well used nor well judged of, but of the wiser sort.' The eyes are 'the life of the picture', and should be 'perfect round for so much thereof as appeareth.' The difficulty is to catch 'the grace in countenance by which the affections appear', that is, the expression which is an index to character; for expressions, 'witty smilings' (wit means intelligence), 'stolen glances', are all fleeting and must be caught swift as a swallow on the wing.

Art is arduous, and Hilliard desiderates a condition of life that is both aesthetic and ascetic, temperate and select. The artist should live for his art, everything in his life subordinated to it, in an atmosphere of refinement: limning demanded that there should be no dust or hairs, no spittle or dandruff, on the tiny precious object – better to wear silk, exclude smoke or ill odours, provide music or discreet discourse for the sitter, above all no interruption. Like most Renaissance people, Hilliard had no opinion of critics: the artist himself was the best judge. Common men's opinion was of no value, and one need take no notice of the criticism of sitters: they never know – the wiser suspend their judgment. In any case, the art of the miniature 'tendeth not to common men's use, either for furnishing of houses or any patterns for tapestries, or building, or any other work whatsoever.' Painting after the life was a gift of God, to be followed up with diligence and much labour: a dedicated life. It is an uncompromising statement that stands for artist and aesthete alike.

Unfinished, the manuscript has a supplement of a technical kind on how to mix colours and so on. Hilliard was particularly fascinated by precious stones, their qualities and lore, and he had some interest in minerals, mining and alchemy. Others saw his manuscript and reproduced passages in their works, for example, Peacham and Marcus Gheeraerts.

In his later decades Hilliard was rivalled by his pupil Oliver, who developed a quite different style, as valid and accomplished, in some ways easier to appreciate. While it is a mistake to think of Hilliard's as a two-dimensional style, without volume, it was essentially linear, and the portraits in large, after his style, are enlarged miniatures. Oliver's miniatures are, in contrast, reductions of large-scale pictures to small, built up by shadowing rather than line. In this Hilliard's work is unmistakably English, where Oliver's affiliations are Flemish, like the group that came to dominate sculpture from Southwark, Janssens, de Critzes, Gheeraerts; Oliver was the son of a French Huguenot goldsmith, but married into that group. His work had not the refinement or the fantasy of Hilliard; it was more realistic, it rendered character more powerfully, and it had its own sentiment, including a religious sense that is absent from the pure aesthete. Art was Hilliard's religion. Yet Oliver's art is not inferior; in its own terms it is equal, and comparable. It is indeed illuminating to compare subjects and themes in which the younger man has challenged the master: the poetry of Hilliard's young man leaning against a tree with Oliver's black-hatted and -clad young man seated solidly on a tree-trunk; Hilliard's recumbent man with an open book in a formal garden – we cannot make out the symbolism – with Oliver's Lord Herbert of Cherbury, shield on shoulder, lying at the foot of a tree in a landscape which has more depth and poetry. Their palettes, too, are in recognisable contrast: Hilliard likes simple and brilliant colours, cerulean blue, spring- and apple-greens, cherry-reds, yellow and gold; Oliver's colouring is darker and warmer, fawn and brown, silver-grey, russet and mauve, toned down with black.[20] We see Oliver's altogether looser, freer style in the flowing draperies of his fine Lucy Harington, the blue-stocking Countess of Bedford.

When James came to the throne, honours were divided:

Hilliard became limner to the King, Oliver to Queen Anne, whose hooked nose he rendered unflatteringly in profile. The junior predeceased his master, dying in 1617, Hilliard following in 1619. With Robert Cecil dead in 1612, Shakespeare in 1616, Byrd in 1623, it was the end of an age.

It is only in recent years that the work of lesser painters has begun to be separated out from the mass, distinguished from each other's, and in a few cases brought together. A generation ago people did not distinguish clearly between Hilliard and Oliver; a generation before that everything was lumped together, in country houses, under the name of Zuccaro. It is a pity that the Elizabethans wrote no more about their artists than about their dramatists: we could readily have spared the whole of their theology for lives of their artists and writers.

In our time George Gower has become a distinct personality. By birth a Yorkshire gentleman, in youth he was led away from 'arms and virtue' while his gift, he tells us, long slept; now, revived by gain, he took to living by 'the pencil's trade' and became a successful portrait-painter in the 1570's. We find him supplying five pictures to the Kitsons of Hengrave in 1573: among them Lady Kitson with her smug self-assured pose, arms crossed and *mignonne* face, tall stuck-up white plume in hat, full of character. The detail of the gauze overdress is rendered in Hilliardesque fashion. But Gower's self-portrait is more sombre and searching, more in Bronkhorst's manner. It is emblematic: in the balances in the background the compasses of the trade weigh down the arms of his gentility, his large characterful hand holds palette and brush. He is a fine portraitist: 'hands stand out as though lit by a beam of strong light, the flesh high and even in tone with concentrated shadows.'[21] One notices a certain sharpness of line in the Kitson portraits, there is always definiteness and precision in his outline. In 1581 he became Serjeant-Painter, when much of his time would be taken up with decorative painting. He lived in the parish of St. Clement Danes, and died in 1596. Until 1953 a fair number of his pictures were at Hengrave: now all dispersed.

Among contemporary foreigners Arnold Bronkhorst is now identified – partner with Hilliard in prospecting for gold in Scotland.[22] He signed a portrait of Lord St. John of Bletso, full of personality, bluff, rustic, shrewd; and another of Burghley, elegant, cool and composed, that reveals his native distinction, with the long tapering fingers of the Cecils. Cornelius Ketel is a more forceful painter, with his powerful evocation of fighting Frobisher, large pistol in hand, in the Bodleian. The joint work of the Segars, William and Francis, is being put together, in great and in miniature: from the encrusted and jewelled lace coat over black armour of the Essex portrait in Dublin one would say miniaturists enlarging.[23] Certainly Sir William was a Herald, as some other illuminators were, so their style of painting may be affiliated to that grouping. Everyone is charmed by the picture of young Elizabeth Bridges at Woburn – as Essex was in life (she seems to have been his mistress) – a shyly deprecating girl in elaborately figured dress, with hands chastely folded before her. This is the best work of Hieronimo Custodis,[24] a foreigner much inferior to Marcus Gheeraerts the younger, whom the English called Mark Garret. Brought to England as a child from Bruges, he became a fashionable Court-painter in the 1590's.[25] Sir Henry Lee was his patron, of whom he did a full-length in Garter robes, and this set a model for Jacobean state-portraits. We are told that, nevertheless, Gheeraerts' 'innate modesty' gave way before the new invasion from the Low Countries that brought in Mytens and Van Somer. With them we are in the flood-tide of James's reign, with its opulence and vulgarity.

All this is evidence of the milch-cow the prosperous country was for so many immigrants taking refuge from the distracted times abroad.

Lomazzo's standard treatise on painting, *Trattato dell'Arte della Pittura* (Milan, 1584), was translated by Richard Haydock in 1598, *A Tract Containing the Arts of Curious Painting, Carving, Building*, a book exceptionally well printed at Oxford. The fine title-page has a portrait of Haydock in doublet and ruff, beard and moustache, hair receding from high forehead. He was a doctor and a friend of John Case, who prefaced a commendation to the book. Its importance for us is not so much as a translation of a standard Italian work – though it informs us as to received aesthetic doctrine – as for the additional information it provides us about English matters. It was dedicated to Thomas Bodley whose famous Library was already begun; fragments of the scheme of painted ceilings, with the portraits of scores of worthies, have been recovered in our time.

Haydock had a circle of connoisseur friends in Oxford. He himself had been diligently practising the art for the past seven years – so among unidentified pictures in the neighbourhood may be some of his. Thomas Allen of Gloucester Hall, 'that unfeigned lover and furtherer of all good arts', brought Haydock an imperfect copy of Lomazzo, which could not be 'matched in Paul's churchyard' till a friend procured a perfect copy from Italy. These friends helped Haydock with rare foreign books and by their critical conversation. Owing to Lomazzo's blindness there were many errors in his book: these Haydock corrected, and added matter of his own. He considered, with the usual Renaissance superiority towards medievalism, that the knowledge of painting 'though it never attained to any great perfection amongst us, save in some very few of late, yet is it much decayed amongst the ordinary sort from the ancient mediocrity' – he means in general use, on a lower level. On the other hand, 'some of our nobility and divers private gentlemen have very well acquitted themselves, as may appear by their galleries carefully furnished with the excellent monuments of sundry famous ancient masters, both Italian and German.' But he had noticed signs of careless keeping, 'divers goodly old works finely marred with fresh and beautiful colours and varnishes.'

As for criticism of the more distinguished painters, 'I rather wonder how they have attained so near unto the ancient perfection with so few helps as our country – for aught I could ever learn – hath afforded them.' This gives us a precious insight into what informed opinion thought of the situation that confronted native painters; Haydock wished that he had the pen of Vasari to immortalise the best of them. There follows an enthusiastic encomium of Hilliard, with whom Haydock agreed that limning was 'the perfection of painting' and whom he had persuaded to write his treatise based on his own practice. He admonishes the reader, 'the slenderness of thy capacity showeth the exceeding difficulty of the art.' He intended a second part in which he would list all the eminent English painters. This he never accomplished, any more than Heywood got round to writing his lives of the dramatists: what losses both were to the information we should value most!

It is not my purpose to go through Lomazzo's book, admirably thorough analysis of the subject in every aspect as it is; but we should note his definition of the art as that to which Elizabethans subscribed. 'Painting is an art which, with proportionable lines and colours answerable to the life, by observing the perspective light, doth so imitate the nature of corporal things that it not only representeth the thickness and roundness thereof upon a flat but also their actions and gestures, expressing moreover divers affections and passions of the mind.'

Where the Italian had recommended classical authors for the ways and motions of animals, Haydock recommends English painters to read Sidney, Spenser, Daniel, etc. He adds notes clarifying the nature of 'murrey' as dark blue and revealing his technical knowledge of minerals; he had discussed confusing passages in the original with 'many good painters and chemists'. He incorporated his own criticism of Lomazzo's section on Colours as too abstract and philosophical, preferring an empirical approach as more beneficial to the practitioner. So he inserts his own account of English practice, particularly for limning, 'wherein much art and neatness is required. This was much used in former times in church books . . . as also in drawing by the life in small models, dealt in also in late years by some of our countrymen, as Chute, Bettes, etc., but brought to the rare perfection we now see' by Hilliard and his scholar, Oliver. Haydock shared the Italian view that of all painting, i.e. other than limning, fresco is 'the most workmanly and beautiful'.

As a doctor Haydock adds a section on the ill consequences of women's painting their faces with sublimate, 'some bray it in a marble mortar with quicksilver . . . all ways deletorious to the flesh; 'ceruse' or white lead mixed with vinegar dries up the skin and greys the hair; scaling with plum alum scales off the skin to make it seem red; juice of lemons decays it, oil of tartary takes stains out of linen but mortifies the skin; so too with rock-alum or salt-nitre to procure a flushing of the face. All embellishings made from minerals are deleterious. From these hints we see what contemporary practices were.

Henry VIII may be regarded as the first effective collector among our monarchs[21] and Elizabeth added to the royal collection; but it was in her reign that connoisseurship and collecting first took root. It is not surprising to find good old Archbishop Parker, with his love of antiquities and care for music, assembling a collection of pictures, mostly portraits, and maps at Lambeth. Leicester, with his Italianate tastes, whose handsome presence was portrayed by so many painters – Zuccaro, Hilliard, Gheeraerts, among others – was a more sophisticated connoisseur. At his death he owned two hundred and twenty pictures, mainly portraits, in his various houses. He kept his historical, mythological and genre paintings, Italian and Dutch, at Leicester House in London (familiar to Spenser, whose descriptions of scenes often read like transcripts from tapestries or paintings) : this represented both a more advanced taste in collecting, as well as wider opportunities, and a consciously deliberate disposition of his pictures.[27] Even the chief connoisseur of the time, Lord Lumley, had not such a wide collection, though he had more: over two hundred and fifty pictures, in addition to his remarkable library, his sculptures and the ancestral monuments he built up in his parish church at Chester-le-Street. He had some religious pictures – his sympathies were Catholic – but his main idea was to make Lumley Castle a shrine of family pride, with portraits grouped round those of his line: a reputable ambition, with its fortunate aesthetic consequences. When he discovered an ancient portrait of Richard II, 'fastened on the backside of a door of a base room' in her palace, he gave it to the Queen.[28]

Lumley's was but the extension of the usual idea on a grander scale. It became the fashion to collect portraits of the family as a nucleus, then to add royal portraits and those of notabilities, sometimes from abroad, more usually those at home, such as Burghley or Leicester. We still see such collections, essentially, at Hardwick or Hatfield. The Long Gallery was the place where most pictures hung, mostly portraits; only one or two in other rooms.

With these works and interests we have exhibited what was characteristic of the time. We learn that 'by 1616 a new trend was apparent in English painting, revealing itself in a class of intimate portraits wherein the sitter is caught . . . in a private moment.'[29] A new trend is indeed observable in the work of Sir Nathaniel Bacon, of that exceedingly talented family – he was a grandson of the Lord Keeper, and died fairly young in 1627. He is the most eminent English painter after Hilliard; though an amateur he trained in Italy, and his altogether more ambitious compositions, well designed and free-flowing, betoken a new age. There is little more to detain us. Such familiar pictures as the Queen's Visit to Blackfriars in 1600, or the Spanish and English Plenipotentiaries making the peace of 1604, are 'rather more than mere group portraits'.[30] Hoefnagel's Wedding at Bermondsey is 'unique as showing a bourgeois scene in a recognisable English setting.' It is no less recognisably Flemish, sub-Breughel. Altogether these things do not amount to much.

Similarly with flower-painting and water-colour. One of the consequences of the Renaissance publication of the classics was the immense stimulus it gave to botany. Though the eminent botanist, L'Ecluse, well known to Sidney, knew all the chief languages of Europe, he naturally did not find it necessary to know English.[31] Lobel, however, spent many years as Lord Zouch's gardener in England, and the Willoughbys of Wollaton possessed a volume of flower-paintings from this circle. A charming flower-painter was Jacques le Moyne, whom Ralegh supported in Blackfriars, where he published his *La Clef des champs* in 1586. Inferior English printing was capable only of rather crude wood cuts, but the water-colour drawings on which they were based have freshness and charm, with exactness of rendering. Le Moyne had been with the French colony in Florida; John White was the cartographer and illustrator of Ralegh's first colony in Virginia. Here we are concerned with him only as an artist; among the first of our water-colourists, his renderings of Indian life at Roanoke, the flora and fauna, 'have served at second, third, and fourth hand as material for all book-illustrations of the natives of Virginia ever since.'[32] Though not a professional, White had 'obviously received a training from some professional artists'. Binyon considers his affiliations to lie not with le Moyne but with the Low Countries; 'it was with the art of the Low Countries that English art was then most in contact.'

However, with John White we take a leap to the New World, his drawings the first artistic product of English America.

CHAPTER VI

DOMESTIC ARTS

CLOSELY allied to painting, or subsidiary to architecture, are the domestic arts; they display developments and even pro-fusion in accordance with expanding wealth and comfort, but also – as ends in themselves – varying accomplishment. Em-broidery and tapestry-weaving, for example, come forward at one stride in the magical 1580's: the first achieves its highest develop-ment since *opus anglicanum* was appreciated all over Europe in the thirteenth and fourteenth centuries, while tapestry-weaving, im-ported from abroad, remains at a provincial level. It is something of a mystery how embroidery arrived at this sudden excellence – as with the architecture and the poetry, music and the drama. For almost a century, between the ulcerated Wars of the Roses and the middle years of Elizabeth there is 'a blank period from which little has been recovered.'[1] Explanations must be partly social, as with the other arts: economic and political disturbance, insecurity and impoverishment, the upheaval of the Reformation and the relegation of the Church to a secondary position in the state. The direct influence of political events upon the arts may be neatly illustrated by the way in which the embroideries coming down in the Carew-Pole family stop with the Civil War, to begin again in the security of the eighteenth century.[2]

'Yet about 1570 or 1580 we are abruptly faced with the type of embroidery illustrated' in the rich collections of the Victoria and Albert Museum, in the incomparable private collection at Hardwick, or the Carew-Pole and Middleton treasures – 'a fully formed tradition, showing an overflowing vitality and, in most cases, a considerable technical competence. Nor is this compet-ence restricted to embroideries we may reasonably suppose to be professional: it characterises the great majority of pieces which must be household work. The greatly improved economic position of the English middle class explains how the housewife and her assistants had the necessary leisure; the importation of silk direct from the Levant and the manufacture of steel needles, replacing the older drawn-wire ones . . . explain how the result obtained was technically possible.'[3] Beneath these propitious circumstances instinctive urges are at work: in the beautiful flowered embroideries, especially in blackwork wrought in silk upon linen or canvas – in which purely aesthetic attainment is at its highest – 'the native medieval tradition of linear surface pattern survives', as we have seen it come to the fore in the painting.[4]

Embroideries fall mainly into two groups, those for costume and those for furnishing. With the immense demand for both – in itself evidence enough of increased wealth and comfort, as well as of the larger leisure women had at their disposal – it is not surprising that a large quantity has come down to us: some hundreds of worked caps alone, though they hardly at all appear in the portraits, have survived. The bulk of the work was done in the household, but the number of professional embroiderers naturally grew too: the Broderers' Company, to maintain good standards, received its charter in 1561, by 1580 it had eighty-nine master-craftsmen in London.[5] A great household often employed a professional – hence the excellence of the designs; peasant-work, honest enough, had no such excellence. We know that Mary Stuart and Bess of Hardwick worked together on their embroideries, from the remains of their work at Hardwick and at Oxburgh: Mary had time on her hands – such time as she could spare from her perpetual plotting – though it is surprising that Bess could take time off from making money, family interests and building, her chief passions.

Blackwork had been known since the fifteenth century, but from Elizabeth's time we have hundreds of specimens, tunics, shifts, bodices, gloves, pillows, coifs, caps. Impossible to enumerate them, though we may well remember individual pieces for their shapeliness and elegance, their combination of naturalness and rich foliation – such as the tunic that once belonged to the Queen, now in the Victoria and Albert Museum, embroidered with emblems from Whitney's book. We must be content to generalise: the whole art expresses once more the age's love of symbolism. Since the symbolism has become secular it is chiefly devoted to flowers and plants[6] – as if the charming formal gardens of the time were transplanted into the house – or with animals and insects. Marina, in *Pericles*,

> with her needle composes
> Nature's own shape of bird, branch, or berry,

That even her art sisters the natural roses:
Her inkle, silk, twin with the rubied cherry.

We see the ladies at their work in Helena's words:

We, Hermia, like two artificial [i.e. artistic] gods,
Have with our needles created both a flower,
Both on one sampler, sitting on one cushion.

Something of the medieval spirit lingered on in English embroideries: they did not go in much for the human figure of sophisticated Renaissance fashion. In the love for circular coiling stems with their patterned exfoliation authorities have seen a long continuous history going right back to early Anglo-Celtic ornament. They have their affiliation with title-page borders, and printers' and publishers' devices, as very often their designs come in turn from emblem or natural-history books, foreign or English. There is a unity about Renaissance culture all through.

Then, too, the books themselves were often given embroidered bindings: when these were of perishable velvet they have mostly disappeared. Elizabeth liked embroidered bindings for her books: 'one of the most decorative and in many ways the finest of all the remaining embroidered books of the time' is the bible that her printer, Christopher Barker, presented as a New Year's Gift in 1584.[7] Of crimson velvet it is embroidered all over with veins of gold, Tudor roses and seed-pearl. It was a happy thought in our time to use the pattern for a Wilton carpet design. Such precious books needed a cushion to place them on, if big; if small, a bag: these too were embroidered. Everything was enriched, encrusted or decorated.

Cushions were a new addition to comfort and decorativeness. Harrison tells us that cushioned chairs were, by the 1590's, in every merchant's house; he waxes too lyrical about the hangings and carpets in farmers' houses: I do not believe that they appeared much below yeoman's rank – in the Arden house at Wilmcote, for example. Houses were sparsely furnished by our standards – thus giving the effect of spaciousness, while tapestries or hangings on the wall, curtains and valences for the big beds, carving and plaster-work on friezes and ceilings, table carpets and cushions gave richness and colour. To unupholstered furniture cushions added comfort: hence their importance, their numbers and size, with the opportunity they afforded for decoration. 'These cushion covers survive as the most complete testimony of Elizabethan embroidery, both from the point of view of design and the aesthetic quality of the work. Moreover, they were produced in professional workshops as well as being made domestically in the great houses.'[8] Many still survive – perhaps the largest collection is again at Hardwick, a dozen of them recognisable still from Bess's Inventory, though we must remember how much more brilliant the colours were four hundred years ago. A superb cushion cover at Petworth, centring upon a medallion with the Dudley bear and ragged staff within the Garter is another pointer to Leicester's sophisticated taste, for 'it is a first-rate example of the craft of a professional workshop in cosmopolitan style.'

Carpets were for tables, or the tops of cupboards; rugs, a somewhat later term, for floors. Carpets – decorated with wools, silks, linen embroidery on canvas – presented a fine surface for decoration and are therefore among 'the most splendid and original of Elizabethan embroideries . . . those which, together with hangings, were worked on the largest scale.'[9] Turkey carpets meant those imported from the Near East; 'Turkey work' meant those made from those models in England. The English were apt to adapt them to their own taste – the addiction to flowers developed a recognisable English style: Bridget, Countess of Bedford, notes in her inventory 'two window carpets of my own making, one of them wrought with roses and marigolds.'[10] Cardinal Wolsey, with his princely Renaissance tastes, exerted keen pressure to get Damascus carpets via Venice; at one time a consignment of sixty arrived from Antwerp, which he inspected with pleasure, one by one.

Anxious to acquire anything for the good of its up-and-coming country, the Muscovy Company instructed its agents to learn the methods of Persian carpet-making.[11] In 1579 the elder Hakluyt directed that a dyer be sent to Persia to learn the art of dyeing thrummed wool; and if it were possible to procure 'a singular good workman in the art of Turkish carpet-making, you should bring the art into this realm.'[12] As the result of their forethought we have such splendid carpets as those made for Sir Edward Montagu in the 1580's, still at Boughton, with their octagonal-lobed and diamond-shaped panels with coats-of-arms. An even earlier and no less splendid carpet has come down in the Earl of Verulam's family at Gorhambury: the prevailing green colour reflects the English taste, with border of honeysuckle and oak-stems, and the inevitable coats-of-arms. 'It is of excellent workmanship and in such wonderful condition that it need not shrink from comparison with any Oriental carpet of its age . . . The English craftsmen

after a short apprenticeship produced carpets which in workmanship and design were scarcely, if at all, inferior to those
evolved in the East by centuries of effort.'[13] The Inventory of
Leicester's possessions after his death shows a large number of
Turkey carpets, one of them specified as of Norwich work. We are
beginning to appreciate what a connoisseur he was, what a patron
of the arts. An entry states, 'one of them sent to the Queen by
order of my Lord' – evidently a last present before his death: on
his way to it he had received a token from her at Rycote, 'your
old lodging . . . ready to take on my journey.'[14]

Both Henry VIII and Wolsey had had a passion for collecting
tapestries. Wolsey bought hundreds for Hampton Court, and on
his fall Henry took his entire collection from him – no wonder
that the acquisitive king left some two thousand at his death.[15]
Though there had long been individual tapestry-weavers in the
country – tapestry is woven, where embroidery is applied work –
it was the Elizabethans who first set up a factory or workshop. In
fact two were established, at Barcheston in Warwickshire and on
the site of Bordesley abbey in Worcestershire. This was upon the
initiative of William Sheldon, who built his fortune upon the suppression of Pershore abbey, bought many of its properties and of
the belongings of Bordesley.[16] He remained a Catholic, as did his
son who, dying 'in the verities of the Catholic Church', built a
chapel on to their parish church at Beoley, where they lie under
their monuments. Leicester was personally concerned in West
Midlands affairs and, when the town clerk of Warwick came to
see him about its poverty, he said, 'I marvel you do not devise
some ways among you to have some special trade to keep your
poor on work, such as Sheldon of Beoley devised: which, me-
thinketh, should be not only very profitable but also a means to
keep your poor from idleness.'[17] Sheldon had sent his son Ralph
to the Netherlands with Richard Hicks, the chief arras-worker
in the Great Wardrobe, to learn the art, and they brought back
a Dutch tapestry-weaver. Hicks returned to Barcheston in 1588,
where he was subsequently joined by his son. Around Hicks the
two establishments took shape and developed their style of work: in
his will Sheldon styles Hicks, 'the only author and beginner of this
art within this realm.' Leicester became a patron, as he was of all
the arts – including that of love. Since he was a connoisseur he had
the finest tapestries woven for him: four of them were formerly
at Drayton, with his arms and all their quarterings – for, contrary
to popular belief, the Dudleys were an old medieval family.[18]

For two or three decades the Sheldon workshops turned out a good deal of material – enough for us to observe development towards maturity and to recognise their products as having an idiom of their own. Of decent and enduring craftsmanship, at their simplest they have a rustic vitality, a pride in country ways that links them with the Cotswold Games, the poet Drayton, Justice Shallow's Gloucestershire orchard or the induction to *The Taming of the Shrew*. A number of their tapestry maps of counties, evidently based on Christopher Saxton's atlas of 1579, remain. We have Worcestershire and the western Cotswolds with the endearing familiar names: Stanway and Doddington, Temple Guiting and Upton Snodsbury, Ledbury, Bosbury and The World's End, with at the foot the proud inscription, 'This southerly part which here below towards Gloucester fall / Of corn and grass great plenty yields but fruit exceedeth all.' There is the Elizabethan pride in their country – it was a country one could be proud of then. The Bodleian happily has five of these tapestry maps: they adorned the Sheldons' own house at Weston until it was demolished, when they were purchased by the discerning Horace Walpole.

Most popular were the heraldic panels, for which there was a good demand among the gentry, for cushion covers long or short. The grandest of this class to survive is that with the Pembroke arms within the Garter, now in the Victoria and Albert Museum: this is exceptional in having seated female figures, with an elaborate display of trellis-work, fruit and flowers, on a blue and green ground – peacock colours. The Lewkenor table-carpet one sees in the Tudor room at the Metropolitan is simpler and more heraldic: the coat-of-arms has *putti* supporters, on a mound with wild flowers, the border displaying fourteen coats of the family's alliances. This piece has an interesting provenance: first at West Dene, then at Jane Austen's Chawton.

At Chastleton on its steep escarpment looking towards Stratford, there were five large panels – four of them biblical scenes, from Genesis, and one of Paris awarding the golden apple. And the house once had four large maps, besides cushion covers. For the Joneses were friends of the Sheldons – one room was known as 'Mr. Sheldon's chamber'. The house had been owned by a Throckmorton and then by Robert Catesby – of that restless stock (since Richard III's days). The handsome Catesby sold it in 1602 to Walter Jones, a wool-merchant of Witney, to raise money to pay the large fine for his part in the Essex Rebellion and then, like a fool, went on to lose his life in Gunpowder Plot. The sensible Joneses occupied themselves with furnishing their exquisite new house with objects of beauty: one sees some of them still, one of the Judah series of panels in the Birmingham gallery, others at Oxford and elsewhere, the house essentially unchanged on that pastoral slope, though sadly denuded of its quondam contents.

In 1592 at Hardwick the Countess 'paid to Mr. Sheldon's man for seventeen armses to set upon hangings, 30s 4d' – that would be to set the stags' heads of the Cavendishes in place of Hatton's arms on the tapestries she had bought – with a reward of 10s for hanging them.[19] The undoubted mas.erpieces of the Sheldon workshops are the set of the Seasons still in place at Hatfield. Based on the engravings of Martin de Vos, they at last achieve a real elegance in the elongated figures – especially of Summer, with long tresses and crowned with flowers. Along with figures of Hiems, Bacchus, Ceres, they have an extraordinary elaboration of medallions with Latin tags, landscape backgrounds, fruits, gourds, melons, peacocks in green, blue and gold profusion among the fruited trees. Autumn has a splendid antlered stag, a couchant lion and a spotted leopard in a Douanier Rousseau world of verdure. Profusion, richness, vitality, with a certain country *naïveté*: there we have the English Renaissance.

When the country came to commemorate the defeat of the Armada in a set of ten tapestries to hang in the House of Lords, the national commission was given to the Dutch, for a painter of marine pictures was required for the designs, each one portraying an episode in the famous story, from the Spanish fleet off the Lizard to the pursuit into the North Sea. Lord Admiral Howard was to confer with Cornelius van Vroom of Haarlem, and the leading tapestry-weaver of the time, Francis Spierincx, directed the work. Numerous medallions portrayed the English commanders, Howard, Cumberland, Hawkins, Drake, Frobisher and the rest, with lavish decorative figures and trophies. But the sea-scenes were the thing and, to record the events as accurately as possible, some sacrifice was made in composition. However, they remained the glory of the old House of Lords until the Houses of Parliament burned down in 1839 – fortunately they had been recorded in engravings half a century before.

We are familiar with the costume of the age from its portraits, many of which are indeed costume pieces. Impossible as it is to

go into detail here – the subject would need an encyclopedia* –
we must confine ourselves to what characterises the time, what is
revealing of the society. Costume clearly reflected not only class
and rank, but also profession – the clerical and academic, legal
and mercantile. Some fossil elements remain with us today in
clerical, academic and legal garb. In those days the expression of
class-status in one's costume was regulated by statute, though
there must have been wide margins of divergence. Middle-class
women were not supposed to dress in velvets, except for sleeves;[20]
blue was the colour for servants, so the upper classes forwent that
delightful colour. Peasantry and working people wore serges and
fustians of drab, natural colours, like themselves. Here we are concerned with costume only as a minor art; as such it offered unlimited scope for the application of embroidery, not only over
the whole area of dress but also on shoes and headgear. In general
we may say that the grand costume of the leading classes, nobility
and gentry, was immensely rich and exhibitionist, conspicuous
and competent, atrificial, addicted to hard, brilliant colours.
There was much use of black, but that served as a background to
bring out other hues. Renaissance society was extravagant and
extrovert, so was the costume. The Queen's, in the end, went
beyond everything, for she *was* beyond everything.

Henry VIII's Court departed from the sobriety of his Lan-
castrian father, to resume and increase the masculine magnificence of his Yorkist grandfather. There was a new assertion
of masculinity, in the massive trunks, the padded-out broad
shoulders, the enlarged codpieces that impressed Lytton Strachey.
Under the reign of a lady codpieces diminished, and from the
1590's disappeared. Masculine styles became more refined and
more artificial, as we see in portraits of the earlier Leicester, of
Ralegh and Essex, all shimmering silks and satins, sometimes all
white and silver. (It was the men who more commonly wore
earrings.) Under Elizabeth's aegis feminine costume became ever
more extravagant: though aggressive enough in appearance, there
was something rigid and static about it – there was no free flow
of *déshabille* such as one sees in the canvases of Lely. Authorities
on costume consider artificial restraint as reflecting social superiority (what are we then to think of the *louche* ladies of the Court
of Charles II?)

---

* An advantage of C. W. and P. Cunnington's *A Handbook of English Costume in the
Sixteenth Century* is that the illustrative drawings come from well-known recognisable
portraits.

Costume being obviously, as well as more deeply, related to sex it is natural that there should be such a contrast between Henrician and Elizabethan fashions. As against the sombre spectrum of his brutal Court – black and tawny, green and gold – we have the gay palette of Elizabeth's, Hilliard's colours, cherry and ruby, blue and silver, black, but set off by white and ivory. Special features of the age were the padding out of garments – 'bombast' they called it – and the narrow waists, especially for women above their farthingales. They looked like gorgeous, mailed wasps. Elizabeth's slim, virginal figure gave her an advantage here: she wrote to Philip, at the time of the *rapprochement* with Spain in the 1570's, that he would hardly recognise her she had become so thin. (She ate and drank little.) Knitting was a new feature, it is curious to think, introduced at mid-century by the 1580's it gave considerable employment. Lace, i.e. open work, another introduction from abroad, and drawn work, originally Italian, both became popular only in the second half of the century.[21]

Rich stuffs were what Renaissance people liked. Here the spoils of the medieval Church came in very handy. In Scotland we find the not particularly religious Mary Stuart handing over church vestments to make gayer the body of Bothwell. At Hardwick we can still see the copes and chasubles that were turned to secular purposes, an indication of what happened all over the country. Good materials lasted, and clothes were handed on from one generation to the next. At the top of society there was immense elaboration and *panache* – the costume set off the swagger of the time. We see it most resoundingly in the earlier portraits of Leicester, before he became fat and full with good eating and drinking. Burghley must have been well aware of the contrast his grave sobriety of dress and demeanour made with the perfumed, though highly masculine, favourite: there was politics in that no less than taste, and the Cecils have survived, the Dudleys not. Colour effects were emphasised by slashing and slitting, with different materials showing through. The brilliant doublets pointed to the peascod belly; trunk hose were inflated to strut in the more grandly – as the farthingale was accompanied by a tripping grace in women's steps, 'an excellent motion to thy feet in a semi-circled farthingale.' A man's head was set off by a ruff, given emphasis, while a woman's ruff gave a framework to her appearance, almost a picture-frame. With the Renaissance all was emphasis: no under-emphasis the motto, never miss an opportunity.

In women's dress the kirtle, or skirt, was the dominating feature which the gown, open in front, revealed in all its decoration. The shape depended on the farthingale underneath. These were of two kinds – that which emphasised the back, or in vulgar Elizabethan the 'bum-roll', and the full circle or wheel-farthingale such as the Queen is wearing in the Ditchley portrait. The farthingale is probably of Spanish origin, though there was an Italian kind that was much favoured, and a French farthingale that was very exclusive and not in fashion long. We know to what lengths decoration went, incrustation with seed-pearls, gold and silver thread, black work, embroidery, in addition to the masses of jewelry worn. We should think it gaudy and ridiculous – but what does our opinion matter?: this is the way it was. Towards the end of the reign figure-decoration was extended from the embroideries to the women's dresses, so that there was a brief period when they crawled with insects, lizards, butterflies, moths, birds, an occasional serpent in a paradise of fruits and plants and flowers. What fantasy! – like the gardens or the poetry. And since the age was so extrovert and so competitive, the costume itself has become an outer shell with which to confront the world – contrast the meditative drabness of medieval monasticism. Costume has become a carapace, a kind of armour.

Here we are not concerned with arms and armour from the military point of view but the artistic – and armour became more a matter of art and decoration the less utilitarian it was. The development of fire-arms – the dominant fact in sixteenth-century warfare – made armour cumbersome, and the long internal peace meant that many an 'unscoured armour hung by the wall'. Yet it retained its prestige-value for tilt and tournament; never was greater display made in the matter than under the impulse of the Renaissance. Some of the parade-casques lost sight of their original purpose under their elaboration of design and embossed decoration, but this was Italian or French, not English. The Renaissance reintroduced classical models in the Roman manner: parade-bucklers sported scenes of ancient mythology, sometimes in embroidery, sometimes 'damascened', with gilt inlay in lines engraved in steel. Hence the famous black-and-gold armours.

English armour was influenced essentially by German. An Armourers' Company was already in existence on a small scale, but Henry VIII, to equip his Court with all forms of Renaissance magnificence, brought in German master-craftsmen and established a Royal Armoury at Greenwich. Hence the famous

Greenwich school of armour that dominated the tilt-yard through Elizabeth's reign. The earlier sixteenth-century Gothic style gave way to rounder, blunter forms, with breast-plate globose, toes broad not pointed, separate-fingered gauntlets, enriched and enchased with art. Nevertheless English armours display a certain 'solid simplicity of form by which they can be recognised': though often beautifully decorated, they never went in for embossing.[22] It is fortunate that an album of designs for armours made by Jacob Halder, the Greenwich master, for leading figures in the tilt-yard, display the art in all its careful detail. No less than three suits were made for Sir Henry Lee, one of which remains fairly complete with its bands of exquisite ornament, interlocking knots, strapwork, or borders of pines and pomegranates.[23] The grandest and most complete of all Greenwich armours, with additional pieces for display, is Cumberland's armour, formerly at Appleby Castle, now in the Metropolitan.[24] Looking at it we see that the whole suit of many pieces is covered with decoration, incised love-knots, strapwork, roses, *fleurs-de-lis* while the background metal is darkened to bring out the gilt etching more brilliantly, the effect of black and gold: embroidery in steel.

At Raglan Castle before the Civil War there was an immense armoury; today at Badminton we see portraits of sons of the house, Sir George and Sir Charles Somerset, their magnificently patterned armours setting off their handsome virility. Hatton's armour and Prince Henry's are still at Windsor. The splendid Pembroke suits, hardly less complete than Cumberland's, have joined his at the Metropolitan, where we can freely study them. John Aubrey remembered the armoury at Old Wilton as a very long room, previously the monastic dorter: 'before the Civil Wars I remember it was very full.'[25] Some of it had been captured at St. Quentin, but when the 1st Earl of Pembroke ordered his suit from Greenwich it cost the enormous sum of £500, the price of a small manor. Only the grandest courtiers could afford such luxuries, but theirs was a Renaissance world of display. Art and craftsmanship went as much into the arms as the armour: the finely tapered rapiers with the steel lace-work of their hilts, the engraved and inlaid pistols, the powder-flasks with their ivory and silver. Even the means of destruction were rendered beautiful by the overriding desire for beauty.

The familiar themes of this book are brought home no less by the jewelry. In the Middle Ages, apart from royalty and nobility, the Church was the chief repository, and exhibitor, of jewelry. The Renaissance extended its use to the secular world, and made it extravagant and ostentatious. The Reformation quite simply transferred the jewels, confiscated them from the Church, as with lands, vestments, plate: many a secular cup of the time is decorated with jewels from chalices, as many chalices were shaped into secular cups. Medieval designs and techniques continued to the end of the century; it was not until then that the rose-cutting of diamonds was developed to bring out their full brilliance. So the age was really the age of pearls, worn on every conceivable jewel, in the hair, in the ears, studding costume, even edging the prodigious outspread ruffs like peacocks in their pride. Since the art of diamond-cutting had not achieved its full potential, it was usual to foil stones, i.e. back them with coloured enamels or painted metals. Display was the note of the time, and everyone saw magnificence in profusion. 'Naive design and childish fancy, wrought in work of considerable technical skill in materials of real beauty, are not without their charm; but it is not the charm of great art. With the end of the reign the Renaissance art of goldwork reached maturity. Growing French influence and a later stage of development in England itself brought a stronger sense of dignity and proportion.'[26]

The initial foreign impulse again was taken up by the natives. Holbein gave a prime impetus to goldwork as to miniatures. There then followed Elizabeth's mainly French jewellers. Hilliard combined both inflexions in his own, but English, style. Miss Joan Evans allows that 'English jewels are the most national of all goldwork and have the defects of their qualities.' Gold and enamel were hardly less important than jewels: only in a few exceptions, such as Drake's Star-jewel, does the object consist of jewels alone. The foreign craftsmen are succeeded by English: Derick Anthony and Peter Trender by Hilliard, two Herricks – the father and uncle of the Caroline poet – Hugh Keale and Sir Richard Martin.

The upshot is that several famous extant jewels – whoever made them – are comparable with the best work abroad: most of them relate to the cult of the Queen, whose appearance and profile, no less than her fame, offered the artist the finest potentialities of subject. Thus the Armada Jewel, probably made by Hilliard, 'exquisite in design and workmanship, is purposefully thought out and carefully planned.'[27] The Queen is given the classic profile of an ancient empress, the medallion bordered in red, white and green enamel, set with square-framed rubies and diamonds. The back has the Ark sailing safely through the waves. *Saevas tranquilla per undas.* The Drake Pendant opens up to disclose a Hilliard miniature of her within; outside, an elaborate cameo of sardonyx with a Negro profile imposed upon a white one, the enamelled border set with rubies, diamonds and pearls, a grape-like cluster of pearls depending from it, then one huge pearl. The Queen had it made for Drake: a portrait of him wearing it came down in the family. Similar in style is the Barbor pendant, with small cameo profile of her outside, Hilliard miniature of himself within, a grape-cluster of pearls hanging from it. The Phoenix Jewel, now in the British Museum, comes from the early 1570's, is also based on a Hilliard miniature, with imperial profile wreathed in white enamel roses and green leaves, studded with pearls; at the back, the phoenix rising from flames. There are other famous jewels, the Lennox or the Penruddock, that do not relate to her. But we are reminded that 'the fashion for emblems fulfilled men's need of symbolic expression at a time when the medieval tradition of Christian symbolism had decayed in an age of metaphor.'[28] With the Reformation it was denied rather, so that the cult of the Virgin Queen offered a substitute.

Pendants in the form of a ship had been favoured earlier in Italy: Drake gave her one, which she gave to Hunsdon. It came to Berkeley Castle: hull of ebony, mast and rigging of delicate gold, blue-white-green enamels set with seed-pearls; in the ship Victory blows her horn, while Cupid crowns her with a wreath. The cases in which miniatures were kept were often works of art, of gold or *champ-levé* enamel in various colours, set with precious stones.[29] Fans were now first imported from Italy, their handles similarly jewelled; pendants in the hair became the fashion, but were dropped in the next generation. The Civil War saw an immense destruction of such jewels. Rock-crystal, rare before the sixteenth century, came into use; the cameos rivalled the antique in beauty. Jewels filled with aromatic gums came into use in the highest circles. A most elaborate pomander has come down at Burghley, one side of which opens out into six segments like an orange, with the name of the perfume on each lid.[30] When a globe-pomander of the time was found centuries later by a bargeman on the Surrey side of the Thames – lost by someone on the way to the Globe? – it still retained some of its original scents.[31]

Everything for display: as we see from the portraits it was the fashion, in the earlier part of the reign, for men of station to wear a gold chain, sometimes wound three or four times round: the design became lighter as they became more abundant. Watches, then coming in, were highly decorated. Elizabeth had over a score, one enamelled with the History of Time, another with a jewelled frog on one side, a pomegranate on the other – almost certainly a present from Alençon, her 'frog'.[32] The leading courtiers, especially Leicester and Hatton, vied with each other in designing such emblematic presents for her: those she gave away avoided the dispersal of the royal possessions in Civil War and Commonwealth, some came down in historic families to face the wider dispersal of today. The Philistine Puritans would have approved; all these things aroused Philip Stubbes's ire: 'at their hair, thus wreathed and crested, are hanged bugles, ouches, rings, gold, silver, glasses and such other childish gewgaws.'[33] He particularly disliked pomanders, with their exotic scents: no doubt he preferred his own sour smell.

These deplorably aristocratic tastes spread to the middle-class. If they could not afford diamonds they did at least buy 'Cornish diamonds' – quartz-crystals from the mines there, or 'Bristows' from the Mendips. The Cheapside Hoard, the stock of a jeweller or goldsmith found beneath the ruins of a house in our time, reveals what a wide variety of jewelry of admirable workmanship was available to citizens. And – what was an eye-opener – the geographical expansion going forward enormously increased the range of materials: 'emerald from Colombia, topaz and amazon-stone probably from Brazil, chrysoberyl cats' eyes, spinel and iolite from Ceylon, Indian rubies and diamonds, lapis lazuli and turquoise from Persia, peridot from St. John's Island in the Red Sea, as well as amethysts, garnets, opals and other stones from nearer home.'[34] Though this collection naturally does not vie with the famous jewels made for the Court, some of the pendants are sufficiently elaborate and delicate, little works of art. Throughout the craftsmanship is admirable, not least in those objects, the chains of enamelled roses and daisies, in which the native inspiration is most evident.

It raises the aesthetic question: what constitutes the English quality in English art? In so subtle a realm, where the ocular is a better guide than the argumentative – if one has an eye – one can only suggest, a certain restraint and modesty as against the brilliant audacity of French art, the torrential creativeness, the elegance and originality of Italian. The English are at their best in keeping close to the sources, and inspiration, of nature: this is true for the most fertile (and fertilising) imagination they have ever produced, just at this time.

We may regard the medals of the age as a specific Renaissance importation. Indeed the first portrait medal of an Englishman is a Florentine one of 1480. Henry VIII and Thomas Cromwell were similarly commemorated, while there are Italian medals of Philip and Mary (with the hungry look on her *dévote* face) and of Sir John Cheke togged up in Roman costume. Early in Elizabeth's reign a front-rank medallist from Antwerp, Stephen van Herwick, came over to make 'some of the most admirable cast medals that were ever produced in this country. His medals excel in depicting in unassuming form the features and fashions of everyday life of his time; the strong modelling of the features shows quiet assurance in seeing a likeness and adapting it . . . to medallic form.'[35] They are rather Teutonic and Holbeinesque. The better-known medals of Elizabeth are anything but unassuming. There is the Phoenix badge, which is a companion to the Jewel, an Armada Badge, and the Dangers Averted Medal, of the Queen in full regalia – all of gold. Several English medals were made to commemorate the defeat of the Armada – though many more Dutch (whom it saved) – besides Leicester in the Netherlands and Drake's Voyage round the World. The series ends in 1602 with the Minerva Medal at Windsor: Minerva triumphing over dragon and snail alike, with the paean, 'A thousand shall fall beside thee, and ten thousand at thy right hand, O Elizabeth, Queen.'

We have to see the glitter and colour of costume, jewelry and decoration against the sparse and somewhat sombre background of Elizabethan furniture. For this was the 'age of oak', and where medieval people usually painted their furniture Elizabethans more often left it in its natural state, rubbed it with poppy or linseed oil, or dyed it with alkanet root. They were very proud of their oak, which Harrison, with his usual patriotism, thought 'the most beautiful in the world for fine quality, rich colour and endurance.'[36] And they proceeded to enrich it as much as possible. The number of pieces was very restricted: beds offered the widest scope for design and decoration; next, cupboards, tables, chairs, chests – there was little else. Panelled framing had come in earlier from the Low Countries; now it was extended to bedheads, chairs and chests. Occasional variety was given by inlay in different coloured woods, particularly holly or bog oak. A rather tasteless introduction from the Netherlands were the bulbous excrescences given to table-legs and bed-posts, and carving was applied with undisciplined elaboration – strapwork, demi-figures, masks, grotesques. There is the *naïveté* of the age again; of course, when disciplined and restrained, the finest pieces were achieved.

The Great Bed of Ware, now in the Victoria and Albert Museum, is not over-elaborate for its monstrous size: it has a richly carved head with inlaid panels and caryatids, but the end-posts rest on a graceful open-columned structure.[37] Probably made for the Fanshawe house at Ware, it is famous for having been mentioned by Shakespeare.[38] The Cumnor bed – formerly at Sudeley Castle, now in the Metropolitan – has particularly good carving, with the uncommon feature of a concealed crucifix within the headboard.[39] A Devon bed at Great Fulford has practically its whole surface carved, the headboard with figures. The Sizergh Hall bed of 1568 shows more classic simplicity, the headboard of limewood panels with Renaissance figures, the elegant posts of French walnut. For walnut was an importation – only towards 1600 was black walnut beginning to be planted. Hardwick has 'the most interesting English table in existence': it has a walnut top, inlaid with musical instruments, notation, cards and other games, with flowers, fruits and a heraldic border with Bess's three coats-of-arms.[40] Other rarities there are a marquetry table with playing cards at the corners, legs of Doric columns with inlay; a walnut drawtop table inspired by Du Cerceau (like some of the chimney-pieces), with heraldic monsters as supports; Gilbert Talbot's classic chest with drawers, and a little iron ring to tie a dog to; a cupboard of oak and walnut with doors of an architectural design. This is quite exceptional, probably French in workmanship: further evidence of the great woman's search for excellence. For draw-top tables did not come in from abroad till the second half of the century – Protector Somerset was the first person to have one. (In those days power went with taste.) Writing cabinets originated in Italy, conquered Spain and France, but were very rare in England: people kept their papers and books and clothes in chests. Walnut is more frequently to be seen in Nonsuch chests – fairly familiar to us with their arcaded panels, occasional marquetry with the windows and turrets that reminded people later of Nonsuch as their signature.

Chairs were less frequent than one might suppose: often only two for the master and mistress – the mistress's might be without arms to accommodate her monstrous farthingale – other people sat on joint-stools or benches, as in a college-hall today. Tables that were works of art came in from abroad, their forms spreading from Mannerist Italy, or influenced by Continental pattern-books, whence they got their sphinx-supports or heraldic lions, which particularly appealed.[41] A number of marble-top tables were imported from Italy: novelties to place at the end of a long gallery, or opposite the fireplace as at Hatfield. There is a difference of inflexion in the foreign influences: in the West Country, radiating out from Exeter, the rounded forms of Southern France – coming in through trade and political connexions – spread in Devon and persisted into the next century.[42] One can see its peculiar richness in the pilastered panelling from an Exeter house now in the Victoria and Albert Museum, as well as in such a country house as Great Fulford or Bradfield. In the Home Counties the influence came from Flanders and Northern France, as one sees in Sir Paul Pindar's house: radiating from London, this had a much wider extension across the country, all the way to beautiful Levens in Westmorland.

The opulence of a great house appears in Shakespeare's description of Imogen's bed-chamber: the tapestry of silk and silver, the chimney-piece carved with 'chaste Dian bathing';

> the roof o' the chamber
> With golden cherubins is fretted; her andirons
> – I had forgot them – were two winking Cupids
> Of silver, each on one foot standing, nicely
> Depending on their brands . . .

Comically enough, it might be Bess of Hardwick's bedchamber. The visiting Duke of Württemberg in 1592 was much impressed by the magnificence of Hampton Court, fretted ceilings, tapestry, pictures, furniture: he thought none more sumptuous anywhere. This was a German view: a visitor from Rome or Florence, Fontainebleau or the Escorial, would hardly be so impressed. But all foreigners agreed on the pleasantness and comfort of English houses in general. 'The neat cleanliness, the exquisite fineness, the pleasant furniture in every part wonderfully rejoiced me,' wrote a foreigner early in the reign, 'the nosegays finely intermingled with sundry sorts of fragrant flowers in their bedchambers and privy rooms with comfortable smell entirely delighted all my senses.'[43]

There was a simply enormous increase in the making, use and display of silver, to an extent we can hardly realise. Individuals and institutions such as corporations, gilds, colleges, thought it proper to equip themselves with bowls, cups, standing dishes, candlesticks, snuffers, spice-boxes, what not – not only for use and display, but as investment and for prestige. Ambassadors sent abroad were regularly equipped with several hundred pounds-weight of plate to make a show; foreign ambassadors on leaving a country were often presented with as much. Every New Year a couple of hundred gifts, mainly of plate or jewels, were made to the Queen; the givers received plate in return. Wherever she went on progress gifts of plate were apt to be made. There was a perfect mania for the exchanging of plate as presents, spreading from the top downwards to the middle class; it was quite frequent for country folk of the yeoman class to bequeath silver that today would be worth a small fortune.

In addition, there were the consequences of the religious revolution, direct and indirect. An enormous mass of church-plate of every kind was nationalised, transferred to the state, was broken up or came into secular hands. Chalices were made over into secular cups; precious stones, especially the transparent crystals of reliquaries that had enabled the Precious Particles to be seen, were re-used for drinking purposes. Then, too, indirectly a vast amount of money that had formerly been given to the churches were freed now for secular investment, of which the two chief forms were lands and plate. Chalices were called in throughout the land, and the order went forth that in their place each parish was to equip itself with a communion cup: plainer but larger. This immensely increased the work for goldsmiths and silversmiths, so that a number of local centres prospered in addition to the accretion to the luxury industries of London. Norwich was an important centre, whose work came up to London standards. Exeter was hardly at all behind – we have examples of Richard Hilliard's fine craftsmanship, though John Johns provided many more communion cups, almost a quarter of the Elizabethan plate in the diocese.[44] Barnstaple was a subsidiary centre, with a goldsmith called Matthew producing work of high quality. Other towns, too, had their goldsmiths – York, Chester, Lincoln, Coventry, Bristol and to these Newcastle, Hull and others were added. There are hundreds of early Elizabethan communion cups in existence throughout England – Cornwall and Dorset showing about a hundred each, Northampton 126, Suffolk 233.[45] Norwich supplied the requirements of Norfolk; the four goldsmiths at Bury St. Edmunds those of West Suffolk.[46] Is it any wonder that, with all these factors at work, with its stability and prosperity, England became a haven for foreign craftsmen driven from their own countries by religious and social disruption? The leading Norwich goldsmith, Peter Peterson, was of Dutch descent, and much Norwich work reflects a Dutch accent;[47] after the Massacre of St. Bartholomew there was an influx of French craftsmen. Do we need any other evidence as to the increase of wealth – though we have seen that everything else corroborates it – or to the sense that contemporaries had that they lived in a fortunate island?

We must confine ourselves to gold- and silver-work as an art: at once we see the signs of the times, comparable trends, as in the other arts. Renaissance design comes in in Henry VIII's reign, in secular work: Gothic style prevailed in church-plate up to the Reformation.[48] But medieval forms continued, while Renaissance ornament was applied to the surface. In this field the new impulse came from Germany, and in particular from Holbein's work for Henry VIII. But 'a strong Teutonic flavour' continued in English silver through the century, not only through the work of German and Dutch craftsmen and through the import of silver, but from the designs circulated by their pattern-books and followed by native craftsmen.[49] Again one observes the English catching up, and Elizabeth patronising her countrymen – her goldsmiths were Hilliard's father-in-law, Robert Brandon and Hugh Keale. In her later years the German influence diminishes – it is not noticeable in the increasing number of cups; while simpler English designs are applied, like those of the embroideries. Dutch influence may be seen in the occasional sea-monsters that appear; one needs no source to explain the fantasy of the age when let loose.

The consequence is that by 1600 more English silver (like English cannon) was circulating in Europe than is generally realised. An unexpected repository, where more Elizabethan silver can be seen together than in any one place – short of a special exhibition – is the Kremlin. These are presents from the English monarchs to the Tsars that have silted up, though there have been some sad losses, in particular a gold cup set with a cameo of Elizabeth that would have been unique.[50] The most conspicuous objects that remain are a pair of big silver-gilt leopards of 1600, presents to the Queen sold by Charles I, a pair of great flagons embossed with sea-monsters and fruit, a pair of large water-pots or jugs, besides standing-cups, livery pots, ewers, cups, salts.

Salts were a characteristically English institution – I do not

know that the idiom 'to sit below the salt' exists in other languages
– and by 1600 they had developed new designs. The earlier
pedestal salt, on ball-feet, had a cover raised on scroll-brackets
for easy access to the salt. The bell-shaped salt had two divisions
fitting into each other, the upper being for pepper or spice, the
lower for salt. All covered with decoration, brackets, scrolls, masks
of animals, swags of fruit and flowers. There are exceptional
designs, like the Mostyn Salt – pedestal and ball-feet but shaped
like a cup – which has a German look to my eye, though made in
London 1586–7.[51] The grandest salts were square-shaped and of
elaborate design, like the Vyvyan Salt from Trelowarren in Cornwall. This has a French look, with its delicate painted panels
behind glass (*verre églomisé*), the cover elevated on slender scroll-
brackets and set with classical medallions, an elegant figure of
Justice on top.[52] The painted designs are from Whitney's Emblem-
book. This finest specimen of its type, made in London in 1592–3,
came back to London in our time, happily to the Victoria and
Albert Museum. The Stonyhurst Salt, of 1577, has an oval crystal
set under the bowl, probably from a reliquary, while the columns
of crystal use up over fifty cabochons (i.e. unfaceted gems), the
main fabric having originally been a silver-gilt pyx.[53] In the
Walker Salt at Trinity College, Oxford, the crystal stem encloses
a gilt Lucretia in place of the sacred relic; in the Holmes Salt of
1577 Neptune and Venus with *amorini* disport themselves in the
former reliquary. A beautiful mace presented to Norwich in 1550
is made of graduated prisms of crystal mounted with silver-gilt,
enriched with cabochons and pearls, probably from reliquaries.
A sufficient number of examples remain, even though 'English
jewelled secular plate of the Renaissance has so very rarely survived that only the inventories of palaces and great houses can
conjure up the quantity and variety which once adorned Elizabethan England.'[54] The greatest losses were, of course, owing to
the idiotic Civil War,

> When civil fury first grew high,
> And men fell out they knew not why.

The Parliamentarian leader, Sir John Eliot, was transported
when he thought of Elizabeth's treasury of plate. 'O, those jewels!
the pride and glory of this kingdom! Would they were here,
within the compass of these walls, to be viewed and seen by us, to
be examined in this place! [Parliament] Their very name and
memory have transported me.'[55] This was, of course, politics –

because Charles I had had to sell some of them to raise money. Elizabeth had no need to buy much – she received such vast quantities as presents, and handed them on; earlier in the reign she still had a supply of church plate to draw on, chalices, reliquaries, crosses, jewelled mitres, pontifical rings. She possessed ten gold cups with covers, toothpicks of gold, hour-glasses and watches of gold, an agate salt, silver-gilt pieces in scores. She did buy French gilt salts of Affabel Partridge, a silver-gilt fountain from Robert Brandon, tapestry-hooks of silver-gilt for the Privy Chamber.[56] Among hundreds of gifts Lady Sidney gave her a lapis lazuli salt in 1579, and Philip Sidney a crystal cup with gold and enamelled rings. There is no end to it.

We must, however, mention what is very characteristic of the time – the fashion for mounting everything in silver, not only rare and fantastic objects, but German earthenware, which was quite common. There is the brown Rhenish stone-ware, or tiger-ware, susceptible of a high mottled polish, and the Siegburg ware, cream in colour, like biscuit-ware. It was the fashion to give these stone flagons a silver-gilt pedestal, neck, cover and addition to the handle, all embossed and enchased. They did the same to beautiful Turkish and Persian earthenware, as well as to rare Chinese porcelain just coming in – as we see from the blue-and-white pieces, said to have been Burghley's, in the Tudor room at the Metropolitan Museum. Mother-of-pearl, ostrich-eggs, coconuts, crystal cups were similarly mounted and embellished. And though English imagination did not run riot in making cups regularly in the form of birds and animals, as the German did, there was plenty of scope for fantasy – particularly, and appropriately – in the form of ships for salts, or elegant, swan-necked ewers. One cup remains in the form of a Pelican in her piety, another in the form of a falcon. Figure-work is much rarer, though it appears at its highest in three splendid series of fruit-dishes executed in the late 1560's and early 1570's.[57] One set of six, made for the Montagu family in Northamptonshire, has a series of scenes from the stories of Abraham and Isaac, one each on a boss in the centre of the dish, surrounded by superb engraved decoration. Another such set by the same unknown maker is engraved with the Parable of the Prodigal Son. A third set illustrating the Labours of Hercules has disappeared into Collectors' Limbo. From their rarity and their sophistication one would suppose them, though made in London, to be the work of a foreign craftsman.

Pewter was in common use in all houses, except the poorest, and vast quantities of it survive. It varied in quality from the finest – an alloy of tin with as much copper as the tin would take – to the poorest quality, for candle-moulds and small commercial articles. The top quality was given a burnish to come as near to silver as possible; searchers kept standards up by travelling the country to punch faulty pewter with an arrowhead, though the Pewterers' Company also awarded a lily-pot sign or a strake for good quality.[58] Decent in design and workmanship as good pewter is, it hardly comes into the realm of art. The most famous object that remains is the Grainger candlestick (in the Victoria and Albert), with drum foot, highly decorated like silver, with delicate lines and lip.[59] There are other footed cups remaining with arabesque designs, while West Shefford church in Berkshire has an elaborate bowl of 1616 – domed foot, knopped stem, flowers and birds, the figure of the donor: 'What have we that we have not received of the Lord.' These things are the height of the craft. New developments in it were being made: from 1588 engraving, towards 1600 beakers and porringers, i.e. dishes with one or two ears to hold by, used as bleeding bowls, or for candles and possets.

New developments in earthenware were made by foreigners. Jasper Andries and Jacob Jansen settled at Norwich in the 1560's, and helped to extend the range of colours with enamels from the dominant medieval greens (from copper) to blues (cobalt), purple (manganese), red and yellow (iron and antimony).[60] The earlier types of decorative ware, jugs that came from West Malling church, followed Rhenish patterns. In 1571 Jansen, anglicised to Johnson, moved to London and set up a factory in Aldgate which employed a number of Flemish pot-workers and -painters, who turned out a mass of dishes, drug-jars, vases, jugs, tiles. The earliest Stafford ware goes back to the same time,[61] but a distinctively English ware does not appear until a couple of generations later.

Higher as art we may rate the Venetian glass made in London by Verzelini, 'whose name is deservedly the most celebrated in the history of English glass.'[62] Actually it was Jean Carré of Arras who was first licensed, in 1567, to make the new Continental glass in London. The growth of luxury is witnessed by the fact that no less than fifty shopkeepers engaged in importing crystal glass direct from Venice opposed the move.[63] But a wise government was determined to domesticate new arts and crafts in the country, whatever the opposition from shopkeepers and stupid workpeople (as in the case of the new draperies).[64] Carré called in Verzelini as manager and overseer; the good work prospered and in 1575 Verzelini was given a monopoly of the manufacture of Venetian glass for twenty-five years on condition that he 'teach and bring up our natural subjects in the said art and knowledge of drinking glasses.' The result is the group of beautiful glasses, so rare and prized today: the 'Dier' cup of 1581 (in the Victoria and Albert), engraved with the royal arms, animals and arabesques – could it have been made for that man of taste, Sir Edward Dyer? Similar glass goblets we know to have been engraved by Anthony de Lysle (probably from Lille).

The art of stained glass received a blow at the Reformation from which it never recovered: the destruction of glass with the monasteries, and subsequently in cathedrals and churches, was a terrible loss. (In excavations at Shaftesbury, not a large monastic house, three cartloads of shattered glass were found.[65]) In Elizabeth's reign it continued: at Durham the odious Protestant bishop Pilkington destroyed all the glass in the cloister because it depicted the life of St. Cuthbert. Later on, the Elizabethans began tentatively to revive the art on a secular basis, heraldic glass with scrolls and masks,[66] and Archbishops Abbot and Laud encouraged the Dutch painters, van Linge, to settle at Oxford where they did a good deal of work in college chapels and halls – something to repair the damage. But the Civil War put an end to all glass-painting. We see the spirit in a petition of the idiotic Women of Middlesex in 1642: 'We desire that profane glass windows, whose superstitious paint makes many idolaters, may be humbled and dashed in pieces against the ground. For our conscience tells us that they are diabolical and the father of Darkness was the inventor of them, being the chief patron of damnable pride.'[67] This is revealing. Nothing gives the inferior such a sense of their inferiority as works of art: this is the real reason why they wish to destroy them.

There was nothing to offend in wall-paper or leather-goods: more utilitarian, less a subject for art, more middle-class anyway. The sixteenth century saw the beginning of English wall-paper. Just as rush-matting was evolved out of rushes on the floor, so painted cloths on the wall were a stage in the evolution of wall-paper.[68] It seems to have been known as 'water-work': witness Falstaff, 'a pretty slight drollery, or the story of the Prodigal, or the German hunting in water-work, is worth a thousand of these bed-hangings and these fly-bitten tapestries.' The Painters and Stainers came together to form a gild in 1500, and received their charter in 1581. Early wall-paper was printed from wooden blocks in direct imitation of embroidery, but monochrome, printed in black on a buff ground. Old Tudor houses have turned up specimens, patterned with royal arms, roses or lozenges, sometimes used to line chests. The Ashmolean has a box of 1615, lined with paper of true English feeling in its arrangement of flowers and leaves, honeysuckle and acorns. By 1600 different types had developed, armorial, floral, formal, diaper-patterned; shortly flock-paper begins, more durable, designs printed with glue or oil, wool blown over the paper to stick, *papier velouté* from abroad.

Leather hangings were imported, particularly from Spain, 'Córdoba leather': vegetable-tanned, they could be gilded and coloured.[69] As such we can still see them as 'sling seats' or chair-backs, the latter often patterned in relief. Leather served for a wide variety of containers, for boxes, cutlery, jacks (pitchers, of which the largest were known as 'bombards'); bags, pouches, wallets; for jerkins, breeches, gloves, shoes; harness and saddlery; coffers, trunks, cases for many things, such as musical instruments. Bookbindings, with their gold-tooling, offered notable scope for art. Italy took the lead, to which France succeeded with Grolier (d. 1565) and has kept it ever since. 'Gold-tooling came to England during the reign of Henry VIII . . . but no distinctively English style was evolved until the 17th century.'[70] Here, again, the Reformation was responsible for a vast destruction, with Edward VI calling in all the medieval service books, forbidden to be kept under penalty.[71] Once more we see the Elizabethans setting about to repair the damage, picking up the pieces and making a fresh start. Connoisseurs like Thomas Wotton, Sir Henry's father, employed a French binder: hence the beauty and finish, the flowing lines of the patterns on his book-bindings. Good Archbishop Parker established a binder at Lambeth; he told Burghley that he had 'within his house drawers and cutters, limners, writers and bookbinders' – and we have seen that he employed Whythorne for the music of his chapel. Some splendid examples of his bookbindings remain, some of them in velvet with embroidery in gold and silver thread, rose-bushes, roses, snakes and flowers.[72] Burghley and his wife were both book-collectors and had good bindings. Leicester had a large library, with a preference for the French style in his bindings. French book-binders, like Jean de Planche, were established in London, several of them from Lyons. The English learned from them to improve their art, though their bindings lacked the finish and refinement of the French; they worked mostly in brown calf, morocco not coming in till after 1600. By then an English binder, Williamson, who owned the well-known stamp of a crowned falcon holding a sceptre which we recognise on his bindings, was the first to tool the title of a book on the spine. Modernity is beginning.

The only keyboard instrument to be made in England now existing was made by a foreigner in 1579, the son of an Antwerp virginals-maker.[73] It has the arms of the Roper family, over-painted by those of Hoby and Carey, evidently having passed from one connoisseur-family to others. As early as 1579 there was a maker of virginals at Leicester, Andrew Marsam – an unexpected appearance for the provinces.[74] The best known English instrument-maker was John Rose, who lived in Bridewell. The Ashmolean has a splendid viol made by him, painted with the Somerset arms; this has a baroque outline of toad shape, with wreathed mask on the head, the back has calligraphic lace-work as on embroidery or furniture. Another viol of his in the Victoria and Albert, simple and undecorated, was evidently made for a professional, not a courtier. Bologna lutes were considered the best, but even an Italian like Vincenzo Galilei admired English makes.

English craftsmen did not begin to make watches and chamber-clocks till 1600, though Bartholomew Newsam had already achieved a position as a clockmaker.[75] The British Museum has a fine striking clock of his that shows him a master of his craft: a domed and perforated top, with plates and barrels of brass. Newsam succeeded Nicolas Urseau as clockmaker to the Queen. When he died he left tools to another Newsam, clockmaker at York, the rest to his son 'with condition that he become a clockmaker as I am'; to a friend 'a striking clock in a silken purse and a sundial to stand upon a post in his garden', to another friend 'a sundial of copper gilt'. By this time the English had cottoned on to making time-pieces, and soon were making pretty watches.

Their time-lag in printing, for whatever reasons, was longer. Before 1500 some 360 books were printed here, but 2000 English books or for English use were printed in the Low Countries. It was not till mid-century that the country's needs were satisfied by its resident printers, a number of them – and among them the best, like Vautrollier – immigrants.[76] These, both printers and type-founders, helped to raise standards. From mid-century to 1583 the number of printing concerns in London about doubled, from twelve to twenty-three, and the reign saw some improvement in book-production – if not altogether in printing – typified by the work of John Day. A Marian exile, while abroad he studied the art of printing to good purpose. On his return Archbishop Parker gave him his patronage and support; the scholarly and humane archbishop liked the new Italic type so much that 'he made Day import specially an excellent fount of it.' As a result of their efforts to raise standards, 'now, for the first time, we can find books printed in England which do not suffer so greatly when compared, not with masterpieces . . . but with the ordinary work of the great Continental firms like Plantin at Antwerp.'

This went along with the increased use of good Roman and Italic types, in place of the old Gothic black-letter: better types were imported, there was no original designer in England. Day called upon a good artist to engrave his finest title-page, that of *The Cosmographical Glass*, designed by John Betts. This allegorical piece was so much admired that it was used for six more books. Day's most famous book, however, was John Foxe's *Acts and Monuments* – the Book of Martyrs that had a wider influence than any other book in damning Catholicism; in this as in other wood-cut illustrations the influence of Holbein continues paramount.[77] In the 1570's Hilliard was called in to design a couple of title-borders – it was a pity that he did not do more in this field. He had a distinguished successor in William Rogers, 'the greatest of the English engravers in the Tudor period, and a worthy peer of such foreign artists as the Hogenbergs, Gheeraerts, de Bry and Hondius, who worked for part of their careers in this country.'[78] Rogers will be known to readers by his elaborate engraving of the Queen, crowned and sceptred – and old – with vast far-thingale covered with knots, standing by a window, a chair of state behind her. Rogers comes at the end of the development – he died the year after her: with him English book-engraving at last reached maturity.

A. M. Hind thought it unfortunate that our earliest engravers should have formed their styles on the Netherlands School, and adopted the conventions of Flemish and Dutch immigrants – as with the monuments, we may add. France and Italy would have been better. But it was an advantage when it came to map-making and map-engraving, for Antwerp was the leading geographic centre, succeeded by Amsterdam. The foremost spirits there were closely in touch with London and the English geographers and voyagers. This had the effect of rapidly maturing English map-engraving – though here we trench upon the field of science.

Thomas Geminus first brought line-engraving into the country; here again his interests were scientific and anatomical. We may regard John Shute, with the illustrations to his book on architecture, as the first Englishman in this special field.

It was Mercator who conquered the world of map-making for the Italic script.[79] Even in the matter of handwriting we see Renaissance Italy overcoming the Gothic medieval world. The Italic hand arrived in England about a century after its first appearance in Italy, and it spread with the group of Cambridge Edwardian humanists whom we have seen to exert a seminal influence in other fields of Elizabethan culture.[80] Roger Ascham taught Elizabeth to become a practitioner of it; she was followed by Leicester and Robert Cecil, who both wrote beautiful, flowing hands, Burghley more crabbedly, Essex clearly, Ralegh idiosyncratically. It is interesting, and in a way appropriate, that that conservative man, William Shakespeare, should have kept to the old hand.

Ralph Edwards sums up that 'by the end of the Queen's reign, though traces of the Gothic still lingered, almost everything designed for use or ornament had undergone a complete transformation.'[81] And he points to 'the unity brought about over a wide field by the steady advance of Renaissance influences.' This is perhaps too strong for the Elizabethan age as a whole – as we have seen in its architecture, its poetry and drama: its very creativeness seems to have sprung from the fusion of diverse elements, in which the Renaissance represented what was new and modern.

CHAPTER VII

SCIENCE AND SOCIETY

T HE beginnings of modern science may be traced to the Renaissance. For some decades now there has been a tendency to overemphasise the medieval continuity in the sixteenth century, and it is quite true – as always – that most men's minds remained at a medieval level. But it is the minds of the elect who constitute the *differentia* between one age and another. There was a broadening of men's outlook with the discovery of a New World and the voyages into unknown oceans, a moving away from old moorings, an increasing restlessness of mind: the former moulds were to be broken, some of them resoundingly shattered. But the direct impact of the rediscovery of the classical world is as marked in regard to science as in any other field. Copernicus learned from his reading of Plutarch in humanist Italy that some of the Greeks had thought that the earth rotated on its axis and revolved around the sun.[1] Mathematics became the key to science, a quantitative construction of the cosmos; but modern mathematics derive essentially from Greek, not medieval, mathematics.[2] Even the sciences of observation owed something to that sharpening of vision which, allied to the analytical intellect, was to be seen at its height in Leonardo.[3] The rediscovery of ancient knowledge in science, as in architecture and the arts, provided a base for further explorations which transcended the originals. As the rediscovery of Galen and Ptolemy meant an improvement on much medieval nonsense about medicine and geography, so in the next phase Vesalius went beyond the one in anatomy as Copernicus did the other in astronomy.

Where did the Elizabethans stand with regard to the remarkable extensions and transformations of scientific knowledge in the century? What contributions did they make, and of what character?

We observe the same cultural lag, the marked speeding up from the 1580's as in other fields – the beginning of the movement to flower at the end of the age with such first-rate figures as Thomas Hariot, William Gilbert, Bacon and William Harvey.

Until then we are in the region of honest investigators of the second rank, true to the character of budding English empiricism, with such men as Thomas Digges, William Borough, Robert Norman, Edward Wright. We should begin with the precursors who pointed the way and laid out the programme.

The earlier humanist impulse produced work of distinction with Linacre and Tunstall. Linacre's importance is almost wholly medical, but it was European: he translated a number of Galen's works into Latin, his commentaries on Aristotle's physics and meteorology remained unpublished. Tunstall's *De Arte Supputandi* was a standard summary of arithmetical knowledge to date, without adding anything new to it. Since it was in Latin it had an appreciative public abroad; then, caught up in the frantic religious controversy let loose by Luther, Tunstall turned aside into the useless wastes of theology.

With the Edwardians we notice at once a change, in which Robert Recorde (a Welsh Rickard and a Fellow of All Souls), who came to grief in prison under Mary, is a decisive figure. Significantly, he wrote his works in English; they were immensely popular, and his new practical methods of mathematical teaching made him his country's chief educator in the subject for the rest of the century. Since he wrote in English, he was unknown abroad, though his work in this field was far more important than that of Ramus, who has garnered all the credit for a similar approach, somewhat later. Moreover, it is not generally realised that Recorde introduced a new feature, 'the most original and historically important sign = for equality'; the signs + and − he brought for the first time into an English book.[4] Other symbols he adopted from German mathematicians, Stifel and Rudolff. His critical attitude towards Aristotle's authority was more moderate and sounder than that of Ramus – it was more like that of Bacon later. Indeed Bacon might have written the words that admirably express Recorde's attitude to authority: 'it is commonly seen that when men will receive things from older writers and will not examine the thing, they seem rather willing to err with their ancients for company, than to be bold to examine their works or writings. Which scrupulosity hath engendered infinite errors in all kinds of knowledge, and in all civil administration, and in every kind of art.'[5]

Recorde was intellectually ambitious – one sees something of a kindred spirit with those other Celts, William Thomas and John Dee. He proposed to cover the area of scientific knowledge to date, making it known to the English in a series of books, and before his early death – though some of his books are lost, others were not completed – he had gone a considerable way to achieving it. His first was *The Ground of Arts*, the most popular arithmetical work of the century, which went through numerous editions. It was Recorde's admirable grasp of method that made it so, expounding general principles first, making their applications, then putting exceptions, meeting difficulties, with careful criticism of authorities. This orderly exposition, in dialogue form, was observed in each of his books. Even so, this did not cover all his interests: 'he was also a learned physician, an able Greek scholar, a historian interested in the antiquities of Britain, and one of the earliest students of . . . Anglo-Saxon.'

The sequel to this book was *The Whetstone of Wit*, the first English algebra, as *The Pathway to Knowledge*, of which Recorde completed only two of four books, was the first geometry. In the latter he segregated the theorems from the problems – an arrangement that made for more clarity in teaching that Ramus adopted later – and gave simpler and more practical definitions than Euclid, of whom he promised a translation he did not live to make. A book which dealt with mensuration, with descriptions of instruments and how to work them, is lost. But *The Castle of Knowledge* treats of the use of globe and sphere, and again was a pioneer English text-book on astronomy, where preceding works were translations or epitomes of ancient or medieval authors. Here again Recorde is the first to reveal his knowledge of Copernicus's thesis, with a tribute of respect to the master and a promise to go into it more thoroughly on a future occasion. To the objection of the scholar that the earth's rotation on its axis and its revolution round the sun are contrary to common sense and the consensus of learned writers, Recorde answers, 'it passeth far your learning, and theirs also that are much better learned than you, to improve his supposition by good arguments, and therefore you were best to condemn nothing that you do not well understand.'[6] Recorde undertook to expound in such a way that his pupil would be as earnest then to credit it, as now to condemn it. I think this shows where his sympathies lay; there is no real doubt that Copernicus regarded his position as no mere hypothesis but the truth of the matter; he submitted it to the judgment of mathematicians not of the ignorant. Even so, he knew so well the idiocy of men's prejudices that it took the heterodox Rheticus to impel the cautious Copernicus to publication.[7]

Recorde did not live to complete his promised *The Treasure of Knowledge*, which was to deal with the theory of the planets, and the practical application of astronomy to navigation. Or many others of the works he put into his programme, such as that on the making of dials, the origins and wanderings of peoples; but he did publish *The Urinal of Physic*, a practical manual of medicine, for he was a practising doctor. Besides this he made large historical collections and was an authority on coins and coinage.[8] As such he was made surveyor of the mint at Bristol, and surveyor of mines and money. A remarkable man, it was a pity that he should have ended his life in a Marian prison – though not before he had handed on a fruitful heritage. He was 'the pioneer in taking up the advanced educational theories of the 16th century and applying them systematically in a series of textbooks on the mathematical sciences.'[9] Like Ramus he emphasised order and method in exposition, the practical applications of the subject instead of endless disputation *in vacuo*, the dominant method in university education – with its excruciating results in both religion and politics. He had a continuing influence upon the Elizabethans; 'the great value placed upon applied mathematics by the Elizabethan middle class is one of the most significant characteristics of the age.' Among Recorde's followers are to be reckoned Thomas and Leonard Digges, Humphrey Baker, William Bourne and Thomas Blundeville.

That characteristic Edwardian, Sir Thomas Smith, had Copernicus in his library, but his real interest was astrology: he confessed that his passionate absorption in it was such that for some years he could scarcely think of anything else or make a move without it. Dee – more in touch personally with European scientists than any Englishman – was familiar with Copernicus and the latest astronomical thought on the Continent. He persuaded John Field to base the tables and calculations he published in his *Ephemeris* in 1557 on the Copernican hypothesis, since this had put the old ones out of date. Like Recorde he put off expounding the new view of the cosmos himself, and in his usual unsatisfactory way it is impossible to tell whether he regarded it as physical reality, though he realised that it was mathematically superior. There is no doubt that Dee was the best mathematician until the rise of Hariot: all the intermediate generation looked up to him as their master and several of them were his pupils.

He is indeed a transitional figure, far more medievally minded than Recorde, who was a complete modernist in outlook: Dee was ambivalent in his. On one side he shared the practicality of the English school: he was interested in 'the practical applications of astronomy and geometry, whether for casting nativities or advancing navigation, for reforming the calendar or mapping subterranean mines.'[10] On the other, he was imbued with the nonsense of hermetic philosophy, for ever chasing the will-o'-the-wisp of a monad to which all the diverse phenomena of nature could be reduced – it was as a by-product of this that he introduced the word 'unit' into the language.[11] Ultimately, this useless pursuit overbore the more valuable contributions he had to make, and tipped the precarious balance. So that his more useful mathematical contributions are in his earlier works, and even so *parerga* to other people's.

For example, he did not translate Euclid – that was done by Henry Billingsley – but Dee contributed a *Preface*, which is always treated with respect as having had an impact 'upon young men of the middle class . . . setting out as it did the ways in which geometry could advance technique and foster inventions.'[12] It was certainly programmatic, rather than strictly mathematical, concerned with definitions and the naming of parts rather than theory and exposition. The definitions are sufficiently common-sense: the principal kinds of mathematics deal with number, i.e. arithmetic, and magnitude, i.e. geometry. 'But that name contenteth me not' – and he goes off into an ecstatic celebration of Number, 'the principal example or pattern in the mind of the Creator.'[13] He considered geometry too base a name: it should be megethelogia'. 'A marvellous neutrality have these things mathematical, and also a strange participation between things supernatural, unmortal, sensible, compounded and divisible.' Probability and sensible [i.e. of the senses] proof may serve in natural matters, but this is not sufficient in mathematics, where only a perfect demonstration of truths certain and necessary will do. This is unexceptionable, but in Dee sense is so much mixed up with nonsense that reading him in the original is enough to give one Hotspur's reaction to Glendower. (It is likely enough that Shakespeare drew upon the Welsh *magus* for his portrait of Glendower.)

As with some other Celts Dee was his own worst enemy; on the other hand it is his acutely personal inflexion, with its paranoiac obsession – for which, alas, the world gave him good reason – that makes him so alive to us, when so many of the others are dead beyond recall. His writings are tingling with personal reminiscences. In urging the military need for mathematics in the ordering of ranks, Dee cites Northumberland's young heir, with his addiction to arithmetic on the field of war: he kept the rules in a gold case round his neck. Dee was close to the Dudleys: he pays tribute to the scientific interests of the young Warwick; but of all those able sons of the great man there remained only one bastard grandson to continue their talents, with his spectacular production in the next century, *Arcano del Mare*. This was Sir Robert Dudley who – such are the ironies of history – left England for Italy, to become a Catholic, recognised by the Pope as Duca di Northumberland!

Dee distinguishes properly between astronomy and astrology, and inveighs against those who refuse to allow the sun, moon and stars 'so much virtual radiation and force as they see in a little piece of magnetic stone. And perchance they think the sea and rivers . . . to run in and out of themselves at their own fantasies. God help, God help.' In statics he cites the propositions of Archimedes, such as that the surface of every liquor at rest is spherical, recommends the utility of the subject for gunnery and experiments with cubes, with demonstrations and theorems upon Euclid's propositions. He propounded 'pneumatithme', hollow geometrical figures which might take shape to enable two or three men to go to sea-bottom by keeping air under a big cauldron – in other words, a diving-bell; and 'menadrie', how to multiply force, for example, by a crane to lift weights. In 'thaumaturgie', the making of strange works, he once observed self-propulsion at Saint-Denis, in company with Orontius, i.e. the celebrated Oronce Finé. (Dee knew everybody.) He had seen wooden doves to fly, moved by secret springs. And then – 'shall the folly of idiots . . . so much prevail that He, who seeketh no worldly glory or gain at their hands be robbed and spoiled of his name and fame?' The idiots spoiled his fine library all right, as they did Lord Mansfield's and Joseph Priestley's later.

Dee dedicated his *Propaedeumata Aphoristica* to his friend Mercator in 1568, promising works he had in manuscript on mathematics, the planets, celestial globes, the perspective glass. (The Earl of Pembroke presented a copy from the author to the Queen.) He possessed a perspective glass, 'without which astronomy cannot be well grounded or astrology verified and avouched.' Dee's *Paralliticae Commentationis Praxeosque nucleus quidam* of 1573, with its trigonometrical theorems for determining stellar parallax, was recommended to the reader by Thomas Digges on behalf of his 'dearest friend and mathematical companion.' In fact Dee published little: his knowledge, his library and scientific equipment were all generously available to students, but he regarded knowledge as the proper realm of the intelligent and not at the disposition of ordinary people, let alone the ignorant whom he despised – as most Elizabethans did.

Thomas Digges was the strongest and most influential protagonist of Copernicanism, not merely as mathematical hypothesis but as physical reality. Nevertheless the greatest shake given to Aristotle's view of the cosmos came from the heavens themselves, with the brilliant super-Nova that shone in the firmament, brighter than Venus, for some seventeen months in 1572–3 before it became invisible.[14] This apparition upset everyone; to most ignorant minds it portended disaster, even Lord Burghley was fain to consult Digges as to what to expect. The super-Nova in Cassiopeia did far more to shake Aristotelian physics and cosmology to ordinary minds than any amount of mathematical demonstration, for was it not received doctrine that the upper firmament was changeless and pure, nothing new could disturb its finite and eternal constancy? Only what was beneath the moon was subject to change, hence the inferiority of the sublunary sphere. And yet it was obvious to all intelligent observers that the new star was way out beyond the moon. When it disappeared from view people's apprehensions were allayed and orthodoxy resumed its sleep. But they received a further shock with the comet of 1577.[15] Lord Henry Howard records the consternation at Richmond and the decision with which the Queen herself threw open a window to view it, with '*Jacta est alea*' (the dice is thrown).[16] Intelligent observers who had ceased to believe in the immutability of the heavens had been watching for a further test: here it was. For, with their improved perspective glasses, it could no longer be believed that comets were sublunary, mere exhalations of the earth's atmosphere, as was generally held.

Digges's book on the Nova, *Alae seu Scalae mathematicae*, was the best on the subject, highly regarded by the great astronomer, Tycho Brahe. Digges ended with a tribute to Copernicus, *nunquam satis laudatus*, and since it was in Latin, not English, it could be appreciated on the Continent. For the English reader Digges came out more aggressively in his *Prognostication* of 1576, in which he roundly stated that Copernicus had not meant his view as mere hypothesis but as fact, and answering Aristotle's arguments for the earth's stability. 'If therefore the earth be situate immovable in the centre of the world, why find we not theories upon that ground to produce effects as true and certain as these of Copernicus?' He proceeded to throw away the lumber of Ptolemaic complexities, the equants to provide for unaccountable irregularities in the movements of the planets, etc. It was not until after the turn of the century that Kepler, on the basis of Tycho Brahe's observations, was able to calculate the orbits of the planets as elliptical, instead of the perfect circles they were supposed to describe in the heavens. In fact Digges went further than Copernicus, in drawing the conclusion that the universe was infinite, and realised the huge size of the stars that followed from the acceptance of the new view. Digges appended to the book his own translation and adaptation of the core of Copernicus, for English readers, *A Perfect Description of the Celestial Orbs*. This had edition after edition, and was much the most influential manifesto of the new system. Moreover, the diagram that Digges drew to illustrate it became its most familiar representation to the Elizabethans.[17]

Digges insisted in this, as in all his work, that observation and experiment were the only way, theories based on facts were alone valuable. As Sir Charles Sherrington observes, 'A fact does not decay', with the implication, theories do. Digges considered that 'the ancients progressed in reverse order – from theories which were clearly false, to seek after true parallaxes and distances, when they ought rather to have proceeded in inverse order: and from parallaxes which have been observed and are known, they ought to have examined theories.'[18] This, of course, is the right way round – the way that man has progressively acquired knowledge in science. Digges set admirable examples of scientific method in his own work: 'his *Pantometria* was designed to teach the application of correct geometrical methods to difficult problems in surveying and all types of mensuration. His *Stratioticos* showed the application of similar methods to military fortification and ballistics.'[19] He intended to write a Commentary on Copernicus, 'by evident demonstrations grounded upon late observations to ratify and confirm his theories.' Here his hopes were frustrated. He had hoped, I think, to be able to use the Nova of 1572 to prove the Copernican hypothesis; but this was not possible, it merely demonstrated the falsity of Aristotle's physics. It was not until Kepler that the physical facts of the Copernican universe were confirmed.

Digges consciously appealed to the practical work of artisans, such men as William Bourne, as chief instigator of valuable work on navigation, Robert Norman who first demonstrated the dip of the magnetic needle, William Borough who worked on the varia-

tion of the compass, John Blagrave a leading designer of astronomical instruments, who proclaimed his adherence to Copernicanism
and constructed a splendid astrolabe in accord with it. We can
observe the gradual acceptance of the new view among informed
spirits and, though we cannot expect the poets to be among them,
John Davies at least knew what was coming to be accepted:

> Although some wits enriched with learning's skill
> Say heaven stands firm and that the earth doth fleet
> And swiftly turneth underneath their feet . . .

In the Cambridge quarrel of Harvey, Nashe and Greene, the last
two stood for orthodox, old-fashioned sense; Harvey was a modernist – that was one of the objections to him. Actually, nothing
is more remarkable about this mis-estimated and ill-recognised
man than the width of his sympathies. It was rare for a classical
scholar to be able to appreciate the work of mechanics and artisans; but he had their books in his library and pays them a
generous tribute. 'He that remembereth Humphrey Cole, a mathematical mechanician, Matthew Baker a shipwright, John Shute
an architect, Robert Norman a navigator, William Bourne a gunner, John Hester a chemist, or any like cunning and subtle empiric'
– they 'will be remembered when greater clerks shall be forgotten
– is a proud man if he condemn expert artisans, or any sensible
industrious practitioner, howsoever unlectured in schools or un-
lettered in books.'[20] These were not university men: it was
remarkable of the most academic of persons to perceive their
quality. But Harvey was himself an original man – who now
remembers the third-rate dons who disconsidered him and frustrated his ambitions? In the event, the English scientific school in
this early period was characterised by its painstaking, practical
and experimental nature.

Geography has its roots in astronomy; as astronomy was the
characteristic science of antiquity, so in a sense geography was of
the early modern era – as nuclear physics is of its end, the new
Dark Ages. In the Renaissance geographical knowledge was vastly
more exciting and obvious to the ordinary man than Copernicanism, which was grasped by few. Everyone could appreciate that
a New World had been discovered, new lands and seas were opening up before men's astonished eyes: it was unsettling, but immensely stimulating to the imagination. And also to science:
the recovery of Ptolemy was as important for navigation as cartography.[21] But the discovery of new lands transcended Ptolemy as

Vesalius's anatomy went beyond Galen. By the end of the age, Samuel Purchas was to regret that the ancients had not known the habitability of the tropics or the antipodes.[22] There was a close and continuing dialectic between the voyages and the extension of knowledge, and of a twofold character: not only the necessary discussions with the cosmographers, the provision of maps, charts, instruments, preparatory to the voyages, but the specific instructions to keep continuous observations as to course, bearings, stars, latitude and longitude (however unsatisfactorily, for the latter problem was not effectually solved till the chronometers of the eighteenth century), in addition to other phenomena of climate, anthropology, etc., and bring it back to the scientists thirsting for new knowledge. It was a period 'during which Englishmen of all ranks were forced gradually by circumstances to think geographically as they had never done before.'[23]

Once more we find the impetus released in the latter half of Henry VIII's reign, carried forward by a notable group of Edwardians to a significant expansion and improvement later in the century. Henry became keenly interested in military engineering as well as shipbuilding, employed Germans and Italians, like Portinari, on his works, and advanced native talents such as Sir Richard Lee and John Rogers.[24] His foremost cartographer, Richard Cavendish, made admirable charts of the Thames and Orwell estuaries, though it is not known who executed the pictorial map of the Channel coast, as informative as it is beautiful, now in the British Museum.[25] The Edwardians were ready to go further, and were closely connected with the Netherlands, which became the centre of geographical knowledge. As usual the new knowledge at first came by translation: Richard Eden dedicated his version of Munster's *Cosmography* to Northumberland, the promoter of the first voyage to find a North-East Passage to the Orient, which inaugurated the Elizabethan opening of the sea-route to Russia via Archangel. Later Eden turned his attention to the NewWorld, acquiring his information from Spanish sources, and adding original material from the English voyages to the Guinea Coast. He translated the most up-to-date manual on navigation from Spanish, then spent some years in France, acquiring the cartography of the school of Dieppe. The dynamic centre was moving northwards: Eden was a close student of Gemma Frisius, and annexed his explanation of determining longitude with a timepiece.[26]

An immense amount of geographical knowledge was acquired

by translation – virtually the whole of what was available, at first by Richard Eden, Richard Willes and John Frampton, later by the directive, organising energy of the younger Hakluyt. Such Protestant exiles under Mary as Leonard Digges took the opportunity to learn the wisdom of the Egyptians while abroad, and shortly the English were making their contributions to Continental knowledge. Humphrey Lluyd provided his friend Ortelius with a map of England and much information about Wales, while Anthony Jenkinson's journeys to Persia gave Mercator information for his world map of 1569. We might regard Lluyd's summing up of Welsh characteristics – some are recognisable still – as human geography. 'They be somewhat impatient of labour, and overmuch boasting of the nobility of their stock, applying themselves rather to the service of noblemen than giving themselves to the service of handicrafts . . . There is no man so poor but for some space he setteth forth his children to school, and such as profit in study sendeth them to the university, where for the most part they enforce them to study the civil law. Whereby it chanceth that the greater part of those which possess the civil and canon laws in this realm are Welshmen.'[27]

Celtic defects, as well as qualities, are evident in the geographical work of Dee as in other aspects of his mind. Nevertheless he was the chief transmitter of cosmographical and navigational knowledge from the Edwardians up to the rise of Hakluyt and the younger generation, the later Elizabethan school. He had introduced the globes of Frisius to Cambridge and absorbed information from a wider circle of acquaintance than any living person, from Sebastian Cabot and Richard Chancellor to Mercator. Thus he became the leading consultant in the voyages to find the passage, either by North East or North West, to the Far East. He was called in especially to advise concerning the Frobisher voyages, though it is not suprising that the leaders found his instruction too theoretical, while the instruments with which they were generously provided were beyond their capacity to use. Dee took credit to himself for two inventions, the 'paradoxal compass' and the 'compass of variation': indefinite and vague as usual, these seem to have been an adaptation of Pedro Nuñez' method of laying a course along a succession of rhumbs which would approximate to great circle sailing.[28] However, one would hardly care to trust oneself to the oceans under Dr. Dee's guidance: he had a fixation upon the Strait of Anian, which was supposed to obviate the necessity of rounding North America. On one of his charts he suggests an entry from about Hudson Bay to emerge somewhere about the Gulf of California.

When one reads for oneself Dee's *General and Rare Memorials pertaining to the Perfect Art of Navigation*,* one finds that it is more paranoiac than ever, and yet out of the mish-mash something emerges. There is a perfect obsession with the word British – he is himself the 'Briton gentleman', it is the 'British Kingdom', the 'British monarchy' – and in the end we owe to him the phrase the 'British Empire'. He took over from Spain the idea of a school of English pilots, which he advocated with his usual passion. It indeed seemed urgent enough, when Henry VIII had needed to employ no less than sixty French pilots in his service.[29] Yet such was the enterprise released by the Elizabethan expansion that by 1600 foreign countries were recruiting English navigators, such as Henry Hudson and John Davis, for the most arduous and remote voyages, to the Arctic and the Far East. While the visionary and transitional individualist, Dee, was superseded by the sober and indefatigable Hakluyt, a master of directed co-operation.

By the end of the century there was a marked improvement in the quality, as well as an increase in the quality, of English maps – from those of Humphrey Lluyd, say, detailed as those were. The Bodleian has a couple of his maps, that of Wales naturally more accurate than that of England: both very decorative, with mountains and woods in colour, delightful ships and dolphins at play in the Irish Sea.[30] The 1580's saw the first good detailed maps; based at first on Dutch originals English atlases gained footing, and by then London had become a centre for making instruments and distributing navigational charts.[31] By 1579 Christopher Saxton had completed his pioneer national atlas, a splendid work in twenty-one sheets still familiar to us today: he had been backed by Burghley in this patriotic endeavour, and helped financially by Sir Thomas Seckford of Seckford Hall in Suffolk, an Elizabethan house we can still see today on the road to Woodbridge.[32] Robert Adams prepared the charts of the Armada campaign engraved by Ryther – copper engraving achieved a clearer precision. A number of his charts remain among the State Papers, chiefly connected with the fortification of Plymouth and Scilly. He and Thomas Digges were employed in the difficult engineering problems posed by Dover harbour, where the imprint of their work can still be

---

* The Huntington Library possesses Dee's own copy, with his note: 'Trebon in the kingdom of Bohemia the 10th of November 1588. John Dee.' It has a fine plate of a ship in full sail, with 'Elizabeth' crowned, seated in the prow.

seen under subsequent layers. John Norden showed triangular distance tables on his maps, and was first to introduce roads into them. The admirable scientist Edward Wright produced a fine world map for the 1600 edition of Hakluyt. It was not until 1627 that Speed compiled the first general atlas by an Englishman.

Navigation was the first and indispensable science to the Elizabethans, because – as its protagonist, William Bourne, wrote – 'we lie environed round about with the sea.' Of the two parts into which it falls, the first, pilotage is empirical; we are concerned here with the second, oceanic navigation, which is scientific, dependent upon astronomical observations and calculations, involving mathematics. The opening up of the oceans added a new dimension to the science, posed a host of problems, practical and theoretical, in short revolutionised it. Naturally, with their discovery of the seaways to the Far East and of the New World, the Portuguese and Spanish school of navigation took precedence: English mariners learned directly from them, writers on navigation translated their books. The Portuguese had been the founders of the new school of astronomical navigation, but English sailing to northern latitudes, not only in search of a North-East or North-West Passage but across the Northern Atlantic generally, posed more complex problems. There was the variation of the compass, for example, which put seamen out of their reckoning, in some places, several hundred miles. There was the necessity of improved instruments for more exact courses, by great circle sailing, the complexities of global navigation, needing geometry, compared with which Mediterranean navigation had been plain sailing. There were oceanic currents to reckon with, taking ships off course, fog and obscured skies when observations could not be taken. Conditions brought forth the effort. Just as the exceptionally high tides Breton sailors had to deal with (which had surprised Caesar in his day) called forth the best tide-charts,[33] so the English school took the lead in regard to the variation of the compass, 'in scientific observation, experiment, and speculation.'[34] It is extraordinary to notice what a concentration of talents this field of investigation called forth and the further developments it inspired.

William Bourne, a native of Gravesend, no university man but a gunner at Tilbury, not only mastered the arts of gunnery, surveying, and navigation but wrote manuals of the first importance on these subjects. He was a propagandist for them, and encouraged other people's work at them; the whole cast of his mind was aggressively practical, he addressed himself to practical men. In his *A Regiment for the Sea*, 1574, he provided 'the first complete English nautical declination table'[35] – i.e. tables of the sun's declination north or south of the celestial equator, by which to calculate latitude – for the cycle of four years 1573–6, 'which will serve for twenty-four years without any great error.'[36] At several significant points Bourne was able to add to knowledge from the experience of the English in northern navigations – for example, his original chapter on how to find the latitude 'where the sun doth not set under the horizon, and also to take the sun at the lowest being due north.' He provided the rule with a diagram for ascertaining 'how many miles will answer to one degree of longitude in every several latitude', giving many examples of the differences of length at different latitudes. He realised that as yet longitude could not be determined instrumentally – a hope that inspired many books and tracts among the English (even our old friend Simon Forman came out brazenly with one in 1591, *The Grounds of the Longitude*) – but that the best hope was simply to keep 'a perfect account' by dead reckoning. On the variation of the compass Bourne recommended all masters to record the variation 'at every place they come to' – it would be a great help, empirically. At that date scientists did not know that even the variation itself was not constant but varied in the course of a century, the 'secular variation', so that one sees how complicated things were for their simple techniques and instruments. A characteristic of this book was that, with excellent diagrams, it instructed people how to *use* the instruments. It thoroughly merited its success as the prime manual of navigation for Elizabethans, and continued to be useful well into the next century.

Several people expressed themselves indebted to Bourne for encouragement, as he was indebted to Dee's *Mathematical Preface*, and he seems to have had a hand in the marked improvement of instruments taking place. Yet he wrote three more books; *Inventions or Devices*, 1578, expounds a large number of such, useful mainly for fireships, 'how to discomfort a whole navy riding, and make them slip their anchors', which was put into practice with devastating effect against the Armada off Calais ten years later. Among many other inventions – such as to enable an armed man to swim, with a girdle inflated with air – we learn that John Skinner, 'one of her Majesty's men, has devised a screw under the tail of any piece of ordnance to bring her to what level you list.'[37] Bourne devotes a whole section to gunnery, as he did a separate book,

The Art of Shooting. Waters tells us that 'the unrivalled reputation of English seamen as gunners' dates from these years. We observe the art all the way from the Armada to Trafalgar.[38]

His *Treasure for Travellers* is even more diverse, and it was 'important for many reasons: because it contained the first popular explanation of surveying by triangulation; because it was the first English book to describe the volumes, capacities, and proportions of ships' hulls, and the methods – based upon calculations of cubic content – of getting ships over bars or shoals; because it was the first to describe the sizes and weights of cordage, with rules for their computation; because it contained one of the first descriptions of the currents of the ocean, and explained in popular language the value of mathematics to the seaman.'[39] Popular language was indeed his forte; when one reads him one finds oneself confronted by an aggressively lower-class, Protestant anti-intellectual, with not so much an inferiority complex as an assertive pride in being but 'a poor gunner', and 'not learned'. He had not much use for useless aristocrats: he wished rather that all people of substance and living should 'practice something by which they may do some good upon the face of the earth.' He hated superstition, waste and conspicuous consumption: good old Bourne deserved well of his country, he was also something of a portent.

Bourne's *protégé*, Robert Norman – by profession a seaman and compass-maker – announced the important discovery of the dip of the magnetic needle from the horizontal plane in *The New Attractive*, 1585. This has been described as 'one of the first truly scientific books ever published in England.'[40] It was based on some twenty years' observations at sea and the making of many compasses: he found that after magnetising the iron with the loadstone 'the north part would decline downwards under the horizon', so that he was 'constrained to put wax in the south part to make equal again.'[41] Norman was also constrained to include a discourse on the loadstone and its magnetic properties, as also on the variation of the compass itself. At every point Norman based himself on observation and experiment. Theoreticians supposed that the variation was 'proportional' to the eccentricity of the magnetic pole; but Norman had observed the recoiling and coming back again westwards of the Pole between the North Cape and Vaigatz: it was 'very strange and against the opinions of all that have before written.'[42] In fact there was no proportion or uniformity in the variation. As for explanations, 'I will not offer to dispute with the logicians in so many points, as here they might seem to over-reach me, in natural causes.' Norman stuck to his observations and experiments, refusing to theorise – and actually it was in following these lines that the English discovery of the *secular* variation was eventually made.

Meanwhile Norman's discovery raised hopes in many minds that it would provide an instrumental means of determining latitude, 'just as it was hoped to use variation to determine longitude.'[43] Neither hope was destined to be fulfilled, but it gave birth to a number of books and tracts which do not call for treatment here. Norman confined himself to the practical, continuing to make his compasses and selling his invaluable book, with its chapter on different types and how they were made, from a bookshop at St. Magnus Corner convenient for seamen. Two years later he produced a translation and adaptation from the Dutch, *The Safeguard of Sailors*, a practical guide to the navigation of Western European coasts. It is fascinating to read the detailed directions for entering 'Foy [the sensible Elizabethan spelling for Fowey], a hard haven', for anyone who knows that harbour.

By the 1580's a whole group of practical men, several of them bound by ties of mutual respect and acquaintance, were engaged in advancing knowledge. Thomas Hood, a Cambridge man, did not disdain to carry on Norman's compass-work after his death. Hood devised a cross-staff of novel design of 'importance in the chain of developments, that led up to the modern sextant. It was perhaps the first nautical instrument devised to measure the sun's altitude by indirect observation.'[44] Hood explained its use in a tract with admirably clear diagrams. He also wrote a tract on the use of the splendid pair of globes, terrestrial and celestial, now at Grenville and Drake's Buckland Abbey – which the far-sighted merchant, William Sanderson, had constructed by Emery Molyneux, the master instrument-maker, both for the use of seamen and the instruction of students.[45] By this time another leading merchant, Thomas Smith, was financing a mathematical lecture by Hood for a similar audience, for whom Hood published various mathematical translations and tracts.[46] Robert Hues – one of the scientific circle of Ralegh and Hariot – outclassed Hood with a far more detailed Latin treatise on these globes, *Tractatus de globis*. An Oxford man, Hues accompanied Cavendish on his circumnavigation of the globe; coupling theoretical knowledge with practical experience, his work remained the standard authority for nearly a century.

William Barlow, a bishop's son, made an eloquent plea for just this combination of science with practice, and made his own contribution not only by his writings but by devising an improved compass, 'a model which remained in use virtually unchanged up to the 19th century.'[47] Thomas Blundeville was a prolific writer on these subjects, but in addition he appears to have 'the distinction of devising the protractor', for measuring angles.[48] To his *Theories of the Seven Planets* Blundeville appended an account of two instruments by which to find the latitude by variation, invented by his friend, Dr. William Gilbert. Later, considering that the use of these instruments 'will be too troublesome for the most part of seamen', Gilbert got Edward Wright to append tables, made according to Gilbert's *De Magnete*, 'by which the magnetic declination being given, the height of the Pole may be most easily found.'[49] These tables had been calculated trigonometrically by Henry Briggs, the first Gresham professor of geometry in London. The Scot Napier invented logarithms, to simplify arithmetical calculations; Edward Wright translated Napier's book, and with Briggs added further devices and tables. Apparently 'for the logarithms in most common use today, the world is chiefly indebted to Henry Briggs.'[50]

With Edward Wright we come to a Cambridge mathematician who went to sea with Cumberland specifically to apply his expertise to navigation. The result, after some years and discovering that Jacobus Hondius had appropriated some of his findings, was his masterly *Errors in Navigation*, 1599: many of them arising 'in the geometrical lineaments of the meridians, parallels, and rhumbs' described in the book, when a knowledge of geometry, or at least its application, was wanting.[51] One catches something of the contemporary atmosphere of excitement with 'the wonderful discoveries of this our age made to the furthest parts of all the earth . . . So much the less ought any notorious error to be tolerated therein.' Wright proceeded to correct wherever he could the errors from transferring global realities to plane charts, without geometrical reduction, which resulted in faulty courses. Mercator's projection, for example, was useless for high latitudes: Wright made his own projection, 'one peculiarly well suited to the navigational needs of English and other northern navigators.'[52] Wright's book 'by its chart projection introduced order out of the former cartographical confusion', and, packed with learning sifted by experience, was the best summary of navigational knowledge at the end of the century. By then Spain and Portugal, formerly in the van, had fallen well behind; while in Italy there was a marked decline of interest in these matters in the last quarter of a century.[53] The lead was with the English and the Dutch: the magnet indeed pointed northwards. Like the thoroughly competent mathematician Wright was, with a completely scientific mind, he wrote a number of other books covering the whole cognate field, surveying, cosmography, dialling and, himself familiar with the making of instruments, he gave valuable assistance to Gilbert's great work on the magnet.[54]

Perhaps the most original scientific intellect among Elizabethans was Thomas Hariot. He was born in the shadow of St. Mary's at Oxford, within sight and sound from All Souls where I write these words. From Oriel College, where Ralegh also had been a student, Hariot passed into his service as mathematical instructor. Thus he devoted himself first to the problems of navigation and cartography, and as its scientist accompanied Ralegh's first plantation in America, the Roanoke colony of 1585–6. On the basis of his close and objective observations he wrote his famous *Brief and True Report of the new found land of Virginia*, which was published by Hakluyt and afterwards by De Bry in four languages. It became the leading authority on the flora and fauna, natural commodities, people and their habits, of North America for the next century. We need only say of it here that it may be regarded as the first English work of anthropology, its method is so inquiring, objective and concise. In order it first describes the commercially viable products, then food and victuals with methods of agriculture – including here an account of tobacco, which became so important to Virginia. Next came roots, fruits, berries; then animals, birds, fishes; commodities for building and planting. Lastly, anthropology proper: the nature and manners of the people, their religion and beliefs, priests and medicine men, their diseases – he noticed that many of them died after being visited by the white men, evidently from infection. He expressed his humane disapprobation of the whites' too prompt readiness to kill. He learned enough of the language to communicate with the Indians and gather their ideas. His book, a marvel of compression, became a classic. It was based on notes and materials that were lost at Roanoke; we learn later that – interested as he was in ciphers and secret scripts – he drew up an alphabet in which to express the language.[55] John Aubrey tells us that the characters were 'like devils' – everything about Hariot was regarded as enigmatic, questionable, and slightly sinister.[56]

This is undoubtedly one of the reasons why so much of this great scientist's work was never published, was known only in his own circle, remained in manuscript, or was irretrievably lost. A mass of his mathematical papers has survived, but in inextricable confusion. The chronicle he wrote of the crucial early voyages of 1584–7 has vanished. So has the *Arcticon*, the manual of navigation he wrote for instruction for Ralegh's voyages. He applied himself to constant and continuous observation, and his mathematical knowledge to correct conclusions. He compiled the first table of amplitudes for sea, i.e. of the angle wide of due east or due west at which the sun rises or sets, given its height and declination, calculated by spherical trigonometry. He made continuous observations on the Pole Star, concluding that 'owing to the precession of the equinoxes, the figure [polar distance] altered by about 24' in a century.'[57] He prepared correction tables for every tenth degree of latitude, to obtain the true height of the Pole Star, from different observation points. Much greater errors at sea arose from the inadequacy of instruments, and the parallax of the eye in using the cross-staff. So Hariot designed several variants of a back-staff, for observing the sun and avoiding glare – though he himself preferred direct observation of the sun when rendered possible by mist or light cloud. Even so, this dedicated observer found his sight dimmed for an hour after one such observation. By his tables of amplitudes he made it possible to correct the compass daily at sea, at sunrise or sunset. Since they were for Ralegh's use, they were not published: not until 1664 did English tables appear.

This, alas, was characteristic of so much of Hariot's work, precursive and unrecognised. Hariot, like Wright, occupied himself with 'the problem of the plain chart . . . by which a correct course could not be laid down.'[58] Again, Hariot did not publish his *Canon*, but from a first draft that survives, *The Doctrine of Nautical Triangles Compendious*, it appears that 'he had begun the calculation of meridional parts (M) by the equivalent of the modern formula $M=K \log \tan (45°+\frac{1}{2}\phi)$ although the integral calculus had not yet been introduced or logarithms invented . . . A tribute to his mathematical genius.' Hariot was closely involved not only with Ralegh's plans for Virginia but with his hopes of Guiana: we find him making charts and maps for Ralegh's voyage of 1595 and in correspondence with Sir Robert Cecil, always urging the need for secrecy.[59] He had need to, for private reasons as well as public: he was unorthodox in his beliefs, he did not accept the biblical account of the Creation. Christopher Marlowe, who called Moses but a juggler, thought that Hariot could do better; the orthodox Nashe inveighed against 'the mathematicians abroad that will prove men before Adam.' Hariot had as much need to be careful in England as Galileo had in Italy – more so, because Hariot was involved with the dangerous Ralegh and the suspect Northumberland. At the time of Gunpowder Plot Hariot also was imprisoned for casting the King's horoscope for the 'Wizard Earl'.[60]

By this time Hariot was concentrating more on astronomy, with the aid of the new telescopes made for him by Christopher Tooke. Both Leonard and Thomas Digges had been interested in optics, and in 1585 William Bourne, at the request of Lord Burghley, gave the best account of the effects of the new 'perspective glasses' with convex lenses.[61] These revealed new stars and celestial phenomena never before glimpsed by the human eye. For one thing they confirmed these people who doubted Aristotelian orthodoxy; they enabled Kepler and Galileo to make their discoveries. In 1607 Hariot was down at Ilfracombe and in South Wales taking observations of the comet, and comparing notes with Kepler and Sir William Lower, a Cornish military man of scientific interests.[62] A year or so before Lower had reported to Hariot from Cornwall that the 'cylinder' had at last enabled him to see three distinct stars in Orion. Now he was greatly excited by Galileo's three-fold discovery, as to the irregular surface of the moon, like the earth's; the telescope's addition of myriads of new stars; the four moons circling round Jupiter. 'I am so affected with this news,' Lower wrote; he too had observed spottedness over the moon, but had no idea that they were shadows.

Lower followed up with 'We are here so on fire with these things that I must renew my request and your promise to send me of all sorts of the cylinders . . . Send me also one of Galileo's books if any yet be come over . . . Concerning my doubt in Kepler, you see what it is to be so far from you: what troubled me a month you satisfied in a minute . . . Answer other points concerning Vieta [the algebraist, Viète], Kepler and yourself.' We see Hariot as a key-figure, instructing his circle of English *savants*, while corresponding with Kepler and Galileo, respected by them. In July 1609 Lower reported the observations he was making, under Hariot's instructions, upon 'the moon in all his changes. In the new manifestly I discover the earthshine a little before the dichotomy; that spot which represents unto me the man in the moon (but without a head) is first to be seen. A little after, near the brim of the gibbous parts towards the upper corner appear luminous parts like stars – much brighter than the rest; and the whole brim along looks like unto the description of coasts in the Dutch book of voyages. In the full she appears like a tart that my cook made me last week: here a vein of bright stuff and there a dark, and so confusedly all over. I must confess I can see none of this without my cylinder.' In February 1611 Lower was urgent for more lenses, and reading Kepler has 'so thoroughly seized upon my imagination as I do not only ever dream of them [the stars], but oftentimes awake, lose myself and power of thinking with too much wanting to it.'[63] Lower has difficulty in understanding all the details, he needs Hariot to explain to him, but sees that Kepler has overthrown 'the circular astronomy', as Hariot stated.

Hariot himself had arrived at the notion of the elliptical orbit of the planets, and in the two years 1611–2 had made 199 observations of sunspots, by which he determined the period of the sun's axial rotation.[64] All without announcing his discoveries: think what a furore there would have been if he had! He had already had too much trouble from his dangerous associations, and the charges against his orthodoxy, to challenge human foolery superfluously. He agreed with Galileo, who had adopted the teaching of Copernicus many years ago and adduced arguments in support, refuting opponents, 'which so far I have not dared to bring into the public light, frightened by the fate of Copernicus himself, who – though he acquired immortal fame with some – is yet to an infinite multitude of others an object of ridicule and derision, for such is the number of fools.'[65] For years Galileo had gone on teaching the old out-of-date astronomy at the university, though he knew better.

Lower was justifiably concerned at Hariot losing the credit for his own discoveries – as he did. 'Do you not here startle to see every day some of your inventions taken from you; for I remember long since you told me as much, that the motions of the planets were not perfect circles. So you taught me the curious way to observe weight in water [specific gravity], and, within a while after, Ghetaldi comes out with it in print. A little before, Vieta prevented you of the garland of the great invention of algebra. All these were your dues, and many others that I could mention; and yet too great reservedness had robbed you of these glories.'[66] Secretiveness was probably in Hariot's nature, as well as enforced upon him by circumstances. But the faithful Lower was sure that there was yet more in Hariot's storehouse of invention, and there was.

The effect of all this upon an alert mind capable of appreciating its significance may be seen in Donne's immediate reaction:

> Who vagrant transitory comets sees
> Wonders because they are rare; but a new star
> Whose motion with the firmament agrees
> Is miracle, for *there no new things are.*

But the scientific truth is that there *are*, and it was therefore no miracle. Donne shortly drew one apposite conclusion:

> Man has weaved out a net, and this net thrown
> Upon the heavens, and now they are his own.

For it was by way of scientific observation and experiment, not by *a priori* theorising, that man eventually reached the moon.

During 1606–9 Hariot was in correspondence with Kepler, who wanted to know his views on the origin and essential differences of colours, on the refraction of rays of light, and the causes of rainbows and haloes round the sun.[67] Hariot sent back a table of the results of his experiments with thirteen liquids and transparent solids, with their specific gravities. He discussed the reason for refraction, and thought that the rainbow was explained by reflection on the concave superficies, and refraction at the convex, of each drop. He pointed out some errors in Vitellio's second table of refractions, and promised to exchange meteorological observations with Kepler over the last two years. Dr. Gilbert had recently died, leaving a manuscript *De Globo et Mundo . . . contra Peripateticos,* i.e. against the Aristotelians, and Hariot had read some chapters; Kepler had not yet seen Gilbert's work on magnetism.

Lower was right: Hariot did not publish even his fundamental contributions to algebra. From 1615 he was suffering from cancer on the face; nevertheless his scientific curiosity led him to write several letters in Latin to his doctor at Court, describing the symptoms and progress of the disease. In 1618 he was observing the comet of that year, and corresponding with Allen and Standish at Oxford regarding it. In 1621 he died, leaving a box of maps and charts to Northumberland – Ralegh having been executed in 1618 – and, movingly,'my two perspective trunks wherewith I use especially to see Venus horned like the moon and the spots in the sun.'[68] The rest of his telescopes, tools to grind lenses and two of his furnaces he left to his instrument-maker, Tooke. His mathematical papers and two big new globes he had borrowed from him he left to Lord Lisle – Philip Sidney's brother. He appointed Nathaniel Torporley executor of his mathematical writings, a proper choice since he had been amanuensis to Viète and could understand them, to consult with Warner and Hues where he did not. All his accounts with Ralegh, in a canvas bag, were to be burnt, alas!

The Reverend Nathaniel Torporley was a clergyman and, as such, could not wholly approve of the man of genius whose mathematics he could understand, if he could not the man. So he expressed his reservations thus:

T.H.

An an excellent mathematician one who very seldom⎫
As a bold philosopher one who occasionally   ⎬ = erred
As a frail man one who notably   ⎭

This gives one a tantalising reflection upon Hariot's private life; he was a bachelor, approved by Marlowe: did he divagate in matters of sex? What a pity he did not consult Forman! – but, then, Simon was beneath him, and he could cast his own horoscopes. The clergyman-mathematician indited *A Compendious Warning* against the 'pseudo-philosophic atomic theory revived by him [Hariot] and, outside his other strange notions, deserving of reprehension and anathema.' So Hariot, close friend of Ralegh, really was an unbeliever, an atomist, and had good reason to be silent. Yet Torporley did his duty by Hariot's algebra, and from his papers published his *Artis Analyticae Praxis* in 1631.

Mathematicians today pay tribute to Hariot's genius, and place him alongside Viète. 'Hariot's algebra is less rhetorical and more symbolic than perhaps any other algebra that has ever been written . . . Hariot admits into his system positive and negative numbers, but rejects imaginary or complex numbers . . . His *Praxis* stands out as a remarkable treatise for the beginning of the 17th century.'[69] Cajori tells us that Hariot 'brought the theory of equations under one comprehensive point of view, by grasping that truth in its full extent to which Viète and Girard only approximated: namely, that in an equation in its simplest form, the coefficient of the second term with its sign changed is equal to the sum of the roots; the coefficient of the third is equal to the sum of the products of every two of the roots, etc. He was the first to decompose equations into their simple factors . . .'[70] His work was no less important in the development of mathematical notation. Though we cannot here go into it in detail, some of his usage prevailed and became standard in mathematics today: for example, his signs $<$ $>$ for 'less than' and 'greater than'.[71] Where Viète had used capital letters, Hariot used more conveniently small letters, as we do today. He used the dot for multiplication, for example, 2.ccc. This received no attention in his own century, even from Wallis, who stood on Hariot's shoulders; but in the eighteenth century it was generally adopted, with no credit to Hariot, as usual.

However, Wallis accused Descartes of adopting Hariot's theory of equations, without acknowledgment. In the Bodleian copy of the *Praxis* – given by Bess of Hardwick's son, Charles Cavendish – Wallis has a note: 'This treatise of Mr. H.'s was (it seems) so well liked by Descartes that he hath in a manner described the whole of it for the substance (though in other order and words) into his Geometry (but without so much as naming the author): which was first published in the year 1637 in French, six years after this [*the Praxis*] was first extant. There were many other worthy pieces of Hariot's doing left behind him and well worth the publishing.' It was Hariot's own fault that he got no credit for his work: he should have adhered to the principle, 'Publish, and be damned.' As for charges of plagiarism, so common in the history of science, the explanation is simple: several people are working out the same ideas at the same time.

Today we are promised further research from the mass of papers Hariot left behind him. 'He was led to develop important and highly original theories of the conformality of stereographic projection [a long-winded way of stating what I have said above about charts], the rectification and quadrature of the logarithmic spiral, the exponential series and interpolation formulae, and to apply these results to his great unpublished logarithmic tables of meridional parts of 1614.'[72] Let that be as it may be, his *Praxis* 'set down algebra in its modern literal form, virtually that familiar to pupils of elementary mathematics today.' Of his work on projectiles and impact 'very little has so far been analysed . . . He described and proved not only the parabolic orbit of projectiles, but also the tilted parabolic orbit . . .' On impact there exists his manuscript, prepared for the press, *De Motu et Collisione Corporum.* 'His work on specific gravities and weighings in fluids has also not been studied in any detail.'

Hariot's is really a very curious case – not unlike the discovery of Hopkins' poetry in our time. Though his name is unknown to the general public that knows the names of Kepler, Galileo and Bacon, there is little doubt that this secretive, taciturn man was the most searching, the widest ranging and the most original intellect among Elizabethan scientists.

Dr. William Gilbert, by contrast, was a well-known public figure and received ample recognition in his own time. For one thing he was the most eminent doctor in London, a leading figure in the Royal College of Physicians, of which he was President in 1599, and became personal physician to the Queen in 1601, whom he attended in her last illness. For another, he published his great work, *De Magnete*, in his lifetime in 1600. On the other hand, he left a second work of hardly less, and more varied, interest – the *De Mundo* to be published posthumously; while all the papers, instruments, globes, cabinets of minerals, which he left to the College of Physicians, perished in the Fire of London. The records of a long series of chemical experiments which he conducted are now lost. So that of him too we know much less than we could wish. He was a grumpy, crusty bachelor – it is revealing to think of the achievements of those philosophic bachelors, Hariot, Hobbes, Locke, Newton, without the impedimenta of wives and children. Their children were their works. Gilbert's portrait shows a stoutly built, very masculine, somewhat constipated figure, with wide-awake eyes, giving nothing away – except his intellectual interests, hand on globe, compass on table. He, too, was in correspondence with the European *cognoscenti* of the time – it is a regrettable loss that the letters between him and Fra Paolo Sarpi have been destroyed – and he received the tribute of a famous couplet from Dryden:

> Gilbert shall live till loadstones cease to draw,
> Or British fleets the boundless ocean awe.

To understand his work and appreciate his importance we must visualise the excitement generated by the phenomena of magnetism at the time. Gilbert laid the foundations of electrical science – he introduced the word into the language – and was feeling his way towards the concept of gravitation. From a study of his works it seems that he was no more orthodox than Hariot: that may partly account for the element of tension present, and he was altogether more aggressive. Only those who have read Gilbert know how exasperated he was by people's stupidity, the repetition ol accepted commonplaces instead of going to the facts, the contempt he had not so much for the mob (all Elizabethans had that) as for the ordinary run of academics, the professors hanging on to Aristotle contrary to the evidence, theorisers and doctrinaires. Himself was interested only in facts. He must have been a rather uncomfortable man to know.

Born at Colchester in 1540, he went to St. John's College, Cambridge – nursery of so many earlier Elizabethans – and followed this with foreign travel, including a spell in Italy. Though his profession was medicine, his intellectual interests from early on were more generally scientific: his first observations of a comet were at Cambridge, 2–12 November 1569, followed by those of the Nova in 1572, and again in 1577–8.[73] He was writing down his *meteorologia* probably in the early 1580's, his *physiologia* in the 1590's. In London he lived on St. Peter's Hill, near Upper Thames Street, where, in addition to his fellow-physicians, he had a more select company of practical scientists, artisans, instrument-makers. The company he sought were those who were experts in navigation, and the instruments he depended upon were nautical. He retained his contacts with Colchester, died there – in the plague-year 1603 – and was buried in Holy Trinity church (where John Wilby joined him some years later).

Sarton describes Gilbert's *De Magnete* as 'one of the greatest books of Science.'[74] It certainly is a book of power and originality, of marked homogeneity and thoroughness, of striking character corroborative of the man. The first (and last) thing to notice is that it is based mainly on experiments, some three hundred of them. Gilbert had also read the entire literature of the subject, but mostly to dismiss previous speculations about magnetic and electrical phenomena as fanciful nonsense, not vouched for by observation or experiment. He is particularly hard on Aristotle's physics, though a number of contemporaries come in for his reprobation for their unsupported speculations, Fracastorio, Ficino, Paracelsus, Cornelius Agrippa, Cardan, Scaliger. He may be aligned with the anti-Aristotelian school of Telesio and Patrizzi – in that like Bacon; but he hardly mentions them, Patrizzi only twice.[75] He was rather an isolated figure, with a strongly individualistic temper. There seems to have been no co-operation between him and Hariot, for example: a pity, for Hariot could have helped him with his mathematics. But Gilbert's interests were not so much academic as technological: he was interested mainly in physical experiments, nautical instruments and navigation, mining and metallurgy. In his sphere he, too, was a portent of the future of Britain.

His mind was severely utilitarian. He disliked theorising and was quick to deride theorists. And yet, in the end – so variable is nature – he opened himself to just this charge: he could not resist erecting the deductions he so accurately and with such patience drew from his experiments into a general magnetic philosophy, with the earth itself operating as a magnet (though he mistakenly connected its field of force as such with the fact of its diurnal rotation). He thereby earned Bacon's stricture upon him for the very thing he disliked in others – making a general system out of his experimental findings, in themselves admirably scientific. Bacon was not the one to let such an arguing point pass.

However, the bulk of his work was experimental and objectively observational. Zilsel tells us that several of his devices are still in use, his discovery that to dress the poles of his loadstones with iron made them more effective: that is, his invention of the armature of magnets. One of his invented instruments was 'the first of its kind in the history of physics – an electroscope, still somewhat imperfect, constructed after the pattern of the magnetic needle.'[76] His book is a classic of scientific method and construction. Zilsel sums it up as 'the first printed book written by an academically trained scholar and dealing with a topic of natural science, which is based almost entirely on actual observation and experiment.' It preceded by a few years both Galileo and Kepler. But it is not easy to assess Gilbert: 'he is usually as critical-minded as a modern experimentalist, does not rely on any authority, and always tests reports of others by his own experiments.'

The book came out with a Preface by Edward Wright which was a manifesto for the new science – it was by favour of the magnetic compass that a whole new continent had been discovered. Wright was a whole-hearted Copernican, but in this book Gilbert confined himself to accepting the diurnal rotation of the earth.[77] Gilbert followed with an outspoken Preface complaining how difficult it was to win support for anything new: his doctrine of magnetism contradicted most of the received axioms of the Greeks. So be it. Book I proceeded to expose in detail the nonsense hitherto thought and taught on the subject, for example, St. Augustine's myth that the diamond would take away iron from the magnet. All this was a rational clearing of the ground, with a perhaps salutary arrogance, along with a good deal of unexpected information, such as that the Chinese knew that the tails of comets were turned away from the sun. Gilbert knew that comets were not sublunary exhalations of the atmosphere, but were above the moon, in the supposedly perfect and immutable heavens. There follows a thorough investigation of iron, its mining and metallurgical qualities, and medicinal uses. As opposed to the alchemists' fixation on gold, Gilbert thought of iron as the first of metals, with its polarity like loadstone – of which a large quantity had been recently discovered in a Devon mine of Adrian Gilbert's – and being of one substance with the earth itself. All the movements of the loadstone are in conformity with geometry and the form of the earth (an Aristotelian concept he could not do without), and controlled thereby. He constructed a little Earth, a terrella, by which to demonstrate these forces and movements – this word also, and 'verticity', he contributed to the language.

Book II contains most of what Gilbert has new to offer. Aristotle admitted only two basic motions, of light objects upwards and heavy objects downwards. Gilbert enumerated five. To refer the metals to their respective planets was the notion of raving astrologers and simpletons. He distinguished, by many experiments, the loadstone's properties from those of amber (electron). Not only amber but many substances attract light bodies – jet, diamond, rock crystal, hardened wax; best when dry, they lose their electric attraction when wet. All bodies are attracted by electrics save in flame or fire, or when too rarefied; but many electrics do not attract till rubbed. Without friction few bodies give out their natural electric effluvium. The loadstone attracts only magnetic bodies, electrics attract everything; but what is it that produces movement – something imperceptible flowing out of the substance? He had noticed that electric power was at its best, in England, in a dry east wind. He discovered that electric actions would not pass through flame, while magnetic actions would; that electric actions could be screened off by interposing the thinnest layer of fabric, while magnetic actions would penetrate thick slabs of every material except iron. He found that the specific amount of magnetism was greater if the loadstone were elongated in shape. Kelvin summed up that Gilbert's *orbis virtutis* is simply his expression 'for what Faraday called the field of force, that is the space round a magnet in which magnetic force is sensibly exerted on another magnet . . . Gilbert's word *virtue* expresses even more clearly than Faraday's word *force* the idea urged so finely by Faraday, that there is a real physical action of a magnet through all the space round it, though no other magnet be there to experience force and show its effects.'[78] We see that Gilbert's experiments laid the foundations of electromagnetism: it would seem that, with the existing means and instruments as a limiting factor, he could hardly have gone further than he did.

Subsequent Books deal with the use of magnetic needles, the direction of the compass, the discovery that its variation is not constant, on the dip of the needle. Gilbert concludes with a Book on the globe of the earth as a loadstone. He was convinced that the moon was in accord with the inner parts of the earth by its nearness and likeness of form. He regarded the earth's centre as the centre of its magnetic movements, which he correlated with its rotatory motion, as to which he constantly quotes Copernicus against Aristotle. He concluded that 'all magnetics conform themselves to the globe of the earth in the same ways and by the same laws by which another loadstone or any magnetics do to a terrella' – the model he had constructed for demonstration.[79]

In the *De Mundo* Gilbert went further in two important respects. He described earth and moon as each affecting the other, the earth more effectually owing to its greater mass. He accepted Copernicus's wider system of the course of the planets round the sun, and his discovery of the anomalies in the motion of the earth's axis; along with a good deal of downright abuse of fools, particularly learned fools, for not seeing the point he has a generous tribute to Copernicus as 'the restorer of astronomy'.

It is this consideration that makes me think that the *De Mundo* consists partly of later and partly of earlier work, and this may be supported by the fact that on the title-page we are told that the work is edited from two manuscripts.* In the *De Mundo* Gilbert's conception of the universe is more fully expounded and better integrated. He expanded his view of the similarity between earth and moon into several chapters, with a description of its surface, a map of it, and an account of its motion around the earth. Only in the *De Mundo* did he state that the planets revolved round the sun: this marked further progress upon the *De Magnete*. He denied Aristotle's view that the universe was made up of four basic elements – earth, water, air, fire – which had been fundamental in the whole of European thought. He considered earth as basic, a pure magnetic substance, of which other things, winds and clouds, were effluvia. All the stars were globes with their effluvia (atmosphere), and between them was void. There were two classes, the light-giving globes and those which do not give out light. He regarded the earth's light as a reflection of the sun's. There were many globes too far away to be seen. The fixed stars, furthest from the earth were *not* attached to any sphere and did not move round the earth. He located comets beyond the moon and used their existence to deny planetary spheres and fixed star

---

* *De Mundo nostro Sublunari Philosophia Nova*, Amsterdam, 1651 – 'ex duobus mss. codicibus editum.' It would be a service to the history of science if this important book were translated and edited with notes.

spheres. He accepted Democritus's view of the Milky Way as a collection of many stars.

In electro-magnetism he expounded his views further. His basic position was that matter attracted portions of matter like to itself: hence the interaction among planets and stars. He put a definite boundary to the earth's atmosphere, with a void beyond. He looked to magnetism to account for the daily rotation of the earth and the captive orbiting of the moon, and for the earth or other celestial bodies to attract like bodies, thus accounting for falling bodies like meteors. We must remember that all this was written before 1603, some years before Galileo. It is not fanciful to say that Gilbert was well on the way to Newton.

Book IV dealt with the winds and spectrum of the rainbow, springs and waters – about which he had collected a good deal of information from all over Britain – the tides, with the pulls of both moon and sun, and the saltness of the sea. He denied that the Flood had formed the mountains, and derided the view of the mob (*vulgus*) that fossil forms had been left by the flood. When one thinks that this nonsense continued right up to the nineteenth century, one sees what a very modern mind Gilbert's was and how much before his time. When one compares him for example with the unquestioning, traditional views of the cosmos that writers like Spenser or Shakespeare accepted . . . we are already in a different world: the world of the Royal Society after the Civil War. Gilbert wrote contemptuously of the belief, still accepted by almost everybody, of the immutable firmament, 'as if it were the habitation of the gods' – he did not dare to say God, as everybody believed. We shall observe the mountainous obstruction to science and sense raised by the Bible in people's minds; in general it was too much for them to scale, but it does not seem to have meant much to Gilbert or Hariot.

We do not need to go in detail into the small flood of works that accompanied and followed Gilbert's. They all acknowledged him as the master; they had no original contributions to make, but some made refinements upon his experiments, useful corrections or distinctions, while they provide information as to the progress of science abroad. Around 1600 was a watershed: one is on the threshold of the scientific century.

Mark Ridley, for example, in his *Short Treatise of Magnetical Bodies and Motions*, 1613,[80] registers for us how difficult it had been hitherto to believe the earth's motion, yet now Galileo and Kepler

have observed by telescope that Jupiter rotates upon its axis in
less than a day, with four moons revolving round him, and that
Venus moves round the sun in ten months. The new science of
magnetism was something the ancients never guessed, that polarity was to be found in the earth's globe and in a round loadstone.
Ridley took patriotic pride in Norman's discovery of the dip of
the needle, and included in his book Henry Briggs's table of degrees and minutes of the angles of the inclinatory needle with the
horizon, calculated for every elevation of the Pole. How important
this was for more exact navigation we know from various stories
of how far out of course seamen often found themselves. Ridley
added a recommendation of his own maker and capper of loadstones, which reminds us, as several of these works do, of the number of instrument makers that had grown up in London by 1600.

William Barlow, prebendary of Winchester – of the episcopal
family which did so well out of the Reformation – animadverted
against Ridley in a most unchristian spirit: one thing at issue was
their respective closeness to the great Gilbert. Barlow was the
nephew of Roger Barlow, the Henrician pioneer in the navigation
to South America; though the nephew detested the sea, he had a
lifelong interest in the scientific problems of navigation. He dedicated his book – *Magnetical Advertisements*, 1616 – to Sir Dudley
Digges, a leader among the group in the City forwarding these
interests and backing new voyages of discovery. Barlow had been
converted to the new science of magnetism by Gilbert's book,
though he totally disagreed with its Book VI endeavouring to
prove the earth's rotation by its magnetic force. Many gentlemen
were anxious for a translation of the *De Magnete*, but few were
competent to undertake it for they could not understand it. Barlow claimed that his experiments registered a further distinction
between magnetic bodies, which exhibited a mutual attraction,
and electrical bodies where power resided only in the body itself,
not in the thing attracted. Barlow backed his own Winchester
workman for the making of loadstones – Gilbert had had his fashioned and capped by him. A good deal of Barlow's book was
practical, about needles, compasses, loadstones, their making and
qualities. He quotes a letter from Gilbert expressing pleasure at
'the wonderful liking of my book' among the *cognoscenti* of Venice
and Padua – this would have included the young Galileo, who
became professor of mathematics there in 1592.[81]

We learn something more from Ridley's reply, *Magnetical
Animadversions, 1617*. Some time before Gilbert's death a powerful

magnet was fashioned that took up an anchor of 24 lb. weight, though 'with what great variety of tricks and devices did they wonderfully content the common people.' It was now becoming realised in the universities that Aristotle's anatomy and astronomy were both at fault. Nor was there any doubt that the earth is not the centre of the universe, but that the sun is. Edward Wright had been an instructed Copernican from his youth up – he had been a Fellow of Caius, 1587–96 – while Gilbert had not plumbed the depths of Copernicus. Here Wright had helped him, and contributed Book IV, chapter 12; he had not written the controversial Book VI, on the earth's rotation and magnetism. This is significant: it reveals that Gilbert was weak on the side of mathematics: his interests were in physics, metallurgy and technology.

There is no reason to suppose that we have not got the whole of Bacon's thought, because he left several of his works incomplete, others mere sketches. For in fact they are very repetitive: he repeats over and over what he thinks, almost compulsively, such was his intellectual urgency and absolute conviction that he was right. His writings were much broken into by the pursuit, and the work, of office – no Elizabethan could resist its lure, though in moments of truth Bacon knew that he was made for a literary, rather than a political, career, that he was an intellectual rather than a practical politician. We should keep in mind, therefore, the date and circumstances of his writings, and remember that some – that on the tides, for instance – are early and before Galileo had written; others date from the last five years of his life, when disgrace released him (reluctantly) to devote himself to the more lasting works of the mind. These are more mature, more fully informed of the progress made by science. Nevertheless all his writings, however diverse in form and subject, have a remarkable unity: he is always after the same thing, urging the same campaign. His crowded life did not leave him time to make many specific contributions to science, but his influence on its development was prodigious, especially in Britain, and to a lesser extent overseas.

In fact, though he respected the mechanical arts far more than he did theorising, systems of philosophy, he did not aim at making advances and discoveries in the mechanical arts and sciences himself so much as laying out a programme in which all could take part co-operatively in advancing science – in this a precursor of today – and on the basis of this work to erect something like a system of general scientific thought. (His dislike of philosophical systems was so great that one hesitates to use the phrase, a 'philosophy of science'.) His attitude of mind is made clear over and over again, nor is it so difficult to place him in the history of thought. He also was anti-Aristotelian, though more moderately so than Gilbert – he pointedly says that he is anxious to retain the best of the past while advancing new knowledge. But his sympathies were with the pre-Socratics, as Gilbert's were, his affiliations in his own time with Telesio and Patrizzi, both strongly anti-Aristotelian, with a materialist emphasis in their account of nature.

Bacon is popularly supposed to have been an advovate of the inductive method in science; in fact, he expressed himself as vehemently opposed to simple induction. He thought equally little of the deductive syllogisms that prevailed in the schools: he held that no new knowledge could be obtained from them. He advocated, with complete conviction and some passion – for his passions were mainly intellectual – what might be described as the method of elimination. One should always collect fact after fact, instance after instance, until one comes up against a fact or instance that negates the generalisation being formed; he says that the negative factor always has the greater force. Thus one continues, eliminating at every stage of the process, until a general axiom may be concluded. From this general axiom further investigations will be suggested, which one should follow out according to the same procedure – and so forward.[82] Bacon believed that a general system of scientific axioms would be arrived at this way. With immense optimism he thought that this work could be achieved in the next two generations; that it would be a co-operative work calling for no individual giants of intellect but for the complementary industry of people of more equal ability and skills.

Things did not work out quite this way. For a couple of centuries to come the chief contributions to science were made by individuals of genius working on their own – Newton and Darwin, for example. On the other hand, in a couple of generations – after the disastrous folly of the Civil War – the Royal Society was founded to carry forward Bacon's programme of work very much in accordance with his ideas. Wilkins and Boyle, from whose Oxford group the Royal Society sprang, were inspired by Bacon's ideas. Then, too, it is remarkable how often Bacon is cited by American thinkers in the eighteenth and early nineteenth centuries,[83] and there could be no better example of Bacon's 'mechanical man' than Benjamin Franklin. Today, the organisation of science has taken on a dominantly co-operative character, international in scope. Bacon's forward-looking ideas have received ample, if belated, vindication: he was a prophet indeed.

It remains to inquire how far Bacon's method of scientific investigation – by which he set such store and for which he has been unduly disconsidered – is in keeping with the way scientists work. Evidently, not precisely: one must take the evidence of a scientist, rather than a philosopher or logician, on the matter. Partington distinguishes the three stages of the process. First, one constructs a table of positive instances, giving all the known cases in which the particular phenomenon under investigation is present, for example, heat. A second table should follow of negative instances of related cases in which the phenomenon is absent. A third table should give degrees of comparison, in which the phenomenon is present in different degrees. The variation must be given quantitatively. Following this method, Bacon apparently arrived at a correct conclusion as to heat: 'Heat itself, its essence and quiddity, is motion and nothing else'; it is a particular kind of motion, 'expansive, restrained, and acting in its strife upon the smaller particles of bodies.'[84] Partington tells us that Bacon had a competent knowledge of contemporary work in chemistry: he seems to have taken his views on heat from Cardan. We must remember that his aim was to establish generally valid axioms, and that the elementary character of science at the time, the simplicity of instruments and means, imposed frustrating limitations. He thought that the advance of science could be much more speedy, not only if, as he wished, people would set their brains to it instead of wasting them upon theology, the fabulous, the merely curious (so beloved of Elizabethans), but faster and easier than was possible in the nature of things – which alone he respected.

He wanted an immensely wide foundation of knowledge of particular things, as the primary material for sound general principles of science. His directives were categorical – away with citations of authors, away with everything rhetorical or mere verbiage, adhere to a plain style straight to the matter.[85] (This became the direct motto of the Royal Society.) Away with curiosities, superstitions and magic. Pronounce only on the basis of many instances, and after rigorous elimination at every stage until the higher axioms are reached. Everything relating to natural phenomena is to be numbered, measured, weighed or defined, not merely speculated about. (It is fascinating to notice how much he despised people's speculations: he knew them for what they were, and with very little sympathy.) Later in the process, mistakes in experimenting will be detected by testing them in accordance with the general principles established. Opinions and speculations are endless and useless – as a politician he would know. But the programme was for others to carry out, 'for I care little about the mechanical arts themselves: only about those things which they contribute to the equipment of philosophy.'

This rather lordly dictum has allowed him to be much misrepresented. For we must remember that by philosophy he meant 'natural philosophy' – in the sense in which, carrying out his ideas, the older science professorships at Oxford are entitled in natural philosophy. For Bacon this was a common field of knowledge constituted by all general axioms not peculiar to the particular sciences, but which applied in common. Secondly, he did respect the mechanical arts: 'the most useful inventions are due to experience, and have come to men like windfalls . . . not from vain and babbling doctrines about the nature of things.'[86] We shall see how much he respected the practical sciences, the mechanical arts; though he had little enough time for experimenting, he even turned his hand to the banausic arts when he could. The very word 'invention' had been a term in rhetoric, as we have seen; Bacon changed its meaning: nothing was ever invented by rhetorical invention, he roundly declared. What a world away from the earlier Elizabethan rhetoricians we are with him! The ultimate purpose of science, of mechanical invention, of progressive discovery, was the amelioration of man's condition. We see in him what a modern man he was: a prophet and a portent, utilitarian and humanitarian, essentially secular and materialist; for all his protestations, an intellect without religion or that other refuge for those who have not faith (according to Newman) – essentially without poetry.

His constant refrain is that we should get closer to nature and work in and along with it. In medicine we should revive the Hippocratic method of recording the nature of the disease, its treatment and issue.[87] He urged the study of comparative anatomy, the use of vivisection upon beasts to advance knowledge, euthanasia to ease the pains of the dying. Anyone who knows the full horrors of Elizabethan purgings will sympathise with his wish for inquiry into 'more easy and less loathsome purgings.' He favoured the 'altering of features' – a very early forecast of plastic surgery. Spectacles had been developed to aid sight, why not hearing-aids? Magnifying glasses were now in use, why not microscopes? Always the method was to be from experiment to experiment, eventually to general axiom, thence opening up fields for further experiment. We can see sympathetically into this extraordinary man's forward-looking mind from his Wellsian fable, *The New Atlantis* (again unfinished). There, in Solomon's House we have a society furnished with the aids he envisaged, a picture of 'our own world as it might be if we did our duty by it.'[88] There were aquariums for experiments with fishes, dispensatories for medicines, laboratories for chemistry; perspective houses for demonstrations of lights and colours; microscopes, furnaces and retorts; engine-houses, and sound-houses for experiments with harmonics. It is not fanciful to say that these suggestions looked forward to radio and television. That anything might be achieved is his constant refrain, if only people would drop their useless disputes in theology and politics, and deploy their energies of mind to more useful purpose.

On the practical side, Bacon made his own modest contributions, showing that he in no wise disdained the practical arts. His governing idea here was that investigation into conditions in nature should result in being able to produce them artificially for man's benefit.[89] Mineral medicines, for instance: might one try to imitate natural baths and mineral springs?[90] He describes the quantitative experiments he had made in dissolving gold, looking forward to its medicinal use – as today in the treatment of tuberculosis. He pursued similar elementary experiments with mercury, lead, silver, copper, noting the quantities of acid that would dissolve a certain weight of metal and no more. Probably he was influenced here by his reading of Paracelsus – to whom he was less hostile than Gilbert had been – Cornelius Agrippa and Cardan; for, with the aid of amanuenses like Dr. Rawley and young Hobbes, Bacon was able to keep abreast of the work being done abroad. And he drew upon the widest range for suggestions. He himself suggested hot-houses for plants, not known in his time. He made experiments with wheat, steeped in dung, urine, etc., to achieve speedier growth or greater fertility. He was greatly interested in the phenomena of distillation, and of fermentation. He used thermoscopes, 'those glasses which indicate the state of the atmosphere in respect of heat and cold', and proposed a number of experiments in which they might be used to detect heat and cold in bodies.[91] It is well known how this led to his death, a martyr to scientific curiosity. The ailing ex-Lord Chancellor got out of his coach at Highgate one cold day to gather snow with which to preserve a chicken – an experiment in refrigeration; from which he got pneumonia and thus died.

On the critical side, we must remember the date at which he was writing and the discouraging, disjointed circumstances in which so much of it was done. More of his work is analogous, in its primitive way, to the processes of modern science than we may suppose. His tables of comparative instances offer a counterpart to our statistical analysis.[92] Science is not a set of static discoveries, but an unending dynamism generating new problems – but does not his dialectical process of experiment-axiom-further experiment amount to much the same thing? 'Had science at his time been more fully developed, he might have been the first to emphasise this point.' He has been underestimated by scientists for his failure to appreciate the scientific discoveries of his time. It is true that he himself underestimated both Gilbert and Hariot, though he knew Gilbert's work and Hariot's investigations into specific gravity. But Bacon's interests were not in mathematics, physics or astronomy, and he remained a pre-Copernican. This was not obscurantism on his part: he thought that the evidence was as yet insufficient. We do not know whether these individual, isolated spirits knew each other: it shows how much a Royal Society was needed. Bacon was completely disappointed in his hopes of the wise Scotch owl that sat on the English throne, whose intellectual interests were dictated by Calvinist theology. Bacon's fundamental separation of science from theology enabled science to go forward relatively unimpeded and independent.

For all the scope of his intellectual imagination Bacon kept his eyes on the ground – 'it is the mechanical arts that give the better insight into the secret places of nature.'[93] The groundsmen, particularly the surveyors, artisans, instrument-makers, gunners, navigators, improvers, were all making their small individual contributions, with a general indifference to theory and a recognisably English empiricism. With a confidence in their times, belief in their country, optimism as to the future. 'Why then should we think so basely of ourselves and our times?', asked Sir Hugh Plat, the agricultural improver.[94] 'Are the paths of the ancient philosophers so worn out or overgrown with weeds that no tract or touch thereof remaineth in our days whereby to trace or follow them?' Various improvements were brought forward to aid in surveying, applying mensuration to surfaces and solids. Leonard Digges described his instruments in several books – his methods in the *Pantometria* – and invented the theodolite. Similar applications were made in ballistics and gunnery, which made their mark against the Armada. The log-and-line method of measuring distance by sea was an English development.[95] Advances were made in metallurgy, not only by the great Gilbert but by the tantalising Adrian Gilbert (about whom we should like to know so much more) and with the aid of foreign mining experts like Burchard Cranich, to be summed up shortly by Dud Dudley in his *Metallum Martis*.

Thomas Hood writes in 1590, 'it is but late since the mathematical sciences began to be in request within this city.'[96] Of this movement towards the remote industrial and technological future Bacon was the prophet. Though his own main interest was the discovery of scientific laws, he rejoiced that 'the mechanical arts ... as having in them some breath of life are continually growing and becoming more perfect.'[97] When the first historian of the Royal Society summed up its foundation and character, he pointed to Bacon as 'the one great man, who had the true imagination of the whole extent of this enterprise, as it is now set on foot.'[98] The Royal Society was Solomon's House come to life.

I LONGLEAT HOUSE

2 HARDWICK HALL

3 HARDWICK HALL

4 HARDWICK: THE PRESENCE CHAMBER

5 JOHN DONNE,
THE POET

6 MICHAEL DRAYTON
AS LAUREATE

7 DR JOHN BULL

8 NICHOLAS HILLIARD:
SELF-PORTRAIT

9 AN UNKNOWN YOUTH: A HILLIARD FANTASY

10 SHELDON TAPESTRY: SUMMER

11 HATFIELD HOUSE

12 TOMB SCULPTURE
BY EPIPHANIUS
EVESHAM

13 THE DORMER TOMB,
WING

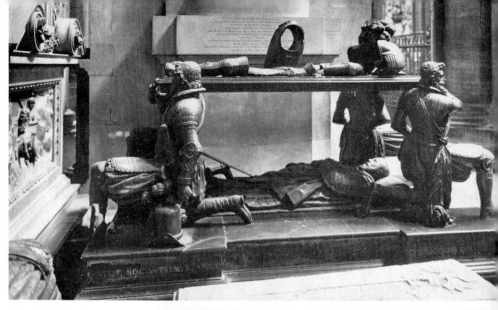

14 THE VERE TOMB, WESTMINSTER ABBEY

15 A LADY'S COSTUME

16 A TABLE CARPET

17 THOMAS DIGGES'S DIAGRAM
OF THE COPERNICAN UNIVERSE

18 THE SURGEON'S CHEST

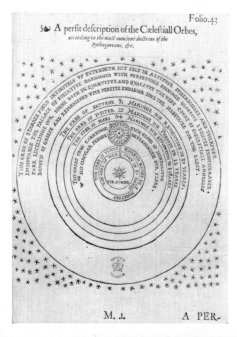

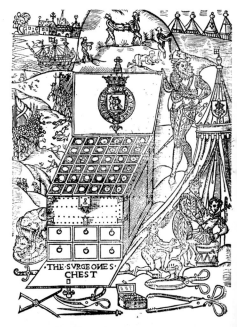

19 DR WILLIAM
GILBERT, THE
PHYSICIST

20 JOHN BANISTER
DELIVERING AN
ANATOMY LECTURE

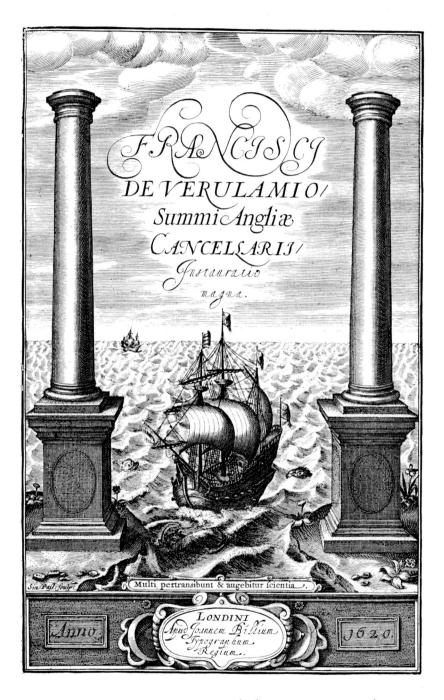

21 TITLE-PAGE OF BACON'S 'NOVUM ORGANUM'

23 SIR GEORGE SOMERSET
IN ARMOUR

25 THE VYVYAN SALT

26 LADY WROTH WITH AN ARCH-LUTE

27 QUEEN ELIZABETH: A COMMEMORATIVE PORTRAIT

CHAPTER VIII

NATURE AND MEDICINE

ALREADY all over Western Europe, from the earlier decades of the century, men were engaged in extending the boundaries of their knowledge of nature. This was of the essence of the experience that we mean by the Renaissance and exemplifies similar characteristics to those we have observed in other fields. The rediscovery of ancient naturalists, like Dioscorides and Theophrastus, had comparable effects to that of Galen in anatomy and medicine. At first they were absolute authorities, not to be questioned; then, as they inspired new work and further discovery, they were transcended. There was this difficulty with the naturalists of antiquity, that the flora they described was that of Greece and Italy not of Northern and Western Europe. Once more, as with architecture, the Italians were much closer to, and in keeping with, the source of new inspiration in the revival of antiquity. It imposed an added challenge to the naturalists of Northern Europe to make their flora fit the ancient descriptions and make the correct identifications. In the end, the effort necessary inspired a finer achievement. The new naturalism was inspired first by Italians such as Mattioli or Calzolari (from whom we derive calceolaria); but their work came to be outclassed by the naturalists of Northern Europe, such as Brunfels, Bock, Fuchs (from whom we get fuchsia) or Conrad Gesner; Dodoens, L'Ecluse and Lobel (whence lobelia), the English form for de L'Obel.

Naturalists in general – botanists, herbalists, zoologists, ornithologists, entomologists – were usually doctors by profession: their studies grew up in proximity to, and out of, medicine. This was natural, indeed the way they developed; for what was characteristic of the medieval attitude was the use to which the object was to be put, flowers and herbs were studied for their medicinal uses, ascribed their astrological affiliations – the astrological lore was as important as the botanical. The Renaissance changed this attitude: men became interested in the study of natural objects, as indeed of man, as ends in themselves. This gave a powerful stimulus to naturalistic, as to anatomical and medical, studies. Men were now profitably engaged in accumulating and investigating the facts upon which in the next – the scientific – century they would be able to base natural laws.

As yet, this would not be possible: students were still dogged by the idea of spontaneous generation, so they could not formulate a sound genetics. Until the development of the microscope they could not watch the smaller processes of generation, the hatching from minute eggs, let alone bacterial processes. They did not know but what lice were generated from human sweat – still less then could they know the connection between lice and typhus. Though a few observers noticed the collocation of mosquitoes in the West Indies and fever – even the often deadly consequences of mosquito-bite – they could not observe how it worked: after all, it was not until this century that the process was worked out. They did not know but what minute insects might be generated from dust or from putrefaction – as indeed their revered biblical and classical authorities assured them. Once again, as we saw with the cosmology of writers such as Spenser, Marlowe, Shakespeare, Donne, we are in a betwixt-and-between world: they are never quite sure what might not be possible. It is a world immensely stimulating to the imagination, but not wholly scientific. We watch it becoming increasingly scientific, until it graduates with the achievements of Gilbert and Hariot, Bacon and his doctor, the great Harvey.

In this movement of mind, at the dawn of the modern age, we shall see the Elizabethans making their characteristic contributions, greater or smaller.

I

For convenience let us separate natural history from medicine, the naturalists from the doctors, though these interests were often present in one and the same person, the studies closely interrelated and interacting upon one another.

As in other fields the Renaissance impulse may be first seen at work in the group of Oxford humanists, of whom Linacre was the leading scientific light. Edward Wotton, who became a Fellow of Linacre's Royal College of Physicians and also studied at Padua, produced an encyclopaedic *De Differentiis Animalium*. But it is a work of humanist book-learning: the way of scientific advance was to be from book-learning to facts. Sir Thomas Elyot's

Castle of Health showed him interested not only in dietary and medicine but also plants and birds. He wrote in English, and this offended the doctors, the more so because he did not belong to the profession. Leland, who – like Linacre – was attached to All Souls, was omnivorously curious on his itineraries throughout the country: 'with him we may surely say that the exploration of Britain for its natural resources and fauna has begun.'[1] With the next generation we have seen the Renaissance impulse burn more brightly at Cambridge with a Protestant light, and Cambridge produced the leading English naturalist of the century with William Turner.

Turner was a Northumbrian with recognisable North Country characteristics, a *protégé* of Ridley and the Wentworths. He was very forthright, rude about people's silly superstitions, with an aggressive commonsense that went to the heart of a matter and sharpened his scientific insight. His bent was for scientific observation from his boyhood. Apparently he was a good-looking man, with a boisterous humour. In dealing with the birch-tree, he comments, 'it serveth for many good uses, and for none better than for beating of stubborn boys, that either lie or will not learn' – a piece of salutary knowledge that our age has forgotten.[2] We still remember him by a number of plant-names he domesticated, stone parsley, hawkweed, goat's beard, ground pine – though not all his suggested names stuck. The identification of plants by the ancient authorities was difficult, though Turner had a sufficient knowledge of Greek; 'he achieved a real success in bringing the ancient catalogues into a close and often accurate relationship with the actual flora of England.'

'On birds little or no work had yet been done, and identification was a difficult and complicated process.'[3] Turner was accurate and scholarly, citing his authorities classical and modern (in particular, German). His life-long training as an observer was no less close: 'cranes nest among the English in marshy places and I have very often seen their pipers [half-fledged young]: this some people born outside England declare to be untrue.' Contemporary household accounts bear him out: we are reminded how much more richly endowed with nature's creatures was England then, and how much denuded now for too many humans.

These studies occupied Turner happily at Cambridge, and he put forth his *Libellus de re Herbaria* in 1538. A man of promise he was rewarded by becoming Somerset's physician and with the

Deanery of Wells, when the unexpected catastrophe of the Marian episode befell the country. Turner was a combative Protestant and fond of his master, Ridley, whose judicial murder by fire horrified him. Himself did not wait to be purged by theological brutes, but took the more sensible course of exile. This was the making of him as a scientist: he went to Italy, learning of the school of Bologna; he travelled all over Germany, Switzerland, the Netherlands, observing plants and birds wherever he went. He laid in an immense store of information on which he could work for the rest of his life; he made friends with other masters in his field, above all with Gesner with whom he kept up a correspondence. We observe, especially with naturalists, the high degree of cosmopolitan co-operation they maintained, the generosity with which they exchanged specimens, the readiness with which they contributed to each other's works to advance the cause of science.

He had already produced a book on birds, while on an earlier visit to Germany: principally the birds mentioned by Pliny and Aristotle. 'The book is an excellent piece of pioneer-work: most of his identifications are sound and all are careful; his descriptions especially of habits are very good.'[4] Near Bonn, when the field-fares fed on juniper-berries, 'the people eat the field-fares un-drawn, with guts and all, because they are full of the berries of juniper.' The red kite was common then in England: 'it often snatches food from boys' hands in our cities and towns.' In Germany he describes the habits of the golden oriole, whose note was like 'that of the big flute which takes the bass part in accompanying.' The shrike, which was a carnivore and preyed on its own kind, was naturally at home in Germany.

During his Marian exile he wrote his treatise on the use of baths.[5] But his masterpiece was his *Herbal*, which came out in three parts, with heavy revision and large additions, from 1551 to 1568. Nothing is more admirable than his scientific conscientiousness: he declared early on that he would not put his book into Latin until he had studied the West Country flora, for he was persuaded that it was fuller than any other part of Britain. On Elizabeth's accession he was restored to his deanery. This enabled him to complete his great *Herbal*, which included 'the first scientific records of no less than 238 of our native plants.'[6] As a doctor, he was also interested in their medical uses. What is new with him is the passion for nature and natural observation as ends in themselves. 'It is this attitude of objective interest in nature

... which is the source and impetus of the scientific movement ...
He examined and collated his authorities; he scrutinised his species
in the light of them; he laboured with nomenclature ... Identification is for him, as for every true scientist, never an end in itself
but a means to appreciation, to the discernment of characteristics
and the study of form and function.'[7]

If he had found time to put his *Herbal* into Latin, he would
have had a far greater European name – for no one could be
expected to read English – and he would himself have introduced
a new flora to European science. Nor did this exhaust his interests.
He had collected much material about British fishes, some of which
he contributed to Gesner's vast *Historia Animalium*. In his last
years Turner was hoping to write a work on fishes, which would
have laid the foundation for that study in Britain as securely as
his work on plants and birds. But, being a man of his time, he
wasted time in controversy on subjects and with people who, for
all their prominence then, were ultimately beneath the notice of
a first-rate scientist. For though, as a controversialist Turner took
a moderate Protestant line, what does that signify compared with
the fact that 'he was the true pioneer of natural history in
England'?[8]

Dr. Caius' main importance is as a doctor. He spent over five
years studying at Padua, under Montanus, and became acquainted with Vesalius. This may have helped him with his studies
of animals, in which he became a pioneer. He too was a correspondent of Gesner, to whom he sent reports on the animals he
was able to observe at the Tower, which had a kind of zoo. These
he worked up into a book, *De Rariorum Animalium atque Stirpium
Historia*, 1570. In the same year he published his standard account
of English dogs, *De Canibus Britannicis*, pleasantly translated by
Abraham Fleming. Both books exemplify the good scientific
method Caius had learned abroad and taught at home. His interests were more dispersed than Turner's and one cannot place
him in the same class as a scientist. A conservative and a Catholic,
he was for one thing more credulous; a humanist, who thought
ill of writing in English, he was rather given to absurd etymologies.
His book upholding the greater antiquity of Cambridge university, as against that of a Fellow of All Souls (Thomas Key)
defending Oxford's, was not only inaccurate but showed no
critical sense.[9] As if it mattered which was older! – he was much
better on the subject of dogs.

A more original naturalist was a Cambridge man of a younger generation, Thomas Penny, a practising doctor who spent most of his spare time gathering a mass of material about insects. Though he was a good botanist too, he was really the first of English entomologists. Since he did not get round to publishing his work but left it to a pushing Scot to do so, Thomas Moffet, the latter got all the credit – including the folklore transformation of sex into Little Miss Moffet confronting the Spider. Penny studied at Montpellier and in Germany and corresponded with Gesner, L'Ecluse and Lobel, to all of whom he communicated numerous finds. He travelled widely in Europe, going as far as Prussia and making a pioneering expedition to Majorca for field work. It was at Orléans that he made his significant study of the bed-bug, and found that it was not generated from rotten timber, but laid eggs – the beginning of sense in a field where there was still much confusion of thought.

Penny's work was subsumed along with that of others, in Elizabethan fashion, into Moffet's *Theatrum Insectorum*. Raven tells us that Penny was the only true scientist among them, and that if only we possessed the whole of his work he would rank high. 'Certainly he grasped the importance of beginning with identification, with the proper discrimination and description of the different species and types, and with observation of them rather than traditions about them . . . Penny's work, despite the sad accident of its delayed publication, is the true foundation of entomology.'[10]

Moffet himself wrote books on Silkworms, and Diet; a dependent of the Herberts, he was the author of a brief Latin biography of Sir Philip Sidney. A writer not without charm, let us use him here rather for the light he throws on his time, the worse than bestial cruelty meted out to animals by humans. Though one can hardly bear to transcribe it, this shows what they are capable of. As a doctor Moffet warns against unwholesome meat from unnaturally shut up and crammed capons, or birds deprived of light by stitching up their eyes.[11] Serving in France, he had had the opportunity of observing Norman butchers' methods of killing young heifers: felling them, making a hole about the navel and blowing air through a swan's quill till the whole skin swells like a bladder; while this is going on, two or three others beat the heifer as hard as they can with cudgels, the hide being bruised the flesh is tenderer to eat. 'As for the common way of brawning boars by stying them up in so close a room that they cannot turn themselves round about, and whereby they are forced always to lie on their bellies, it is not worthy the imitation; for they feed in pain, lie in pain, and sleep in pain.' Nevertheless, 'after he is brawned for your turn, thrust a knife into one of his flanks and let him run with it till he die. Others gently bait him with muzzled dogs.'

Of such are human kind.

There gradually grew up in London, and in some parts of the country, intelligent circles to encourage and respond to these newly flowering interests. A cultivated few were able to make contributions to developing the subject: the Knyvet brothers, for example, Sir Thomas and Edmund Knyvet of Ashwellthorpe in Norfolk, where they had a remarkable scientific library and whom we see today on the staircase at Faringdon House, Berkshire, in all their elegance and native distinction. The Knyvets contributed several Norfolk specimens to Penny, crickets, moths, beetles, or else drawings done by themselves, or observations on insect-habits. In Lancashire Thomas Hesketh was collecting plants all over the county, and sending them on to John Gerard in London.

In neighbouring North Wales, at Lleweni, Gerard had another correspondent with herbal interests and a garden: this was Sir John Salusbury, to celebrate whose married love the poets contributed to Chester's *Love's Martyr*, Shakespeare sending 'The Phoenix and the Turtle.' Salusbury's father had compiled a Welsh herbal: the Christ Church copy of Gerard's *Herbal* belonged to the son and we can discern Sir John's mingled interests in herbs and plants, diet and health, from his notes in it.[12] He wrote 'Certain Necessary Observations for Health'; but the following poem, which we will keep in the decent obscurity of Elizabethan spelling, is clearly a recipe for pleasure, for an aphrodisiac.

> Good sir yf you lack the strengthe in your back
> > and wolde have a Remediado
> Take Eryngo [ginger] rootes and Marybone tartes
> > Redde wine and riche Potato
>
> An oyster pie and a Lobsters thighe
> > hard eggs well dressed in Marow
> This will ease your backes disease
> > and make you a good Cocksparrowe.
>
> An Apricock or an Artichoke
> > Anchovies oyle and Pepper
> These to use doe not refuse
> > twill make your backe the better

The milke of an Asse will bring to passe
all Thinges in such a matter
When this is spente you must be contente
with an ounce of Synamon water.

A number of observations of wild flowers are recorded, with their locations, mostly in 1606. 'English saxifrage in the coppice in Lleweni park next the new stable over the high stile upon the right hand of the footway that leadeth from Lleweni Hall to Denbigh: I found it the 23 May 1606.' He found herb paris 'in a place called Cadnant, where a fairy well springeth called St. Michael's well, ffynon Mihangel, within a bolt-shot of the well down the spring . . . where likewise is found the herb twyblade. By reason of the rankness of the place there are found a great store of herb paris with five leaves apiece, but the year 1606 I found the same with six leaves.' A couple of years later he is planting these last in his garden. He was a herbalist, and gives a number of recipes. Here is one for a sample: 'Take a certain amand milk [aperient] made with these herbs: Take plantain, ribworth, knot grass, cheaper purse, comfrey, of everyone a handful, strawberry leaves, sanicula, ditto. Let this be boiled in a quantity of fair water: of this liquor make an amand milk. This is excellent against a consumption, waste or running of the reins, or breaking of a vein and within the body, or any foul matter within man's body.'

It reminds us that at this time most medicines used were herbal. As to its value, it can hardly have been so deleterious as the noxious concoctions of the apothecaries, powdered unicorn's horn, the liver of a newt, sliced snakeskin, and the rest of it. There is indeed a verse against the apothecaries:

Apothecary's shop of drugs let not thy stomach be:
Nor use no physic till thou need, thy friend adviseth thee.

This was good advice; probably better – to use none at all.

On the other hand, the best apothecaries took part in the extension of botanical knowledge. The Queen's apothecaries, John Rich and Hugh Morgan, had herb-gardens. Morgan was a real botanist who had a special interest in West Indian plants and kept constant touch with the sea-captains bringing home exotics from overseas. (We find several references to Drake doing so.) Thus Morgan was able to make new contributions to Lobel, as Richard Garth was able to do to L'Ecluse. Lobel spent the last years of his life in England. He paid a first visit early in Elizabeth's reign, when he made friends with the excellent Penny, but went back to take charge of the Prince of Orange's garden. After his assassination, Lobel returned and made himself a focus of botanical scholarship, as he had been the pioneer of bulb-culture in Holland.

He enjoyed a somewhat ambivalent friendship with the disingenuous Gerard, whose mistakes he did his best to correct. Perhaps most misleading were the attributions of illustrations to wrong plants. For the English were dependent on foreign plates for their illustrations. Here there had been a noteworthy advance in the art of botanical illustration abroad, partly encouraged by the marvellously observed work of Dürer and Leonardo, which was a factor in the progress of the science.[13] This went along with an increase in gardens and gardening that was a feature of the century. Still more the introduction of new flowers and plants, from the Near East, the Mediterranean, the New World, whence we got such familiars now as sunflowers and nasturtiums, tobacco, the potato, Indian corn. In Jacques Le Moyne, Ralegh maintained a charming artist who was personally acquainted with the flora of North America. Thence he produced his *La Clef des Champs* with woodcuts from his delightful drawings in 1586. While John White gave us what must be our first portrayal of the banana.

John Gerard was no scientist but a gardener of long experience and wide acquaintance. For twenty years he was gardener to Lord Burghley, whose passions were architecture, genealogy and gardening. The basis of Gerard's book, and his reputation, was not his own but someone else's, and he behaved disingenuously about it. The foundation of his vast folio was Priest's translation of Dodoens; Gerard rearranged the order in accordance with Lobel's better scheme, produced the book and got away with it. Numbers of gardeners and readers have been indebted to Gerard ever since – including those amateur gardeners, Adam and Eve, and that very professional reader, John Milton; for Milton's idea of the fatal Tree comes from Gerard's description of the banyan. Other associations touch us with their wing in his book. 'Walking in the fields next unto the Theatre by London' – where walked the Elizabethan dramatists – Gerard found a double buttercup; and he noticed saxifrage growing 'upon the brick wall in Chancery Lane, belonging to the Earl of Southampton.'[14]

Gerard wrote better than most scientists have done, and that keeps his large book fresh and alive. Full of mistakes as it was, it was corrected by Lobel; and then again by a young botanist of brilliant promise, Thomas Johnson, so that Johnson's edition of Gerard's *Herbal* was by far the best. Johnson just had time to produce it before he was killed in the Civil War.

II

In the early sixteenth century England was naturally behind Italy and France in medical science, but also behind the standards in the German cities, the sanitary arrangements of which favourably impressed Montaigne on his tour in 1580–1. Some of these had their codes with something like medical officers of health to supervise them.[15] The reign of Henry VIII saw the first attempts at modernisation, more efficient organisation, in these as in other respects. The Royal College of Physicians was founded in 1518, its charter admitting that its aim was progress following in the steps of well-regulated cities abroad. The same year saw the first government orders for prevention of plague: they followed foreign models. In 1532 the first Commissioners of Sewers were appointed throughout the country: though these dealt mainly with rivers and riparian problems, they also included drainage and effluents.[16] In 1540 the two separate gilds of Barbers and Surgeons were brought together, and given better status and regulation, as the Royal College of Surgeons.

Meanwhile, the first effects of the Reformation, as in the educational field, were damaging – disorganisation and disarray. In London this was to be repaired and placed on a sounder footing. The two chief hospitals, St. Bartholomew's and St. Thomas's, were salvaged by the public spirit of London citizens. On his death-bed Henry VIII took further steps of reparation. In the end London emerged with a sound, and functionally articulated, system of five Royal Hospitals, provision for the sick, poverty and unemployment. 'Poor householders received outdoor relief; the sick were tended at St. Bartholomew's, the permanently infirm at St. Thomas's; the children of poor persons were fed, clothed and educated at Christ's Hospital (founded in the buildings of the Grey Friars); the insane were treated at Bethlehem Hospital [Bedlam]; the undeserving, vagabonds and worse were made to work in Bridewell.'[17] This was a palace quite recently built by Henry, looking out on the Fleet river. The country, however, was slower to catch up: many small hospitals were not refounded and *ad hoc* provisions had to be – and often were – made.

In mid-century the Royal College of Physicians had a dominant figure in Dr. Caius, as the Surgeons had in Thomas Vicary. Caius devoted his energy to building up the prestige of his College, on a disciplinary and ceremonial basis. The College did little to advance medical education, so leading doctors continued to study at the foremost European centres, Padua, Montpellier and (towards the turn of the century) Leyden. However, members were actively in touch with the overseas adventures of the age – in the army and navy, on the voyages, and in providing a succession of English doctors to attend the Tsars in Moscow. As the result of the close control over the licensing of doctors it was necessary to call in foreign physicians, qualified abroad; we find a surprising number of them serving, not only in London but in such a provincial town as Exeter. But most of its collegiate energy was devoted to pursuing unlicensed practitioners and illicit practices: between 1572 and 1603 the College dealt with over a hundred such cases.[18] In spite of this there was a considerable increase in the number of recruits to the profession – as we should expect, with an expanding society.

The College conducted its campaign on two fronts. It was out to assert the primacy of physicians, with their academic learning and qualifications, over surgeons, with their lowly companions, blood-letters, midwives, barbers. A physician might practise surgery, a surgeon might not practise physic. Secondly, there was its campaign against the unlicensed, empirics, quacks. Behind this was the College's consistent Galenism; it sets its face against the new chemical treatments coming in from abroad, especially under the influence of Paracelsus, with their dangers in the use of mercury, antimony, stibium etc. Still, with the increase of syphilis, it was hopeless to try and stop the mercury treatment, the only useful one, though dangerous in excess. New medicaments were necessary.

On the other hand, with so inadequate a number of doctors, what were people to do? Women delivered all the children born; old wives, with their traditional lore, their herbs and their spells, effected as many cures as most Tudor doctors, and probably fewer deaths. We find constant interventions on behalf of such people, by more open-minded grandees at Court, some of whom had benefited by their ministrations (or thought they had), against the stone-walling of the College. The College rarely gives way. In 1573 it was argued in the Lord Mayor's court whether surgeons might give inward medicines for the French pox, sciatica or any ulcer or wound.[19] The bishop of London and the Master of the Rolls argued in favour, but Dr. Caius proved its illegality and all gave way to him. On another occasion Walsingham intervened on behalf of Margaret Kennix 'for the readmitting of her into the quiet exercise of her small talent' – using simples to heal wounds. She had been prohibited 'contrary to her Majesty's pleasure'; the College did not yield to her Majesty's pleasure. In 1588 Peter Piers was sent to prison for giving pills of antimony, turbith and mercury sublimate, by which he had killed several persons.

It was natural that our old friend 'Dr.' Forman should have been a target of the College.* In the 1590's he was several times before the doctors. He had pretended to cure many 'hectical and tabid' (i.e. consumptive) people by an electuary of roses in wormwood water.[20] He boasted no other help in diagnosis but ephemerides (calendar calculations) and by aspects and constellations of the planets. The doctors, of course, believed as much as Simon in these; but when they examined him in astronomy as well as physic, he answered so absurdly that there was 'great mirth and sport among the auditors.' He was interdicted from practice and fined £5. Two or three years later he was up before the doctors again, found very ignorant, sent to prison and fined £10. After a month or so he was released by order of the Lord Keeper. Dr. Smith and four other doctors waited on the Lord Keeper to recommit 'so notorious an impostor'. Nine months after, Simon admitted that he had prescribed a compound water to a gentleman in a burning fever, who died on taking it. Examined a third time, by the Queen's physician, he was found as ignorant in astrology as in physic. He was again committed to prison, and on coming out took refuge across the water at Lambeth, where he could not be got at. He had 'practised' for fourteen years in the country. We learn that it was his friend, Dean Blague, who procured a letter from the Archbishop for his release. He was freed on giving bond not to practise; the College wrote to Whitgift in June 1601 not to protect him.

All this completely corroborates the truth of Forman's diaries, from the other side.

These prescriptions, complicated potions, compound waters and chemicals offer a contrast with the simple diet prescribed by a country parson in Cornwall, Hugh Atwell, rector of St. Ewe, who relied chiefly on a diet of milk and apples, and effected many cures – to people's surprise.

* For him *v. The Elizabethan Renaissance: The Life of the Society*, 144 foll.

Let us look at the London hospitals to see exactly what went on. Richard Grafton, the printer, impoverished himself by the public work he did for them; innumerable gifts were received from citizens, money, clothes, cheeses, coals, but he ended as a pensioner. Dr. Caius had a house in the Close, with a hall big enough to give the College's first feast; Grafton printed Caius' book on the Sweating Sickness in 1552.[21] Lopez was a physician at Bart's until 1580, when he was succeeded by William Turner's son, Peter. Dr. Timothy Bright, who wrote his celebrated *Treatise of Melancholy* while at Bart's, was often warned for neglecting his duty: he evidently preferred writing, and ultimately found refuge in the Church. Three surgeons were appointed in 1549, the leading one being Vicary, head of his profession, with a house in paradise, i.e. the monastic garden. In 1585 one hears a familiar note: the surgeons asked for more pay – but it was for more work, not less.

Numbers were expanding: where the governors aimed at 120, they went up to over 180, and could be reduced only to 160. One is struck, here as elsewhere, by the charitable spirit towards the poor. And not only towards the innocent poor: in 1596 David Doo was dismissed 'for unkindness towards the poor condemned prisoners of Newgate.'[22] In 1571 Weston was the apothecary who served out drugs to the poor; he complained that he could not make ends meet because of the increase of numbers. His salary was increased to £26. 13. 4 a year; in 1585 he was dismissed for neglect of duty. Roger Gwynn was apothecary, 1587–1614, as also for St. Thomas's; he was sometimes paid extra for effecting a cure, then his salary was increased, 'so long as the governors should see the poor better looked to and sooner healed.' In addition to oils, ointments and plasters, he had to prepare scurvy-grass for drink: it had a vitamin content. There were a matron and eleven sisters, each looking after nine or ten and a ward, with 'a fool' to provide light relief.

St. Thomas's had already been at a low ebb before the Dissolution, with poor women in childbirth refused admission and dying at the church door; the Master was selling the plate: 'the world is naught, let us take while we may.'[23] Since the repentant Henry VIII, on his deathbed, abolished the stews on the South Bank, St. Thomas's was used by some of the Southwark whores for lying in.[24] However, the prudent historian suppresses some of the charges against the sisters – they were apparently no better than they should be; the matron during 1572–80 was three times had up for drunkenness, the third time dismissed – evidently an Elizabethan Sarah Gamp. Very many of the poor here had syphilis: after their cure they were to be punished for their lewd life.

At Bridewell entertainments were more variegated. In one week in 1581 William Fleetwood, Recorder of the City, shut up 146 masterless vagabonds in Bridewell and chased the rest out into the country.[25] But when he took evidence from the frail sisterhood as to visits from the staff of the Portuguese ambassador, the ambassador had Fleetwood put in the Fleet for a few days for spoiling the fun. Some of the women in Bridewell had been arrested at the notorious Black Lucy's or at Diogenes' house in Seething Lane. So Henry VIII's death-bed piety had not proved wholly effectual. There were religious entertainments, too, when recalcitrant Puritans were shut up with recalcitrant Catholics, who loathed each other. There was open preaching in Bridewell; Margaret Maynard, one of Penry and Barrow's following, said 'There is no church in England, and she hath not been to church these ten years.' On the other hand, Thomas Doulton would not work on the Assumption of the Virgin, so he was put in the hemp-house. While Father Watson, 'a little man with a squint he could look nine ways at once', called out in the service, 'You call it the service of God, but it is the service of the Devil.' Later ecumenical discoveries would seem to indicate that he was mistaken. Unfortunately for himself he was let out – to get into far worse trouble and lose his life for the Main Plot under James. He did not know when he was best off.

The aim of the Royal College of Physicians was to keep medicine and surgery separate, and thus preserve the primacy of medicine and enforce a monopoly. Their very conservatism gave increasing opportunity to both surgeons and apothecaries to move into the field of the new drugs coming in from abroad. It was impossible to keep medicine, surgery and pharmacy separate, even in London – still less in the provinces. A general form of practice gradually grew up, with much less regulation than on the Continent. From 1603 to 1643 there were almost ten times the number of physicians outside London than were licensed by the College to practise in London.[26] Evidently the profession largely escaped control. The licences to practise that continued to be given by the bishops were certificates of honesty and good conduct rather than of medical qualification. As Richard Carew said of Cornwall, 'the most professors of that science in this county, saving only one – J. Williams – can better vouch practice for their warrant, than warrant for their practice.' Experience meant more.

In the country at large surgeons and apothecaries were becoming general practitioners, and were far more numerous. In the Exeter diocese, i.e. Devon and Cornwall, from 1568 to 1640 there were 81 licences for surgery, 12 for medicine and surgery, thirteen for medicine alone.[27] The city of Exeter had four physicians at one time, besides a couple of Spanish doctors; surgeons and barbers could do the regular seasonal bleeding even the healthy thought necessary. The leading doctor was John Woolton, son of a former bishop, who had had the full eleven years formal education at Oxford, becoming a Fellow of All Souls and ending with the M.D. His open quarrel with a successful, but unqualified, local practitioner, Thomas Edwards, reached the courts. Something of a sensation, it takes us into the heart of the issue in dispute – abroad as in England – and into the life of the time.

Edwards had been apprenticed to a local apothecary and then employed by one of the Spaniards, Dr. Francis Bryna. Edwards had been at Oxford for a short period to brush up his Latin; from 1597 he began to practise medicine and in a short time was highly regarded by the local gentry. This was important, for they had large households in need of purging, dosing and bleeding, apart from accidents. Edwards' success aroused Dr. Woolton's ire, who sent him an abusive letter at Christmas 1603: 'Mr. Trivett, your master, taught you not to go beyond your mortar and pestle . . . You ought not to administer so much as a clyster or open a vein without licence of a physician.' Edwards had taken away a leading patient from Woolton, young Sir William Courtenay, to whom Edwards had administered 'stibium [sulphuret of antimony], mercury crude, precipitate, sublimate, turbith mineral, borax crystalline, ratsbane, vitriol, brimstone, *aqua fortis*.' It looks as if young Courtenay had syphilis. Woolton ended by telling Edwards to burn his prescriptions and make salt of the ashes, 'which you, I know, can do, being a perfect Paracelsian.' There was the point.

Dr. Woolton charged Edwards with letting 100 oz. of Courtenay's blood in the past twelve months, and administering in the past fortnight eight strong purgations, one vomit and other desperate practices. When the doctor met Edwards on the road, he shouted at him to 'go home to his pestle and mortar'. Edwards' apprentice testified that his master worked differently from any physician, but that his use of mercury was successful in treating ulcers and cancers, while his use of opium was normal. Young Courtenay, the heir of Powderham, had served with Essex in Ireland, one of his knights, in 1599: he shortly died, in 1605.[28] This did not prevent the local gentry, Pollards and Champernownes, from speaking up on behalf of their favourite practitioner. The case dragged on for three and a half years and ended with a characteristically savage sentence by Lord Chief Justice Coke, who fined Woolton the ruinous sum of £500, ordered him to pay Edwards £170 damages, to stand in the market-place at next assizes at Exeter with twelve feet of interrogatories about his neck, and to be imprisoned till then.

It was not to be supposed that the odious Coke would ever go against the freedom of choice of the local gentry and we know that he hated any kind of control, except that of the common law. But it may have added to his venom that Woolton was a bishop's son – the father had deserved his bishopric for the exemplary way in which he had stayed in the city tending the sick throughout the plague of 1570. It may be that Woolton had an unpopular social position in Exeter, the other physicians being friendly with each other. After this experience Dr. Woolton retired to his estate in North Devon – and no wonder! Thus the apothecaries gained the right to practise in the country.

The reference to opium in this case is interesting, for few exotic drugs reached England till about 1600. Dr. Woolton's objections were to the mineral prescriptions of Paracelsan medicine, where he was taking the orthodox line of the Physicians in London.

Apothecaries were usually members of the grocers' or mercers' gilds in the cities, and appropriately in the city-plays they performed *The Three Kings of Cologne*, with their offering of frankincense and myrrh. At Oxford they had their shops next to University College, and here Boyle and Hooke later performed their chemical experiments – on the site of the Shelley Memorial.[29] The apothecaries sold confectionery, sweets and fancy goods as well; a Canterbury apothecary sold necklaces from the loot of ships wrecked in the Goodwin Sands: he had his shop in the High Street, next to John Marlowe, shoe-maker, in 1593, the year of Christopher's death. The royal apothecaries were in a very good way of business. The Serjeant-Apothecary supplied urinals for the lords meeting in Council at 3d each.[30] Perfumes were a considerable expenditure. When the Queen moved from one palace to another, 2 oz. perfume were supplied to air the great chamber and the privy chamber after cleaning. 'The perfume pan in the private chamber' was frequently refilled with rosewater. Then there was orris powder and damask powder for her bedchamber. There was even a bath, an elongated wooden oval bound with hoops, which was carried back and forth between palaces. It seems that this was only in use when medically ordered, when it cost 10s. to prepare – bags of herbs, musk, civet, highly aromatic – for immersing or sitting in, inhaling the fumes. It was used every six months, so that the old Hatfield joke that 'the Queen taketh a bath once in six months, whether she needeth it or no,' may be founded on fact.

Hugh Morgan, as Queen's apothecary, was a leading figure in this world, one of the inspectors of drugs, Master of the Grocers' Company. Treacle was the most common medicament. Morgan claimed that he could make treacle as good as that of Venice or Constantinople, and complained at the import of 'a false and naughty kind of Mithridatum and treacle in great barrels' at 3d. or 4d. a lb. Himself charged 11s. for a confection of bezoar stone and unicorn's horn. He not only grew herbs obtained from the West Indian voyages, but had rare trees from Eastern Europe, and a judas-tree in his Battersea garden. His tombstone there said: 'Hugh Morgan, late of Battersea, esquire, sleepeth here in peace. Whom men did admire for worthful parts. To Queen Elizabeth he was Chief Pothecary till her death.'

Her ladies he had provided with pills and lotions, pectoral powders and bitter electuary, oxicrocin plasters, Venice turpentine, almond milk, camomile flowers, roseleaves, oil of vinegar, roses. They also had preserved cherries, sugar candy, liquorice and 'dredge' comfits, that is, sugar-coated dragees very popular in apothecary shops. Sometimes an unfortunate one had need of a midwife, when she would have to scuttle from Court. Professional midwives were also licensed by the bishops – and sometimes turned their talents to abortion. 'Agnes Hobson of Alne [in the bishopric of Durham] administers love potions or apothecaries' potions of her own preparation, wherewith she destroys the foetus in the womb, and even the mother. She has given the said potions to very many women. She has made expiation.'[31] Agnes Marshall, of Driffield Parva, performed as a midwife without proper experience: her chief line was incantations. These, of course, were very common at childbirth, as was baptism by midwives. This was unpopular with Protestants, and James I made it felony – because of the danger of witchcraft.

Naval surgeons needed a knowledge of physic as well as surgery. One sees how impossible it was to maintain a rigid distinction, with so well known a surgeon as John Banister, author of several text-books. He had shared the military experiences of William Clowes in 1563 and again in 1586, and at forty-two sailed in the *Leicester* for the East.[32] A general practitioner at Nottingham, when he combined physic with surgery, the College came down on him. The Queen directed that he be given a licence; the College complied, but stipulated that he was to call in a Fellow in dangerous cases. The overseas voyages were having an effect upon the profession by the 1580's, aloes coming in from Malacca, senna from Mecca, *nux vomica* from Malabar. But it was an adventurer, not a doctor, George Watson, who first described the tropical diseases of the West Indies in *The Cure of the Diseased in Remote Regions*, 1598. Under 'taberdilla' he gave an account of yellow fever, of sun- or heat-stroke under 'calenture'; he recommended beer in which grain and red pepper had been soaked, against scurvy. One of the Caribbean voyagers noticed that the native medicine was more effectual than the needle for the itch of chigger-flea beneath the skin. John Lock, calling at Famagusta in 1553, gave the first English description of trachoma; the merchant Henry Hawks, at Vera Cruz in 1572, noticed the suspicious connexion between the mosquito and malaria.

III

Of diseases the one most characteristic of the age, which we do not have with us today, is plague. Since the Black Death in mid-fourteenth century it had been endemic in Europe. In England, as elsewhere, it was a factor of the utmost importance that people had to accept and live with for the next three centuries, until, after the frightful outbreak of 1665, it tapered off. One can hardly begin to estimate its effects, physical, let alone psychological. Its impact on population has never, so far as I know, been fully appreciated. Plague was always in being, increasing in summer, declining in winter; then, every decade or so, there would be a severe outbreak, killing something like one-tenth of the population. Within two or three years the population figures had recovered, the cistern had welled up again. That shows that, without the plague, there would have been a population-explosion beyond the means of subsistence. It indicates, too, that its cessation must have been an important factor in the eighteenth-century increase of population. What its effects on men's minds must have been no one can describe: one can understand the readiness to accept the fact of death, the chanciness, the transitoriness of life, the inescapable inequality of men's lives and conditions. Perhaps there was a brighter radiance upon life, because of its uncertainty:

> Adieu, farewell earth's bliss!
> This world uncertain is:
> Fond are life's lustful joys,
> Death proves them all but toys.
> None from his darts can fly:
> I am sick, I must die:
> *Lord have mercy on us.*

There is the inscription written upon infected houses; it is probable that the author of those lines himself died of the plague.

Not until the nineteenth century was the plague bacillus isolated. There were two forms – bubonic, which affected the lymphatic glands, and pneumonic, which caused acute inflammation of the lungs, of which people usually died. The two forms often operated together. The sixteenth century knew about infection and contagion but did not suspect that the carrier was the small black rat, whose fleas carried the bacillus. Evidently heat brought out the fleas: the plague was at its hottest in the summer months. From the fifteenth century it became more of a disease of town-life, though epidemics of it spread to the country, where at intervals there were severe visitations. Then, too, infection arrived from abroad. The heavy epidemic of 1563 was brought back by the army from the Le Havre campaign. By 1564 it had arrived at Stratford, where it might easily have swept away John and Mary Shakespeare's first-born in his cradle.

Statistics in the sixteenth century are notoriously unreliable, and not too much should be built on them. But plague-statistics are fairly reliable, for the London bills of mortality and the parish registers roughly corroborate each other. We may infer that parish registers in the country are not far out. The reader should not be burdened by figures more appropriately placed in a footnote: a few may be sufficiently revealing. Stow gives the deaths from plague in London from June to December 1563 as some 17,500, and in its suburban out-parishes, some 2,750.[33] There were about 20,000 plague-deaths out of a total mortality of 23,600: that is, in this severe epidemic about five in six deaths were owing to plague. Less severe epidemics occurred every decade or so. During the years 1583–92 when there was no large outbreak, merely a few hundred up and down from year to year, the population of the city alone – apart from the suburbs – leaped from 120,000 to 150,000. The year 1603 saw a bad outbreak: of the 38,000 people who died that year in London 30,500 died from plague: again something approaching five out of six.[34] Of a total population of some 200,000 something like one-sixth perished. They were soon replaced. People moved in from the country and from abroad; by the end of 1605 the number of births had almost recovered.

Perhaps a few more figures may be borne with, to illustrate what a scourge plague was at intervals and how the epidemics went up and down. London figures are the fullest and most reliable:[35]

Year	Total Deaths	Of Plague
1578	7830	3568
1579	3406	629
1580	2873	128
1581	3931	987
1582	6762	2976

It would be possible to compile comparative figures for country towns and parishes: we do not need to, the point is sufficiently clear. Every ten years or so the parish registers show a severe outbreak. In 1575 a bad epidemic swept Bristol and the West of England; in 1590 another: in little Totnes, with a population of some 2000, 246 died of plague during eight months.[36] In 1627 at Dartmouth, with a comparable population, there were 110 plague deaths in the summer months; some people left the town for the country. Nevertheless, after 1610 plague began to abate in country districts.

When a bad outbreak was at its height – and this is an important point – people were really helpless: they could only wait, fatalistically, for it to abate. Society in the sixteenth and seventeenth centuries was 'insufficiently organised to carry out with success an elaborate set of unpopular orders . . . when the pestilence became virulent the populace got out of control, and the authorities were forced to sit with folded hands until the plague had spent itself.'[37] Contrary to orders people would crowd over plague pits, or heaps of the dead – curiosity (or cupidity) no doubt being as great as grief. Sixteenth century people were highly emotional – like Middle Easterners or the inhabitants of Belfast or West Side, New York, today: nothing could induce them not to crowd to the burials. When the authorities failed they were liable to receive a rating from on high. In 1583 the Privy Council administered a stinging reproof to the City, on behalf of the Queen, for not providing an isolation hospital: 'whereat her Majesty doth the less marvel when she considereth how slenderly you respect the preservation of your own lives, preferring your desire of trade and gain before duty and nature ... Wherein many cities of less antiquity, fame, wealth, circuit and reputation are to be preferred before that of London, as being in all countries provided of such a place.'[38] Not until ten years later, after the severe epidemic of 1592–3, did the City start to build a pest-house; by 1604 Dublin had one, by 1606 Manchester.[39] When the Queen visited Ipswich she herself gave it a rating, the clergy for their laxity, the town authorities for the state of the streets.[40] This was followed by a significant improvement; paternal government answers: people are always and everywhere children.

The plague-orders of the authorities were sensible enough, if only they could have been strictly executed. Infected houses were to be shut up, the inhabitants not to move in or out for twenty or so days, their wants supplied by the richer members of the parish – obviously this could not be adhered to in a big outbreak. Those owning wells were to sluice the channels; fires in the streets at night to burn all rubbish. Dogs were greatly blamed – and the streets swarmed with them; hundreds of them were killed – but this may not have been a good thing, since they killed the rats that were not suspected. Rats were encouraged by the awful habit of throwing out entrails, tripes etc. into the water-channels, and the numerous barber-surgeons casting blood out of doors after their blood-lettings. Thomas Lodge pleaded in vain that slaughter-houses should be abolished to the outskirts near the river, so that garbage and refuge might be swept away by the tide. He suggested that infected garments of the well-to-do be burnt, as in Italy. The authorities ordered that the dead be taken straight away to their graves, but 'people of the poorer sort, even women with young children, flocked to burials and out of sheer bravado stood over open plague-pits to show the world that they did not fear the infection.'[41] The theory was that 'it was impossible to take the infection during the act of worship'; fortunately the authorities did not act on this nonsense: they forbade people from suspect houses, whether themselves infected or not, from attending church. As the years went on scavenging orders became stricter; surveyors of parishes and nurse-keepers were appointed in London.

Apart from the fundamental fact that the cause of the infection was unknown, medical treatment was sensible enough in general. Victims were recommended to stay in bed, in a warm temperature, on a low diet. No doubt this indicates one reason why, in the plague of 1603, far more men died than women: the women stayed in bed, while the menfolk had to stay on their legs to the last to get a living. Of course, people preferred fancy remedies, cordial waters, arsenic under the armpits, the holding of plucked pullets or pigeons to the plague-sores until the poor birds died. 'The pullet will gape and labour for life, and in the end will die; then have another pullet and do the like to the patient, and if that die, yet still apply the patient with pullets so long as any do die.'[42] The birds were supposed to be drawing out the poison: we see that sympathetic magic was what the savages believed in. More rational doctors lanced the botches in armpits, groin, neck, the enlarged lymphatic glands – though that must have had its dangers in the ignorance of sepsis. Perhaps 'Dr.' Forman did less damage with his waters: he won fame by sticking to his post in 1593, it may have been this that first gave him success. A popular verse testifies:

> Then came the plague in ninety-three
> Whence all these Doctors fled:
> I stayed, to save the lives of many
> That otherwise had been dead.

Bamford, a Southwark clergyman, held that magistrates and the clergy should remain at their posts – as they did – being public persons; but doctors should consider their own lives and ability to do good, 'in regard they are no public persons and live, not by a common stipend, but by what they can get.'[43] He wrote a tract against 'the bloody error which denieth the pestilence to be contagious.' But his reasoning was no better than anybody else's: 'doth not the ordinary experience of laying live pigeons to plague-sores and taking them presently dead away, and that one after another, demonstrate mortal infection?'

We know how prudent and responsible citizens behaved in time of visitation from the letters of the actor, Edward Alleyn, to his wife in the summer of 1593: 'keep your house fair and clean,

which I know you will, and every evening throw water before
your door and in your back-side, and have in your window good
store of rue and herb of grace.'[44] Her stepfather replied that the
plague has been 'almost in every house about us, and whole
households died. My friend the bailiff doth escape, but he smells
monstrously for fear and dares stay nowhere.' Last week some
1130 had died of plague, the largest number yet. The actor,
'Robert Browne's wife in Shoreditch and all her children and
household be dead, and her doors shut up.' Henslowe had a
receipt for a drink for the pestilence: 'take and wash clean a lily
root and boil it in white wine till the one half be wasted. Then
give it the patient to drink and he shall break out full of bladders
as he were burned or scalded with hot water and then they will
dry and the person wax whole.'[45] It was thought that if the bubos
did not come out, the plague went inwards and the patient died;
but people did not distinguish between the bubonic and pneumonic symptoms.

So frightful a phenomenon has left many evidences in literature, medical and otherwise. Or there were the losses to the arts:
Robert White, one of the most brilliant composers, died a young
man in his thirties in the epidemic of 1574, with his wife and
three daughters.[46] In 1603 Ben Jonson was staying with his old
master, Camden, at Sir Robert Cotton's in Huntingdon when
he saw, in a vision, his eldest boy, then seven, 'with the mark of a
bloody cross on his forehead.' The child died of the plague:

> Farewell, thou child of my right hand, and joy;
> My sin was too much hope of thee, loved boy . . .
> Rest in soft peace and, asked, say here doth lie
> Ben Jonson his best piece of poetry.

The Globe Theatre was closed for some eleven months in 1603–4.
F. P. Wilson suggests that since the second quarto of Shakespeare's
Hamlet was printed 'according to the true and perfect copy' towards the end of the year, 'it is possible that in these months he
revised and enriched the play which has done most to immortalise
his name.'[47] It is at any rate now certain that the crisis of the
plague years 1592–3, with the closing of the theatres for the
greater part of two years, gave him the time in which to write
Venus and Adonis, *The Rape of Lucrece*, and most of the Sonnets.

After the crabbed works of the physicians and preachers –
Bullein, Kelway, Bamford – it is a relief to read the tracts of
Lodge, Dekker, Middleton, who all wrote on the plague. In the

epidemic of 1603 numbers of people had come flocking to Lodge in Warwick Lane for his cordial waters; but, a gentleman, he objected to making himself vendible, 'unworthy a liberal and gentle mind, much more ill beseeming a physician and a philosopher'.[48] Even he, a doctor, was in favour of the use of arsenic cakes under the armpits or about the heart: 'by a certain similitude one venom draweth another out.' But, besides, let the wind be between thee and the sick person, or hold some odoriferous perfume in the hand; fly narrow ways and streets where there are dunghills, haunt no assemblies or feasts. Best of all – keep out of the way of it. Dekker's moralistic pamphlets condemn the runaways; but, indeed, what more sensible than to run away?[49] In the epidemic of 1563 the Queen remained at Windsor; a gibbet was erected in the market-place for persons coming from London. Dekker's descriptions of the scenes in London in 1603 are vivid, tear-jerking journalism, though his tributes to the stricken city are sincere, for he was a born Londoner, in love with his nursing mother, and in his verse *News from Gravesend* he is moved to poetry.

The two heaviest epidemics of plague came in from abroad: that of 1563, as we have seen, and that of 1603, which was thought to have been brought back by soldiers from the Netherlands. It is fairly clear that the Sweating Sickness, which came to be known as the English Sweat, was brought in by Henry VII's Norman mercenaries who fought for him at Bosworth. Epidemics of this were severe in 1485, 1506, 1517, 1528, 1551; after this the disease seems to have lost its virulence.[50] It was probably a kind of 24-hour influenza, with a very high fever; if the patient sweated freely he usually recovered, if not he died. The disease is noteworthy to us as the subject of the first English classic of medicine, Caius' *A Counsel against the Sweat*, 1552. Caius apologised for writing in English, but he had been asked by friends for his advice – and very sensible modern-minded advice he gave.

Middle-aged and middle- and upper-class people were mostly affected by it – Caius thought that it had something to do with their over-eating (by contrast with Italians and Spaniards). He thought also that it might be carried by fogs, mists and damps; he did not exclude the influence of the constellations. His advice was in accordance. Instead of superstitious waters and treatments, a pure and moderate diet; avoid infected fruits, drinks and meats. Clean houses – voiding rushes and dust; perfumes and odours within, fresh air without. Clean clothes, plenty of exercise and ease of mind; clean ditches and waters about the house. Nature is pleased with a little: no surfeiting (Henry VIII was given to surfeiting, his daughter to a low, moderate diet). Caius' advice was in keeping with Hippocrates: help nature to do its work.

Typhus grumbled away unspecified among the poor, with their lice; but it made history when it emerged into the light of day, as gaol-fever, at the notorious Black Assizes at Oxford in July 1577, and at Exeter in 1586. There are horrified accounts of both, because of the persons affected.[51] At Oxford there died two judges, the sheriff, two knights, eight of the J.P.'s, several gentlemen and their servants, the whole of the grand jury with one or two exceptions. No one knew how it happened – some idiots suggested that it had been let loose upon the court by the papists of Louvain. Sir William MacArthur has suggested that dust from the lice of the prisoners may have been blown about the court by a breeze on a hot July day. Among those who died were a Harcourt, a Fettiplace and Anthony Forster, owner of Cumnor Place when Amy Robsart fell down the stairs there. The infection spread to the town, where some 300 died. At Exeter Sir Bernard Drake of Ashe had cast the crew of a Portuguese ship into a foul deep pit of the Castle. At Assizes he paid for it with his life; so did Sir Arthur Basset, Sir John Chichester, Thomas Carew of Haccombe, Robert Cary of Clovelly, John Waldron of Bradfield (his Elizabethan house still stands), John Fortescue, Thomas Risdon. There were risks in being a J.P. in those insanitary days. No one had more pitied the poor prisoners than the Lord Chief Justice, who took order for their better keeping in the Castle. They had their revenge.

Diseases vary in virulence according to conditions, internal and external, the strength of bacillus or virus, the resistance built up to its attack, etc. Smallpox made no such figure in the sixteenth as it did in the seventeenth and eighteenth centuries – the Queen suffered an attack and recovered with no ill effects; Philip Sidney's mother, who attended her, went down with it and was disfigured for life. The French pox, *morbus gallicus*, as the English called it, was a worse scourge. People then had no doubt that it came to Europe from the West Indies: hence the attachment to guaiacum as a remedy – on the theory that God provided a counter-agent wherever a particular disease came from. Syphilis was brought to Naples by Spanish soldiers from the New World; it came north with the French, after Charles VIII's Italian campaign ni 194–5. It spread rapidly and widely, from the bottom to the top of

society: Francis I had it, so had the Emperor Charles V – Vesalius
was his doctor (Dr. Caius lived with Vesalius at Padua while he
was writing his epoch-making book on anatomy). It does not
appear that Henry VIII had it – his disease was glandular; and
young Edward VI died of tuberculosis.

A number of tracts on this new disease, one or more being
translations, appeared in English. We may confine ourselves to
the best, by the leading surgeon of the age, William Clowes. As
surgeon in army and navy, and at the London hospitals, he had
a wide experience of treating it. In addition to his expertise,
Clowes was an excellent writer, vivid and veracious; his stories
alone are an introduction to the social life of the age: they have
much in common with Forman – of whose type Clowes strongly
disapproved. Nevertheless, Clowes was not without his troubles.
On one occasion he was sued by a husband for not curing his wife
of the pox, and had to pay 20s.[52] This reminds us that people
expected a medical man to cure them, and were apt to hold him
responsible if he did not. On another occasion Clowes fought with
a fellow-surgeon in the fields. No bones were broken, and subsequently the fellow added the useful appendix on mercury treatment to Clowes' book on syphilis.

Clowes was yet another Warwickshire man, born in 1544. In
the French campaign of 1563 he served with his senior and life-
long friend, John Banister, who wrote a number of popular, if un-
original, books on medicine. It is significant that the surgeons
were more voluble in English, where the physicians were still
constipated in Latin; but none had a quill as sharp as Clowes.
From 1564 he was surgeon in the Queen's ships based at Ports-
mouth; in 1580 he got the Bishop's licence to practise medicine,
by her direct favour. He served with Leicester's army in the
Netherlands, became surgeon-in-chief to the Fleet in '88, and
retired in 1596 to Plaistow where he died in 1604. His house, with
its fine chimney-piece and coat-of-arms, was demolished in our
time for a cinema.

Several editions of his book on syphilis were called for: the
disease was now widespread in England as elsewhere, and in his
opinion increasing. In five years he and his three fellow-surgeons
at St. Bartholomew's had cured – so they thought – over 1000
persons there, besides those at St. Thomas's and other hospitals
about the country. At St. Bartholomew's he says fifteen in twenty
had the disease, in another book he says ten in twenty – one sees
how loosely Elizabethans talk about figures.[53] He thought that the

disease was not always contracted from unclean women, for often the private parts exhibited no symptoms while other parts of the body did – one observes the confusion here. Some children were infected by the milk of corrupt nurses; he does not seem to have suspected that they might have inherited it. Others got it by wearing the clothes of infected persons, or touching them, or sitting on the same stools of easement. The disease's characteristic 'flowing matter, being once entered into any part of the body, proceedeth on from part to part, never resting: especially when it toucheth any such part as hath in it an apt disposition to admit such infection.' He meant the mucous membranes – a correct observation. The best doctors abroad defined it as an affection of the liver, for it corrupts the blood; but the symptoms varied according to 'the humour which most ruleth in them' – we see the mingling of medieval with modern characteristic of the age.

Here again: 'I judge it very dangerous to touch any part of man's body with lancet or knife whenas the moon hath motion in that sign [of the Zodiac] which governeth the part that should be stricken. As to open a vein in the head when the moon is in Aries; or in the neck when she is in Taurus, in the arms the moon being in Gemini,' etc. 'If the moon be in Leo by the which the heart is governed, it hath been thought, then dangerous to let blood at all.' We learn that children were not usually let blood till puberty, nor elderly people after sixty. Many people thought to cure the pox simply by purging, especially when it was newly taken and the patient strong and lusty. We may remark here the lightheartedness with which this dreadful scourge was treated on the stage, a subject for jokes about people losing their noses or their members. Shakespeare jokes about it often enough, though in his bitter play *Timon of Athens* he has a passage on its horrors – and Clowes had seen or read about Timon.[54] He gives detailed instructions as to opening the obstructed passages by syrups and waters, and rules for blood-letting. This should be done only by practised doctors, not by 'painters, glasiers, joiners and, I think, tinkers and cobblers . . . too too far.'

On diet he is very sensible, as also on massage, procuring a sweat, ointments and so on. If the ointments are not sufficient, add more mercury, always first mortifying it with *aqua vitae*, or something to check its corrosive biting. Mercury is objected to as hurting the sinews, but we must take that remedy till better be found. Most people shunned the use of mercury as poison, but the doctors favoured it. Different lotions are prescribed for washing the mouth, till the ulcers are cured, the teeth fastened, the throat healed. Guaiacum is held very useful, though not all the guaiacum in the Indies would suffice to treat the numbers suffering from the disease.

One of Clowes' cases will serve to introduce us to the horrors people suffered. A man thought he was suffering from 'an involuntary flux, or looseness of the reins, called gonorrhea.'[55] The aetiology of these various diseases was of course unknown, but doctors could distinguish different symptoms. Clowes diagnosed an advanced case of syphilis: 'the roof of his mouth was pierced through with corruption of the bone, and many sharp and putrefied humours continually distilling from the brain . . . Also he was still troubled with *gonorrhea foetida* and his body greatly pined and wasted, as it were in a lingering consumption.' Clowes could do nothing for the poor fellow, who shortly called in a quack, 'who did administer unto him his fume [brimstone and mercury] . . . he received the smoke thereof chiefly in his mouth, being in his bed sitting upright, and a cloak or mantle cast over his head . . . to keep in the smoke or fume. At the second perfuming suddenly his head was taken with a convulsion, and a marvellous shaking and trembling over all his body, and so he died.'

It throws a lurid light on Falstaff's not unkindly words to Doll Tearsheet: 'You help to make the diseases, Doll. We catch of you, Doll, we catch of you. Grant that, my poor virtue, grant that.'

Sixteenth-century civilisation saw rapid progress in the firepower of guns, and so the treatment of gunshot wounds became more urgent. Most people believed that these wounds were poisoned: this was the first hurdle that intelligent surgeons had to get over. The second was the horrible treatment by cauterisation, or with boiling oil. Here the great French surgeon, Ambroise Paré, introduced new methods.[56] Clowes was in touch with the best French thought, and quotes receipts of Paré. But he does not seem to have practised Guillemeau's method of double ligatures to stop bleeding: he stopped the veins with restrictive powders, caustics. Nevertheless he had good success in dealing with these wounds. He tells us that in Leicester's army in the Low Countries in 1585, 'there did not die, to my remembrance, one man that was then hurt with gunshot so that he was not first wounded to death, but that he was shortly after perfectly cured.'[57] In this case what a pity Clowes did not attend Sir Philip Sidney! We know that Clowes was not far away, for 'when I was at

Arnhem at that time when Nymegen was besieged,' the knowledge of Paracelsus' plaster was imparted to Clowes as a secret by
Jerome Fermor, 'a great favourer and lover of chirurgery': whom
we see upon the wall of the chancel at Towcester, who lived 'in
wedlock with his wife 42 years, and he attained to the honour of
a great grand-uncle', dying in 1602.

Clowes' accounts of his cases are fascinating, if sometimes
horrifying. He cured a man who fractured his skull and thighbone
on the famous occasion when the gallery at the Bear Garden fell,
killing a number of people. Clowes performed a successful tre-
panning operation upon him, first darkening the room till it was
without air or light, save for a candle, 'because in this case the
air is very hurtful.'[58] A London cheesemonger overcharged his
dag (i.e. pistol), which flew up into the corner of his eye and
fractured the bone. The surgeons allowed the wound to close up,
the man grew weaker and weaker and at length speechless, so
that 'divers times the bell tolled for him.' Clowes opened the
wound and took out the screw of the dag with the fractured
bones. The cheesemonger 'liveth to this day.' Clowes never minded
claiming his due: nor did any Elizabethan. And it is good to find
him speaking up for the unfortunate Dr. Lopez, who was 'both
careful and skilful not only for his counsel in dieting, purging and
bleeding, but also for his direction of Arceus' apozema.' This was
a concoction of glycerine, cummin seed, a contusion of bugloss
roots, etc.: 'I have found it a treasure for the curing of wounds
in the breast.'[59]

If gangrene sets in (as it did with Sidney) then the limb must
be amputated, in accordance with Thomas Gale's directions, of
the previous generation, who published his book on gun-shot
wounds in 1563. Great care was necessary over the operation,
and close attention paid beforehand to the state of the body 'for
evacuation and dieting.' Two hours before the operation a good
warm caudle should be administered, and a brisk exhortation by
a preacher. Two strong men are necessary to hold the patient
down on the form and grip the leg so firmly that it will numb
the incision and stay the bleeding; the surgeon to have a sharp
saw with a steady, quick hand. There follow two pages illustrating
surgeons' instruments, directions for stitching etc. One is reminded of Paré's horrifying description of operating for stone in
the bladder.[60] What people went through! One would imagine
that the best thing would be to be dosed with laudanum. They
did know its use, for Clowes tells us how to make it: take opium,

slice and dry it in an earthen platter, 'gather the roots of white henbane in March, the moon being full, and dry them in the shadow.'[61] In the treatment of syphilis, if there is much pain from the mercury treatment, 'a little opium may be put to it.'

Surgeons were much more open to the new Paracelsan remedies than the physicians were, who stuck to Galen. Clowes recommends turbith mineral, an oil of sulphur, for taking away dead or proud flesh after treatment for the pox. And what extraordinary things people suffered from! – he has a powder 'to take away warts that grow about the *praeputium*', a collirium for ulcers of the yard, an unguent to open a bubo (plague-swelling) when it suppurates.[62]

Clowes' last book was on the Struma, or King's Evil. This was a kind of scrofulous abscess or glandulous tumour, hard, knotty and kernelly, in the neck or under the chin, on the breast, under the armpits or in the groin, sometimes with large veins or arteries. Clowes states, 'it is hard to cure a noisome, corrupt and malignant ulcerous struma, which doth many times degenerate into incurable cancerous and rebellious fistulous ulcers.' He held that if the disease was inherited it could not be cured by surgery. 'These kinds of scrofulous abscessions do rather presage a divine and holy curation, which is most admirable to the world, that I have seen and known performed and done by the sacred hands of the Queen's most royal Majesty.' It must have been a disgusting spectacle for her to look on – the penalty of her sacramental vocation. All European monarchs performed, at a certain stage of civilisation – as it might be Chaka or Cetywayo. The common-sense Hanoverians discontinued it when they came to the English throne.

No medical writer of the time comes up to Clowes in personal observation or perhaps in his roving spirit of inquiry – his personality comes through and keeps him alive when others are forgotten. His friend, John Banister, wrote quite as many books: the next generation thought it worth while to publish them in collected form in 1633. Both Clowes and Banister were imbued with the desire to instruct the younger members of the profession and to bring medical knowledge abreast with the latest developments on the Continent. Banister says, in dedicating his compendium of anatomy, *The History of Man*, to Sir Francis Willoughby – that amateur of science – that he sought above all 'the advancement of chirurgery in England, in the which cogitation my zeal hath long time turned.'[63] Living in Silver Street Banister would have had Shakespeare for a neighbour about 1600.

Banister's line was to adapt for English readers information from foreign writers, so we find him repeating and commenting on Tagault and Fernel, Colombo, Fallopius and Vesalius. He has a sour comment on the last, 'whose whole work seemed as tedious as his Epitome over-culled and short', and he takes the opportunity to follow Colombo in saying that in the yard is neither vein nor nerve, 'notwithstanding that Vesalius is of clean contrary opinion.'[64] One would suppose that Banister was so addicted to books that he could not use his own eyes. The limitation of his mind is evident in his omission to describe the private parts of women: 'I am from the beginning persuaded that, by lifting up the veil of nature's secrets in women's shapes, I shall commit more indecency against the office of decorum than yield needful instruction to the profit of the common sort.' He did get so far, however, as to say, 'it seemeth certain that Aristotle was not a little deceived in matters anatomical' – he thought that the hinder part of the head was destitute of brain.

Banister and Clowes gave each other moral support. It would seem that they were under attack by third-rate members of their profession, now forgotten, for writing too much. Clowes says, in commending Banister's *Antidotary Chirurgical*, 'one chief cause of their great impatience is for publishing of such like works as is this your *Antidotary*, saying forsooth that only their mere practice is sufficient without so many books.' But, of course, *they* couldn't write, and intelligent colleagues would find the book useful. Elsewhere Clowes states that he has himself experienced 'carping envy' for his recent book, *De Morbo Gallico*:

> But who so ready to control, [criticise]
> or fit to carp and clatter,
> As he that hath the dimmest sight
> and judgment in the matter.

This ulcerated self-consciousness and sensitiveness to criticism was characteristic of Elizabethans.

We need not linger over the naive works of Andrew Borde or Thomas Vicary, who were Henricians, or even of William Bullein, a prolific writer who died in 1576.[65] Borde and Bullein were both sharp observers with sharp pens. Among Bullein's works was a *Dialogue on the Fever Pestilence*. He wrote a good deal in dialogue form; his stories, reminiscences and folklore are more interesting than his medicine. In his book on the plague, for instance, there is a reminiscence that takes us back to the Wars of the Roses and Barnet Heath where Warwick the Kingmaker fell. The battle was fought on Palm Sunday, 1471, and Roger's 'grandfather was also here with twenty tall men of the parish whereat I was born, and none of them escaped but my grandfather only. I had his bow in my hand many a time . . . Also his harness was worn upon our St. George's back in our church many a cold winter after, and I heard my grandame tell how he escaped.' He climbed up an oak-tree and, being a thatcher, climbed well out of danger, and after hid thereabouts.[66]

It brings home to us that the Wars of the Roses were not far away from the Elizabethans; after all, it was Elizabeth's grandfather who won the Battle of Bosworth.

Psychiatry, as a medical subject in itself, was something new. Timothy Bright's *Treatise of Melancholy*, 1586, is the best-known work in the field. Blood-letting and purgation were the standard treatment for melancholia,[67] but Bright probed into its physical and psychological causes and suggested more sympathetic treatment. He diagnosed two kinds of melancholy, either 'a certain fearful disposition of the mind, or else an humour of the body.'[68] His account of how the grosser part of the blood mounts up into the brain by 'vapours' was to have a notable future in the eighteenth century. Along with a good deal of nonsense in the Elizabethan manner – about ostriches' feeding, about God and coleworts and cabbages – there is some sound sense about the effects of climate and occupations on people's make-up. We learn that butchers were not employed on juries in capital cases; 'they being accustomed with slaughter', the difference between man and beast was not so sensitively appreciated.

Fear, in Bright's opinion, was the root of melancholic sorrow, the apprehension of danger even if there was none, fantasy making it worse than it is: he is describing, in our phrase, the state of *Angst*.[69] He goes into some of the phenomena of hysteria, and how these psychological states affect the body and *vice versa*. He has a chapter on the afflictions of conscience of sin – what we call guilt-complex. He recommends a light vegetable and fruit diet to thin the blood; rest and sleep, and avoidance of the labours of the mind, since 'studies have great force to procure melancholy, if they be vehement and of difficult matters and high mysteries.' Along with contemporary nonsense about the use of stones, especially carbuncles (rubies or garnets), he prescribes cheerful music 'and such as carrieth an odd measure.' Avoid 'dumps and fancies and set music . . . which serve rather for a disordered rage', for music can be a magical charm upon men's minds. That Bright found it so we know from his will: it mentions his books of music theory, his two volumes of Zarlino in Italian and 'those my instruments of music called the theorbo and the Irish harp, which I most usually played upon.'[70] The past tense is affecting.

We know from several indications that Shakespeare read Bright's book before writing *Hamlet*, not only the characteristic verbal transformation of 'the brain as tender as a posset curd' into 'it doth posset and curd . . . the thin and wholesome blood.' The Huntington Library copy of Bright's book belonged to one C. P. A contemporary hand has scrawled 'Love Love Love LLL' a score of times; then, 'no more thou little winged archer O no more as heretofore thou', 'love is an eating care a cross. Love is an eating', 'Love Love no love', 'quis liberavit.' At the end, 'Lord if thou wilt thou canst make me clean. Lord speak the word and thy servant shall be cleansed from all her sin.'

Perhaps this takes us into the heart of an Elizabethan psychiatric case.

The first English book on hysteria was written by Edward Jordan, *A Brief Discourse of a Disease called the Suffocation of the Mother*, 1603. A student at Padua, Jordan was familiar with the work of Cardan, whose name for it was *passio hysterica*. Once in the Santo at Padua Jordan had seen five or six idiots 'at one sermon interrupting and reviling the preacher until he had put them to silence by the sign of the Cross and certain powerless spells.' One recognises across the centuries the common sense attitude of the English abroad, contemptuous of Continental credulity and its manifestations. But we have seen that at home there were Catholic priests at work encouraging hysteria in foolish women, to gain credit for the faith by exorcising demons from them.* Jordan's tract was written to expose this nonsense and show that the phenomena 'which in the common opinion are imputed to the Devil have their true natural causes.'

He began his attack by a very cogent claim for a doctor to be heard in his own proper province. Why should we not prefer the judgments of physicians in a question concerning the actions and passions of man's body – the proper subject of that profession – before our own conceits, as we do the opinions of divines, lawyers,

* Cf. *The Elizabethan Renaissance: The Life of the Society*, 267 foll.

artificers, etc. in their proper elements?' This is a convincing
Elizabethan approach, by contrast with the modern assumption –
quite untrue in fact – that everybody's opinion is of value and to
be heard. Jordan wrote his book that people's 'unlearned and
rash conceits might be thereby brought to better understanding
and moderation who are apt to make everything a supernatural
work which they do not understand.'

He showed that many hysterical symptoms were observable
in other diseases; for example, insensibility, not feeling when
pricked by a pin, accompanied apoplexy or palsy; convulsions
appeared in epilepsy. Women were much more liable to hysteria
than men; the symptoms were those of a retention of the 'mother'
or womb, the breathing being affected, accompanied by a choking
in the throat. Jordan cited cases of a woman who had a fit every
Saturday for ten weeks, another at a particular hour, and a
young man who had fits on incurring his father's disfavour and
recovered on reconciliation. We recognise the psycho-somatic
pattern nowadays. Jordan knew a gentlewoman 'who upon the
sight of one man would always feel an uterine affect.' No doubt.
Some women suffering a syncope should not be buried for three
days, for some have come to life again. This accounts for the well-
known story in the Mount Edgcumbe family – of the Countess
in her coffin restored to life when a servant bit her finger to get
her rings – as also of many miracles. Some hysterics can induce
epilepsy, feign possession, etc.: of such was the Holy Maid of
Kent who got Bishop Fisher, More and other holy men into
trouble. Jordan describes the symptoms clearly, recites what was
thought to be the causes, and prescribes sensible treatment: light
diet, moderate religious instruction, allowing patients to enjoy
their desires, and sometimes 'politicly confirm them in their
fantasies.' It all sounds quite modern.

Many years later Jordan wrote a second book on *Natural
Baths and Mineral Waters*, 1631, for he had become a resident
doctor at Bath. A first book on the English Baths had been written
by Dr. William Turner in 1562; he inveighed against their poor
equipment, to anyone who knew the spas abroad, and at how
little appreciated the natural resources of the country were – as
good as anywhere else, if only people knew. Jordan made practical
proposals for the cleansing of baths every day, their draining
from the bottom, separate baths for women and for those suffering
from infectious or contagious diseases.[71] At Bath there were some
five baths, the warmest of which was the King's Bath; the waters

were strong in bitumen, people drank them and bathed in them. At the Dissolution the baths passed from the priory ultimately into the control of the corporation.[72] A new 'Lepers' Bath' was constructed for people with 'horrible' diseases; people came in increasing numbers to the little town, doctors set up there – Turner's son, Peter, the well-known Dr. Sherwood, Jordan. Conditions improved, better buildings and protection from the weather, but stricter regulations could not prevent mixed bathing in the nude.

The later sixteenth century saw a marked advance in the cult of baths and in the use of mineral waters at health resorts. In place of the miracle-working holy wells with their saints, health resorts with their resident doctors. In backward places the old cults continued – at St. Madron's or St. Nun's well in Cornwall, or St. Winifred's near Flint, to which Catholics chiefly resorted. By 1572, when Shrewsbury put up the buildings, Buxton became a place of resort, second only to Bath. Mary Queen of Scots spent a month there in 1573, profiting from the waters, and paid several visits in the years following.[73] Burghley was there in 1575, rather to Elizabeth's suspicion, though she encouraged him to return in 1577 – herself had no use for the waters and rather laughed at the fashion. She drafted a comic letter, prescribing a minimal diet for Leicester, who was a frequenter. So were the hypochondriac Cecils, Burghley and his two sons, who patronised both Bath and Buxton. Burghley took a course of drinking the waters for ten days before going into the bath. We have plenty of information from the chamberlain's accounts at Bath about the aristocratic patrons of the place.[74] Among the most frequent visitors were Burghley's eldest son, the Swedish Marchioness of Northampton, the Queen's cousins, the Hunsdons, Leicester and Warwick, Ralegh and his relations, Sir John Gilbert and Sir Thomas Gorges.

We have an immense amount of information about people's illnesses among the upper classes – as with Americans today their letters are full of their physical complaints. Courtiers and officials have frequently to excuse themselves from attendance at Court or upon their duties on account of ill health, their rheums and agues, their aches and pains, their purgations and blood-lettings. One sympathises with the plaintive Egerton who accounts falling into the physician's hands a curse. Burghley's letters are wearisome with endless complaints of his woes. One has only to turn over a few pages of the Cecil correspondence to find everybody complaining.[75] Lord Stafford has left Court for fear of the pox (small), but now has ague. Lord Shrewsbury has the stone – like a large number of people. The second Lord Burghley has taken a course of physic, but dares not rely on York (where he is Lord President) for the apothecaries are all recusants. Lord Hunsdon has not derived much benefit from a visit to Bath, and he has been half turned into an apothecary's shop. Lord Cobham finds that there is never a good bone-setter in London; on the other hand, Sir Edward Hoby's knee has received much good from the thumber's hands – evidently an osteopath. Lord Burgh has 'been cut all over my leg with a lancet, and abidden loathsome worms to suck my flesh' – incisions made for leeches – 'and of all this have I more anguish than I would wish almost my enemy to feel.' Lord Cobham warns his brother-in-law, Robert Cecil, that Lord Treasurer Buckhurst's two daughters have small pox, and 'you know he doth ever wear furs. There is no one thing that doth carry infection so much as furs doth. I have heard you often say that you more fear the smallpox than anything else. Respect your health above anything, and think upon yourself and your poor friends if such a misfortune should now befall you' – Cecil would be sitting in Council with Buckhurst that afternoon. Bishop Bancroft is suffering from a tertian ague, of which he has had five fits: he is in bed 'expecting for a fit the sixth in number.' He was not a healthy man; he suffered agonies from stone, sometimes having to have sick-leave from attending the House of Lords. He was archbishop for only six years before he died.

It appears that one form of 'ague' was malaria. 'For centuries malaria was firmly established in certain endemic centres in England, particularly the Fen country, the marshes of the Thames estuary, the marshes of south-east Kent, the low-lying country around Bridgwater, and the Ribble district in Lancashire. In London itself the Lambeth and Westminster marshes were notorious.'[76] Not all the malaria was contracted on the spot, people carried it about and infected others; it is probable that the 'Irish ague' that afflicted so many people serving in Ireland was malaria. 'The variety of malaria most prevalent in England was that known as benign tertian – "benign" in contrast to malignant tertian of warmer climates; and "tertian" because in man the parasites take 48 hours to mature and burst, thus causing a paroxysm or ague-fit every third day. Quartan malaria was also present, but to a less extent on the whole. Here the parasites take 72 hours to mature, so that the ague-fit recurs every fourth day.' We hear of both, but much more frequently of 'tertian' – a familiar complaint.

IV

To complete the picture: we have relics with us today – portraits, painted scenes, monuments, medical cases, drug chests, surgical instruments, books, prescriptions – from which we may derive a visual reminder of what Elizabethan medicine and surgery were, as in other fields and disciplines.

At Caius College, Cambridge, is the fine Renaissance tomb of its second founder, with its eloquent inscription, *Fui Caius*. At Oxford, St. John's College has a Gheeraerts portrait of the eminent Dr. Paddy, President of the College of Physicians, painted in 1600; and an earlier portrait of the beneficent Dr. Case, holding his medical book with a small skeleton on the table before him. We have portraits of Clowes, Gale and Gilbert, among others. A picture has come down to us of John Banister delivering the Visceral Lecture at Barber-Surgeons' Hall in 1581. There is the realistic scene: the two Masters of Anatomy, with lancet and scalpel, stand beside him, on a reading desk an open copy of Realdo Colombo's text-book on the subject. Banister has one hand on the open viscera of the body, while pointing with stick to the diaphragm of the standing skeleton. Banister, an underlipped man of forty-eight with brown beard, wears black hat and gown with white sleeves. Above the heads of the students looking on are the arms of the Barber-Surgeons, around the skeleton's head the striped bandages we still see symbolised on barbers' poles all over England and America.

Among other objects shown at an exhibition to illustrate Elizabethan medicine at the Wellcome Historical Medical Museum were two gold angels hung round the neck of patients by the Queen at her Healing for the Evil: the Archangel Michael on one side, on the other *Factum est istud et est mirabile*. From time to time the Virgin Queen hieratically performed her disagreeable duty. A copy of William Tooker's *Charisma*, 1597, with the Office of Healing makes clear from the rubrics that the Queen touched the sore place with her sacred hand. An oblong box covered with beautiful needlework of contemporary design turns out to be a medicine case of the Bacons of Redgrave, with their crest of the boar, with instruments, probes, files, etc. A case of surgical instruments, from Heydon Hall, Norfolk, is dated 1570: everything finely decorated, handles, flanges, hafts. There is the large saw surgeons did their amputations with (like a butcher's meat-saw), hinged axe and cleaver; a long forceps for extracting arrow-heads, bullet-extractors, lancets, probes, showing traces of gilding; decorative trepans and seton-clamps becoming common in the sixteenth century. A drug cabinet of 1614 is of polished oak, with coat-of-arms and pretty hasps; six tiny drawers, with one long one at the bottom. Then there were the ointment jars of delft-ware, brought in by Jaspar Andries, the making of which became located at Lambeth; earthenware crucibles and pots, green glass alembics for distillation, glass phials excavated from all parts of London, including half a dozen from Bridewell.

As for prescriptions we are fortunate to have the case-book of Shakespeare's son-in-law, Dr. John Hall, at Stratford. Hall had a large practice not only among the townsfolk but among the surrounding gentry and nobility. He gives us a full account of the illness of his daughter Elizabeth – Shakespeare's granddaughter – at sixteen, its symptoms and how he cured her. 'Thus she was delivered from death and deadly diseases, and was well for many years.'[77] We learn that 'she eats nutmegs often' – an odd addiction, perhaps an aperient. In the town and round about Dr. Hall looked after Shakespeare's relations and friends, Nashes, Greenes, Quineys, Combes, Underhills – though not, apparently, his poor relations, the Harts, Judith Shakespeare's family. Further afield were the Comptons, now Earls of Northampton, Lady Rouse of Rouselench, the Catholic Sheldons and several other Catholic families. Not far away, across the pastures at Clifford Chambers, were the Rainsfords. This was 'the Muses' quiet port' of Drayton, their life-long friend. And, sure enough, Shakespeare's friend appears in his son-in-law's case-book: 'Mr. Drayton, an excellent poet, labouring of a tertian, was cured by the following: Rx the emetic infusion, syrup of violets a spoonful: mix them. This given, wrought very well both upwards and downwards.'

V

As a consequence of the English being first to open up Russia's relations with the outside world via the northern route, and holding a privileged position in Moscow, it fell to them to provide physicians for the Tsar and his Court. In 1557 Dr. Ralph Standish, a Cambridge man, with an apothecary accompanied the returning Russian ambassador.[78] Ten years later Dr. Reynolds followed, at a salary of 200 roubles. In 1570 Dr. Elisaeus Bommel, another Cambridge man, was on the staff of the English ambassador in Moscow; but, a German by origin, he could not resist meddling in politics and died there after torture.[79] The wife of Ivan the Terrible's son and successor, the Tsar Fedor, had no children and Queen Elizabeth's help was elicited. Her virgin status did not prevent her from sending the Tsarina her advice, and she selected one of her own physicians, Dr. Jacob, for the post.[80] He was skilled in female complaints, the Queen herself having often benefited from his advice; she assured the Tsarina that he knew more about lying-in than any midwife. Next followed Dr. Mark Ridley, whose interest in electro-magnetism we have observed. He was a remarkable man, who used his four years in Moscow, 1594–8, to good purpose in compiling the first of Russian-English and English-Russian dictionaries.[81] Dr. Jessup was next recommended,[82] but died before he could take up the appointment. There followed an unsatisfactory episode, with the mission of Timothy Willis, who fumbled his diplomatic task, was not well qualified as a doctor – nor did it help him that he arrived without equipment or books, which had been impounded on the overland route.[83] From the letters of Baldwin Hamey, a Dutchman who served in Russia 1594–7, we get a vivid picture of the atmosphere of suspicion and fear, the medieval superstition.[84] He subsequently became naturalised in England. James I recommended Dr. Dee's son, Arthur, who remained as physician at the Russian Court for as long as fourteen years.[85]

In its way this succession was a tribute to the standing of English medicine. Belated as the College of Physicians was, compared with abroad, in arranging for a pharmocopoeia to be compiled – an authority by which drugs might be allowed or dismissed – when it ultimately appeared in 1618, it was the first to cover a whole country.[86] From all the evidences progress was being made, if nothing spectacular. But under the surface a decisive leap forward was being prepared. From the 1580's anatomy was coming to be regarded as part of physic, as well as surgery: it was impossible to keep the disciplines apart, and within the Royal College of Physicians a decisive step was taken, which furthered the integration of medical knowledge and research. This was the foundation of the Lumleian Lectures, in anatomy and surgery, by Lord Lumley and Dr. Caldwell, within the College itself.[87] When it came to Dr. William Harvey to make his dissection, in 1616 – the year of Shakespeare's death – he quietly announced a discovery as revolutionary as that of Copernicus: the circulation of the blood.

He knew that he was breaking with views held for centuries, though – like other men whose original genius has brought about a revolution in thought – he was curiously conservative, with a proper respect for antiquity, especially Aristotle. Though Harvey was right about the circulation of the blood, and its mode of operation, the physiological processes – the word 'physiology' was just coming in, from 1597 – the microscope was not yet sufficiently developed to be able to see corpuscles moving from the arterial into the veinous system.[88] Harvey's deductions were correct, but were not then provable; and, as with Copernicus, many would not accept them. Aubrey, who knew him well, tells us that after his epoch-making book came out, *De Motu Cordis*, 'he fell mightily in his practice, and 'twas believed by the vulgar that he was crack-brained; and all the physicians were against his opinion and envied him: many wrote against him.'[89]

Not all the physicians were against him, but Aubrey is corroborated, as usual, by the fact that there was no sign of the new teaching in the College text-books for many years. It took some twenty or thirty years for it to penetrate the universities of Europe. But Harvey lived to be very old, and so, as Hobbes said, 'he is the only man, perhaps, that ever lived to see his own doctrine established in his own lifetime.'[90] Harvey did not much care for what other people thought: he was contemptuous of contemporaries and 'was wont to say that man was but a great mischievous baboon.' (At the battle of Edgehill, while the fools were fighting, he sheltered under a hedge and took out a book.) He was 'a solitary worker', whose science – like other men's art, including the historian's – was 'intensely personal'.[91] He achieved his results, for all the world to see, through his absolute dedication to his work: the work was an end in itself. To this we must add his uncompromising passion for truth, and the genius which was, of course, intuitive. Wenceslas Hollar told Aubrey that when Harvey was travelling with the Earl of Arundel in Germany as his physician, 'he would still be making of excursions into the woods, making observations of strange trees, and plants, earths, etc. naturals, and sometimes like to be lost.'[92] In fact he wrote a book *De Insectis*, for which he had made anatomical observations over years: this, and other writings on Respiration, on the Function of the Spleen, an *Anatomia Medicalis*, were all lost when his lodgings at Whitehall were rifled by Parliamentarian soldiery at the beginning of the Civil War.[93] He could never retrieve his papers for love or money, and told Aubrey that "'twas the greatest crucifying to him that ever he had in all his life.'

The fact that Harvey died only a year before Oliver Cromwell need not prevent us from regarding him as an Elizabethan in his training and *Bildung*. Born at Folkestone, 1 April 1578, he was at King's School, Canterbury – Marlowe's old school – from 1588 to 1593, the year of Marlowe's death.[94] He was at Dr. Caius' old college at Cambridge from 1593 to 1600, and followed in his footsteps to Padua 1600–2. He was already in practice at the time of the Queen's death. With him English medicine emerged from its apprenticeship to give a lead to Europe.

CHAPTER IX

MIND AND SPIRIT

MUCH of the mind and spirit of the age has already been made evident to us in this book, in different respects and various fields; now we must concentrate and elicit, if we can, its intellectual formulations, its more formal thinking and modes of feeling about ultimates. Here we come up against our greatest difficulty; for, where on one side there was little pure philosophising – in that respect a marked contrast with the Middle Ages – most people's thought was dominated, permeated, overcast by religion, and in that they were medieval enough. Once more, departing from their own perspective and putting things in a different proportion – there is no reason why the historian should adhere to theirs – we give more consideration to the elect minds of the age, whose difference from ordinary standards made it what it was. We shall attend to what Bacon, Ralegh and Donne have to say rather than Bishop Jewel or Whitgift, Cartwright or Father Parsons; just as we attach more importance to the geographers, mathematicians and astronomers than to the geomancers, alchemists and astrologers. Of course there were many more of the latter class – there always are: that is not what is so significant, either historically or philosophically.

We may agree with the philosopher, if somewhat less excitedly, that 'the mathematical science of physical nature' is 'the most stupendous intellectual conquest of modern times';[1] or, to put it more broadly, that the development of science is the characteristic achievement of the modern age, mainly since the seventeenth century. The Elizabethans were only on the threshold of all that. As the philosopher diagnoses, the chasm between the universe of nature and the world of the mind had not yet opened up:[2] there was still integration, man and the universe were still one, there was even a chain of being from the summit ('God') to the humblest unit at the bottom.[3] Hence, in one way, the inspiration there was in the creative works of the age, and the excitement and consolation we find in them. Hence, too, the difficulty we have in understanding the age, for though we may share many of its values – and even those decreasingly – we do not share its beliefs.

Let us, to offset personal bias in the matter, give two examples in the words of writers of our time who still subscribe to some form of religious belief. Calvin (*cette âme atroce*, Voltaire called him) dominated the theology of Protestant England: most of the bishops were Calvinists in theology, though not presbyterians we need hardly say, in regard to church organisation. Even Archbishop Whitgift was a Calvinist; so was James I, whose personal tastes, one would have thought, were more in keeping with Arminianism. Carew Hunt sums up, 'the dogmas which underlie Calvin's system are so remote from our present modes of thought that it has become hard to see how anyone can ever seriously have entertained them.'[4] (There is no nonsense that human beings will not believe.) 'The system itself is an attempt to unite, and to justify on grounds of Scripture, a series of propositions upon the nature of God and upon his dealings with Man, which are left unresolved because they are logically irreconcilable. Calvin's claim to be the greatest systematic theologian of the age is indisputable. Unfortunately, his insistence upon the divine inspiration of all parts of the Bible made him fail to see in it the record of a progressive revelation, and gave him no adequate standard with which to compare the morality of the Patriarchs with that of the Gospels. Thus, when Renée of Ferrara sensibly observed that David's hatred of his enemies was unsuited to the new dispensation, Calvin sternly replied that "such a gloss would upset all Scripture", as indeed it would have done much of his interpretation of it. Where the basic presuppositions of his creed were concerned, his treatment was often arbitrary and showed a remarkable facility for reading into the texts whatever he wished to find in them.' Of course: as always, with all believers, however mutually exclusive their interpretations, in accordance with their interests, their social groupings, their personal fantasies: more a matter for anthropological investigation than rational discussion, taking them seriously. 'None the less, he set out with an unexampled clarity a system of belief which was capable, under the conditions of the time, of kindling the faith not only of the *élite* but of the masses.'

So much for what a Protestant descendant of Calvinism can find to say for it today. His conclusion leads straight to the central, and the saddest, fact in human history: that it is not the truth of what men think that matters so much as the effectiveness of what they think, its appeal – in the case of either the *élite* or the masses

– to their emotional leanings, their prejudices, their interests, their illusions. So that in the human record, though the devotion to truth is on everybody's lips and men will equally die or kill in thousands for this or that mutually contradictory 'truth', there is in fact very little of truth in the record, and little devotion to it among human beings, or any comprehension of what it means or entails.

All politicians – that is, all who wish to exert power over other human beings, to lead them very often for their own good – know that the mass of men, if not precisely idiots, are at any rate children, not adult in matters of thought. It is doubtful whether they ever will be any other. But the leaders of men, in action, do not let on: it is not so much that it would spoil the game (a too cynical view), as that there would be no point in it (a more realistic consideration). On the other hand, a mere thinker may inquire – since so much lip-service is paid to the masses today – should the knowledge of the fact, in a democratic society, be withheld from them?

Francis Bacon's thoughts about this are as much to the point today as when they were written – unlike the theological trash he so much despised. 'There is in human nature generally more of the fool than of the wise; and therefore those faculties by which the foolish part of men's minds is taken are most potent.'[5] And he points out that 'in all wise human governments those who sit at the helm can introduce and insinuate what they desire for the good of the people more successfully by pretexts and indirect ways than directly.' Even in regard to thought, believing a traditional system is no more than giving credence to a stage-play, an ideological smoke-screen: 'all the received systems are but so many stage-plays, representing worlds of their own creation after an unreal and scenic fashion.'[6] It might be Pareto writing. (Bacon had a low view of stage-plays: he thought that only academic plays served any purpose, in education – and yet many idiots have supposed that Bacon wrote Shakespeare's plays!) Bacon was acutely aware that anyone of independent thought was 'like one who rows against the current.'

As for 'intellectualists', Bacon thought little of them, tumbling 'up and down in their own reasons and conceits . . . who, by continual agitation of wit do urge and, as it were, invoke their own spirits to divine and give oracles unto them' – instead of studying facts as they are, which alone Bacon respected.[7] 'Doctrines which find most favour with the populace are those which are either contentious and pugnacious, or specious and empty', aimed at 'entangling their assent', or tickling and taking them in.[8] Much more worthy of respect are writers like Machiavelli, 'of that class who openly and unfeignedly declare or describe what men do, and not what they ought to do.' Bacon thought that, in ethics, moral philosophers proposed 'a higher elevation of man's nature than it is really capable of'; in philosophy men were apt 'to suppose the existence of more order and regularity in the world than it finds.' So he preferred the world of fact and of experience: 'I consider history and experience to be the same thing, as also philosophy with the sciences', that is, he equates philosophy with the knowledge of nature. Thus he acknowledged the force of historical experience, the authority of fact, as against fables and deductive argument. 'History, of all writings, deserveth least taxation, as that which holdeth least of the author and most of the things themselves.' He made no secret of the fact that he regarded the accumulations of knowledge hitherto, particularly philosophical and theological systems – that is, the great bulk of what men had previously given their minds to – as a useless heap, 'fruitful of controversies and barren of works.' And he especially disliked the method of disputation upon which they had spent their mental energy: he thought it adverse to the discovery of truth. 'All the disputation of the learned never brought to light one effect of nature before unknown.'[9]

Observe that, in the realm of religion and theology, the sixteenth century spent most of its mental energy on dispute.

There was, to take our second example, the Bible. Calvin, in his extremist fashion, was more conscious than his twentieth-century critic that literal interpretation of Holy Writ had to be maintained at its weakest point, where it was otherwise indefensible, against all sense and reason, or the authority of the whole would be overthrown – since the whole has no more authority than its parts. It is only in the past century that scholarship – with much effort, against a mountain of prejudice, a veritable taboo on the subject – has established the true character of the Old Testament, that it is largely 'subjective' history, of events arranged with the definite aim and purpose of Ezra and his priestly caste and time;[10] that the Pentateuch, with its reconstruction of earlier Jewish history (even if incorporating earlier fossils) is largely later than the literature of the Prophets – as Bishop Colenso faced a lifetime of obloquy and abuse for pointing out. The Elizabethans had no idea of the historical evolution of the Bible, that it was compiled in the course of 'only a few centuries', that 'only in modern times have we come to know something of the circumstances amid which it grew up.'[11] To the Elizabethans it presented a mountain-wall, a solid block to the intelligence behind which they could not get. It was inconceivable to most minds to go behind the orthodoxy of the age, with its subjection to received ideas, let alone set aside the accepted scheme of things.[12]

At any rate, it required great originality and equal hardihood to do so, but that there were people who doubted the orthodox account of these things and even suspected the truth, we may infer from the not infrequent charges against 'atheists' and 'atheism' – terms of abuse applied imprecisely to any who were at all heterodox. Marlowe, for example, was reviled as an 'atheist'; he was not: he seems to have been a deist or a pantheist, with an impersonal, cosmic conception of deity:

> . . . he that sits on high and never sleeps,
> Nor in one place is circumscriptible,
> But everywhere fills every continent
> With strange infusions of his sacred vigour.

It was very original of Marlowe to have thought himself so far out of the rut; we know that he took pleasure in pointing out the contradictions in the Bible, that he thought (with Hariot) that there were men before Adam, and that 'the first beginning of religion was only to keep men in awe.'[13]

We shall see the insuperable difficulties that the taboo upon criticism of the Bible created for Ralegh when he tried to make sense of the Old Testament story of the Jews in his *History of the World*. Actually at this time Scaliger first began to treat Old Testament history as an integral part of ancient history, and the sceptical Selden in the next generation followed with his researches into Semitic mythology.[14] But, on the whole, 'Protestantism, with its doctrine of verbal infallibility, hindered the progress of criticism.' The conflict between Reformation and Counter-Reformation set back the intellectual progress made by the Erasmian Renaissance and confirmed people in their prejudices and fancies. Believers might well have welcomed the insane religious disputes and wars of the later sixteenth and earlier seventeenth centuries, for they riveted their mutually conflicting nonsense on men's minds. Tolerance came only with the relaxation of belief, as the growth of science was connected with that of latitudinarianism, not Puritanism.[15] Only very independent minds, like Selden and Hobbes, dared to make direct criticisms – and were called names for their pains; Spinoza called attention to the chronological impossibilities of the Old Testament, which had made nonsense of Ralegh. But these were later.

Indeed it is strange that so alien a corpus should have so entered into the English tradition, and that English historians, to a man, should be so proud of it. 'The Old Testament reflects a world of thought and ways of thinking very different from our own.'[16] There is the unceasing cult of hatred, the vindictive spirit of the deity portrayed in it – Saul is ruined, for example, simply for his refusal to kill; there is the odious and 'inveterate belief in the sanctity and efficacy of blood.' All this must have had unfortunate consequences upon the generations leading up to the Civil War, increased the savage temper of the Puritans, sharpened their nasty language, encouraged blood-thirstiness and the resort to war. Nevertheless, as our Biblical scholar says, the Bible 'won a unique place as the foundation of Western religion and theology, and influenced the course of Western thought more than any other book', and claims that its God is revealed as 'the God of all history'.[17] But this clause, too, should be subjected to the limitation of the West, and even then for only a brief period of its history. The decline of Christianity accompanies – it even preceded – the decline of the West. It is indeed a local, a provincial, manifestation – like other religions: European, not an expression of China, India, Japan, Africa or of the Muslim world. The importance of the Bible – apart from the parochial importance of the Old Testament to the Jews as their sacred book (Persians, Egyptians, etc., had theirs) – was due to the historical triumph of Christianity with the Roman Empire.

It is an interesting speculation how different Europe might have been if Greek thought had won, *per impossibile*, and become an influence on the English mind. Jewish monotheism was neither unique, nor necessarily a 'higher' development;[18] its excruciating ethicality and morose moralism, its earnestness and lack of humour, its legalism and concentration upon 'righteousness', i.e. rights, its aesthetic insensitivity compared with the miraculous achievements of Greek art, make it infinitely unattractive compared with later Hellenism.*

---

* Cf. Cook: Jewish religion 'must have been thoroughly barbaric, with its wine and feasting, its noise, the smell of countless animal sacrifices, its unrestrained dancing and, on occasion, practices that made Baal-peor an abomination. The frenzied rites gave reality to the sense of communion with deity.' *Cambr. Ancient Hist.*, II. 451.

However, we cannot expect the Elizabethans to think themselves out of their own skins. Few can. With these provisos,
and with the relativism proper to history, we may regard what
the Elizabethans naively regarded as absolutes, in their con-
text.

Bacon did not specifically express this point of view, but he
certainly implied it. He knew well that in the excited state of
men's minds in the later sixteenth century, compared with what
it had been before Luther's resort to unreason against Erasmus
and the reaction from the other side, it was not safe to inquire
into the mysteries of faith. He was as dismissive of theology as he
was of teleology. 'In natural theology I am so far from noting any
deficience that I find rather an excess',[19] he says with cautious
irony – thus dismissing one-half of the mental effort of the age.
With regard to all the writers on angels and spirits he could dare
to say outright what he thought – 'superstitious, fabulous and
fantastical'. Nor did he respect any more the doctrine of final
causes that dominated traditional philosophy, 'for to say that the
clouds are formed above for watering the earth, or that the solid-
ness of the earth is for the station and mansion of living creatures,
and the like' may be good enough for metaphysics but in physics
is 'impertinent'.[20] 'For the inquisition of final causes is barren and,
like a virgin consecrated to God, produces nothing.'[21] He went
further; he regarded this whole traditional mode of thought –
the addiction to a tautologous and self-defeating teleology – as a
mere hindrance and the chief cause why 'the search for physical
causes hath been neglected and passed in silence.'[22]

We perceive the revolutionary clearance of intellectual junk
that Bacon effected for himself and proposed for others – theology,
metaphysics, bogus science – which together occupy a large area
of the Elizabethan *speculum mentis*. How superior a mind we feel
him to be compared with most of his contemporaries, with their
credulities and infantilities, their lack of critical intelligence even
when devoted scholars, their pursuit of curiosities and will-o'-the-
wisps. We breathe a purer air of sense with him after the inspis-
sated fogs, the contortions and convolutions, the envenomed disputes about the non-existent among the divines – that cost the
historian Buckle a paralysis of the mind. Of course it is possible to
criticise Bacon for this or that, as text-book dullards do, for his
downgrading the place of hypothesis in science or of deductive
logic, or for the lack of a consistent philosophical system, but we

must remember that it is at least possible that he has himself anticipated the criticisms. His aim was to overthrow all the traditional systems of philosophy, which, he considered, obscured the study of the facts of nature.

No wonder the nineteenth century, which was itself riddled with religious disputation – compare the obstinate opposition to the theory of evolution, or to the Higher Criticism of the Bible – found the mind revealed by the *Essays* uncongenial. It has been usual to deplore Bacon's reading of men as 'cynical': it is more important to inquire whether it is not true. He coolly exposed the distortions that arise in men's very modes of thinking, the illusions and the deformations of which they are for the most part unconscious. He effects a salutary clearance at the beginning of the *Novum Organum*, with the wonderfully perceptive section on the various 'Idols which beset men's minds' – an approach much more in keeping with twentieth-century thought than it was with the nineteenth century.

Bacon distinguished four classes in the factors and influences that form men's thinking and deform their understanding.[23] First, 'the Idols of the Tribe have their foundation in human nature itself . . . for it is a false assertion that the sense of man is the measure of things.' We can at once see the bearing of this for religion and theology: man creates God in his own image, and interprets the universe by his own measure. Second, 'the Idols of the Cave are the idols of the individual man': each man lives in his own den, interpreting things by his own experience or prejudice, in accordance with his own nature and temperament, the impressions by which he is affected from his surroundings. The third class Bacon calls Idols of the Market-place, 'on account of the commerce and consort of men there. For it is by discourse that men associate, and words are imposed according to the apprehension of the vulgar.' That is, most men are led, or misled, by words instead of attending to things, correlating one with the other, adhering to exact usage and consistent definitions. 'Lastly, there are Idols which have immigrated into men's minds from the various dogmas of philosophies . . . all the received systems are but so many stage-plays, representing worlds of their own creation after an unreal and scenic fashion.' So he called these Idols of the Theatre. He cites for an example the philosophical fiction that the movements of the celestial bodies must be perfect circles – which had long impeded the apprehension of the facts. He concludes, 'but the corruption of philosophy by superstition and an admixture of theology is far more widely spread and does the greatest harm.'[24] He clearly equated the two.

There is in all this a great deal that it has taken the twentieth century to catch up with, with Pareto and Veblen, Freud and Russell, or the modern analytic school.

As a homosexual, Bacon's view of human nature was singularly penetrating and *désabusé*: not for him the illusions with which normal men seem unable to dispense. 'There is little friendship in the world, and least of all between equals.'[25] 'Great persons had need to borrow the opinions of the vulgar to think themselves happy.' 'Men in great place are thrice servants: servants of the sovereign or state, servants of fame, and servants of business. So as they have no freedom, neither in their persons, nor in their actions, nor in their times. It is a strange desire to seek power, and to lose liberty; or to seek power over others and to lose power over a man's self.' 'The rising unto place is laborious, and by pains men come to greater pains. And it is sometimes base, and by indignities men come to dignities. The standing is slippery, and the regress is either a downfall, or at least an eclipse.' Bacon foreknew it all: he wrote these words years before he experienced it in his own person. 'Retire men cannot when they would, neither will they when it were reason. Certainly great persons had need to borrow other men's opinions to think themselves happy; for, if they judge by their own feeling, they cannot find it.' 'While we seek honours we lose liberty.'[26]

Bacon knew it all in and for himself, as well as by watching the world with his sharp viper-like eye. He applied his knowledge to himself, correctly – 'a man naturally fitted rather for literature than for anything else and borne by some destiny, against the inclination of his genius, into the business of active life.'[27] Born in his station, the brilliant son of a Lord Keeper, he could not but embark on a public career. But he was a divided man. One should watch how one's temperament agrees or not with the state of the times, he says; if they are discordant, he recommends withdrawal, retirement. But his age offered golden rewards to initiative and brilliance; he would have no call to waste his gifts on public life in ours. His lifelong participation in public affairs qualified him to condemn the perpetual doctrinairism of intellectuals: 'the writing of speculative men on active matter for the most part seems to men of experience . . . to be but dreams and dotage.'[28] As for the people, 'what is popular judgment worth as a test of good and evil?'[29]

In psychology the first object is to study 'the different characters of natures and dispositions': here 'the common discourse of men – as sometimes, though very rarely, happens – is wiser than books.'[30] The aims: first, 'a scientific and accurate dissection of minds and characters and the secret dispositions of men'; second, 'the affections and perturbations of the mind' – here the best authorities are historians and poets. The most reliable source for the knowledge of human character is the wiser sort of historians: 'a character so worked into the narrative gives a better idea of the man than any formal criticism and review can.' Bacon naturally favoured the study of history, for it paralleled, in the world of man, the knowledge he sought in the realm of nature. He regarded the essential as political history, a simple narrative of events coupled with their causes; and the best material to be found in state papers. His conception of historic periods was akin to that of the Enlightenment. There were only three periods of learning, those of the Greeks, the Romans and the Renaissance.[31] After Christianity was established the sharpest wits devoted themselves to theology – he would have agreed with Gibbon about that; the Romans were too much taken with moral philosophy; natural philosophy was at its height only briefly among the pre-Socratics: Democritus, 'who removed God and Mind from the structure of things', penetrated further into nature than Plato and Aristotle.[32]

Nevertheless there was an idealistic element in Bacon, in the human sphere as in that of science. We have seen that the motivation of his passion for scientific knowledge was to alleviate men's lot. In the human sphere he looked beyond national conflicts and desiderated an international language: it should be possible for 'a number of nations whose languages are altogether different but who agree in the use of such characters [of symbols or emblems, as in Egyptian hieroglyphs or Chinese ideograms] to communicate with each other in writing; to such an extent indeed that any book written in characters of this kind can be read off by each nation in their own language.'[33] He observed the different characters of peoples as expressed in their languages, the Greeks more fitted for the arts, the Romans for business. Thus he was against the imposition of classical measures upon English verse as incompatible with the structure of the language. His was indeed an ecumenical mind, as we see in his comprehensive toleration in religion: 'consciences are not to be forced, but to be won and reduced by the force of truth, with the aid of time.'[34] As he himself put it, the best authority is time.

Even in the individual sphere one's heart inclines to a man who wrote, 'a crowd is not company, and faces are but a gallery of pictures, and talk but a tinkling cymbal, where there is no love.'[35] But he did not mean sexual love, he meant friendship: 'it is a mere and miserable solitude to want true friends, without which the world is but a wilderness.' And he thought that the first fruit of friendship, though not the last, was that 'it redoubleth joys, and cutteth griefs in halves.'

Bacon was a true Elizabethan in disliking specialisation: he appreciated the fruitful cross-fertilisation of different subjects, the insights afforded by comparative views. Ralegh exemplified this in his life; essentially a man of action, even so he was very much a reading man, constantly alert to study in different fields, an intellectual who supported Hariot to teach him mathematics and cosmography. He experimented in chemistry as in poetry and politics; in the end he settled for history, and wrote his *History of the World*, a masterpiece which retained its authority for much of the seventeenth century. He had intended to embark on it earlier,[36] but only the Tower gave him the leisure and the concentration.

Like everything of Ralegh the book is intensely personal: that keeps it alive and readable. He put everything he knew into it: his experiences in France as a young man, and at sea, Cadiz in 1596, in Guiana, in Ireland; the reading of an omnivorous mind; his knowledge of cosmography, his philosophy and beliefs; his disingenuousnesses and ambiguities; his reflections on politics and religion. A prisoner under suspended death-sentence, hated by James I, with so many enemies, he had to be so careful. One has to be familiar with the age to catch all the nuances. On the surface he is flattering in his references to the king; but no one would mistake his portrait of Ninias, a sovereign who was 'no man of war at all but altogether feminine, and subjected to ease and delicacy'; who followed a mighty empress and 'proved no less feminine than she was masculine.'[37] Under Ninias 'undertaking spirits wanted the employments' they had been given in the previous reign, and had to 'remain at home unregarded whilst others, more unworthy than themselves, were advanced.' No one could mistake the reference to the advance of the unworthy Howards: while at every point where the history gave him an opening, Ralegh poured scorn on sodomites. This would not be lost on the homosexual Court of the first Stuart, on James himself or his young men, Hay, Carr, Villiers; or, for that matter, on Lord Henry Howard, now Earl of Northampton, or Lord Chancellor Bacon.

Ralegh prided himself on his masculinity, and to the Elizabethans it was more highly thought of to be masculine than feminine. Woman was 'given to man for a comforter and companion but not for a counsellor.'[38] Eve's motive was 'a desire to know what was most unfitting her knowledge, an affection which hath ever since remained in all the posterity of her sex.' In this, as in other respects, there is a direct affiliation from Ralegh to Milton, who published some of his papers later.

We must confine ourselves here to Ralegh's intellectual outlook, the frame of his great work. He begins with an incorporeal, impersonal, invisible God, 'a power uneffable and virtue infinite; a light by abundant clarity invisible; an understanding which itself can only comprehend; an essence eternal and spiritual.'[39] 'The manner and first operation of his divine power cannot be conceived by any mind or spirit compassed with a mortal body.' Though this may be reconcilable with orthodoxy, it is more likely to represent a fundamental deism when we consider Ralegh's lifelong association with Hariot and its affiliation, if a tenuous one, through that group with Marlowe; and, further, the absence of much reference to a personal deity, let alone Christ, in the course of the History.

On the other hand, Ralegh clearly made a deliberate resolution to accept the literal reading of the Bible: this made for the immense success of the History in his own time, especially with the Puritans (whom he despised), and its devaluation subsequently. He was, as usual, playing to the gallery – and received his reward. There was, in any case, the extreme difficulty, the impossibility, for an Elizabethan to surmount the mountain-chain that walled him in: it was beyond any Elizabethan to overthrow the whole system of religious belief. One had to choose – so Ralegh opted for complete literalism and the historical account of the creation of the world as veracious, written by the finger of God through Moses – though Moses, Ralegh noted, 'forbare to speak of angels.'[40] 'God knows what a multitude of meanings the wit of man imagineth to himself in the Scriptures', and Ralegh for once chose the safer path. On a point of lesser import he went so far as to say, 'for myself I am persuaded that the waters called "the waters above the heavens" are but the clouds and waters engendered in the uppermost air.' The general rule he enunciated for himself was 'where the Scriptures are silent the voice of reason hath the best hearing'; on the other hand, this meant that many improbabilities 'every Christian must believe for it is affirmed in the Scriptures.'

Questions of doctrine he could leave on one side – that of predestination, for example, 'I leave to the divines'; it was the historical narrative with its impossible affirmations that gave so much trouble.[41] Was Moses' description of Paradise allegorical, as Origen and Philo thought? Ralegh took it more literally, 'yet I do not exclude the allegorical sense of the Scripture' – a typical example of having it both ways, if not of disingenuousness. It is 'contrary to God's Word that more than eight persons were saved from the Flood.' Was the Tree of Life 'a mere allegory'? Ralegh thought not, though he was not sure whether it was the *ficus Indica* or the banyan: 'I myself have seen twenty thousand of them in one valley not far from Paria in America', each of them capable of shrouding four hundred or four thousand horsemen. Ralegh's imagination was always apt to run away with him.

After this we are less surprised that his account of the Biblical Flood loses all touch with sense in his pathetic anxiety to stick to the literal word of Holy Writ. The Flood covered the whole earth, including mountains 'thirty miles upright' – anyone who had seen water-spouts in the Caribbean could justify Moses' manner of speech.[42] And where did the Ark come to rest? – not far from where it was made, Ralegh felt sure. And the animals? 'All those two hundred and eighty beasts might be kept in one story or room of the Ark in their several cabins; their meat in a second; the birds and their provision in a third, with place to spare for Noah and his family and all their necessaries.' Noah begat the first of his sons in his five hundredth year; Noah's three sons peopled all the world 'in both the process of time required to be understood'; 'Methusalem begat at a hundred and eighty seven', Abraham at a hundred and thirty, and so on with all the Patriarchs.[43] Some modernist spirits had tried to explain this away as meaning 'lunar years', i.e. months; but Ralegh sticks to the Bible. 'The truth and antiquity of the books of God find no companions equal, either in age or authority.' Moreover, he warns, 'they which shorten the times make all ancient stories the more improbable.'

The Puritans were delighted: the great infidel had become a

believer. Oliver Cromwell recommended the *History* to his son as the best and most commendable reading.

Little did they understand their man. He had no liking for sectaries: the ornamenting of tabernacle, Ark, sanctuary, which had been imitated in all ages by the Church 'is now so forgotten and cast away in this superfine age by those of the Family [of Love], by the Anabaptist, Brownist and other sectaries, as all cost and care bestowed and had of the Church is accounted a kind of popery.'[44] Moreover, they would subvert all order: 'as many kinds of religion would spring up as there are parish churches within England, every contentious and ignorant person clothing his fancy with the spirit of God and his imagination with the gift of revelation.'

It was not long before the Civil War would reveal this in its ripe absurdity.

We find a direct example of the way in which the Old Testament inculcated, and justified, barbarity in war in Ralegh's citation of the law, from Deuteronomy xx. 10–12, putting a city or camp to the sword after its refusal to surrender – which Ralegh had practised at Smerwick, as Cromwell was to do at Drogheda.[45] Nor has Ralegh any charitable opinion of the people: they are always 'the rascally mob', 'the beggarly, mutable, and ungrateful multitude' – as in Shakespeare; 'it is the delight of base people to reign over their betters.' Ralegh regarded slavery as natural, rooted in natural inferiority, as Aristotle had done in the *Politics*. 'Certainly we find not such a latitude of difference in any creature as in the nature of man; wherein . . . the wisest excel the most foolish by far greater degree than the most foolish of men doth surpass the wisest of beasts.' Modern physiologists find that the inequalities of men's minds are as great as in their corporal capabilities.

Biblical numbers gave Ralegh some pause: 'that Judah and Benjamin, a territory not much exceeding the county of Kent, should muster 1,160,000 fighting men, it is very strange.'[46] In accordance with his settled resolution he tries to make sense of the nonsense. Yet, in all but sacred history, in all secular matters, he took leave to use reason and the rule of probability, 'and this may suffice in defence of the liberty which I have used in conjectures . . . as neither unlawful nor misbeseeming an historian.' He makes a gallant attempt to synchronise ancient Greek history with the Old Testament, to bring together Prometheus with Moses, etc.; yet, with Homer or Hesiod, 'I am not much troubled when this poet lived, neither would I offend the reader with these opinions but only to show the uncertainty and disagreement of historians.'[47] So probability is a fair guide: 'we must be sometimes bold to observe the coherence of things, and believe so much only to be true as dependeth upon good reason or at least fair probability.' In regard to the difficulty of establishing the true account of some events, he thought 'mutual dependency in things of this nature no small argument of truth.'

In all secular matters his critical intelligence is properly exercised. He realised that the predictions of heathen gods were antedated by their priests *ex post facto* – he did not say the same of Scriptural prophecies; he was well aware that men made gods in their own image, that God has bodily shape is 'an error of anthropomorphitae'.[48] As his work progressed, he became freer in mind, or more candid: he had previously thought of the Sibylline Books 'sometimes reverently': he now knew that they and even the books of Hermes Trismegistus were forgeries. Few of his English contemporaries did, but Ralegh was abreast of Continental scholarship: Scaliger, Casaubon, Viperano, Pererius, Torniellus.

Ralegh was aware of the delight men find in histories, 'for the variety of accidents therein contained'; but 'historians desiring to write the actions of men ought to set down the simple truth and not say anything for love or hatred; also to choose such an opportunity for writing as it may be lawful to think what they will and write what they think – which is a rare happiness of the time.'[49] In fact, he wrote partly to get his own back on his time – which had frustrated, mistrusted, disesteemed, and at length imprisoned him in the Tower – as one can see again and again from his asides all through the *History*.[50] That is the real psychological motivation of his didactic use of history to point out the punishment that befalls incompetence and injustice in high places, the refusal to employ the ablest men. The defeated and ill-treated Hannibal is his hero; he points out that the losing side is often in the right. Like Churchill, he thought that 'the ordinary theme and argument of history is war.'[51] Here he is at his most penetrating, constantly illuminating from his own wide experience, war both on land and at sea, the character and advantages of seapower, the uses of shipbuilding, the relation to trade and commerce, with generous, if envious, tributes to Spain's imperial achievements in America.

The usual attitude of Elizabethan historians – as opposed to the chroniclers, who were out simply to record – was didactic: one studied history for the lessons it taught. The more so, Ralegh thought, because there was a 'great similitude' in worldly events: many situations resembled each other, and he believed – like Spengler in our time – that the processes of history were circular. Like many men who have been involved in politics and action, his experience was that 'matters of much consequence, founded in all seeming upon substantial reasons, have issued indeed from such petty trifles as no historian would either think upon or could well search out.'[52] This is of importance for historiography today, where historians often miss the sheer irrationalism of human behaviour in seeking to impose a rationalist strait-jacket upon diversity and inconsistency. 'Hadst thou lived abroad as I have done and seen by what folly this world is governed, thou wouldest wonder at nothing.' This was written on the threshold of the Thirty Years War; at the end of it Oxenstierna drew the same conclusion.

The reverses of fortune left their mark on Ralegh's reflections; indeed, 'rarely or never can we consider truly of worldly proceedings, unless we have felt the deceits of fortune.'[53] Contemporaries were much addicted to maxims and lessons from history; in reading Ralegh's one feels how often they were personal reactions to his own mistakes. 'Great men do study, not only to hold their own, but also to command and insult upon inferiors' – as he had done in his heyday; now held in prison, he could reflect upon it in his own person.[54] 'Men ought in any wise to refrain to do or say anything which may offend' – himself had never been able to refrain. For men who have won reputation, 'to maintain that conceit and eschew envy, there is nothing better than a life retired from daily conversation and chiefly of the multitude' – but neither Ralegh, nor Bacon, nor any other Elizabethan, could ever withdraw unless forced to. 'Men are more mindful of injuries done unto them than of benefits received by them ... thankfulness is accounted a burden, but revenge is sweet and reckoned a great gain.' One does not forget his shocking letter to Robert Cecil urging him to take a final revenge upon Essex. Truly, 'on pensait lire un auteur, on trouve un homme.'

Shafts of light are thrown into the minds of these people by the maxims with which they instructed their sons. Ralegh's are chiefly concerned with the ills of poverty, from which we may infer how bitterly he must have resented his early impecuniosity. 'Marry with money, for love abideth not with want' – he himself had had to marry a girl without a penny.[55] 'If thou be poor withal, thou and thy qualities shall be despised. It is a shame amongst men, an imprisonment of the mind, a vexation of every worthy spirit . . . Thou shalt be driven basely to beg and depend on others, to flatter unworthy men, to make dishonest shifts.' Men forget services rendered them: 'I myself know it and have tasted it in all the course of my life.' Trust no man with your great weakness, 'for every man's folly ought to be his greatest secret.'

Ralegh could not live up to his own wise precepts; the cooler Cecils did. Burghley's Advice to his son, Robert, struck a note of unimpassioned wariness, after three generations of Court life. 'Trust not any man with thy life, credit, or estate; for it is mere folly for a man to enthral himself to his friend, as though, occasion being offered, he should not dare to become the enemy.'[56] 'Be sure to keep some great man thy friend, but trouble him not for trifles. Compliment him often with many, yet small, gifts and of little charge.' 'Towards thy superiors be humble yet generous. With thine equals familiar, yet respective. Towards thy inferiors show much humanity and some familiarity. Yet I advise thee not to affect, or to neglect, popularity too much. Seek not to be Essex; shun to be Ralegh.'

It is striking how little of a Christian spirit there is in the worldly precepts that really expressed these men's minds. It brings home all the more how necessary the Christian religion was to mitigate the struggle for survival, soften the sharpness of suffering, exemplify the healing virtues of charity, console the defeated and those stricken by the wayside, afford some compensation for the horrors of the rat-race and the snake-pit.

Ralegh intended to write a short history of England, from William the Conqueror to the end of Elizabeth's reign, but Cecil would not (understandably) allow him the use of the state-papers. It is a loss to us, for Ralegh knew many of the secrets of the time. Samuel Daniel, who had helped Ralegh with his *History*, wrote an admirable history, so far as it goes. He had the temperament and the gifts for it: 'a natural historian, endowed with a rare sense of the past.'[57] Antiquarian studies made a notable advance; much pioneer work was done in publishing medieval chronicles, in addition to the labours of the Elizabethan chroniclers themselves, Grafton, Holinshed, Stow, Speed and Camden with his *Annals*. But the English were behind the Continent in writing history, and this was Daniel's point of departure: it was 'some blemish to the honour of our country to come behind other nations in this kind.'⁵⁸ Daniel had taken his notions in foreign countries, no doubt from his sojourn in Italy. And 'it concerns them most to know the general affairs of England who have least leisure to read them.' Here, again, is the practical purpose of history – that men of affairs might learn from it.

Daniel exhibited singular independence of mind: he did not borrow his opinions from his contemporaries, perhaps because he lived withdrawn from them; he was free from bias, especially the Protestant bias that disfigured his compatriots – in that like Shakespeare. Indeed, in that like the elect minds of the age: the Queen herself, Bacon and Hooker and Donne; Marlowe, Ben Jonson and Drayton; Ralegh, Hariot, Gilbert and Harvey. Daniel was a patriot, but a moral one and no provincial, condemning ill deeds and pointing out the punishments, deploring the evils of war though with a proper pride in martial prowess. He stands in sharp contrast to the chroniclers, who lacked critical sense; though Camden was an exception, even he derived the legendary pre-history of Britain from Brutus. Daniel was remarkable in refusing to acknowledge anything other than historical evidence beginning with Caesar and Strabo. All the Elizabethan historians went back to Britain and the British origins. An exception was the Teutoniser, Richard Verstegan, whose Dutch background enabled him to appreciate remarkably the Anglo-Saxon elements in the story, in the language and people.⁵⁹

Best of all in Daniel is his historical imagination and judgment in refusing to belittle the achievements of the past in terms of his own age – very remarkable in view of the Renaissance depreciation of the medieval. He respected the monastic chroniclers, as the blinkered Milton could not: 'dubious relaters . . . blind, astonished and struck with superstition as with a planet: in one word, Monks.'⁶⁰ *Per contra* Daniel says, 'it is but the clouds gathered about our own judgment that makes us think all other ages wrapped up in mists, and the great distance betwixt us that causes us to imagine men so far off to be so little in respect of ourselves.' Indeed, it is 'arrogant ignorance to hold this or that nation barbarous . . . Man, wheresoever he stand in the world, hath always some disposition of worth.' In the end, 'we deal with you [the past] but as posterity will deal with us, which ever thinks itself the wiser.'

That is rare historical understanding.

It is surprising that there was not more scepticism in the age, but its rarity is another evidence of backwardness, lack of sophistication. It would have been impossible for England to produce a Pomponazzi or Ochino, a Montaigne or Servetus. We now know that 'The Sceptic' published among Ralegh's papers is a fragment from Sextus Empiricus. Sextus was unknown to the Middle Ages, he was not published until 1562 by Étienne.[61] With this the knowledge of the sceptical school of Pyrrho was released upon Europe. Bayle regarded this rediscovery as the beginning of modern philosophy. The most notable exponent of a Pyrrhonian frame of mind was, of course, Montaigne.

We cannot go in detail into the writings of Sextus Empiricus or into the teachings of Pyrrho as expressed in them.[62] They expounded a sceptical attitude not only as a rule of life, but even with regard to the possibility of knowledge. They taught that peace of mind was attainable only by a non-committal attitude towards the vexatious problems of life and thought; since nobody could be certain about what they were disputing, the sensible attitude was indifference – ataraxy. The relevance of this at a time of religious conflict, when people were killing each other for mutually conflicting propositions – or at least using them as an excuse – is obvious. Sextus' book against the Ethicists expounds a moral relativism. Socrates was thought the first to introduce the distinction between things good and evil; but opinions vary as to what is good or evil, as in regard to beauty. Is he who suspends judgment regarding the nature of things good and evil happy? As the thing in itself is doubtful so is the method of learning doubtful. Is there any certainty in knowledge? Doubt was extended in every sphere, to every discipline. The school doubted the value of logic-chopping, grammar and rhetoric, as much as science or astrology. Astrologers had always assumed that things on earth were in 'sympathy' with those in the heavens – for which there was no basis whatever. Did the gods exist? The arguments for their existence – from consensus of opinion (opinion was always erratic), from the order of the universe, from the absurd consequences that would follow from denying deity, from arguing other people down – the sceptics found unacceptable. All this might with equal force be applied to the Christian view of the universe, and Christian dogmas.

One wonders if many Elizabethans read Sextus Empiricus – we know that Dr. John Chamber, writing on astrology, had done for one.[63] Much naughty information and many heterodox opinions were open to those who read the classics. Their reading of them, at school and at the university, was directed mainly to those writers, or those parts of an ancient author, that were not too obviously in conflict with Christian teaching. The fundamental Latin writer for them was Cicero; but it was the Cicero of the *De Officiis* that they read – Burghley carried the little book about with him in his bosom – not the Cicero of *De Natura Deorum* with its disquieting relativism about deities. From this book it is evident that Cicero did not believe in them – but he performed his religious rites as augur as if he did. And this was the attitude of Continental sceptics. Montaigne thought that one had to be excessively certain, to sacrifice another man's life for the sake of an opinion. The implication was that only fools were. He thought that the merits of all opinions are relative to the cultures that produce them, 'et certes la philosophie n'est qu'une poésie sophistiquée.'[64]

Luther's revolutionary view, that what conscience compelled him to believe on reading Scripture was true, was deeply characteristic of German subjectivism and may be regarded as a source of the German philosophical idealism which has had such disastrous consequences for Europe.[65] Other reformers then used this subjective criterion to condemn their opponents' appeals to conscience as heresy – of course: as the Catholic Church condemned them. Calvin used it against Servetus; and he informed Farel beforehand, if Servetus came to Geneva, 'I will not suffer him to get out alive.'[66] Nor did he, though Farel was deputed to accompany him to the stake. Servetus did not believe in the Trinity; a brilliant doctor, he did know about the pulmonary circulation of the blood. No doubt he was touched with megalomania, as Calvin said; but so was Calvin. Servetus had been out to instruct Calvin, not to learn from him – but no one could instruct Calvin. The conflict was at bottom the conflict between two egos, and the dyspeptic Calvin was probably as ulcerous as he was certainly ulcerated.

In fact the Reformers opposed Rome with another complete dogmatism in religion – they played each other's game, no doubt sincerely enough, hotting up the atmosphere, blowing the flames of theological disputation into religious war, burning with zeal. Erasmus's contempt for metaphysicking was thoroughly justified, his half-expressed hopes for a third world, betwixt and between the fanatics on both sides, shattered. The Reformers' rule of faith, based on the Bible as the Word of God – a non-sense concept –

with their subjective, conflicting certainties, was purely psychological. But an unexpected result of the conflict, among elect minds, was the conclusion drawn, by such people as Castellio and Acontius, that no one could be so sure of truth as to justify killing another human being as a heretic. Castellio's *De arte dubitandi* exemplified a very modern approach, a cautious scientific attitude to intellectual problems as against the ludicrous certainty, on both sides, as to what was in its nature uncertain.[67]

In the glad days of Elizabeth's accession, in the reaction from the horrors of Mary's reign, Castellio had appealed to her to refrain from violence in forcing men's conscience – and this was in keeping with her Erasmian upbringing, her Laodicean outlook. In the 1560's some thousands of refugees came into the country from Alva's terror in the Netherlands: the government welcomed these valuable recruits with their new industrial skills and capital. The Dutch Church was reconstituted at Austin Friars, as in Edward's reign – really to keep a responsible control over the congregation. It appears that it was not so homogeneous or united as was thought: there was an Anabaptist and a Familist element that did not subscribe to Calvinist orthodoxy.[68] The sheet-anchor of Calvinism was the doctrine of predestination, with all the arrogance it implied towards the non-elect:[69] the holy Catholic Church meant the predestined saints.[70] To Luther the Catholic Church meant the assembly of true believers. We perceive that each meant simply themselves. But pastor Haemstede refused to regard Anabaptists and Familists as reprobates; he declined to dispute the theological points, there had been too much theological disputation already. Brought before Bishop Grindal, with his Calvinist outlook, Haemstede was excommunicated and banished in 1562.[71] But the most eminent members of the congregation, van Meteren and Acontius, sympathised with him and were in turn excommunicated.

Acontius (Giacopo Acontio, born near Trent about 1500) was a brilliant military engineer, whose book *De Methodo* reduced mathematics to scientific simplicity and precision. Now in London he set himself to reduce the elements of Christian belief to an irreducible minimum, upon which Christians, he hoped, might agree not to fight each other.[72] His book, *The Stratagems of Satan*, published in Latin at Basel, 1565, was the classic plea of the century for toleration, along with Castellio's. (It was not published in English until 1648, and then only one-half of the book.) Acontius thought it impossible to achieve a doctrinal system embodying absolute truth, and in a lifetime of spiritual search he had not been able to find any unquestionable mark to determine the body of doctrine necessary for salvation. Indeed, he thought that it was the elevation of doctrine to a sacrosanct position that had been responsible for so much contention and bitterness, even among Protestants themselves. He proposed a minimum upon which, hopefully, Christians might 'worship God in a faith which meets the requirements demanded by the Bible. He regarded the bitter controversy over the Lord's supper as idle and foolish. It would be difficult to find another writer in this period who would so boldly discard as unessential an article of faith which had been most highly responsible for the bigotry and persecution which marked the century.'[73] He was, in fact, some centuries before his time. He denied that there was any exclusive salvation, with its concomitant – damnation for others; he condemned forced confessions and persecution of heretics; he did not think it was the business of the civil authorities to interfere in religious matters. I fear that this assumed a degree of enlightened reason out of all keeping with his time.

Anabaptism – a word of opprobrium, like 'Bolshevism' in the 1920's – merely meant rebaptising, a ceremony of conversion: Anabaptists were forerunners of modern Baptists. The Familists were precursors of the Quakers. Adherents of H. N., Hendrik Niclaes, whom the Family of Love looked upon as their founder, they formed a secret freemasonry of remarkable distinction in their upper *échelons*. The famous printer Plantin was one of them; the whole circle of van Meteren, Ortelius, L'Écluse, was touched by sympathy for them.[74] They were 'illuminated', led by the inner light of conscience; remarkably freed from dogma, they did not believe that man was unregenerate, born in sin; pious and charitable, they lived the inner life of the spirit, without partisanship or taking any sides. They attached no significance to the visible and external form of the Church, and thus were able to conform outwardly without giving their inner adhesion to nonsense. This was what frightened people, because they could not be sure who might or might not be adherents in their midst. They were also pacifists and did not think that magistrates should order religion: this was shocking (and indeed before its time).

Adherents of the Inner Light spread from London into East Anglia; Bishop Woolton of Exeter unearthed a little group in his remote diocese. After the religious fires had been banked up by the Papal Bull of Deposition, the Northern Rebellion, the Ridolfi

Plot, the challenge to the Anglican settlement from Catholics and Puritans alike, the days of lenity were over. On Easter day 1575 a considerable Anabaptist congregation was surprised, beyond Aldersgate; some twenty-seven were arrested and sent to prison, from which some escaped, others were banished.[75] 'Four of them bearing fagots' – in the good old Marian fashion – recanted their errors at Paul's Cross: they had to swear that 'Christ took flesh of the substance of the blessed Virgin Mary', that infants should be baptised, that magistrates might exercise Christian authority, and that it was lawful to swear an oath. Two remained obdurate. In July Henry Terwoert, a handsome young goldsmith – alas – was burned with another, older man, 'who died in great horror, with roaring and crying.' There were hardly any more burnings in Elizabeth's England; in Spain, burnings in hundreds continued for more than a century.

In 1580 two yeomen of the Queen's guard spoke up against the Council's imprisoning members of the Family of Love, and were found to belong to it.[76] Their confession revealed the tenets held among such humble folk. They were 'illuminated' and restored to man's state before the Fall; they must be 'deified' in God and God in them, that is, they believed in a quickening of conscience and the life of the spirit. Magistrates should not rule among Christians. Themselves might deny their faith in case of persecution: they should not suffer their bodies to be executed, being temples of the spirit. They did not regard the literal sense of Scripture; Judgment and Resurrection were already past. Van Dorsten tells us that this simple faith of the Family suffered 'constant and almost unequalled defamation, from which it has never really recovered.'[77] In fact, it survived into the later seventeenth century, to be absorbed by the Quaker movement. G. H. Williams concludes that today many Christians are closer to these despised Radicals than to the authoritarian churches. 'The Radicals were to shape the contours of the world that was to come after them far more than they or their Catholic and Protestant opponents realised.'[78] Their ultimate importance was infinitely greater than in their own day; it is for this reason that they have been given larger proportion than the world of Christian orthodoxy around them would have thought warranted. They were its solvents.

The infernal disputatiousness of the age – though its best spirits did not enter into disputation, neither Shakespeare nor Bacon, nor Gilbert, Hariot, Ralegh – arose not only from the perennial aggressiveness of men, but from the whole method of education and mode of mental operations. There was an excruciating concentration upon logic; traditional logic was for the purpose of disputation, with the grand assumption that by dispute men could not only detect error but establish truth. For complete communication between the instructed and the uninstructed, or the as yet not instructed – for these matters apply only to the educable, a small portion of the human race – both a logic and a rhetoric are necessary. 'A theory of communication is an organic part of a culture. As the culture changes so will the theory change.'[79] The movement of the age in logic, flowing from the cultural revolution of the Renaissance, was away from the dominant interest in the accumulated wisdom of the past towards the direct observation of reality. 'Concrete descriptions of reality came to be admitted to the status of sciences alongside the older generalisations of moralist and theologian . . . The great shift in men's thinking between 1500 and 1700 was in part a shift from the preponderant emphasis upon traditional wisdom to the preponderant emphasis upon new discoveries.' This was entirely in keeping with Bacon's expectations and in part due to his advocacy. But the time was not yet, in 1600: it 'was not yet ripe for sciences based upon experiment, observation, and the minute description of particulars . . . A logic of induction in advance of that time would have had no influence.' Once more, as in science, we see the age as something betwixt and between.

The leading figure in earlier Elizabethan logic and rhetoric was Thomas Wilson, whose book *The Rule of Reason* (1551) was the first English logic, straight out of the Edwardian stable.* His aim was the familiar one, 'to make logic as familiar to the Englishman as, by divers men's industries, the most part of the other liberal sciences are.'[80] There was no English vocabulary to describe the terms of logic, but Wilson exhibited a native concreteness in defining logical 'place' in terms of a hare's form or a fox's burrow – in that like Ascham. Wilson published his *Rhetoric* in 1553, the 'year in which the earliest complete account of the rhetorical doctrine connected with all five parts of the Ciceronian theory of oratory appeared in print.' We should note Wilson's protest against 'strange inkhorn terms' and foreign forms of speech instead of 'their mother's language', and Northumberland's personal interest. On Mary's accession Wilson decamped to Italy, where he escaped from the Inquisition's prison in Rome – to return to do

---

* This important figure deserves a full-length biography.

good work as a full-fledged Elizabethan. He was much employed in diplomacy and became a privy councillor, receiving the reward of the fat deanery of Durham, though a layman. Better, he published the first English translations of Demosthenes and a prime work upon economics, his *Discourse upon Usury*.[81] His *Logic* and *Rhetoric* became standard works and received several printings, until the rise of Ramism, which dominated the later period.

Ramus's campaign against scholasticism was an attempt to simplify its complexities, 'seeking to bring learning into a closer relation with the practical needs which it exists to satisfy.'[82] His programme represented a radical reform in method and teaching, applied to all the liberal arts, rather than any revolutionary change in content – for that the intellectual world would have to wait for Descartes. He was really a reformer of the traditional, with a fervent conviction that 'the theory of communication needed drastic revision if it was to satisfy the needs of a new era.' He wanted to simplify the learned arts into a system of universal affirmations, in descending order from the more general to the less. He regarded this as a more natural order of arrangement, as against the scholastic straitjacket of invariable dichotomy (i.e. exclusive alternatives). It was still a deductive method – not in keeping with Bacon's methodology. Ascham, who was the first to appreciate Ramus, saw that, contrary to the misrepresentations of him, he was attacking inept Aristotelians rather than Aristotle, and while removing scholastic accretions he remained traditional.

Ramus's clean reorganisation of these subjects was brilliantly successful in education. After his death in the Massacre of St. Bartholomew his teaching became widespread in Northern Europe, and from the 1580's he enjoyed (posthumously) a dominant position in logic and rhetoric in England. It was particularly influential at Cambridge, where it linked up with the more aggressive Protestantism of Chaderton, Perkins, Downham, Ames – whence it was transplanted to New England – and had a late flowering in Milton. William Temple, a follower of Sidney, had a controversy over it with Everard Digby; Perkins applied Ramus's terms to the art of preaching, Abraham Fraunce to the law. Cambridge was full of these discussions in the 1580's: Guise's indictment of Ramus in Marlowe's *Massacre at Paris* reflects the interest they excited. Oxford was more traditional, though even Hooker admitted the 'marvellous quick dispatch' the method offered: one could learn in a matter of days what formerly took years.[83] Hence the more disputation! Oxford adhered to the middle of the road, and in the end worked out its own *modus operandi*. 'The three [books] that may be said to have been so important as to have taught logic to all England during the 17th century are the product of Oxford men, even as Cambridge men had claimed the same distinction during the 16th century.'

Languet warned Philip Sidney that Ciceronianism was 'the chief abuse of Oxford' – not that he would know: a typical piece of French superciliousness. Actually all instruction in rhetoric throughout the period was based on Cicero. In the sixteenth century 'artistic' and 'non-artistic' proofs paralleled direct and indirect evidence today. 'In an age which lacked the facilities to assemble and disseminate such non-artistic proofs as documents, confessions, eye-witness reports, contracts, laboratory analyses, statistics and the like, it was inevitable that artistic proofs would receive special emphasis.'[84] This gives us the proper perspective in which to see the treason-trials of the time, the bullying of prisoners, the use of every kind of insinuation to incite prejudice, the stringing together of daisy-chains of evidences to construct a 'proof'. And, of course, with the more fatuous disputes of theology, no proof was possible anyway.

The issue of Ciceronianism – of a slavish imitation of manner and observance of words as against content and interpretation – was a European one. Gabriel Harvey – that useful barometer of intellectual trends – was one of the first to fall for Ramus's *Ciceronianus*: in his third year he read it twice in two days, and was at once converted by its transparent honesty. Harvey says that it led him to appreciate the varieties of style of the best Latin authors, not Cicero alone, and hence their diverse characteristics. He compared his conversion as from a merely verbal concern to the marrow of subject and matter. In 1577 he published his own lectures, the *Ciceronianus* and the *Rhetor*, which together 'constitute an admirable statement of the basic philosophy of Ramistic rhetoric.'[85]

We see once more how modern-minded Harvey was, how much in touch with literary movements abroad, widely read both in the classics and in recent literature, with a real enthusiasm for learning and teaching. Generous in his tributes to men of geniune intellectual quality, intensely patriotic about Cambridge, how superior he was to the commonplace people who kept him out. It is sad to think what more he might have accomplished if he had been given his chance, instead of being driven into silence.

(Cambridge much preferred Perkins roaring away.) Harvey must have been a stimulating teacher, with his insistence – as against the learning by rote of the day – on the student applying his powers of interpretation: 'He should focus attention not only on the word, but much more on comprehension, and knowledge.'[86] What better programme could there be, with his pointed questions for students: 'What have I learned today?' 'What progress in what subjects?' – still the essence of any real education, though remote from students today.

Everything about Harvey is personal: that is what keeps him alive. The enigma of his personality still intrigues us. When he refers to those who think of God as 'an infinite and incomprehensible essence, not to be circumscribed by any limits', was he thinking of Everard Digby, or of Marlowe?[87] As against Spenser's high-minded, idealistic conception of love, Harvey's preference for the physical appears to us more human and more sympathetic. An intellectual moderate, but morally respectable, he was no friend to Puritans. He well understood the mutability of men's thinking: 'so it standeth with men's opinions and judgments in matters of doctrine and religion.'[88]

In the lively intellectual life of Cambridge in the 1580's Everard Digby made a singular figure. The last time we met him was in connection with poaching the deer in Sir Thomas Fitzherbert's park in Staffordshire, where Digby was then living.[89] He was a sport; he wrote the first book on swimming, *De arte natandi*, all in due academic form, the rules of the art, then practical demonstration, with full-page woodcuts. Dedicated to Richard Wortley, student of the Muses, it celebrates their Cambridge days together, Socratic talks on the banks of the Cam in Maytime, for they were at St. John's together. Among the verses prefaced to the book were some by E. K. – was this Spenser's E. K.? (If so, he should be looked for among Johnians.) In 1580 Digby played in the college performance of Legge's famous 'Richardus Tertius'. But Digby's sporting instincts, or his sense of humour, got across the humourless Master of the college, William Whitaker, the leading Calvinist in Cambridge. By an exercise of unilateral authority Whitaker expelled Digby from his Fellowship, for preaching voluntary poverty at St. Mary's – a popish position – for blowing a horn and hallooing in the court, not paying his commons, and for describing Calvinists as schismatics: one hardly knows which of these offences was worse.

Digby's intellectual position was very much his own. On one

side he was a traditionalist, and wrote a Latin tract refuting the Ramist method; there followed a controversy with William Temple – puritans were sympathetic to Ramus. In 1579 Digby published his main philosophical work, and a very curious work it is, *Theoria Analytica*. It embraces a wide range of reading, notably among the Hermetics of whose philosophy he was evidently an adherent. It was a mixture of scepticism and mysticism, concluding that we know only that we do not know, that the ultimate is indemonstrable: a principle such that the last term is determined by the first (something like the position R. G. Collingwood ultimately arrived at). The book therefore is largely concerned with other means of apprehension, mainly mystical. The key to knowledge is faith, and there is a good deal about the supra-sensible world, with the number-mysticism of Pythagoras and the Greeks, and the Hermetic obsession of bringing all things to oneness. The argument descends from the summit of the pyramid of light to the human mind in its terrestrial habitation, the origin of the soul, the number and nature of the senses. At this point Digby gives an impressive and complex analysis of formal demonstration in the arts of the quadrivium, arithmetic, geometry, music, astronomy. He reminds one of the nonsensical Hermetic writer, Robert Fludd, except that Digby at least has his feet on the ground when he comes to academic disciplines (if not discipline). Rémusat who alone seems to have studied Digby, thought of him as a precursor of Leibniz; there is nothing in Sir Sidney Lee's view that his classification of the sciences foreshadowed Bacon: it was purely traditional.[90]

Digby's last work was in English, a *Dissuasive from taking away the goods and livings of the Church*. In his dedication to Lord Chancellor Hatton, his patron – a middle-of-the-road man – Digby sounds discouraged: reflecting 'what small account of scholars is made at this day . . . I resolved with myself never to publish anything in print hereafter.' And he never did. After the storms of the Reformation 'a ridiculous generation newly come ashore are not ashamed to affirm that they will dig up the garden anew, that they will reform the superstitious branches of the sweet ancient well-blown rose of England.' This gives us something of Digby's temper. He regarded the Puritan 'fancy' taken against bishops, deans, cathedrals and the order of the Church as the real foundation for their sophistical arguments. Within a couple of generations they would have their way, with no improvement to the state of things, and immense aesthetic loss – what chiefly matters. Digby was evidently an interesting and original man, and vastly more sympathetic than Whitaker, egregiously learned in theology and involved in interminable controversies with the Catholics. He took up, and is still given, too much space.[91]

The most influential, and representative, of the Cambridge theologians was William Perkins: he was aggressively Protestant, but not strictly a Puritan. We have already exposed his barbarous views about witches – our condemnation of them might be re-garded as anachronistic, were it not that there were already humane and civilised persons like Reginald Scot who regarded them as such. A reading of Perkins' collected works in three folio volumes only confirms our reading of him. His books were extra-ordinarily popular and went into many editions: we have to deal with him. The whole system of his theology is set forth in vol. i, *A Golden Chain*: it treats of the nature of Scripture, on which (as with all Protestants) the edifice was based. Thence it exfoliates into the nature and life of God, the persons of the godhead, pre-destination, angels, man and his state of innocency, sin and the fall of the angels, man's fall and disobedience, the union of two natures in Christ, and so on.

We do not need to go in detail into these propositions, which constituted the myth that prevailed over most of Europe at the time – with variations over which different sects within it fought to the death, killed each other, roasted or hanged each other, broke each other on the wheel. It would be unfair to say that this was solely because they were Christians, fairer to say simply, because they were humans. All the same, these nonsense-proposi-tions – in other words, beliefs – exacerbated men's natural aggres-sions and excused (to them) or, as they thought, justified their cruelties. Perkins thought that 'witches' should be put to death because the law of 'Moses' said so. The Presbyterian Cartwright held that 'the death penalty must be exacted for those breaches specified in the Old Testament' – for adultery, for instance.[92] To these the charitable Cartwright would add the death penalty for a Catholic priest, simply for being a priest: no Anglican thought anything so barbarous. 'A nonconformist by force of circum-stances', his defender says, 'and a conformist at heart, he aimed at ascendancy for his own beloved system and not liberty of conscience for all . . . He stood indeed for liberty of conscience, not because he believed in its intrinsic value,' but because he wanted it for himself. But so did the Catholics, and that was all there was to it.

The distinguishing mark of Calvinist theology – predominant in England up to the 1590's, when it began to be questioned (also at Cambridge, where the disputes waxed hot) – was its rigorous version of the doctrine of predestination. Perkins defines it as 'the decree of God by which he hath ordained all men to a certain everlasting estate: that is, either to salvation or condemnation for his own glory.'[93] We perceive that every word and phrase, strictly speaking, means nothing, corresponds to nothing; but over it they killed – the killing was a fact. Perkins proceeds to distinguish four different brands of doctrine on the matter: the Pelagians, who believed in man's free will, either to reject or receive God's grace; the semi-Pelagians or papists; the muddled Lutherans; only the Calvinist view was true, everybody else being erroneous. Since it was all nonsense we do not need to go into the hair-splitting distinctions he makes, merely cite the dominant Calvinist view ('truth'): 'the cause of the execution of God's predestination is his mercy in Christ in them which are saved, and in them which perish the fall and corruption of man; yet so as that the decree and eternal counsel of God concerning them both hath not any cause beside His will and pleasure.'[94] This is to exclude any idea that man's good works can help him at the day of judgment – a popish idea; only God's grace is any good, and only then upon the elect fore-ordained to be 'saved'.

Some more emollient doctrines were being put forth at Cambridge in the 1590's, by Baro and Barrett. These easy-going persons would suppose 'a universal or general election . . . whereby God hath decreed to redeem by Christ . . . all mankind wholly . . . as well the reprobate as the elect.'[95] This was shocking of them, 'fearing belike lest they should make God both unjust and unmerciful' – as they well might! It does not need much knowledge of psychology to appreciate that the tremendous force of the persuasion of predestination came from the assurance it gave that 'we' are 'saved' – whatever that means – and others damned. We may compare it with the aggressive strength it gave Communism in our time to be convinced that history was predetermined its way. This kind of persuasion unleashes the full forces of human egoism, always the strongest.

To turn to a less exalted sphere of Perkins' thought, the more practical one of men's callings in this world, he lays down that 'every man must judge his particular calling wherein he is to be the best for him.'[96] This appears to give a rather more democratic gloss to the Apostle Paul's 'Let every man abide in that calling wherein he was called.' But it is an infidel opinion that we choose for ourselves: we are called by God. Thus many who persuade themselves of their vocations 'have no calling at all. As, for example, such as live by usury, by carding and dicing, by maintaining houses of gaming, by plays and such like.' Thus a Perkins would exclude a Shakespeare from the age: it is a nice example of the puritan temper. Serving men should have some useful calling in addition to their waiting, otherwise they would spend most of their time eating and drinking, sleeping and gaming – most unprofitable members of church and commonwealth. One sees what the godly commonwealths of New England would be like, in which Perkins' precepts were put into practice.

Perkins would have no nonsense about ecumenism, such as the better spirits of the seventeenth century hoped for. 'It is a notable policy of the Devil, which he hath put into the heads of sundry men of this age, to think that our religion and the religion of the present Church of Rome are all one for substance, and that they may be reunited as, in their opinion, they were before. Writings to this effect are spread abroad in the French tongue and respected of English Protestants more than is meet or ought to be . . . This union of the two religions can never be made, more than the union of light and darkness.'[97]

As for Puritans proper, who accepted Cartwright as their leader, their 'quarrel with the English Church was not a theological one. Even adherents of the Bancroftian school acknowledged that the Puritans were in agreement with them on the fundamental points of doctrine. Cartwright's chief goal was the transformation of the Church of England into a Presbyterian State Church.'[98] In other words, it was simply a conflict for power. No one knew the Puritans better than Richard Bancroft, who had been at Christ's, a dominantly Puritan college. For a decade Archbishop Whitgift depended principally on Bancroft in dealing with the Puritans, tracking down the scurrilous Marprelate libellers of the bishops, and so on. Bancroft became extremely well-informed about their activities, in these years during which he worked like a galley-slave for the Church, while a score of his juniors were preferred before him, and he incurred the unpopularity along with Whitgift (himself a Calvinist in theology). No matter: to Marprelate Whitgift was worse than Bonner, sitting upon 'his cogging stool which may truly be called the chair of pestilence.'[99] Bishops were regularly called anti-Christian, robbers, wolves, horse-leeches, etc. Anyone who knows the age intimately from the documents will know what patient, hard-driven beasts of burden the Elizabethan bishops were, getting little thanks from anybody, even the Queen, for their pains. They had to bear all the odium for trying to implement *her* discipline: she drove them on.

It is not too much to say that the unrelenting Puritan propaganda against the bishops sowed a crop of hatred which bore bitter fruit in the Civil War. Bancroft knew his men. In his sermon at Paul's Cross, before the Parliament of 1589, he described them. 'In respect of their conversation they are said to be humble and lowly of outward show, but yet of nature very contentious and unquiet, doting about questions and strife of words: whereof cometh envy, strife, railings and evil surmisings. They are bold and stand in their own conceit; they despise government and fear not to speak evil of them that are in dignity and authority . . . They are libellers and do speak evil of those things which they know not.'[100] Every one of those charges could be substantiated.

In historical writing and tradition the Puritans have had things far too much their own way, the case for the Church gone by default, people like Whitgift, Bancroft and Laud treated with no kind of justice or understanding, often traduced. It was their duty to maintain order – and the Puritans were intolerable; actually the authorities, even Laud, were much more tolerant than *they* were. It was the business of Whitgift, and after him Bancroft, to govern the Church; ordinary intelligences find opposition much easier to sympathise with than the problems and burdens of government. The latter demand maturer minds, more adult judgment – as Oliver Cromwell found when the responsibility became his. Richard Bancroft came of the same social class, the gentry, and he had a mind attuned to government: that is why he has been ill-appreciated. He was an utterly devoted churchman, who cared for nothing else – like Whitgift, a celibate; but though driven by the cares of his position in upon himself, overdriven and not strong in health, he was a human being with a sense of humour, who consoled himself with music and books. After only six years as Archbishop, he died leaving all his musical instruments to his nephew; he revoked leaving his library to Canterbury – he feared that the cathedrals might be despoiled.[101] As they were: he knew what to expect of the Puritan temper.

Bancroft gives a recognisable picture of the Puritan manner. 'You shall see some that, after they have fetched divers great sighs and groans, will presently with great gravity and drawing out of their words, with a heavy countenance, with casting down their heads and with a pitiful voice, breathe out malediction. The which men do rather believe because it seemeth, by such their hypocritical dealing, rather to proceed of a sorrowful compassion than of malice and hatred.'[102] Which of course it was, even more envy – the sociological importance of which sociologists and historians are apt to overlook – and the frustrated desire for power. When they got there, and their humbug set the tone under the Commonwealth and Protectorate, only a military dictatorship kept them there – contrary to all their 'beliefs' and assumptions; and as soon as the dictator died, the sense of average human beings ended the rule of the saints for good and all. Again and again, Bancroft exposed their propaganda-language: they are always the 'godly', they are the 'servants of God', the Church of England is wanting 'a godly ministry'; ordinary church-folk are 'ungodly' (theologically, no doubt, un-elect), bishops anti-Christian, wolves, beasts. It hardly needs a Pareto to expose the method; Bancroft could do it quite well. Intellectually he had the better of the argument: in vain.

Bancroft expounded the position of the Church of England, and made a good case for it, in the circumstances of the time: consonant with Scripture, adhering to the early Fathers as against the accretions of Rome, holding the essentials of the Christian faith shorn of later dogmas such as transubstantiation and of the papal supremacy, which had no primitive warrant. Neither Calvin nor Beza condemned episcopacy in principle, and the Book of Common Prayer had been approved by the Continental Reformers: even Calvin distasted only some 'tolerable fooleries' – with his usual arrogant superciliousness.[103] Though why should Calvin be regarded as an authority for England? The Prayer Book was compiled by such men as he ought to have reverenced – Cranmer, Latimer, Ridley, Hooper, who died for it. Knox had brought back to Scotland the authority of Calvin and Beza, 'as though they had been such Peters for the Protestants as the Bishop of Rome pretendeth himself to be for all Papists.'

The tide was in fact turning for the Church of England: by the 1580's it had developed an ethos of its own, more in keeping with the character of the English people than either Puritanism or Romanism (as subsequent experience proved) and could turn the tables on them. When the Puritans appealed to Beza for encouragement in their opposition to the ceremonies prescribed in the Prayer Book, 'it was a fond part for them to write so unto him, and a very insolent part for him to take so much upon him.'[104] Archbishop Whitgift did not hesitate to rebuke the pontiff of Geneva for 'overbusying' himself with the concerns of the English Church and received a tribute to the English episcopate in reply. Now Beza allowed even of a primacy among bishops – as in effect he would like at Geneva.

Bancroft proceeds to give an unflattering account of Calvin's subjection of Geneva to a much harsher ecclesiastical discipline than ever the bishops had exerted there. Bancroft's political mind thoroughly understood the political penetration of Calvin, who had realised that, without the authority of an ecclesiastical Senate dominated by himself, he would never have been able to rule 'the multitude': it ended in the rule of *one man* at Geneva. Bancroft gives an unfavourable account of Consistorial government there, their interference 'in all the common affairs of the city,' keeping men from communion without giving reason, 'but because some of the godly brethren, forsooth, were offended with them.'[105] He exposes Calvin's methods of vote-snatching – such was the Consistorial Discipline 'daily dashed in our teeth, as though that form of discipline had come lately from heaven.' Then there were Calvin's propaganda methods, regularly painting opponents in the worst colours in his vast correspondence all round the Protestant world, flattering the self-esteem of his followers. Bancroft understood it all.

With a sense of humour he carried the warfare into their camp for a change – 'all out of square from the Apostles' times – till Geneva was illuminated!'[106] He quotes the godly John Wake writing to John Field, the organiser and brain behind the Puritan campaign: 'let me know your judgment particularly – whether it be in any respect tolerable for women that profess religion and the Reform to wear doublets, little hats with feathers, great gowns after the French and outlandish fashion, great ruffs and hair either curled or frizzled, or set upon wires and such-like devices.' (The Puritans had a proper view of the subjection of women – Milton was no exception in this respect.) Another of the godly wants to know 'whether the strict prohibition of not kindling fire on the sabbath be of the substance of the moral precept.' What asses they were! Yet Field's next correspondent reminds him, 'I hope you have not let slip this notable opportunity of furthering the cause of religion [i.e. theirs] by noting out all the places of government in the land for which burgesses for the Parliament are to be chosen, and using all the best means you can for procuring the best gentlemen of those places, by whose wisdom and zeal God's causes [i.e. their own] may be prepared.' When it came to the question of power – which was what mattered – the Puritans had a very strong scent. It was impossible to put them down; not until they had martyred an archbishop in poor Laud could the Church vindicate itself.

Bancroft was able to show that these nasty types detested each other as much as they did the Church. What the Presbyterians said about the Church the Congregationalists said about *them*. Barrow and Greenwood described the 'wretched disciples of Calvin' as 'most pernicious deceivers', and their adored Discipline as 'a silly presbytery or eldership', 'a presumptuous irregular Consistory which hath no ground in the word of God.'[107] Barrow said of Cartwright's followers, 'these Reformists for fashion sake give the people a little liberty to sweeten their mouths and make them believe they should choose their own ministers.' These underground exchanges came into the light of day with the envenomed quarrels of Presbyterians and Independents for power, after the defeat of Church and King. Why all the pother? Because humans like quarrelling: human aggression seeks every outlet, the struggle is always – as with men at all times – simply for power. It is a double reason for disparaging what men think, compared with the works of their hands – jewels, painting, music, architecture, sculpture, theatre – that not only what they think is largely nonsense but that it often provides them with the excuse for destroying what is of more worth.

In a second book, *Dangerous Positions and Proceedings* along with his *Survey of the Pretended Holy Discipline*, Bancroft gave a narrative of the harm these people had already done. He struck out at both sections of disturbers of the peace, seminary priests and Jesuits on one side, Puritans on the other: 'both of them labouring with all their might to steal away the people's hearts from their governors, to bring them to a dislike of the present state of our Church: the one sort for the embracing of such directions as should come unto them from Rome; the other for the establishing of that false and counterfeit hierarchy which they would obtrude upon us from Geneva'.[108] Since the latter wished to introduce Presbyterianism as in Scotland – with what uncongenial consequences we know, when subsequently it was tried under the Commonwealth – Bancroft gave a factual picture, drawn largely from Knox, of the iconoclasm of the Scottish Reformation, with the destruction of abbeys and cathedrals. He drew out the implications of the teachings of Knox, Buchanan and Co., that 'people may arraign their prince', as they – or rather the Army – would do in 1649.[109]

Bancroft gave an informed account of the growth of the Presbyterian campaign, and he showed that these people would stick at nothing: Martin Marprelate had not hesitated to say that reform 'cannot well come to our Church without blood'. A recent event had confirmed Bancroft's warnings. An Oundle man, William Hacket, who had been a servant of the Puritan Knightley and waited on Penry, was converted and set up to announce the Messiah. (Prior to his conversion, he had bitten off a schoolmaster's nose at Oundle.)[110] Whipped out of York, Leicester and Northampton, he arrived in London at Easter in 1591 and had no difficulty in persuading two gentlemen – Coppinger, who had a small post in the Queen's household, and Arthington, a Yorkshireman – that he was the Messiah. Hacket proclaimed that he had been anointed by the Holy Ghost to inaugurate a new era, and that he was immortal. More serious, he announced that the Queen was no Queen, and in July 1591 appeared with his followers in Cheapside calling on the crowd to rise and displace the government. There shortly grew such a tumult that the fanatics had to take refuge in the 'Mermaid' – entertainment there was not merely literary. Hacket died on the scaffold as a traitor – he was, of course, mad; the fool Coppinger, of the royal household, starved himself to death in prison; Arthington was released after a year.

Since we are exposing the mind and spirit of the age, this was a part of it.

In general, a proper appreciation of the Church of England has been wanting in historical writing, particularly in Continental scholarship, which can more easily understand either a Catholic or a Protestant position. The Anglican Church, with an idiosyncrasy of its own, partaking of both, is more difficult. Then, again, the nineteenth century at home was dominated by Protestant historians and was far too sympathetic, unhistorically so, to the Puritans; while the New England Puritans, so essential an element in the making of the American nation, have naturally had a disproportionate influence in the interpretation of the past.*

* Cf. W. K. Jordan whom further study of these questions caused to modify many of the views he had imbibed from his background: 'in particular he has come to appreciate the vast contribution and noble temper of the moderates and to regard more critically the thought of the zealous,' *The Development of Religious Toleration in England from the Accession of James I to the Long Parliament, 1603–1640*, 9.

Until Whitgift became archbishop, the Puritans made the running, and the Church was on the defensive. Now it took the offensive; Bancroft was Whitgift's right-hand man, and Whitgift paved the way for his succession. Bancroft never lost dignity, but for a more personal controversialist we may turn to Matthew Sutcliffe.*

The particular value of Sutcliffe's writings is the detailed information he is able to give us from both the Puritan and Catholic underworlds which he made it his business to explore. For one thing, Sutcliffe clearly knew who Martin Marprelate was – about whom so much mystery has been made, and for whom Dover Wilson, erratically as usual, suggested Sir Roger Williams of all people! From the depositions of printers and other people employed, Sutcliffe was able to point to the obvious persons – chiefly Job Throckmorton, with John Penry, John Udall and John Field, in co-operation. Moreover, Sutcliffe got on the track of Throckmorton's connections with Hacket and Coppinger: they emerged from the excitable background of Northamptonshire Puritanism. Lord Chancellor Hatton, who knew, regarded Throckmorton as 'a man of a lewd and proud disposition, and of a dissembling and factious spirit.'[111] (On the other wing of the family, the Catholic branch, Francis Throckmorton had been executed as a traitor: anything to be out of step.) Sutcliffe knew that Job Throckmorton had been cursed by his mother for his hard dealings with her and thought this a reason for his disturbed spirit, when he might have been quiet. Throckmorton had dissociated himself from Coppinger's manner of extempore prayer, so beloved of Puritans, which was really an art of excoriating their enemies, allowing 'private men to pour out their fancies, prayers made contrary to the rule of faith, yea and to good manners.'[112] This was true enough; but a more effective point was that, though Hacket and Coppinger may have been mad, they had been trained up in the Consistorial discipline, the classis and all that, and were victims of Puritan religious hysteria.

A remark of Sutcliffe's brought out a veteran controversialist against him, the famous Jesuit, Robert Parsons. Parsons insinuated something about Sutcliffe's conduct at Cadiz: apparently he had acted as judge-marshal, while in holy orders. Sutcliffe was a follower of Essex, and so was able to reply, with point, that Essex had been driven on to his fatal course of rebellion by his Catholic associates, his step-father, Sir Christopher Blount, and Southampton. And this was true. For good measure, Sutcliffe

* Sutcliffe would make a good subject for a more extended study.

went on to expose a good deal about Parsons' background, which may or may not be true. It was generally held that Parsons was illegitimate – his putative father a blacksmith, his true father a former monk of Torre abbey. Sutcliffe quoted the account of the secular priests confirming Parsons' bastardy, and that they had informed the Pope. Father Watson also had asserted it, and hence Parsons was never advanced for all his services, his ability, his international notoriety. He meant to be, but Allen was made, a cardinal. Certainly this would account psychologically for Parsons' insatiable need to assert himself, to be in the public eye, his genius for intrigue, his passion for power.

Parsons was hardly an attractive personality: he was a big corpulent fellow – with more energy than he knew what to do with, pustules in his face. Sutcliffe knew all about his troubles at Balliol, where there had been a small minority of crypto-Catholics, against the Protestant majority. There are the usual Protestant insinuations against celibate priests and colleges. During the notorious disturbances in the English College at Rome, against the Jesuits, one Harward gave out that he could name 'seven sodomites in that college': this was no novelty among those who forswear marriage.[113] He has long been the tormentor of the boys of the English College, though his friends say he loves them but too well. 'And namely one Fisher, a fine youth that sometime was a Ganymede to Edward Weston, sometime reader of sodomitical divinity at Douai – although now, for his beastly love, they say, he hath lost his place and lecture, and is sent to Antwerp to love wenches there . . . As for Fisher, he is now at Rome to do penance with R. P., protonotary of Sodom.' This was, of course, but vulgar Protestant abuse; Protestants were all in favour of marriage – a safer option, when all is said and done.

The seductive Fisher became, however, a famous proselytiser. In three years' confinement under James he reconciled nearly a hundred and fifty souls.[114] When Buckingham's egregious mother was leaning towards Catholicism, King James arranged a disputation to save her soul. The Jesuit succeeded in converting this grasping woman, against the efforts of Laud; he did not succeed in convincing the king and his favourite. The Arch-priest Blackwell's colleagues, who were supporters of the Jesuits against the bulk of the English Catholics, brought out a book in Parsons' defence, putting a different gloss on his conduct at Balliol.[115] He had been next to Senior Fellow there, and was envied for his success with scholars. No doubt. Christopher Bagshaw, whom

Parsons had helped to make Fellow, turned against him – a familiar enough situation to anyone who has lived in a college – and tried to take pupils away from him. Parsons was in London one Christmas with friends of a pupil, James Hanley, 'a very proper youth', when Bagshaw took the boy out to certain comedies at night, which Parsons had forbidden 'for fear of inconveniences that might ensue in such a throng.' Bagshaw then kept the youth shut up in his chamber, for fear of Parsons' punishment, who was Dean that year. There ensued a college quarrel, and the Protestant majority charged him with perverting the youths of the house.

Actually Parsons had meant for some time to withdraw overseas, and he left the College before he was expelled – the Protestant crew rang the bells of St. Mary Magdalen (in our time once more the most Catholic of Oxford churches) backward as if there were a fire. Bagshaw was the active agent in all this: it is all very convincing, so like life. Then Bagshaw after many broils was driven out, and Parsons helped him overseas to Rome, where he continued to be a trouble-maker and was dismissed. Parsons' supporters came to his defence over his flight from the mission of 1580–1, leaving Campion to his fate. They said that he had in his care two young gentlemen, George Gilbert and Charles Basset, 'whom he loved dearly', and was forced to fly, having to accommodate them overseas. The rumours about Parsons' birth were contradicted: his parents were honest, his father reconciled by the martyr, Father Bryant, his mother 'living several years in flight and banishment for religion'. He had ten brothers and sisters of his name. It seems that there was a something to explain.

We are not concerned here with the biography of this fascinating personality, who evidently attracted as well as repelled, though he was vastly more interesting than any Puritan, all the more congenial for being less holy. His life-story shows how his mind and thought were shaped by his resentments, his emotions, his feuds and vendettas. He was the most notable and constant of the Catholic controversialists, always in hot water and as irrepressible as any Puritan – the government had bad luck in catching Campion, instead of him. To do Parsons justice we should turn to his *Christian Directory*, an exposition of the Christian religion which was found so useful that Edmund Bunny published an Anglican version of it, shorn of Roman excrescences – the praise of virginity, chastising the body, abstinence and fasting, the doctrine of merits. Wherever Parsons wrote penance Bunny put repentance – a good joke, but it much annoyed Father Robert.

Not for nothing had he been a Balliol man: his exposition was as well founded intellectually as such a thing could be. He began at the beginning and went through in logical order to the end, first postulating 'that there is a God which rewardeth good and evil, against all atheists of old and of our time.'[116] He based himself on metaphysics, on the wonder of the world and its design, the *primum mobile*, Aristotle and Plato. He condemned Galen, a scientific naturalist, as 'a profane and very irreligious physician.' Parsons was all for metaphysics, dominated by teleology, as all the religious were. His third chapter deals with 'the final end and cause for which man was created by God and placed in this world' – we have seen how nonsensical Bacon thought this kind of thinking was. The next chapter shows 'that the service which God requireth of man in this present life is religion.' Thus we go on to the 'proofs' of Christianity, and the conundrum whether God's mercy be greater than his justice, and a warning against the love of this world (himself was very worldly).

The poor Bunny got no thanks from the great Jesuit for his well-meant efforts. He had written in an eirenical spirit, hoping that men of good will would appreciate what common ground there was and deploring so many books of controversy engendering 'inordinate heat'. Unfortunately, controversy was what Father Robert liked – it was mother's milk to him – and he provoked Bunny to some heat in reply. Parsons spelt him Buny throughout. Bunny said innocently that he had never meddled with these things before and had only meant to persuade Catholics to 'more moderate ways and to better agreement in the cause of religion.' So he had willingly left in the book what 'might tolerably stand.'[117] This was very Anglican of him. He had been so unwise as to say that all might be members of one Catholic church, and that to insist on division 'we bring ourselves to needless trouble'. Father Robert thought this puny and pusillanimous – 'this is Mr. Buny's good fellowship in religion!'

We might equate Parsons' religion with politics. The world is not a whit better for anything that he knew or taught or lived – and a number of good Catholics lost their lives on account of him.[118]

Meanwhile, the voluminous Whitaker was engaged in controversy with the equally voluminous Cardinal Bellarmine, and with answering those Oxford men, Campion, Sanders, Stapleton and William Reynolds (Oxford produced far more Catholics, Cambridge far more Puritans). We need not go into any further detail: when one has read a score of these books one has read a hundred, all repeating the same arguments, similar abuse and insults, going over the same ground, trudging the wearisome treadmill. It is all dead rubbish. They never argued the issues – Papal claims to authority, for example, or the propriety of national churches – on practical, commonsense grounds, but always on grounds of authority, of absolute right or wrong. There is no absoluteness in such matters; the significant thing is that sixteenth century people could hardly ever see that, least of all the intellectuals. And this speaks volumes as to the modes of thought of the time.

A wide reading in Whitaker brings out nothing new; only occasionally does he make an observation in the realm of commonsense, as that 'the Papists' cruelty far surpasseth the Protestants' just severity'.[119] This was true enough when one considers the three hundred martyrs, nearly all simple folk, of three years of Mary's reign, as against a comparable number of Catholic martyrs, many of them executed as fifth columnists in war-time, during the whole forty-five years of Elizabeth. Some four people were burned for heresy during her reign; but thousands were burned in Spain, or slaughtered in the Netherlands or France. And this is quite apart from the appalling record of Catholic assassinations of their opponents – William of Orange, the Regent Moray, Henri III and Henri IV, Coligny and the thousands who were victims of St. Bartholemew in Paris and elsewhere. The Pope struck a medal to commemorate the killings of these fellow-Christians.

One need hardly go any further with Whitaker than to note the weakness of the Protestant position, in basing itself upon the authority of Scripture. 'The Church can make no writing canonical, neither doth the authority of it depend on the Church. It hath itself his own authority.'[120] On the other hand, 'the sense [of Scripture] is not that which most hold but which is agreeable to the Scripture.' A simple circular argument. And so we come to the tangles their metaphysical nonsense involved them in. 'Necessity is not opposite to the freedom of will, but to force and compulsion; man lost not his will but the quality of it.' Hence, 'if we say God permitteth sin unwillingly, we overthrow his providence and omnipotency; he willeth, yet alloweth not, that which is evil.' There is full treatment of 'what the image of God was in man before his fall' – the kind of (strictly) nonsense that agitated

C. S. Lewis's mind in our time. Perhaps we may in turn be permitted to descry the cloven hoof in Whitaker's unkind sentence, 'no Jesuit nor any beast can be in heaven [where is this?] because they have the mark of the beast.' Nor are any of the Popes in heaven.

One would suppose that these embittered disputes, and the killings, would have opened more eyes than Christopher Marlowe's. There must have been some who had their doubts about the Christian faith, even in backward England. John Dove, after confuting recusants and Jesuits, turned his attention to unbelievers with his *Confutation of Atheism.** There were not only ancient philosophers, like Lucretius and Epicurus, who held the abominable view that there was no God, but recent writers who mention 'a whole island lately inhabited by such as deny God. And I wish all atheists were banished out of Christian states and kingdoms, and sent into that island.'[121] Then there were such scoffers as Lucian, Julian the Apostate and Doletus 'which called Moses, Elias and Christ the three deceivers of the world. And such atheists are the swaggerers of our age, which are not ashamed to call themselves the damned crew.' There are the Machiavellians, whose divinity is policy. 'These English Italianate and devils incarnate hold these damnable opinions: that there was no creation of the world, that there shall be no day of judgment, no resurrection, no immortality of the soul, no hell. They dispute against the Bible, reckon up genealogies more ancient than Adam, allege arguments to prove the story of Noah's ark and the deluge were fables.'

This thinker was able to expound, not only God, but Noah's ark: there *was* room for seven creatures of every clean kind, two of unclean for increase, since the capacity of the Ark was 300 cubits in length, 50 in breadth, 30 in height, three floors in it – a larger *Queen Mary* laid up on Long Beach. Such was the intellectual level of the argument against atheists. We are not told who they were, but we catch echoes of the charges against Marlowe and Hariot. The causes of atheism were: (1) misinterpreting Cicero's *De Natura deorum*; (2) want of hearing the Word preached; (3) God's long-suffering in not immediately punishing atheists; (4) the malice of Satan; (5) the lenity and overmildness of rulers. 'Where the Spanish Inquisition is it is a very rare thing to hear of an atheist . . . it is better to live where there is too much severity rather than too much looseness.'[122] This man was a cleric; he

---

* For Forman's opinion of him, see *The Elizabethan Renaissance. The Life of the Society*, 149.

evidently had no objection of principle to the tortures of the Inquisition.

It is only the superior intelligences that we respect. When we come to Donne we are on a higher plane than with these academic disputants. And Donne knew the Roman position from the inside: he had been thoroughly indoctrinated in it through the determination of his *dévote* of a mother, who belonged to the family of Sir Thomas More, the Rastells and the Heywoods. Two of her brothers were Jesuits, who suffered imprisonment and died in exile; Donne's own brother died of prison fever, after imprisonment for concealing a priest. Donne was brought up in the feverish atmosphere of Jesuit devotion – not of normal secular Catholicism – and thought that his own morbid inclination to suicide sprang from his 'first breeding and conversation with men of a suppressed and afflicted religion, accustomed to the despite of death and hungry of an imagined martyrdom.'[123] In the end, he came to the conclusion that their cult of martyrdom had no justification: in refusing temporal allegiance to the government of their country they were insisting on suicide.

It took him a long time to think himself clear of these early impressions and, to free himself from the prejudices which had been inculcated into him, he undertook a complete course of divinity, studying all sides of the issues of allegiance, of authority and obedience. 'I had a longer work to do than many other men, for I was first to blot out certain impressions of the Roman religion, and some anticipations early laid upon my conscience, both by Parsons, who by nature had a power and superiority over my will, and others, who by their learning and good life, seemed to me justly to claim an interest for the guiding and rectifying of mine understanding in these matters.'[124] The upshot of his studies was his remarkable book, *Pseudo-Martyr*, in which Donne showed that the Jesuits had no valid reason for withholding temporal allegiance, and in martyrising themselves and others were but pseudomartyrs.

The work set forth in cogent intellectual order 'that the Roman religion doth by many erroneous doctrines misencourage and excite men to this vicious affectation of danger.'[125] He shows how – by inciting the secular magistracy against them, then by extolling the value of merits, and the doctrine of purgatory which made the sacrifice worth while. Next, he showed 'that in the Roman church the Jesuits exceed all others in their constitutions and practice in all those points which beget or cherish this corrupt desire of false-martyrdom'. If priests died simply for their spiritual functions that were martyrdom, but refusing the oath of allegiance vitiates 'the integrity of the whole act' and robs them of martyrdom. By refusing the oath they were bound to risk capital penalties – and there was no need for it, even from the Catholic point of view.

Donne knew Catholic doctrine and precept as no Protestant did. He pointed out that Papal authority could not lay this obligation upon their consciences, for the doctrine itself was not certain, nor presented as a matter of faith.[126] Only Bellarmine defended it, but he varied in his statements of it and was contradicted by Catholics of equal estimation. The Canons of the church give no warrant for this refusal, and nothing in the Oath violates the Pope's spiritual jurisdiction. Nor were the English sovereigns claiming any other rights to the loyalty of their subjects than were recognised in the kings of France, not by virtue of any concordat but by the inherent right of the crown.

Donne laid the blame for the blood of the martyrs firmly upon Jesuit policy, in particular upon 'an ordinary instrument of his [the Devil], whose continual libels and incitatory books have occasioned more afflictions and drawn more of that blood which they call Catholic in this kingdom than all our acts of Parliament have done.'[127] This was the Elizabethan government's contention all along, and no one would have any difficulty in recognising Father Parsons from Donne's description of him. France and Venice had always maintained their own laws of temporal jurisdiction:'which laws Parsons, without any colour of truth . . . says they have recalled.' And Donne was able to cite Cardinal Perron in disproof. Philip of Spain had rejected all attempts of the Pope to interpose between Spain and Portugal – contrary to what Parsons says, 'who is no longer a subject and son of the Church of Rome than as that Church is an enemy of England, for in the differences between her and Spain he abandons her.' Certainly Parsons threw in his lot with Spain, writing a book to justify the claim of Philip II's daughter, the Infanta, to the English Crown. What nonsense! – and as if the succession were any of his business.

Donne had no difficulty in penetrating Parsons' motive – revenge upon England, or the more varied psychological motivation of his disciples and dupes. Donne cries out for them, 'O what spiritual calenture [burning fever] possesses you to make this hard shift to destroy yourselves?' The reason: they are 'carried to this desire by human respects [connections] and by the spirit either of their blood and parents when they do it to please them, or by the

331

spirit of liberty, to be delivered from the bondage and encumbrances of wife and children, or else violently by adversity and want'. He concluded: 'it becomes not me to say that the Roman religion begets treason, but I may say that within one generation it degenerates into it.'

Donne had learned the hard way that the Reformation had justified itself. 'You may have observed the birth and prosperous growth of this Reformation . . . This reformation hath spent less time than the corruption, and the Church hath recovered more health in one age than she hath lost in any two.' Pope Adrian VI had admitted the necessity for Reform, but did not live to perform it, and his successors would not carry it out. Now, 'if you consider the good health and sound constitution of the Reformed Religion and that it is in all likelihood long-lived' – having cut out the dead wood and later accretions – 'and in a few years it hath produced so many excellent authors in the arts and in divinity that neither our schools nor our precepts need be beholding to them who deliver no gold without some dross. And that, for temporal blessings, he hath made us as numerous and as potent as his adversaries.'

It is all the more compelling a justification of the Reform, coming from such a source; perhaps the effort, after all, had been worth while.

A no less compelling justification from a comparable spirit among Italians, Fra Paolo Sarpi. would have been familiar to Donne. Protected by the sympathetic independence of Venice, Sarpi was able to view the universal Church as the sum of all individual churches – Roman, Gallican, Greek, Anglican, Lutheran even Calvinist. And this was the sensible Anglican position. 'His ideal, in fact, was not an organisational unity but a loose confederation of autonomous units.'[128] Sarpi paralleled the dislike of the central Anglican tradition for theological hair-splitting. 'The truths of Christianity could only be approached by faith: hence his bitter criticism of the systematic theological discussions which produced the doctrinal formulations of Trent. To apply the subtle definitions and distinctions of human reason to the content of the faith was for Sarpi a shocking contamination of heavenly with earthly things, the product of human vanity, contentiousness, and presumption. It was therefore doomed to futility. This we can all see clearly enough now, but there were some elect spirits who perceived it in the midst of the conflict even then.

With Sarpi the perception was fortified by the historian's sense that he must avoid all systems as distortions of reality, which is to be found in concrete situations and particular detail.

Donne also saw clearly that where most men held their convictions as absolutes and thought of them as 'true', others as 'false', in fact 'men are moulded in their religious beliefs rather more by the accidents of birth, education, and fate' than by intellectual processes.[129] From this point of view it was the less surprising that history should show that the English Church bore the character of the English people more fully and satisfactorily than either of the deviants on either side. The classic case had already been made for it in Hooker's *Laws of Ecclesiastical Polity*: we have already given an account of it earlier.[130]

We should add what Hooker had to say on this specific issue in his *Discourse of Justification, Works, and . . . the Foundation of Faith*.[131] The Presbyterian-minded Travers had delated and traduced Hooker for his sermon at the Temple daring to suggest that Rome might still have 'the foundation of faith' of a Christian church and that 'the thousands of our fathers' who had lived under the Catholic Church might not be consigned to perdition. This charity of spirit was anathema to Travers and his like, and Hooker had to devote a whole discourse to justifying himself. He did not withdraw from his position; he substantiated it by a course of argument, concluding that 'the best-learned in our profession are of this judgment, that all the heresies and corruptions of the Church of Rome do not prove her to deny the foundation directly.' And he doubted not that God would be merciful to our forefathers, 'inasmuch as they sinned ignorantly.' This charitable interpretation was not one to recommend itself to Puritans, but it showed the Anglican Church in the light of a true *via media*. There is no need to labour that Richard Hooker was a man of the spirit.

The fruits of the spirit were rare, naturally, in so bitter and controversial a time – though Donne reaped them in the end, after the vagaries of his youth. It is natural that we should find them in the arts rather, in music and the poets. Even philosophic orthodoxy is better expressed by the poet Davies in his *Nosce Teipsum* than it is by the theologians. His first section, on the limitations of human knowledge, well expresses the pride of the age in its achievements yet admits defeat before the mystery of man's place in the universe:

> We that acquaint ourselves with every Zone
> And pass both tropics and behold the Poles,

> When we come home are to ourselves unknown
> And unacquainted still with our own souls.

He concludes therefore, like Montaigne, that essential Renaissance spirit:

> So within lists my raging mind hath brought
> That now beyond myself I list not go:
> Myself am centre of my circling thought,
> Only myself I study, learn, and know . . .
>
> I know my life's a pain and but a span,
> I know my sense is mocked with everything:
> And, to conclude, I know myself a Man,
> Which is a proud, and yet a wretched, thing.

What is man's soul? Davies is probably referring to the ancient materialists, like Lucretius, when he says

> And others think the name of soul in vain
> And that we only well-mixed bodies are . . .

For no one in the sixteenth century England would dare to think this.

A sceptical turn of mind made Davies reflect,

> For no crazed brain could ever yet propound
> Touching the soul so vain and fond a thought
> But some among these masters have beeen found
> Which in their schools the self-same they have taught.

And so Davies settles for orthodoxy, as practically everyone did: it would have involved an unthinkable mental effort to overthrow it.

Davies traverses the view of those who thought the soul was but a reflection of the senses. The sense-perceptions provided the information, yet the soul subsists by itself, something beyond and apart:

> Nor can herself discourse or judge of aught
> But what the sense collects and home doth bring.
>
> For though our eyes can naught but colours see,
> Yet colours give them not their powers of sight . . .

He goes on to illustrate the fallibility of sense-perception, and so –

> Are they not senseless then that think the soul
> Nought but a fine reflection of the sense?

God created our souls – and we are at once faced by the insoluble dilemmas of original sin, which have had an absurd revival in our time with T. S. Eliot and C. S. Lewis's Problem of Pain –

dilemmas created by their nonsense-assumptions, and which a rational outlook obviates. Davies argues, as they all do:

> How can we say that God the soul doth make
> But we must make him author of her sin?
>
> For if God make her, first he makes her ill
> (Which God forbid our thoughts should yield unto!)
>
> Fain would we make him author of the wine
> If for the dregs we could some other blame . . .

impossible with the concept of omnipotent and omniscient goodness.

> The soul
> Even in the womb is sinful and accursed,
> Ere she can judge by wit or choose by will.
>
> Yet is not God the author of her sin,
> Though author of her being and being there.

No wonder the intelligent were led to question:

> Yet this the curious [inquiring] wits will not content;
> They yet will know: sith God foresaw this ill
> Why his high providence did not prevent
> The declination of the first man's will.

This was the question Milton was to wrestle with in *Paradise Lost*, and pinpoints what Mr. Empson finds so revolting about Milton's God.[132]

All that Davies can urge for the immortality of the soul is that

> None that acknowledge God or providence
> Their soul's eternity did ever doubt.

But this was not true: even Jewish doctrine had not mostly subscribed. Davies regards man's main motive for believing as his insatiable appetite,

> To learn and know the truth of everything.

But wasn't this supposed to be the original root of the trouble?

> Hence springs that universal strong desire
> Which all men have of immortality.

To this we may say that it has never been universal, nor is it noticeably strong today.

The sceptical mind of Erasmus, impatient of dogma, was left

335

in the end with only a devotion to the person of Jesus; and on his death-bed relapsed into the language of his childhood with 'Love Jesus.' This human devotion inspires the truest poetry with achieved spirits such as Sidney or Spenser. Sidney wrote:

> My true love hath my heart and I have his,
>   By just exchange one for another given;
> I hold his dear, and mine he cannot miss,
>   There never was a better bargain driven.
>   My true love hath my heart and I have his.
>
> His heart in me keeps him and me in one,
>   My heart in him his thoughts and senses guides;
> He loves my heart, for once it was his own,
>   I cherish his, because in me it bides.
>   My true love hath my heart and I have his.

Spenser wrote in his sonnet for Easter day:

> Most glorious Lord of life that on this day
>   Didst make thy triumph over death and sin.
>   And, having harrowed hell, didst bring away
> Captivity thence captive us to win.
>
> This joyous day, dear Lord, with joy begin,
>   And grant that we for whom thou diddest die,
>   Being with thy dear blood clean washed from sin,
> May live for ever in felicity.

For Christmas day Robert Southwell wrote:

> As I in winter's hoary night stood shivering in the snow,
> Suprised I was with sudden heat which made my
>   heart to glow;
> And lifting up a fearful eye to view what fire was near,
> A pretty Babe all burning bright did in the air appear.

These pulses of the human heart we hear in the accents of propitiation for our burden of suffering in Byrd's music:

> Agnus dei, qui tollis peccata mundi . . .

Again,

> Agnus dei, qui tollis peccata mundi . . .

And then with all the urgency of a proscribed faith in a time of strife:

> Agnus dei, dona nobis pacem.

It is in the works of the spirit that myth is justified; for it is poetry and art, not dogma, that redeem the spirit of man.

EPILOGUE

My aim here is not to sum up this book as a whole, still less to repeat the arguments of the preceding volumes in which I have attempted to portray – representatively, if not exhaustively – the society of the Elizabethan Age, but to place it in perspective. Even this brief endeavour must be a double one; there is the placing of it in relation to its own time, and there is the perspective of subsequent time – one should suggest something of its influence upon, and inspiration for, the later achievments of the English and English-speaking peoples and for the world of culture beyond. For both influence and inspiration are living and with us still.

Foreigners coming to the island on a voyage of discovery found the English of that age much more as we conceive of Continentals: they were expressive and eloquent, ostentatious and pleasure-loving, not industrious or hardworking, but bold and self-confident, markedly fearless of death, mercurial and inconstant, loving change, above all, passionate. We already see how this carries over into the plays of Shakespeare, their fullest and most authentic portrayal in literature; and we reflect that the Elizabethans are the English *before* the victory of Puritanism twice over, in the seventeenth century with the Civil War and with the dominant middle classes of the Victorian Age. In trying to describe the nature of Shakespeare's genius, Schlegel pointed to the universality and profusion of his characterisation: 'never was there so comprehensive a talent for the delineation of character .. his human characters have such depth and precision that they cannot be arranged under classes, and are inexhaustible, even in conception...'[1] Secondly, there is 'his exhibition of passion, taking this word in its widest signification, as including every mental condition, every tone from indifference or familiar mirth to the wildest rage and despair. He gives us the history of minds; he lays open to us a whole series of precedent conditions.' We might take Schlegel to mean the astonishing way in which, quite naturally, Shakespeare searches out and explores the unconscious.

He owed this almost as much to the Age as to his own genius,

337

which singularly fitted and expressed it. It is hardly conceivable that an English writer in later centuries could so completely give himself up to the passions, or so fully and freely express them in art. For, in the interval between the Elizabethans and Victorians, the English had been deeply affected by Puritanism and Empire – the two are subtly as well as directly connected. To govern other peoples one has to govern oneself: what one gains in government and empire one may lose in art and literature – for it necessitates self-control and a restriction upon the unlimited enjoyment of the passions. This is one reason, perhaps, why modern French literature has reached deeper levels and achieved greater things in the ruthless analysis of the passions than modern English: Baudelaire as against Tennyson or Matthew Arnold, Proust compared with Henry James or Kipling.

There was no such inhibition upon the Elizabethans. Their age saw a balance between medieval primitivism and violence, at last brought under some control, and the Renaissance refinement of spirit we see in Philip Sidney, Spenser, Shakespeare, pointing to a modern mode of sensibility. The fullness of the portrayal of the passions, of which Schlegel speaks, had its root in the nature of the English experience in that Age – itself a release, both inspiration and fulfilment. When Hazlitt says 'an overstrained enthusiasm is more pardonable with respect to Shakespeare than the want of it; for our admiration cannot easily surpass his genius'; or again, with regard to *King Lear*, 'all that we can say must fall far short of the subject, or even of what we ourselves conceive of it' – it was perhaps only in the Elizabethan Age that such achievements were possible: the atmosphere was drenched in passion and poetry.[2]

We cannot exhaust the characteristics of this naive, youthful, up-and-coming people which diverse foreigners noticed: we must concentrate on the consensus, and then on those aspects which specially struck them. The English liked display, like children; their women wanted to be in at everything, they enjoyed a freer status and more liberty than abroad. The English were very independent, and everybody noticed that they despised foreigners. Other nations had a phrase, 'England is a paradise for women, a prison for servants, and a purgatory for horses.' Jerome Cardan thought that the English were very like Italians, expressive in speech and gesture, temperamental and always gaping after novelties. An Italian cardinal thought that, as they were descended from Angles and Saxons, they were therefore friendly to Germans.

But the Elizabethans found the Germans comic, with their heavy manners, their lack of a sense or humour, and their penuriousness. The Dutch were thought boorish – after all, it is a Dutch word; we reflect that the Dutch had not undergone the refining influence of a Court, or the sophistication of manners radiating outwards and downwards from an aristocratic society.

On the other hand, the Dutch historian, van Meteren, who had lived in London, did not have a very favourable view of the people. 'They are full of courtly and affected manners, which they take for gentility, civility, and wisdom.'[3] He thought them vainglorious and boastful, light and deceiving, and he resented their suspicion of foreigners. Some people abroad considered that the English were cunning and ready to dupe others – as well they might, considering the record of Elizabeth's government for successful duplicity. She regarded herself as a model of truth-telling and keeping her word – the English regarded the French as past-masters at breaking theirs, essentially unreliable and treacherous. (Henry of Navarre's desertion of Protestantism and conversion to Rome gave the Queen much concern, religious as well as political; the English distrust over oath-breaking is a contemporary theme of *Love's Labour's Lost*.) The Spaniards were regarded as overbearing and arrogant, fanatical and cruel.

More specifically: all foreigners were struck by the wealth and comfort of the country, by its greenness and the fact that people could afford to eat meat, in particular by the domestic comforts, the cleanliness, of English houses. Germans were specially impressed by the unfortified towns – evidence of internal security, and of the long internal peace of which Elizabeth's government was justly proud.[4] The poet Daniel gave expression to this:

> All round about her blood and misery,
> Powers betrayed, princes slain, kings massacrèd,
> States all confused, brought to calamity,
> And all the face of kingdoms alterèd:
> Yet she the same inviolable stands,
> Dear to her own, wonder to other lands.

This is no more than the truth when one considers the state of her neighbours, the massacres, ruin and devastation in the Netherlands and France. When one reads Felix Platter's Montpellier Journal, one realises how many French towns suffered damage or destruction in the religious wars that raged contemporaneously – one reason for the immense flowering of French architecture in the next century: so much needed to be rebuilt.[5]

Similar tributes come to her from abroad, and not from Protestants only, to set against the vile insults of the Catholic underworld. The praises sung in the earlier years of the reign, by Ronsard, may be regarded as polite Court-verse; but there is no mistaking the bitter vehemence of the contrast that Agrippa d'Aubigné draws in *Les Tragiques* between the miseries of Valois rule and the success of Elizabeth's which was all too obvious, shining like an island-beacon over the stormy waters of Counter-Reformation Europe. After his savage indictment of the last Valois:

> Rois, que le vice noir asservit sous les lois,
> Esclaves de péché, forçaires non pas rois
> De vos affections, quelle fureur despite
> Vous corrompt, vous émeut, vous pousse et vous invite,
> A tremper dans le sang vos sceptres odieux . . .[6]

then comes the contrast:

> Heureuse Élisabeth, la justice rendant,
> Et qui n'as point vendu tes droits en la vendant! . . .

There follows a description of the menaces and threats that she had surmounted:

> Cet œil vit les dangers, sa main porta le faix,
> Te fit heureuse en guerre et ferme dans la paix.
> Le Paraclet t'apprit à répondre aux harangues
> De tous ambassadeurs, même en leurs propres langues.

One sees that the adulation she received from English poets was not simple flattery, as moderns suppose, on the part of subjects: it was partly Renaissance decorum, and wholly sincere. Even this Old Testament prophet has a passage on the signs and portents of her name and virginity:

> Tes triomphantes nefs vont te faire nommer,
> En tournoyant le tout, grand Reine de la mer.

Even Elizabeth's grand opponents paid tribute to her qualities and the achievements of her reign, let alone professed admirers of her own persuasion, such as Henry of Navarre and William the Silent. Pope Sixtus V, who had a measure of greatness himself and therefore could appreciate it in others, was an enthusiastic admirer: 'She certainly is a great Queen, Just look how well she governs! She is only a woman, only mistress of half an island, and yet she makes herself feared by Spain, by France, by the Empire, by all.' Himself a reluctant subscriber to the Armada, while holding no great hopes of its success, he was also an admirer of Drake. 'Have you heard how Drake with his fleet has offered battle to the Armada?', he asked his cardinals. 'With what courage!' He went on to recount his exploits, and summed up, 'He is a great captain.'

The dramatist Lope de Vega, who went to Lisbon with the idea of serving in the Armada, showed no such generosity. He wrote an epic of ten cantos, *La Dragontea*, devoted to Drake's last campaign in the West Indies, on which he died. It has been said of it that 'perhaps no other instance can be found of a grave epic devoted to the personal abuse of a single individual.'[7] Drake had certainly made his name feared along the coasts of Spain and the Spanish Empire, and celebrated throughout the world. But Spanish feeling was such that Lope de Vega's epic, written to catch the market, had not much success. French pamphlets of the time reflect the breathless interest taken in the fate of the Armada.[8] In Hamburg it was taken as a powerful check to Spanish insolence, though the English did not lack insolence either.[9] The Hamburgers were heavily engaged in carrying Baltic supplies and wheat to Spain, and thus were constantly intercepted by English warships and privateers. They had frequent news of Drake's activities, which greatly impressed foreign opinion. Actually he was not in command of the fleet that fought the Armada – that was Lord Admiral Howard, the Queen's cousin. Foreign visitors coming to Chatham were duly impressed by the sight of the ships that had wrought such damage upon the Armada, riding there at anchor.[10] They had earned for her the title, awarded by the poets, of Queen of the Sea.

The ritual, the stateliness and decorum, of the Court impressed foreigners no less. It would seem to have been the most magnificently ordered in Europe, except for the Papal Court; for the Spanish, though sombrely dignified, was withdrawn and remote under Philip, while the French, under Henri III and Henri IV, was too familiar and undignified. There are several accounts of the impression the Queen made, when old and famous. To take only one: Paul Hentzner, a Brandenburger, described her procession to chapel one September Sunday at Greenwich in 1598, the day before her sixty-fifth birthday. There was a long train of nobles, the sword of state carried before her, the Queen looking 'very majestic: her face oval, fair but wrinkled, eyes small but dark and pleasant; nose a little hooked, lips thin, her teeth black', from eating sweetmeats. Blazing with jewels, all in white silk, 'her stature neither tall nor low, her air was stately, mild and obliging

As she went along in all this state and magnificence she spoke very graciously first to one, then to another, in English, French, and Italian. Whoever speaks to her, it is kneeling; now and then she raises some with her hand. Wherever she turned her face as she was going along, everybody fell down on their knees.'[11]

One recognises the atmosphere portrayed in the *Faerie Queene*, or in the poems of Ralegh. Thus the ageing idol kept order in the nursery. She could not understand her successor's inability to do so in Scotland.

At the beginning of the reign England was a power of the second rank on the margin of northern Europe; by the end, it was a naval power of the first rank, strategically situated athwart the shortest Atlantic crossing to the New World. As North America developed and grew in importance, so did Britain, *pari passu* with it. Outside Europe the Elizabethan achievement was to lay the foundations of English-speaking North America and prepare the way for subsequent enterprises, trading empire and expansion of stocks across the oceans. The European upshot of the reign was to checkmate the Counter-Reformation and deprive it of victory in Northern Europe, and to defeat the combined naval forces of Spain and Portugal. The military interventions on the Continent prevented Spanish conquest of the Netherlands, helped to bring into being a brilliant new nation in Holland, and assured Henry of Navarre's victory in France.

It was natural enough therefore that Navarre and the Prince of Orange – the former with gallantry, the latter with circumspection – should express their sense of obligation, and that 'à la fin du XVI' siècle le nom d'Elisabeth est singulièrement populaire parmi les protestants de France.'[12] Du Bartas, whose Protestant epic was a best-seller in its English dress and exerted widespread influence – even upon Milton – has an *éloge* of Elizabeth as

> Qui fait que le Breton, dédaigneux, ne désire
> Changer au mâle joug d'une femme l'empire . .

certainly there was no advantage in changing her rule for James's, except that the latter brought with it the unity of the island. More pointed was the judgment of Du Bartas' commentator, on her achievement 'qui depuis quarante ans a gouverné ce royaume-là en grande prospérité, durant les troubles et misères des autres pays.'[13]

The long struggle with Spain exacerbated feeling on both

sides, and to this was added religious bitterness. The English, especially the seamen, hated the cruelties of the Inquisition; the Spaniards have always been retarded fanatics, but the behaviour of English Protestants towards their customary superstitions was no better and aroused resentment. Further fuel was added by the exiles, with their familiar *émigré* mentality. Perhaps here is the place to notice the influence of, and losses consequent upon, the emigration of English Catholics abroad, against the immensely greater gains - to industry and the arts - of the immigration into the country of foreign Protestants. We may sum up, symbolically, by saying that, if Father Campion was a loss, Father Parsons was not; while the realm of music - where Pearson and Phillips and Dr. Bull were recruits to the Netherlands, as Cooper and Dowland were for some years to Italy and Denmark - is international. There were Spaniards who appreciated English humanity - those taken prisoner by Drake were surprised by their kindly treatment;[14] and it seems that Essex's chivalrous conduct at the capture of Cadiz contributed as much to Spanish disillusionment with the war as the failure of the Armada. (It was vastly in contrast with the horrors of Alva's behaviour in the Netherlands or the 'Spanish Fury' let loose upon Antwerp in 1576.) It seems that the peace of 1604 was more widely welcomed, and more whole-heartedly, in Spain than in England. Both English and Spaniards were strongly nationalistic and disagreeably xenophobic. But the lofty spirit of Cervantes, who saw through suffering to the heart of things, transcends national exclusiveness with the human sympathy of 'La española inglesa', and even begins his story with a tribute to the conquerors of Cadiz 'from the famous Northern Island, governed then by a most noble Queen.'[15]

We have already seen something of the relation of the arts and sciences, the modes of thought, in England to those in Europe at the time in treating each of them, and the immense indebtedness of the small, backward, northern country to Renaissance influences, mediated above all from Italy, France and the Netherlands. It remains to speak of the place of Elizabethan cultural achievement in the tradition of Europe. Here, too, we have seen that the Elizabethans gave something back, already made a contribution, particularly in the realm of music and drama. Elizabethan keyboard technique entered into the origins of modern keyboard music; and English players radiated their drama across Germany: there is a direct line from the original Faust-book which Marlowe used, and his *Dr. Faustus* – the most popular of all Elizabethan plays – on to Goethe.

During the century or more of French cultural ascendancy that followed Italy's decline, any general impact of the Elizabethan Age in Europe was inevitably retarded: classical standards prevailed. In the eighteenth century the characteristic admiration for things English was mainly for institutions, laws, commerce, science and practical affairs: Locke and Newton were the tutelary deities. What Bacon had to say was heard chiefly through Locke: the direct consequences of his teaching were felt mainly through the Royal Society. It is only with the premonitory symptoms of the Romantic movement that the tremendous fertilising force of Shakespeare – perhaps all the more powerful for being so long delayed – began to be felt. In England he never ceased to be the most constantly popular of dramatists: audiences remained faithful, and he held the stage from Burbage to Betterton, from Garrick and Mrs. Siddons and Kean, on to today. He was as much admired as a writer: nothing is more remarkable than the devotion of such diverse men of genius, in direct tradition, from Ben Jonson (who knew him) to Milton, from Davenant (who wished to think he was was his son) to Dryden, and on to Pope and Dr. Johnson. But that was at home in England, among those who spoke his language.

Abroad, it was long before people thought it worth learning English or considered that it had anything to offer. Oddly enough Louis XIV had Shakespeare's Works in English in his library, but they can have meant nothing to him. (They had meant a good deal to that amateur of the drama, Charles I, who inscribed in his copy of the Folio at Windsor an alternative title for *Twelfth Night*, 'Malvolio' – very suitably, as he is the most original character in the piece.) St. Évremond was the first French writer to speak of Shakespeare in 1677,[16] but that was after years of residence in England and acquaintance with Dryden's adaptations of his plays for the Restoration stage. The language remained a barrier, but not only the language – there was the dominance of French classical conceptions of theatre. Shakespeare's ultimate conquest of French understanding – which makes a prolonged and difficult story – is not the least of the triumphs of the Age.

Voltaire was the first to reflect a direct influence, though at the end of his life he came to resent depreciation of Corneille and Racine for praise of 'ce Shakespeare .. un histrion barbare.'[17] We need not take his irritation too seriously: in any case, praise of one need never exclude appreciation of others. Already, in mid-eighteenth century, the *Encylopédie* was comparing Shakespeare to 'a vast Gothic building, sublime and various, but inelegant.' Even today when French critics speak admiringly of Shakespeare's 'liberté sans frein', they fail to perceive that it is not liberty without restraint: he has his own aesthetic, his drama imposes its controls, has its own artistic logic.

Already some critics were beginning to praise Shakespeare, in terms similar to Schlegel's, for the extraordinary range of the passions at his command and the universality of his portrayal of human nature. Talma's knowledge of the English stage, dominated by the traditions coming down from the Elizabethan, had its effect in liberating and varying his later style of acting from its classical formation. But still the poetry could not be perceived: the frightful inadequacy of the French translations obstructed the view. The visit of the English company, headed by Kemble and Miss Smithson, dislodged a Romantic avalanche: Miss Smithson was irresistible as Ophelia and Juliet – and the inflammable Berlioz married her.

After Waterloo Stendhal had waged a polemic to disengage literature from politics and free liberals to appreciate Shakespeare admired by the returned royalists.[18] Shortly the *fougue* of Romanticism swept France, carrying the cult of Shakespeare and Scott, most Shakespearean of writers, forward into new fields to fertilise. First were Berlioz in music, and Delacroix in painting: both were inspired by Shakespeare all through their careers. Berlioz began with a fantasia on *The Tempest*, and an early *King Lear* overture; he went on to his mature dramatic symphony, 'Romeo and Juliet', two pieces inspired by *Hamlet*, and a late work, the opera 'Béatrice et Bénédict', based on *Much Ado About Nothing*.[19] For over thirty years Delacroix was inspired by Shakespearean themes, beginning with a painting of Lady Macbeth in 1825, a subject he returned to in 1849; during this period he produced a series of lithographs illustrating *Hamlet*, along with several paintings of scenes from it, the last of them in 1859.[20] Along the way there were paintings of Cleopatra, and of Othello and Desdemona. Meanwhile, Alfred de Vigny made adaptations of *Othello* and *The Merchant of Venice*, and George Sand of *As You Like It*. At last, among the many versions that poured from the press, Victor Hugo's son made the best translation of the complete Plays.

Operas were inspired by Shakespearean drama all over Europe, beginning with Rossini's 'Elizabetta d'Inghilterra' and

'Otello' in the year of Waterloo and the year after. Verdi wrote an early 'Macbeth', which he revised later; there followed a period of some years when he could not create, but hoped against hope to write a *King Lear* (Debussy was similarly defeated). Then Verdi triumphed with his two last and greatest works, 'Otello' and 'Falstaff'. Meanwhile, the youthful Mendelssohn had written his overture, 'A Midsummer Night's Dream'. Many Continental composers and dramatists found rewarding subjects in Tudor themes, for example, Donizetti's 'Anna Bolena'; while Mary Stuart's story provided a subject for Schiller and Victor Hugo, among others. In the later nineteenth century the fertilising seed was carried to Russia, where Tchaikovsky produced a fantasia on *The Tempest*, a symphonic poem, 'Romeo and Juliet', the 'Hamlet' overture along with incidental music for the play.

In England the inspiration of the Elizabethan Age has been continuous and far more varied – not only in the arts, literature, music, architecture, but in science (witness Bacon and Harvey), seamanship (witness the cult of Drake), colonisation and empire (with Ralegh), and even in politics, at times of threatened invasion, as with Napoleon in 1804, and again in 1940. Even in the single field of music, the influence has been much wider and more complex: there has been not only the continuing inspiration of the poetry, but that of the music itself, ebbing and flowing, and the revival of the folk-song in our time. Century after century Shakespeare's plays provided occasion for incidental music, the songs for setting. With the restoration of the theatres after the Civil War, Matthew Locke wrote the incidental music for Shadwell's version of *The Tempest*, and almost certainly for *Macbeth*. Purcell wrote music also for *The Tempest*, for *Timon of Athens* and *King Richard II*, though more important is his opera, the *Faery Queen*. In the eighteenth century the excellent Dr. Arne wrote some of the most beautiful settings that Shakespeare's songs have ever received: 'Where the bee sucks', 'When daisies pied', 'Under the greenwood tree', and so on.

In our time the Age has borne an even richer harvest. No English composer was closer to the spirit of Shakespeare than Elgar, who came from the same West Midlands countryside – all recaptured in his marvellously evocative work, 'Falstaff'. A number of composers have found renewed creative vitality in the music of the Golden Age. Vaughan Williams offers the rare case of a composer who found his own musical identity in the discovery of the music of that earlier, but not vanished, time. 'Sir John in Love' is a light work compared with the grandeur of the 'Fantasia on a Theme of Tallis', the deeper characterisation of 'Five Tudor Portraits', the haunting beauty of the 'Serenade to Music', inspired by *The Merchant of Venice*:

> How sweet the moonlight sleeps upon this bank!
> Here will we sit and let the sound of music
> Creep in our ears; soft stillness and the night
> Become the touches of sweet harmony.
>   . . . Look how the floor of heaven
> Is thick inlaid with patines of bright gold . . .

The whole last act of this play is suffused with music and contains the most extended of the poet's many tributes to its power, to which he was extraordinarily responsive. The music ceases with

> Peace, ho! The moon sleeps with Endymion
> And would not be awaked.

Holst shared Vaughan Williams' inspiration in Elizabethan music, and steeped himself in Shakespeare for his opera 'At the Boar's Head'. They were both deeply indebted to the revival of folk-music and folk-song, to which Cecil Sharp devoted his life, taking it down from the lips of people all over the British Isles and in the older settlements of the United States. These two streams of inspiration, sophisticated Elizabethan music and folk-song – which, as we have seen, were closely connected in the Age itself – again inspired the work of two men of original genius who died young: Peter Warlock and George Butterworth. Indeed, it was hardly possible for English composers who received their training earlier this century, or were pupils of those involved in the revival, not to be touched by the influence, felt in the musical formation of such composers as Britten and Tippet, however much further their development has carried them later. The impulse is direct in composers like Quilter and Finzi, and received full expression again recently in Britten's opera, 'A Midsummer Night's Dream'.

Our literature goes back to the Middle Ages; an educated man can read Chaucer with pleasure, and *Piers Plowman*, if less easily. But there is a sense, as we have seen, in which it was the Elizabethans who created a conscious literary tradition continuing thenceforward; Shakespeare came to hold the central place in it that is occupied by Dante in Italian. So many of the English poets have borne witness to it, from Milton onwards – all the more remarkable because Milton was a world away from him in the nature of his genius, in convictions and temperament. Again, Shakespeare has been a continuing whetstone for criticism – once more it is the more remarkable that, in some ways, the most discerning criticism should have come from a spirit so much in contrast as Dr. Johnson.

Here, too, the Romantic movement felt that it was discovering the Age anew, as it certainly found a new inspiration in it. The historical novels of Scott – which had such a prodigious influence in Europe and America – descended directly from the historical plays of Shakespeare, with their cardinal invention of the mixture of created characters with the personages and events of history. We have cited Hazlitt's enthusiastic appreciation of Shakespeare; to it we may add the critic's perception that his genius was 'a match for history as well as nature'. Coleridge perceived Shakespeare's confidence in his poetry, in spite of the presumed modesty of his nature, and quotes to the point:

> Your monument shall be my gentle verse,
> Which eyes not yet created shall o'er-read.

Coleridge italicises,

> And *tongues to be* your being shall rehearse,
> When all the breathers of this world are dead.

And this, however much it may be a commonplace of the Age – as with Daniel – proved none the less true prophecy.

The Romantic critics believed themselves to have a new understanding of Shakespeare, and attacked the restrictive canons of classical criticism as impoverishing the imagination. One sees this again in the letters and notes of Keats, for whom Shakespeare was the constant companion of his mind. The young poet attributed to him 'an innate universality', and went on to attempt to diagnose the essence of his genius as a quality of '*negative capability*, that is, when a man is capable of being in uncertainties, mysteries, doubts, without any irritable reaching after fact and reason.'[21] (What a contrast, one may note, with Milton; Keats considered that it was this intellectual process that killed the poetry in Coleridge.) Wordsworth wrote a Spenserian poem in 'The White Doe of Rylstone' – on an Elizabethan theme, too, the Northern Rising of 1569. The curious poet, Beddoes, whose early death was a blighting of promise, was much under the spell of macabre Jacobean tragedy. Of all the Victorian poets Browning was nearest to being a dramatist – he had the dramatic sense and the grasp of character; but the Victorian Age was not the Elizabethan Age: hence his drama failed of fulfilment. Paradoxically, Tennyson's verse-dramas were stage-successes; but that was because of the fame of the poet, the plays were not truly dramatic. An image remains in the mind, summing all this up: the old poet lying dead, the moonlight streaming into his room, with *Cymbeline* lying on the table beside him.

At this moment in time, when the arc of achievement which the Elizabethans began is declining to its end and this country is falling back into being just a European country on a parity with others, as it was in their day – though the evidences of all that they set in motion remain about the world – as we journey about our towns and countryside we can piece together in our minds the society, the individual men and women, who accomplished so much, from their tombs. Not only in the cities and great cathedrals – though Westminster Abbey assembles a representative gathering of that society, from the Queen herself downwards: *patriae parenti religionis et bonarum artium altrici, plurimarum linguarum peritia, praeclaris tum animi tum corporis dotibus, regiisque virtutibus* . . . There, too, is her rival, Mary Queen of Scots, with the defensive inscription: *quicum malediceretur non maledicebat cum pateretur non comminabatur; tradebat autem iudicanti iuste.* There in their chapels are so many who cut a figure in the Age: Burghley's clever wife, Mildred with her unhappy daughter who married the gifted but unstable Oxford. There are the politic Russells, the soldierly Norrises, Vere and Bingham, lawyers like Lord Keeper Bromley, Welsh Dean Goodman and his friend Camden, *his* pupil Ben Jonson and the poets, Spenser and Drayton.

If it is a church in the city, like St. Helen's Bishopsgate in the ward in which Shakespeare lived for a time, there is the great financier and philanthropist, Sir Thomas Gresham, in his classic Renaissance tomb; Sir Julius Caesar, Judge of the Court of Admiralty; Sir Andrew Judd of the Skinners' Company, founder of Tonbridge School. More endearing, there is Martin Bond, seated in his tent with the view of the camp at Tilbury, he was captain in 1588 'and afterwards remained chief captain of the trained bands of this city.'[22] If it is Reigate in Surrey, where the Howards got the priory from Henry VIII, there in the vault below is Howard of Effingham, 'Lord High Admiral of England, General of Queen Elizabeth's Navy Royal at sea against the Spaniards' Invincible Navy.' A step further into Kent, and at Chiselhurst is Marlowe's patron, Sir Thomas Walsingham. In the little church of Sutton-at-Hoo, some evidence of the expansion the Elizabethans set going is the monument to Sir Thomas Smith: 'late Governor of the East Indian, Muscovy, French and Summer-Island Companies; Treasurer for the Virginian Plantation; Prime Undertaker (in the year 1612) for that noble design, the Discovery of the North-West Passage; Principal Commissioner for the London expedition against the Pirates; and for a voyage to the River Senegal upon the coast of Africa; one of the chief Commissioners for the Navy Royal and sometime Ambassador from the Majesty of Great Britain to the Emperor and Great Duke of Russia and Muscovy . . .

> From those large kingdoms where the sun doth rise
> From that rich new-found world that westward lies,
> From Volga to the flood of Amazons,
> From under both the Poles, in all the Zones,
> From all the famous rivers, lands and seas,
> Betwixt this place and our Antipodes:
> He got intelligence what might be found
> To give contentment through this massy Round . . .[23]

If we should be in the Midlands, at All Saints, Derby, we come upon Bess of Hardwick in all her finery as Countess of Shrewsbury – her husband lies at a safe distance in the Cathedral at Sheffield: nothing directly said about *her* on his tomb, only an oblique insinuation. In Essex, at Felsted, we look upon the odious Lord Rich, who betrayed his fellow-Catholic, Sir Thomas More, and died in the odour of philanthropy, founder of the school there. In Suffolk, at Sudborne, in his large monument with painted obelisks: 'Here resteth in assured hope to rise in Christ Sir Michael Stanhope, Knight, who served at the feet of Queen Elizabeth, of most happy and famous memory, in her privy Chamber XX years.'

And so one could go round the country north, west, east and south: to Titchfield, where one sees Shakespeare's young Southampton as a boy on the family monument; Ludlow, where Philip Sidney's little sister, Ambrosia lies; the Abbey church at Shrewsbury with Richard Onslow, Speaker of the House of Commons, in long gown, with peaked beard (like Justice Shallow) and thick stumpy hands; or the small church of Harefield in Middlesex, where we see Alice Spencer in her marble four-poster, patroness of poets and widow of Ferdinando, Lord Strange, who loved the theatre-folk and died young. Thus around to the Beauchamp chapel in St. Mary's, Warwick, where are the princely Leicester, his cosier brother Ambrose, Earl of Warwick, and Leicester's little boy, 'the noble imp'. At Clifford Chambers by the Stour, where Michael Drayton used to spend the summers with the Rainsfords, there they are on their monument in the little church, looking across the meadows to Stratford, that noble spire reflected in the waters of the Avon. There is the heart of England; wherever we go the dust comes alive for us.

NOTES

Chapter I

1. M. C. Bradbrook, *The Rise of the Common Player*, 243.
2. Cf. G. E. Bentley, *Shakespeare and his Theatre*, 19, 21.
3. *Records of the Borough of Leicester, 1509–1603*, ed. M. Bateson, Index under Plays, and *passim*.
4. E. K. Chambers, *The Elizabethan Stage*, I. 335.
5. Bateson, 160, 246.
6. *Accounts of the Chamberlains of the City of Bath, 1568–1602*, ed. F. D. Wardle (Somerset Record Society). Index under Plays, and *passim*.
7. *Ibid.*, 178, 185.
8. *Ibid.*, 68.
9. T. H. V. Motter, *The School Drama in England*, 240.
10. *Ibid.*, 209, 211.
11. *Ibid.*, 32, 59, 225.
12. *Ibid.*, 87, 108.
13. Cf. *The England of Elizabeth*, 506–9.
14. *Mulcaster's Elementary*, ed. E. T. Campagnac, xiv.
15. Chambers, II. 14–17.
16. *Ibid.*, II. 4.
17. L. Bradner, 'The Rise of Secular Drama in the Renaissance', *Studies in the Renaissance*, III. 7 foll.
18. Cf. K. M. Lea, *Italian Popular Comedy*, I. 3.
19. Cf. F. S. Boas, *University Drama in the Tudor Age.*
20. Cf. H. S. Wilson, 'The Cambridge Comedy *Pedantius* and Gabriel Harvey's *Ciceronianus*', *Studies in Philology*, 1948, 578 foll.
21. Cf. C. F. Tucker Brooke, 'The Life and Times of William Gager (1555-1622)', *Proc. American. Phil. Soc.*, 95, 401 foll.
22. *v.* Tucker Brooke for the controversy.
23. Boas, 391.
24. *Ibid.*, 267.
25. D. L. Edwards, *Hist. of the King's School, Canterbury*, 80; J. T. Murray, *English Dramatic Companies*, I. 26.
26. Boas, 290; and cf. L. Bradner, 'The Latin Drama of the Renaissance, 1340–1640' *Studies in the Renaissance*, IV. 31 foll.
27. *The Three Parnassus Plays (1598–1601)*, ed. J. B. Leishman, 242–4. Notice that this is in keeping with what John Aubrey tells us about Jonson going about observing people's humours. There is usually something in Aubrey's information.
28. *Ibid.*, 336–7, 350.
29. Cf. *The Elizabethan Renaissance: The Life of the Society*, 150–1.
30. S. Harsnet, *Declaration of Popish Impostures*, 149.
31. Chambers, II. 87–8.
32. *Henslowe's Diary*, ed. W. W. Greg, Pt. II. 1, 23.
33. *Henslowe Papers*, ed. W. W. Greg, 34 foll.
34. *Ibid.*, 48
35. Chambers, II. 341.
36. These references fall into two groups, Sonnets 27, 50, 51, and Sonnets 110 and 112; *v.* my edition of Shakespeare's *Sonnets* for the dating.
37. *Greene's Groatsworth of Wit, Shakespeare Allusion-Books*, ed. C. M. Ingleby (*New Shakespeare Soc.*, Series IV), Pt. I. 29–31.
38. *Ibid.*, 23–4.

39. Cf. E. I. Fripp. *Shakespeare, Man and Artist*, 383.
40. Chettle's *Kind-Heart's Dream*, Ingleby, *loc. cit.*, 38.
41. Chambers, III. 325.
42. q. B. L. Joseph, *Elizabethan Acting*, 38–9.
43. Cf. John Sparrow, *Visible Words: A Study of Inscriptions.*
44. Cf. John Winthrop's 'Experiencia' in my *Elizabethans and America*, 142–3.
45. q. M. C. Bradbrook, *The Rise of the Common Player*, 101.
46. q. A. Harbage, *Shakespeare's Audience* (paperback edn.) 117.
47. q. Bradbrook, 108.
48. Thomas Heywood, *An Apology for Actors*, 21 (*Shakespeare Society*, 1841). Miss Bradbrook cites this passage as being from Nashe; it is, in fact, from Heywood.
49. *The Works of Thomas Nashe*, ed. R. B. McKerrow, I, 212.
50. q. E. K. Chambers, *William Shakespeare*, II. 233.
51. q. Joseph, 82.
52. M. C. Bradbrook, *Shakespeare the Craftsman*, 36.
53. G. R. Kernodle, 'The Open Stage: Elizabethan or Existentialist?' *Shakespeare Survey 12*, 2–3.
54. Joseph, 88–90.
55. *Ibid.*, 91.
56. q. Chambers, *William Shakespeare*, II. 214.
57. Joseph, 92–4.
58. Cf. my *William Shakespeare*, 259–60.
59. A. Harbage, *Shakespeare's Audience*, 159.
60. Cf. *ibid.*, 160, 'If Shakespeare exerted the greatest power over the audience, it follows that the audience exerted the greatest power over him. It follows that he expressed it best.' The situation is better expressed by G. E. Bentley: 'the audience that gave a man of genius such a magnificent opportunity to speak to his time in his plays has never appeared again in the commercial theatre; it was lost, apparently for ever, in the reign of James I and Charles I.' *Shakespeare and his Theatre* (paperback edn.), 106.
61. Cf. *The Complete Works of John Lyly*, ed. R. W. Bond, III. 81 foll.
62. Chambers, I. 288.
63. G. E. Bentley has found that his name was Solomon, not, as has been thought, Salathiel.
64. Bentley, 67.
65. Cf. G. Wickham, 'The Privy Council Order of 1597', *The Elizabethan Theatre*, ed, D. Galloway, 21 foll.
66. T. J. B. Spencer, 'Shakespeare: The Elizabethan Theatre-Poet', Galloway, *op. cit.*, 1.
67. q. from Dekker, *Ben Jonson*, ed. Herford and Simpson, I. 13.
68. T. J. B. Spencer, *loc. cit.*, 7.
69. For example, A. Harbage's *Shakespeare and the Rival Traditions*, which, according to Bentley, 'tends to exaggerate the differences between the audiences in the earlier public and private theatres and to minimise the overlapping.' Bentley, 103.
70. G. Wickham, in Galloway, *loc. cit.*, 40.
71. Cf. Chambers, I. 342 foll.

Chapter II

1. F. Brunot, *Grammaire historique de la langue française*, 22 foll.
2. C. S. Lewis, *English Literature in the Sixteenth Century*, 237.
3. q. R. F. Jones, *The Triumph of the English Language*, 13.
4. q. *ibid.*, 18.
5. E. J. Dobson, *English Pronunciation, 1500–1700*, I. 62.

Notes

6. *John Hart's Works on English Orthography and Pronunciation*, ed. B. Danielsson, Part I. 115.
7. *Ibid.*, Part II. 39, 42, 44, 48, 50, 55.
8. q. *ibid.*, Part I. 119.
9. For his career, *v.* my *England of Elizabeth*, 506–9.
10. q. Dobson, I. 125.
11. *Mulcaster's Elementary*, ed. E. T. Campagnac, 469.
12. q. Jones, 52, 69.
13. q. *ibid.*, 7.
14. Dobson, I. 116, 142.
15. q. Jones, 179.
16. Sir Philip Sidney, *An Apology for Poetry*, in *Elizabethan Critical Essays*, ed. G. G. Smith, I. 203.
17. J. Buxton, *Sir Philip Sidney and the English Renaissance*, 112.
18. *The Poems of Sir Philip Sidney*, ed. W. A. Ringler, lvii.
19. Smith, I. 149, 151.
20. Smith, I. 181.
21. Cf. Buxton, 4.
22. Smith, I. 170, 172.
23. *Ibid.*, I. 193.
24. G. Puttenham, *The Art of English Poesy* (Arber's *English Reprints*), chapter heading of c. II. 21.
25. *Ibid.*, 164–5.
26. *Ibid.*, 56.
27. George Puttenham, *The Art of English Poesy*, ed. G. D. Willcock and A. Walker, lxxxv.
28. q. *ibid.*, lxxxvii.
29. Gabriel Harvey, *Pierce's Supererogation*, in Smith, II. 260.
30. C. S. Lewis, *op. cit.*, 339.
31. q. R. A. Lanham, *The Old 'Arcadia'*, 202.
32. Cf. W. R. Davis, *A Map of Arcadia. Sidney's Romance in its Tradition*, 146 foll.
33. q. *ibid.*, 229.
34. Lewis, 338.
35. *The Countess of Pembroke's Arcadia*, ed. A. Feuillerat, 24.
36. *Ibid.*, 103.
37. *Ibid.*, 61.
38. Lewis, 393.
39. D. Bush, *Mythology and the Renaissance Tradition in English Poetry* (paperback edn.), 89.
40. q. A. C. Judson, *The Life of Edmund Spenser*, 206.
41. Bush, *op. cit.*, 121, 123.
42. Cf. my *Christopher Marlowe: A Biography*, c. IX, 'The Rival Poets'.
43. Lewis, 486.
44. G. E. Bentley, *Shakespeare and His Theatre*, 1.
45. *Ibid.*, 11.
46. M. C. Bradbrook, *Shakespeare and Elizabethan Poetry*, 122.
47. *Ibid.*, 82.
48. Cf. *ibid.*, 141.
49. Cf. Bush, 77.
50. q. E. K. Chambers, *William Shakespeare*, II. 194 foll.
51. Lewis, 531.
52. q. J. Rees, *Samuel Daniel*, 43.
53. *The Complete Works of Samuel Daniel*, ed. A. B. Grosart, IV. 76.
54. Daniel, *A Defence of Rhyme*, in G. G. Smith, *op. cit.*, II. 366.
55. Bush, 156.
56. Cf. J. Buxton, *A Tradition of Poetry*, 59, 74.
57. Cf. B. H. Newdigate, *Michael Drayton and his Circle*, 22–3.

58. Buxton, *op. cit.*, 72–3; *Poems of Michael Drayton*, ed. J. Buxton, I. xviii.
59. Bush, *English Literature in the Earlier Seventeenth Century*, 180.
60. In these paragraphs I am much indebted to E. A. Baker's admirable *History of the English Novel. The Elizabethan Age and After.*
61. *The Works of Thomas Nashe*, ed. R. B. McKerrow, I. 287.
62. Lewis, 412.
63. McKerrow, III. 93–4.
64. *Ibid.*, I. 287.
65. q. *Essays by Sir William Cornwallis the Younger*, ed. D. C. Allen, xvii.
66. *Ibid.*, 20, 190.
67. Lewis, 418.
68. *The Poems of George Chapman*, ed. P. B. Bartlett, 49.
69. Miss F. A. Yates first discovered this 'school' in her *A Study of Love's Labour's Lost*; it was further explored by Miss M. C. Bradbrook in *The School of Night*.
70. Cf. F. P. Wilson's admirable *Elizabethan and Jacobean*.
71. q. D. Bush, *English Literature in the Earlier Seventeenth Century*, 106.
72. *Ibid.*, 108.

Chapter III

1. *Music at the Court of Henry VIII. Musica Britannica*, XVIII, trans. and ed. J. Stevens, 60.
2. G. Reese, *Music in the Renaissance*, 763.
3. *The Age of Humanism, 1540–1630*, ed. G. Abraham. *New Oxford Hist. of Music*, IV. xxii; and cf. H. M. Brown, 'Music – How Opera Began', in *The Late Italian Renaissance, 1525–1630*, ed. E. Cochrane, 401 foll.
4. W. Mellers, *Music and Society*, 63.
5. *Ibid.*, 69.
6. *Ibid.*, 74, 75, 84–5.
7. *Ibid.*, 85.
8. *Tudor Church Music*, VI. ed. E. H. Fellowes, *Thomas Tallis, c. 1505–1585*, xxvi.
9. *Ibid.*, I. *John Taverner, c. 1495–1545*, xxvii.
10. *Ibid.*, xxvi.
11. *Ibid.*, xxxi.
12. *English Madrigal Verse*, ed. E. H. Fellowes, 618.
13. This was the number in 1593, H. C. de Lafontaine, *The King's Music: Records 1460–1700*, 38 foll.
14. Abraham, *op. cit.*, 467–8.
15. q. D. Stevens, *Tudor Church Music*, 55.
16. q. E. Brennecke, *John Milton the Elder and his Music*, 9.
17. Cf. H. Barnett, 'John Case – An Elizabethan Music Scholar,' *Music and Letters*, 1969, 252 foll.
18. *Letters and Memorials of State*, ed. A. Collins, I. 285.
19. q. Abraham, *op. cit.*, 468.
20. Stevens, *op. cit.*, 43.
21. He signed it as Richardson, the name he bore earlier, which was his mother's name; cf. D. Lysons, *The Environs of London*, (ed. 1795), III. 534–5.
22. *Tudor Church Music*, VI. xv foll.
23. I owe this suggestion to Professor J. Kerman.
24. Among the Undated Petitions in the *Salisbury Mss.* at Hatfield is one from Byrd craving the Council's letter to the Attorney-General to the like effect and favour for his recusancy as the late Queen and Council gave him. Evidently between 1603 and 1612, when Salisbury died.
25. Cf. J. A. Westrup, rev. of Fellowes, *William Byrd* (2nd ed.), *Musical Quarterly*, 35, 489 foll.

26. J. Kerman, 'Byrd's Motets: Chronology and Canon', *Journal American Musicological Soc.*, 14. 359 foll.
27. W. Shaw, 'William Byrd of Lincoln', *Music and Letters*, 1967, 52 foll.
28. Kerman, *loc. cit.*
29. Cf. W. Palmer, 'Byrd's Alleluias', *Music and Letters*, 1952, 322 foll.
30. Cf. P. Clulow, 'Publication Dates for Byrd's Latin Masses', *Music and Letters*, 1966, 1 foll.
31. For several occasions, cf. P. Caraman, *William Weston*, 71, 76, 77; and P. Caraman, *John Gerard*, 49
32. Mellers, 85; see above, p. 82.
33. Cf. J. L. Jackman, 'Liturgical Aspects of Byrd's *Gradualia*', *Musical Quarterly*, 49. 17 foll.
34. E. H. Fellowes, *William Byrd*, 129.
35. W. Palmer, 'Byrd and Amen', *Music and Letters*, 1953, 140 foll.
36. D. Brown, 'The styles and Chronology of Thomas Morley's Motets', *Music and Letters*, 1960, 216 foll.
37. *Cal. S.P. Dom.*, *1591–4*, 106.
38. D. Brown, *Thomas Weelkes*, 180, 182.
39. *Ibid.*, 143.
40. E. H. Fellowes, *Orlando Gibbons*, 17–18.
41. D. Stevens, *Thomas Tomkins*, 66, 74.
42. New organs were installed at Westminster in 1596, Magdalen and New Colleges at Oxford in 1597 and 1598. Abraham, 472.
43. E. H. Fellowes had originally overstressed the independence of the English school, A. Obertello in *Madrigali italiani in Inghilterra* the dependence on Italy.
44. *The Autobiography of Thomas Whythorne*, ed. J. M. Osborn, 67 foll.
45. Cf. my *Ralegh and the Throckmortons*, 90.
46. J. Kerman, 'Elizabethan Anthologies of Italian Madrigals', *Journal of Am. Musicological Soc.*, 4. 123 foll.
47. Obertello, *op. cit.*, 209.
48. Modern edition (1952), ed. R. A. Harman, 3.
49. R. Steele, *The Earliest English Music Printing*, 16.
50. *Grove's Dictionary of Music and Musicians*, 4th edn., ed. H. C. Colles, III. 519.
51. D. Brown, *Thomas Weelkes*, 60 foll.
52. *The English Madrigal School*, ed. E. H. Fellowes, IX. ii.
53. J. Kerman, *The Elizabethan Madrigal*, 233.
54. Fellowes, *op. cit.*, VI. iii foll.
55. Fellowes, *The English Madrigal Composers*, 226.
56. Fellowes, *The English Madrigal School*, V. xvii.
57. *Ibid.*, XVIII. *passim.*
58. *Ibid.*, XX.
59. *Ibid.*, XXXIII.
60. *Ibid.*, XXIX, XXX, XXXI.
61. *Ibid.*, XXI.
62. *Ibid.*, XXV, XXVI.
63. *Ibid.*, XXIII.
64. *Ibid.*, XXVII.
65. *Ibid.*, XXVIII.
66. *Ibid.*, XIX; for this family see *The England of Elizabeth*, 317–18.
67. *Ibid.*, XVII.
68. *Ibid.*, XXXIV.
69. *Ibid.*, XXXV.
70. *H.M.C.*, *Salisbury Mss.* V. 436–7.
71. *Ibid.*, VI. 68.
72. *Ibid.*, VIII. 273, 498, 501.
73. *Ibid.*, IX. 238–9.

74. *Illustrations of British History*, ed. E. Lodge (2nd edn.), II. 576.
75. *Ibid.*, II. 578.
76. Collins, *op. cit.*, II. 203.
77. B. Pattison, *Music and Poetry of the English Renaissance*, 18–19.
78. C. M. Simpson, *The British Broadside Ballad and its Music*, 269.
79. *Ibid.*, 225.
80. *Ibid.*, 119, 777.
81. *Ibid.*, 446.
82. *Ibid.*, 101, 495.
83. q. Rollins, 'The Black-Letter Broadside Ballad', *Pub. Mod. Lang. Assocn. Am.*, 1934, 258 foll.
84. Nicholas Breton, q. *ibid.*
85. P. Warlock, *The English Air* (there is no point in spelling it 'Ayre'), 18.
86. *Salisbury Mss.*, V. 445–7.
87. *The Works of Thomas Campion*, ed. W. R. Davis, xxiii.
88. *Ibid.*, 15–16.
89. *Ibid.*, 55–6.
90. Warlock, 104, 109.
91. *Ibid.*, 52.
92. For these see Warlock; E. H. Fellowes, *The English School of Lutenist Song-Writers*, First and Second Series; E. H. Fellowes, *The English Madrigal Composers*, and *English Madrigal Verse*.
93. D. Heartz, 'Les Styles instrumentaux dans la musique de la Renaissance', in *La Musique instrumentale de la Renaissance*, ed. J. Jacquot, 61 foll.
94. J. Noble, 'Le Répertoire instrumental anglais: 1550–85', *Ibid.*, 91 foll.
95. E. Brennecke, 'The Country Cries of Richard Dering', *Musical Quarterly*, *42.* 366 foll.
96. E. H. Fellowes, *William Byrd*, 203.
97. B. Schofield and T. Dart, 'Tregian's Anthology', *Music and Letters*, 1951, 205 foll.
98. For the family, cf. my *Tudor Cornwall*, 84–6, 344 foll.
99. *The Fitzwilliam Virginal Book*, ed. J. A. F. Maitland and W. B. Squire.
100. W. Mellers, 'John Bull and English Keyboard Music', *Musical Quarterly*, 40. 364 foll.
101. *John Bull. Keyboard Music*, 1 (*Musica Britannica*, XIV), ed. J. Steele and F. Cameron. Intro T. Dart., 1
102. H. R. Hoppe, 'John Bull in the Archduke's Service,' *Music and Letters*, 1954, 14 foll.
103. Ludwig Finscher, 'English Music for Recorders and Consort of Viols' (Record SAWT 9511 – Bex.)
104. E. H. Meyer, *English Chamber Music*, 79, 82.
105. T. Morley, *A Plain and Easy Introduction*, ed. cit., 296.
106. q. *Jacobean Consort Music* (*Musica Britannica*, IX), ed. T. Dart and W. Coates, xvi.
107. Meyer, *op. cit.*, 159.
108. W. Mellers, 'John Bull and English Keyboard Music', *Musical Quarterly*, 40. 364 foll.
109. W. L. Woodfill, *Musicians in English Society from Elizabeth to Charles I*, xiv.
110. *Ibid.*, 34 foll.
111. (Anon), *The Worshipful Company of Musicians*.
112. My *Ralegh and the Throckmortons*, 294.
113. q. Pattison, *op. cit.*, 16.
114. q. L. Finney, *Musical Backgrounds for English Literature, 1580–1650*, 69.
115. N. C. Carpenter, *Music in the Medieval and Renaissance Universities*, 315 foll.
116. P. C. C., 31 Hayes.
117. *Music in English Renaissance Drama*, ed. J. H. Long, vii foll.
118. J. H. Long, *Shakespeare's Use of Music: Seven Comedies*, xiii.
119. *Ibid.*, 82 foll.
120. *William Shakespeare: A Biography*, 203–5.

Notes

121. F. W. Sternfeld, *Music in Shakespearean Tragedy*, i.
122. J. H. Long, *Shakespeare's Use of Music: the Final Comedies*, 65.
123. Long, *Shakespeare's Use of Music: Seven Comedies*, 195.

Chapter IV

1. A. Clifton-Taylor, *The Pattern of English Building*, 61.
2. W. G. Hoskins, 'The Great Rebuilding', *History Today*, 1955, 104 foll.
3. A. Blunt, *Architecture in France, 1500–1700*, 5.
4. Cf. J. Summerson, *Architecture in Britain, 1530–1830*, 2.
5. Cf. P. Murray, *The Architecture of the Italian Renaissance*, 199.
6. M. Girouard, *Robert Smythson and the Architecture of the Elizabethan Age*, 52.
7. Summerson, *op. cit.*, 22.
8. N. B. L. Pevsner, *The Planning of the Elizabethan Country House*, 24.
9. Girouard, *op. cit.*, 32, 130.
10. M. Dewar, *Sir Thomas Smith*, 122, 195.
11. q. Sir John Summerson, 'The Building of Theobalds, 1564–1585', *Archaeologia*, 1959, 107 foll.
12. q. Girouard, 33.
13. q. *ibid.*, 73.
14. *Ibid.*, 44–5.
15. C. Hussey, 'Burghley House, Northamptonshire', *Country Life*, 1953, 1828 foll., 1962 foll.
16. q. Sir John Summerson, 'The Building of Theobalds, 1564–1585', *Archaeologia*, 1959, 107 foll.
17. J. Summerson, 'Three Elizabethan Architects', *Bull. John Rylands Library*, 40. 202 foll.
18. Girouard, 86.
19. *Ibid.*, 120, 123.
20. S. Sitwell, *British Architects and Craftsmen*, 27.
21. From the *Hardwick Mss.* at Chatsworth.
22. Clifton-Taylor, *op. cit.*, 80, 201.
23. M. E. Finch, *The Wealth of Five Northamptonshire Families, 1540–1640*, 72 foll.
24. Sir Gyles Isham, 'Sir Thomas Tresham and his Buildings', *Northants. Antiqn. Soc.*, vol. LXV.
25. J. Humphreys, 'The Elizabethan Estate Book of Grafton Manor', *Birmingham Arch. Soc. Trans.*, XLIV.
26. F. H. Crossley, *Timber Building in England*, 116 foll.
27. C. L. Kingsford, 'Some London Houses of the Early Tudor Period', *Archaeologia*, 71. 17 foll.
28. A. E. Richardson, *The Old Inns of England*, 6 foll.
29. Professor Jack Simmons was the first to collect evidence on this subject, in 'Brooke Church, Rutland, with Notes on Elizabethan Church-Building', *Trans. Leics. Arch. and Hist. Soc.*, 1959, 36 foll.
30. E.g. there are three in Berkshire, J. C. Cox, *Pulpits, Lecterns, and Organs in English Churches*, 96.
31. q. *ibid.*, 143.
32. H. L. Phillips, *Annals of the Worshipful Company of Joiners*, 10.
33. J. C. Cox, *English Church Fittings, Furniture and Accessories*, 245, 282.
34. M. Clayton, *Catalogue of Rubbings of Brasses and Incised Slabs*, Victoria and Albert Museum, 9.
35. I am indebted to Mr. John Buxton for my knowledge of these.
36. F. A. Greenhill, *The Incised Slabs of Leicestershire and Rutland*, 22.
37. A. C. Bizley, *The Slate Figures of Cornwall*, 3.
38. L. P. Smith, *The Life and Letters of Sir Henry Wotton*, I. 194 foll.

39. Sir H. Wotton, 'The Elements of Architecture,' in *Reliquiae Wottonianae* (edn. 1685), 32, 53.
40. *Ibid.*, 4, 6, 7, 9.
41. *Salisbury Mss.*, XIX. 120.
42. J. Summerson, *Architecture in Britain, 1530–1830*, 51.
43. *Ibid.*, 9.
44. *Ibid.*, 12, 69.
45. *Ibid.*, 64–5.
46. Cf. *The Book of Architecture of John Thorpe*, ed. Summerson. *Walpole Soc.*, 1966.
47. Wotton, 50, 52.
48. *Ibid.*, 59.
49. Cf. L. Stone, *Sculpture in Britain: The Middle Ages*, 232–3.
50. J. G. Mann, *English Church Monuments, 1536–1625, Walpole Society*, 21. 1 foll.
51. Cf. M. Whinney, *Sculpture in Britain, 1530–1830*, 1.
52. q. J. Buxton, *Elizabethan Taste*, 137.
53. As Mr. E. Mercer seems to think, *English Art, 1553–1625*, 219.
54. Cf. *City of Oxford* (*Roy. Com. Hist. Mon.*), Plate 143.
55. *City of Cambridge* (*Roy. Com. Hist. Mon.*), I. 76.
56. Mercer, 251.
57. q. Mercer, 233.
58. *Ibid.*, 231–2.
59. q. My *Ralegh and the Throckmortons*, 196.
60. q. Whinney, 16.
61. K. A. Esdaile, *English Church Monuments, 1510 to 1840*, 80–81.
62. Esdaile, 59.
63. Mercer, 243.
64. R. Freeman, *English Emblem Books*, 47.
65. Esdaile, 53.
66. *Salisbury Mss.* (*H.M.C.*), XI. 382.
67. Mercer, 254–5.
68. *Ibid.*, 254.
69. R. Lister, *Decorative Wrought Ironwork in Great Britain*, 82–4.
70. J. Harris, *English Decorative Ironwork, 1610–1836*, 2.
71. R. Lister, *Decorative Cast Ironwork in Great Britain*, 65 foll.
72. L. Weaver, *English Leadwork: Its Art and History*, 28 foll.
73. M. Jourdain, *English Decorative Plasterwork of the Renaissance*, 1 foll.
74. q. L. Turner, *Decorative Plasterwork in Great Britain*, 35.
75. Jourdain, 8 foll.
76. Turner, 7 foll.
77. Jourdain, V.
78. q. *ibid.*, 3.

Chapter V

1. E. Croft-Murray, *Decorative Painting in England, 1537–1837*, I. 11.
2. Cf. O. Millar, rev. of above, *Burlington Mag.*, 108. 93 foll.
3. F. W. Reader, 'A Classification of Tudor Domestic Wall Paintings', *Archaeological Journal*, 1941, 182 foll.
4. E. Auerbach, *Tudor Artists*, 174–5.
5. Croft-Murray, 27 foll.
6. F. W. Reader, 'Tudor Domestic Wall Paintings', *Archaeological Journal*, 1935, 243.
7. F. W. Reader, 'Tudor Mural Paintings in the Lesser Houses in Buckinghamshire', *Arch. Journ.*, 1932, 118.
8. F. W. Reader, 'The Use of the Stencil in Mural Decoration', *Arch. Journ.*, 1938, 114.

9. J. Pope-Hennessy, *The Portrait in the Renaissance*, xi.
10. J. Buxton, *Elizabethan Tastes*, 111.
11. H. Wölfflin, *The Art of the Italian Renaissance* (paper-back edn.), 206–7.
12. q. E. Auerbach, *Tudor Artists*, 103.
13. Cf. R. Strong, *Portraits of Queen Elizabeth I*, M. 12.
14. Auerbach, 102.
15. q. Buxton, 124–5.
16. For whom v. the previous vol., *The Elizabethan Renaissance: The Life of the Society*, 148–9.
17. q. E. Auerbach, *Nicholas Hilliard*, 44.
18. Buxton, 122.
19. ed. with Introduction, P. Norman, *Walpole Soc.* 1.
20. Cf. G. Reynolds, *Nicholas Hilliard and Isaac Oliver* (*V. and A. Handbook*), 16.
21. J. W. Goodison, 'George Gower, Serjeant Painter to Queen Elizabeth', *Burlington Magazine*, 90. 261 foll.
22. E. Auerbach, *Nicholas Hilliard*, 265 foll.; Roy Strong, *The Elizabethan Image* (Tate Gallery), 31.
23. Auerbach, 271 foll.
24. R. C. Strong, 'Elizabethan Painting . . . Hieronimo Custodis', *Burlington Mag.*, 105. 103 foll.
25. R. C. Strong, 'Elizabethan Painting . . . Marcus Gheeraerts the Younger', *ibid.*, 149 foll.; O. Millar, 'Marcus Gheeraerts the Younger', *ibid.*, 533 foll.
26. Cf. *Three Inventories of Pictures in the Collections of Henry VIII and Edward VI*, ed. W. A. Shaw (Courtauld Institute).
27. Buxton, 99 foll.
28. D. Piper, 'The 1590 Inventory', *Burlington Mag.*, 99. 224 foll.
29. Mercer, 184.
30. E. K. Waterhouse, *Painting in Britain, 1530–1790*, 29.
31. W. Blunt, *The Art of Botanical Illustrations*, 63 foll.
32. L. Binyon, *English Water-Colours*, 1 foll.

Chapter VI

1. *Elizabethan Embroidery* (*V. and A. Handbook*, Introduction).
2. A. J. B. Wace, 'English Embroideries belonging to Sir John Carew-Pole, Bt', *Walpole Soc.*, 21. 43 foll.
3. *Elizabethan Embroidery*, loc. cit.
4. R. Edwards, 'Foreword', *Connoisseur Period Guides: The Tudor Period*, ix foll.
5. A. F. Kendrick, *English Needlework*, 68.
6. J. L. Nevinson, 'English Domestic Embroidery Patterns of the 16th and 17th Centuries', *Walpole Soc.*, 28. 1 foll.
7. *Fine Bindings 1500–1700 from Oxford Libraries* (Catalogue of an Exhibition 1968), 94–5.
8. G. W. Digby, *Elizabethan Embroidery*, 107–8.
9. *Ibid.*, 99.
10. q. C. E. C. Tattersall, *A History of British Carpets*, 41.
11. Kendrick, 67.
12. Tattersall, 36.
13. *Ibid.*, 35, 38.
14. q. Elizabeth Jenkins, *Elizabeth and Leicester*, 360.
15. W. G. Thomson, *A History of Tapestry*, 241.
16. J. Humphreys, 'Elizabethan Sheldon Tapestries', *Archaeologia*, 1923–4, 181 foll.
17. q. E. A. B. Barnard and A. J. B. Wace, 'The Sheldon Tapestry Weavers and their Work', *Archaeologia*, 1928, 255 foll.
18. N. V. Stopford Sackville, *Drayton House, Northamptonshire*, 36–7.

19. *Hardwick Mss.*
20. D. C. Calthrop, *English Costume, III. Tudor and Stuart*, 83.
21. Cunnington, 87 foll.
22. Sir James Mann, *European Arms and Armour. Catalogue of the Wallace Collection*, 1. xxiv.
23. C. Ffoulkes, 'The Armourers' Company of London and the Greenwich School of Armourers', *Archaeologia*, 1926–7, 41 foll.
24. Cf. *Arms and Armour. Guide to the Collections* (The Metropolitan Museum of Art), 13–14.
25. q. J. G. Mann, 'Recollections of the Wilton Armoury', *Connoisseur*, 104. 10 foll.
26. J. Evans, *English Jewels from the 5th Century to 1800*, 109.
27. E. Auerbach, *Nicholas Hilliard*, 189.
28. Evans, 87.
29. Cf. Pl. 24a and 24b, *Elizabethan Art* (Victoria and Albert Museum).
30. Cf. H. Tait, *Catalogue of Jewelry*, F., Gold Room, Shakespeare Exhibition, Stratford-on-Avon, 1964.
31. Evans, 83.
32. *Ibid.*, 107.
33. q. *ibid.*, 95.
34. R. E. M. Wheeler, *The Cheapside Hoard of Elizabethan and Jacobean Jewellery*, London Museum, 5.
35. G. F. Hill, *Historical Medals in the British Museum*, 19.
36. q. J. C. Rogers, *English Furniture*, 15.
37. Cf. Pl. 3, *Elizabethan Art* (Victoria and Albert Museum).
38. G. Wills, 'Another Look at Elizabethan Furniture', *Apollo*, 1964, 313 foll.
39. M. Adams-Acton, 'Early English Oak Tables, I', *Connoisseur*, 98. 111.
40. P. Macquoid, *The History of English Furniture. The Age of Oak*, 93 foll.
41. R. W. P. Luff, 'Sculptured Supports for Tudor Tables', *Country Life*, 1962, 1467 foll.
42. H. Cescinsky and E. R. Gribble, *Early English Furniture and Woodwork*, 299 foll.
43. q. Macquoid, 59.
44. C. Oman, 'Church Plate of West Suffolk', *Connoisseur*, 195. 105 foll.
45. J. T. Evans, *The Church Plate of Pembroke*, xvi foll.
46. Oman, *loc. cit.*
47. C. J. Jackson, *English Goldsmiths and their Marks*, 305 foll.
48. C. J. Jackson, *An Illustrated History of English Plate*, I. 162 foll.
49. C. C. Oman, *English Domestic Silver*, 48.
50. C. C. Oman, *The English Silver in the Kremlin, 1557–1663*, 27.
51. Pls. 21 and 22, *Tudor Domestic Silver* (Victoria and Albert Museum).
52. *Ibid.*, Pl. 24.
53. H. Tait, 'The Stonyhurst Salt', *Apollo*, 79. 270 foll.
54. *Ibid.*,
55. q. A. J. Collins, *Jewels and Plate of Queen Elizabeth I*, 3.
56. *Ibid.*, 551 foll., 561
57. Cf. *The Illustrated London News*, 1946, 192; and *Tudor Domestic Silver*, Pls. 11 and 12.
58. R. F. Michaelis, *Antique Pewter of the British Isles*, 87 foll.
59. R. F. Michaelis, *Antique Pewter*, 88 foll.
60. F. H. Garner, *English Delftware*, 2 foll.
61. W. B. Honey, *English Pottery and Porcelain*, 25.
62. J. Hayes, *The Garton Collection of English Table Glass*, London Museum, 5.
63. J. Manning, 'Jacob Verzelini, Elizabethan Glass Maker', *Apollo*, 79. 299 foll.
64. Cf. *The England of Elizabeth*, 145.
65. J. D. Le Couteur, *English Medieval Painted Glass*, 158.
66. J. Baker, *English Stained Glass*, 212.
67. q. H. Read, *English Stained Glass*, 194 foll.

68. A. V. Sugden and J. L. Edmondson, *A History of English Wallpaper, 1509–1914*, 3 foll.
69. J. Waterer, 'Leather', *Connoisseur Guide: The Tudor Period*, 149 foll.
70. I. G. Philip, *Gold-Tooled Bookbindings. Bodleian Picture Books*, 3.
71. W. Y. Fletcher, 'English Bookbindings', in A. H. Church, *Some Minor Arts as Practised in England*, 8 foll.
72. *Fine Bindings, 1500–1700, from Oxford Libraries*. Bodleian Library, 67 foll.; and cf. C. Davenport, *English Embroidered Bookbindings*.
73. J. Buxton, 'Concord of Sweet Sounds', *Apollo*, 1964, 303 foll.
74. *Register of the Freemen of Leicester*, ed. H. Hartoff, I. 83.
75. F. J. Britten, *Old Clocks and Watches and their Makers*, 130 foll.
76. R. McLean, 'Printing', *Connoisseur Guides: The Tudor Period*, 169 foll.
77. A. M. Hind, *Engraving in England in the 16th and 17th Centuries*, Part I. 6 foll.
78. *Ibid.*, 258.
79. Cf. A. S. Osley, *Mercator*.
80. G. E. Dawson and L. Kennedy-Skipton, *Elizabethan Handwriting 1500–1650*, 12.
81. R. Edwards, 'Foreword', *Connoisseur Guide: The Tudor Period*, ix foll.

Chapter VII

1. E. A. Burtt, *The Metaphysical Foundations of Modern Physical Science*, 37 foll.
2. G. Sarton, *Six Wings: Men of Science in the Renaissance*, 85.
3. H. Butterfield, *The Origins of Modern Science*, 34.
4. F. Cajori, *A History of Mathematical Notations*, 164.
5. q. F. R. Johnson and S. V. Larkey, 'Robert Recorde's Mathematical Teaching', *Huntington Library Bulletin*, No. 7, 59 foll.
6. q. *ibid.*
7. Cf. A. Koestler, *The Sleepwalkers. A History of Man's Changing Vision of the Universe*, 163 foll.
8. Cf. *D.N.B.*, *sub* Robert Recorde.
9. Johnson and Larkey, *loc. cit.*
10. E. G. R. Taylor, *The Mathematical Practitioners of Tudor and Stuart England*, 170.
11. C. H. Josten, 'A Translation of John Dee's *Monas Hieroglyphica*', *Ambix* XII, 84 foll.
12. Taylor, *loc. cit.*
13. *The Mathematical Preface of John Dee*, in T. Rudd, *Euclid's Elements of Geometry*, 1651.
14. Cf. C. D. Hellman, 'Maurolyco's Lost Essay on the New Star of 1572', *Isis*, 51. 322 foll.
15. Cf. C. D. Hellman, *The Comet of 1577. Its Place in the History of Astronomy*.
16. Lord Henry Howard, *A Defensative against the Poison of Supposed Prophecies* (ed. 1620), 77.
17. F. R. Johnson, *Astronomical Thought in Renaissance England*, 165; and *v.* F. R. Johnson and S. V. Larkey, 'Thomas Digges, the Copernican System ... in 1576', *Hunt. Library Bulletin, No.* 5, 69 foll. for reprint of *A Perfect Description*.
18. q. F. R. Johnson, *op. cit.*, 159.
19. *Ibid.*, 170.
20. q. *ibid.*, 192.
21. E. G. R. Taylor, *The Haven-Finding Art*, 151.
22. R. F. Jones, *Ancients and Moderns*, 13.
23. E. G. R. Taylor, *Tudor Geography, 1485–1583*, v.
24. A. H. W. Robinson, *Marine Cartography in Britain*, 17 foll.
25. Cotton Mss., Aug. I. i, 38.
26. Taylor, *op. cit.*, 22.
27. q. *ibid.*, 75.
28. *Ibid.*, 95.

29. Robinson, *op. cit.*, 17.
30. Ashmole Mss., 1820 b.
31. Robinson, 25 foll.
32. R. V. Tooley, *Maps and Map Makers*, 47 foll.
33. E. G. R. Taylor, *The Haven-Finding Art*, 170.
34. D. W. Waters, *The Art of Navigation in Tudor and Stuart England*, 144.
35. *Ibid.*, 132.
36. W. Bourne, *A Regiment for the Sea*, Dedication to Lord Admiral Clinton.
37. This appears as Device No. 38 in the book.
38. Waters, *op. cit.*, 147.
39. *Ibid.*
40. *Ibid.*, 153.
41. Robert Norman, *The New Attractive*, Chap. 3.
42. *Ibid.*, 19 foll.
43. Waters, 154.
44. *Ibid.*, 189.
45. E. L. Stevenson, *Terrestrial and Celestial Globes*, xix, 190.
46. Cf. R. T. Gunther, *Early Science in Cambridge*, 32.
47. Waters, 218.
48. *Ibid.*, 212.
49. Appended to Blundeville's *Exercises*, 1594.
50. Waters, 403.
51. Edward Wright, *Errors in Navigation*, 1599, Preface.
52. Waters, 225.
53. Stevenson, *op. cit.*, 173.
54. E. G. R. Taylor, *The Mathematical Practitioners*, 182.
55. E. Seaton, 'Thomas Hariot's Secret Script', *Ambix*, vol. 5. 111 foll.; *The Roanoke Voyages, 1584–1590*, ed. D. B. Quinn, *Hakluyt Soc.*, I. 55, 387.
56. John Aubrey, *Brief Lives*, ed. A. Clark, I. 285.
57. E. G. R. Taylor, *The Haven Finding Art*, 219 foll.
58. *Ibid.*, 222 foll.
59. *Salisbury Mss.*, VI. 256–7.
60. *Salisbury Mss.*, XVII. 507, 530, 600.
61. H. C. King, *The History of the Telescope*, 29 foll.
62. H. Stevens, *Thomas Hariot*, 114 foll.
63. *Ibid.*, 120 foll.
64. King, 40.
65. q. A. Koestler, *op. cit.*, 356.
66. q. Stevens, 120 foll.
67. Stevens, 178 foll.
68. *Ibid.*, 190 foll.
69. F. Cajori, 'A Revaluation of Hariot's *Artis Analyticae Praxis*', *Isis*, II. 316 foll.
70. F. Cajori, *A History of Mathematics*, 157 foll.; and cf. D. E. Smith, *A History of Mathematics*, I. 388.
71. F. Cajori, *A History of Mathematical Notations*, 199.
72. A. C. Crombie and others, 'Thomas Hariot, 1560–1621' . . . *Times Lit. Supp.* 23.10.69, 1237–8
73. S. Kelly, *The De Mundo of William Gilbert*, 17.
74. G. Sarton, *Six Wings: Men of Science in the Renaissance*, 94.
75. For these cf. L. Firpo, 'The Flowering and Withering of Speculative Philosophy: Italian Philosophy and the Counter Reformation', in *The Late Italian Renaissance*, ed. E. Cochrane, 266 foll.
76. E. Zilsel, 'The Origins of William Gilbert's Scientific Method', *Journal of the History of Ideas*, II. 1 foll.
77. Cf. the translation by P. F. Mottelay, *On the Loadstone and Magnetic Bodies and on the Great Magnet the Earth*, 1893.

Notes

78. q. *ibid.*, xxii.
79. q. S. P. Thompson, *Notes on the* De Magnete *of Dr. William Gilbert*, 51.
80. The Huntington Library copy belonged to John Barlow in the eighteenth century, and may have come down from Ridley's opponent, William Barlow.
81. Cf. Koestler, 355.
82. For a useful brief account of Bacon's method, *v.* Stuart Hampshire, *The Age o Reason*, 19 foll.; but this deals with his method only, not his scientific work.
83. I owe this point to Professor Merle Curti.
84. J. R. Partington, *A History of Chemistry*, II. 393 foll.
85. *The Works of Francis Bacon*, ed. J. Spedding, R. L. Ellis, and D. D. Heath, I. 254, 271.
86. *Ibid.*, I. 326.
87. *Ibid.*, I. 384 foll.; III. 167; I. 417 foll.
88. *Ibid.*, II. 122 foll.
89. *Ibid.*, I. 60.
90. Partington, II. 409, foll.
91. *Ibid.*, II. 404.
92. H. Margenau, 'Bacon and Modern Physics: A Confrontation', *Proc. Am. Phil. Soc.*, 1961, 487 foll.
93. q. *Science, Medicine and History: Essays in honour of Charles Singer*, ed. E. A. Underwood, 447.
94. q. A. R. Hall, *Ballistics in the 17th Century*, 73.
95. Cf. E. G. R. Taylor, 'Cartography, Survey, and Navigation, 1400–1750', in *A History of Technology*, ed. C. Singer and others, 530 foll.
96. R. F. Jones, *Ancients and Moderns*, 10.
97. M. Purver, *The Royal Society: Concept and Creation*, 23.
98. q. *ibid.*, 5–6.

Chapter VIII

1. C. E. Raven, *English Naturalists from Neckam to Ray*, 45.
2. q. *ibid.*, 50; 65.
3. q. *ibid.*, 67.
4. *Ibid.*, 86–8.
5. *v.* later, pp. 280–81.
6. A. Arber, *Herbals: Their Origin and Evolution*, 124.
7. Raven, 134.
8. *Ibid.*, 127.
9. *The Works of John Caius*, ed. E. S. Roberts, vi.
10. Raven, 190–1.
11. Thomas Moffet, *Health's Improvement, or rules . . . of preparing all sorts of Food used in this Nation*, ed. 1655, 43, 60, 67.
12. R. T. Gunther, *Early British Botanists*, I. 238 foll.
13. W. Blunt, *The Art of Botanical Illustrations*, 57 foll.
14. q. Raven, 209, 214.
15. Sir George Clark, *A History of the Royal College of Physicians of London*, 1. 34.
16. Sir Arthur MacNalty, *The Renaissance and its Influence on English Medicine*, 5.
17. *Ibid.*, 16.
18. Clark, I. 144 foll.
19. C. Goodall, *The Royal College of Physicians of London*, 1684, Appdx, 'An Historical Account of the College's Proceedings against Empirics', 314 foll.
20. *Ibid.*, 337 foll.
21. N. Moore, *The History of St. Bartholomew's Hospital*, II. 416, 421, 433, 585, 611.
22. *Ibid.*, II. 293, 704, 706, 757.

23. q. F. G. Parsons, *The History of St. Thomas's Hospital*, 115.
24. *Ibid.*, 185 foll.; 232.
25. E. G. O'Donoghue, *Bridewell Hospital . . . to the End of the Reign of Elizabeth*, 198, 215, 220, 224, 230.
26. R. S. Roberts, 'The Personnel and Practice of Medicine in Tudor and Stuart England. Pt. I. The Provinces,' *Medical History*, VI. 363 foll.
27. *Ibid.*
28. J. L. Vivian, *The Visitations of Cornwall*, 109.
29. T. D. Whittet, 'The Apothecary in Provincial Gilds', *Medical History*, VIII. 245 foll.
30. L. G. Matthews, 'Royal Apothecaries of the Tudor Period', *ibid.*, VIII. 170 foll.
31. T. R. Forbes, 'The Regulation of English Midwives in the 16th and 17th centuries', *ibid.*, VIII. 235 foll.
32. J. J. Keevil, *Medicine and the Navy, 1200–1900*, 119 foll.
33. C. Creighton, *A History of Epidemics in Britain*, I. 127, 304, 345.
34. F. P. Wilson, *The Plague in Shakespeare's London*, 114–15.
35. Creighton, I. 340 foll.
36. R. M. S. McConaghey, 'Medical Records of Dartmouth, 1425–1887', *Medical History*, IV. 91 foll.
37. Wilson, 72.
38. q. *ibid.*, 76–7.
39. *Ibid.*, 81.
40. Creighton, 320 foll.
41. Wilson, 41, 50.
42. q. *ibid.*, 12, 102.
43. q. Creighton, I. 486, 490.
44. *Henslowe Papers*, ed. W. W. Greg, 35–7.
45. *Henslowe's Diary*, ed. W. W. Greg, Pt. I. 212.
46. *D.N.B.*, *sub* Robert White.
47. Wilson, 113.
48. T. Lodge, *A Treatise of the Plague*, 1603. Lodge dedicated the book to the Lord Mayor, sheriffs and aldermen, hoping that they would order the book to be circulated among the sick for their benefit.
49. They are collected and edited by F. P. Wilson, *The Plague Pamphlets of Thomas Dekker*.
50. *The Works of John Caius*, ed. cit., *A Book or Counsel against . . . the Sweat*, 11.
51. Creighton, I. 376, 383.
52. *Selected Writings of William Clowes*, ed. F. N. L. Poynter, 22.
53. W. Clowes, *A Short and Profitable Treatise touching the cure of the Disease called* Morbus Gallicus *by Unctions*, ed. 1579; cf. Poynter, 74.
54. Poynter, 136.
55. *Ibid.*, 73 foll.
56. *The Apology and Treatise of Ambroise Paré*, ed. Sir Geoffrey Keynes, xi-xii.
57. W. Clowes, *A Proved Practice for all Young Chirurgeons concerning Burnings with Gunpowder and Wounds made with Gunshot*, etc. ed. 1588.
58. W. Clowes, *A Profitable and Necessary Book of Observations . . .*, 3rd ed., 1637, 68.
59. W. Clowes, *A Proved Practice*, ed. cit., 9.
60. Keynes, 189.
61. W. Clowes, *A Right Fruitful and Approved Treatise for the Artificial Cure of . . . Struma*, ed. 1602. The Huntington Library copy is inscribed: 'this bke was geven me by Mr. William Clowes ye mak[er] thereof Septb last 1602.'
62. W. Clowes, *A Proved Practice*, ed. cit.
63. J. Banister, *The History of Man, sucked from the Sap of the most approved Anatomists*, 1578. The Huntington Library copy was presented to Egerton by Dr. Valentine Cary, later bishop of Exeter.
Ibid., 88, 88b, 100.

65. Cf. W. S. Mitchell, 'William Bullein, Elizabethan Physician and Author,' *Medical History*, 3. 188 foll.
66. W. Bullein, *A Dialogue . . . a goodly regiment against the Fever Pestilence*, ed. 1565.
67. D. H. M. Woollam, 'Donne, Disease and the Doctors', *Medical History*, V. 144 foll.
68. T. Bright, *A Treatise of Melancholy*, 1586, 1, 2, 95.
69. *Ibid.*, 161, 295, 301.
70. Cf. W. J. Carlton, *Timothy Bright, Doctor of Physic*,
71. R. Lennard, 'The Watering Places', in *Englishmen at Rest and Play . . . 1558–1714*, ed. R. Lennard, 3 foll.
72. P. R. James, *The Baths of Bath in the 16th and Early 17th Centuries*, 15, 26 foll., 43.
73. Lennard, 6 foll.
74. *The Accounts of the Chamberlains of the city of Bath, 1568–1602*, ed. F. D. Wardle, Somerset Record Soc., vol. 38, *passim*.
75. Cf. *Salisbury Mss.* VII. 175, 186; X. 28, 29, 48, 70, 77, 96, 153.
76. Sir William MacArthur, 'A Brief Story of English Malaria', *British Medical Bulletin*, 8. 76 foll.
77. H. Joseph, *Shakespeare's Son-in-law: John Hall, Man and Physician*, 14–15, 44–5.
78. J. J. Keevil, *Hamey the Stranger*, 30 foll.
79. Sir George Clark, *A History of the Royal College of Physicians of London*, I. 116.
80. W. Munk, *The Roll of the Royal College of Physicians of London*, I. 81–2, 101–2.
81. J. S. G. Simmons and B. O. Unbegaun, 'Slavonic Manuscript Vocabularies in the Bodleian Library', *Oxford Slavonic Papers*, 1951, 119 foll.
82. *Salisbury Mss.*, IX. 151.
83. N. Evans, 'Dr. Timothy Willis and his Mission to Russia, 1599', *Oxford Slavonic Papers*, 1969, 39 foll.
84. Keevil, ch. IV.
85. *D.N.B. sub* Arthur Dee.
86. N. Moore, *The History of the Study of Medicine in the British Isles*, 67.
87. F. W. Steer, 'Lord Lumley's Benefaction to the College of Physicians', *Medical History*, 2, 298 foll.
88. Clark, I. QV 296.
89. Aubrey, *Brief Lives, ed. cit.*, I. 300.
90. q. *ibid.*, I. 301.
91. *Medical History*, X. 97 foll.
92. Aubrey, *ibid.*
93. K. D. Keele, 'William Harvey: the Man and the College of Physicians', *Medical History*, 3. 264 foll.
94. L. Chauvois, *William Harvey; His Life and Times*, 50 foll.

Chapter IX

1. E. A. Burtt, *The Metaphysical Foundations of Modern Physical Science*, 95.
2. *Ibid.*, 80.
3. Cf. A. O. Lovejoy, *The Great Chain of Being*.
4. R. N. Carew Hunt, reviewing F. Wendel, *Calvin: sources et évolution de sa pensée religieuse, Journ. Eccles. History*, 1952, 235–6.
5. *Works of Francis Bacon, ed. cit.*, VI. 402; IV. 323.
6. q. K. R. Wallace, *Francis Bacon on Communication and Rhetoric*, 101.
7. q. *ibid.*, 104.
8. *Works*, IV. 15; V. 17, 28; V. 6; IV. 55, 293; VI. 18.

9. *Ibid.*, VIII. 124.
10. Cf. S. A. Cook, 'The Rise of Israel', *Cambridge Ancient History*, II. 352 foll. Biblical history was 'compiled and shaped for popular edification', *ibid.*, 383.
11. S. A. Cook, *The Old Testament: A Reinterpretation*, v, i.
12. Cf. Lucien Febvre, 'parler de rationalisme et de libre pensée, s'agissant d'un époque où, contre une religion aux prises universelles, les hommes les plus intelligents et les plus audacieux étaient incapables vraiment de trouver un appui soit dans la philosophie, soit dans la science: c'est parler d'une chimère.' *Le Problème de l'incroyance au XVIᵉ siècle*, xvii.
13. Cf. F. S. Boas, *Christopher Marlowe*, 250.
14. Cook, 2, 45.
15. B. J. Shapiro, 'Latitudinarianism and Science in seventeenth century England', *Past and Present*, 1968, 16 foll.
16. Cook, 15, 74.
17. *Ibid.*, v.
18. Cf. *ibid.*, 89.
19. *Works*, IV. 342.
20. q. M. Doran, 'On Elizabethan "Credulity"', *Journ. Hist. Ideas*, I. 151 foll.; cf. *Works*, IV. 363
21. q. V. K. Whitaker, 'Bacon's Doctrine of Forms', *Hunt. Libr. Quarterly*, 1970, 212.
22. *Works*, IV. 363, where Bacon gives many examples of such nonsense.
23. *Ibid.*, IV. 53 foll.
24. *Ibid.*, IV. 65.
25. *Bacon's Essays*, ed. W. A. Wright, 200; 39 foll.
26. *Works*, IV. 475.
27. *Ibid.*, V. 79.
28. *Ibid.*, V. 15.
29. *Ibid.*, IV. 459.
30. *Ibid.*, V. 21 foll.
31. *Ibid.*, IV, 77 foll.
32. *Ibid.*, IV. 363.
33. q. Wallace, 10.
34. q. *ibid.*, 29.
35. *Essays, ed. cit.*, 106–10.
36. W. Oakeshott, 'Sir Walter Ralegh's Library', *The Library*, 1968, 285 foll.
37. *The Works of Sir Walter Ralegh*, ed. W. Oldys and T. Birch (Oxford, 1829), III. 30, 35.
38. *Ibid.*, II. 138.
39. *Ibid.*, II. 1, 7.
40. *Ibid.*, II. 7, 23, 45, 358; IV. 757.
41. *Ibid.*, II. 33, 66, 75, 81, 129, 132,
42. *Ibid.*, II. 204 foll.
43. *Ibid.*, II. 145, 248, 250; III. 3, 19.
44. *Ibid.*, III. 151 foll.
45. *Ibid.*, III. 168 foll.; IV. 418; VI. 50, 145–6.
46. *Ibid.*, IV. 577, 617.
47. *Ibid.*, IV. 497; VI. 284.
48. *Ibid.*, II. 47; VII. 766.
49. *Ibid.*, VIII. 94, 111.
50. 'Tout ce que Ralegh écrivit fut au service de sa carrière, de l'action, de ses ambitions libres ou frustrées, et *The History* ne fait pas exception.' P. Lefranc, *Sir Walter Ralegh écrivain*, 333.
51. *Works*, VIII. 253.
52. *Ibid.*, IV. 615.
53. *Ibid.*, VIII. 120.
54. *Ibid.*, VIII. 44, 92, 106, 114.

Notes

55. *Ibid.*, VIII. 557, 565 foll.
56. F. Peck, *Desiderata Curiosa*, I. 47 foll.
57. M. McKisack, 'Samuel Daniel as Historian', *Rev. Eng. Studies*, 1947, 226 foll.
58. *The Complete Works of Samuel Daniel*, ed. A. B. Grosart, IV. 75–6.
59. Cf. his *Restitution of Decayed Intelligence*.
60. q. McKisack, *loc. cit.*
61. R. H. Popkin, *The History of Scepticism*, 17.
62. Sextus Empiricus: *Outlines of Pyrrhonism*. Trans. R. G. Bury, (*Loeb Classical Library*), *passim.*
63. Cf. *The Elizabethan Renaissance: The Life of the Society*, 238.
64. q. Popkin, 44.
65. Cf. G. Santayana, *Egotism and German Philosophy*.
66. q. G. H. Williams, *The Radical Reformation*, 605.
67. Popkin, 10.
68. J. A. van Dorsten, *The Radical Arts*, 16 foll.
69. 'A certain arrogance which, to outsiders, must always seem to be inherent in the doctrine of predestination,' M. E. Aston, 'Lollardy and Sedition, 1381–1431', *Past and Present*, April 1960, 14.
70. Williams, xxiv foll.
71. *Ibid.*, 783.
72. W. K. Jordan, *The Development of Religious Toleration in England from the Beginning of the English Reformation to the Death of Queen Elizabeth*, 303 foll.
73. *Ibid.*, 342.
74. Van Dorsten, 27 foll.
75. J. Stow, *Annals* (ed. 1631), 679–80.
76. J. Hitchcock, ' Confession of the Family of Love, 1580', *Bull. Inst. Hist. Research*, May 1970, 85–6.
77. Van Dorsten, 27.
78. Williams, xix.
79. W. S. Howell, *Logic and Rhetoric in England, 1500–1700*, 9–10, 24, 159.
80. *Ibid.*, 13, 99.
81. Cf. T. Wilson, *A Discourse upon Usury*, with Introduction by R. H. Tawney; and *Wilson's Art of Rhetoric*, ed. by G. H. Mair.
82. Howell, 9, 342.
83. *Ibid.*, 185, 285.
84. *Ibid.*, 376.
85. *Ibid.*, 248.
86. *Gabriel Harvey's Ciceronianus*, ed. H. S. Wilson and C. A. Forbes, 79 foll., 99.
87. *Ibid.*, 51.
88. q. D. Bush, 'The Date of Spenser's Cantos of Mutability', *Proc. Mod. Lang. Assoc.*, 45. 954 foll.
98. Cf. *The Elizabethan Renaissance. The Life of the Society*, 179.
90. Cf. C. de Rémusat, *Histoire de la philosophie en Angleterre*, I. 111 foll.; and *D.N.B.*, under Digby.
91. Cf. H. C. Porter, *Reformation and Reaction in Tudor Cambridge*, where nothing whatever is said as to Digby's intellectual position, but plenty about Whitaker's.
92. A. F. Scott Pearson, *Thomas Cartwright and Elizabethan Puritanism*, 406.
93. *The Works of that Famous and Worthy Minister of Christ in the University of Cambridge, Mr. William Perkins*, ed. 1612–13, 1. *A Golden Chain, or the Description of Theology*, ch. VII. 16.
94. *Ibid.*, Preface to the Christian Reader.
95. *Ibid.*, 117.
96. *Ibid.*, *A Treatise of the Vocations or Callings of Men*, 756 foll.
97. *Ibid.*, *A Reformed Catholic*, 556.
98. Scott Pearson, 407.
99. q. Richard Bancroft, *Dangerous Positions and Proceedings*, ed. 1593, 60.

100. Bancroft, *A Sermon preached at Paul's Cross*, ed. 1588–9, 5.
101. S. B. Babbage, *Puritanism and Richard Bancroft*, 39 foll.
102. Bancroft, *A Sermon*, 92.
103. Bancroft, *A Survey of the Pretended Holy Discipline*, ed. 1593, 45, 49.
104. *Ibid.*, 54, 134.
105. Bancroft, *Survey*, 31.
106. *Ibid.*, 73, 368–9.
107. *Ibid.*, 419, 433.
108. Bancroft, *Dangerous Positions*, chap. 1.
109. *Ibid.*, chap. IV.
110. Cf. D.N.B., under Hacket.
111. [Matthew Sutcliffe], *An Answer to a Certain Calumnious Letter*, ed. 1595, 78.
112. *Ibid.*, 10.
113. [Sutcliffe], *A Full and Round Answer to N. D. alias Robert Parsons*, ed. 1604, 220 foll.
114. Cf. *D.N.B.*, under Fisher.
115. [Anon], *A Brief Apology or Defence of the Catholic Ecclesiastical Hierarchy*, ed. 1601, chap. 12.
116. *A Christian Directory . . . commonly called the Resolution*, ed. 1650, augmented a little before Parsons' death, chap. 11.
117. Edmund Bunny, *A Brief Answer*, ed. 1589.
118. Cf. W. K. Jordan, 'The direct result of the Jesuit policy was a considerable increase in the suffering of their co-religionists in England . . . We may applaud the courage and the singular devotion of the Jesuits to a high purpose, but we cannot commend either their honesty or their methods,' *The Development of Religious Toleration in England from the Beginning of the English Reformation to the Death of Queen Elizabeth*, 373–4.
119. William Whitaker, *An Answer to the Ten Reasons of E. Campion*, trans. R. Stock, ed. 1606, 36 foll.
120. *Ibid.*, 48, 59, 137, 196, 300.
121. John Dove, *A Confutation of Atheism*, ed. 1605, 1 foll.
122. *Ibid.*, 14.
123. q. from *Biathanatos*, E. M. Simpson, *A Study of the Prose Works of John Donne*, 14.
124. [John Donne], *Pseudo-Martyr*, ed. 1610; cf. Simpson, 188.
125. *Ibid.*, cc. III, and VII.
126. *Ibid.*, cc. IX, X, XII, XIII.
127. *Ibid.*, Address to the Reader.
128. W. Bouwsma, 'Venice, Spain, and the Papacy: Paolo Sarpi and the Renaissance Tradition,' in Cochrane, *op. cit.*, 353 foll.
129. W. K. Jordan, *The Development of Religious Toleration . . . 1603–1640*, 39.
130. Cf. *The England of Elizabeth*, 483–8.
131. *Works of Richard Hooker*, ed. J. Keble, revised edn. R. W. Church and F. Paget, III. 483–547.
132. Cf. William Empson, *Milton's God*.

Epilogue

1. q. W. Hazlitt, *Characters of Shakespeare's Plays*, Everyman edn., xiv–xv.
2. *Ibid.*, xviii, 118.
3. q. *England as Seen by Foreigners*, ed. W. B. Rye, 70 foll.
4. *Queen Elizabeth and Some Foreigners*, *ed.* V. von Klarwill, trans. T. H. Nash, 309.
5. Cf. *Beloved Son Felix: the Journal of Felix Platter*, trans. S. Jennett.
6. A. d'Aubigné, *Les Tragiques*, ed. A. Garnier et J. Plattard, II. 32–3; 179 foll.
7. q. H. A. Rennert, *The Life of Lope de Vega, 1562–1635*, 140.
8. J. H. Grew, *Elisabeth d'Angleterre . . . dans la littérature française*, 45.

Notes

9. *The Fugger News-Letters*, ed. V. von Klarwill, trans. L. S. R. Byrne, 169, 211.
10. Cf. Rye, 49.
11. q. *ibid*, 104–5.
12. G. Ascoli, *La Grande-Bretagne devant l'opinion française*, 217.
13. q. *ibid.*, 218
14. Cf. *New Light on Drake*, ed. Z. Nuttal, *Hakluyt Soc,, passim.*
15. Cervantes, *Exemplary Novels*, trans. James Mabbe, ed. 1900, II. 135.
16. A. Dubeux, *Les Traductions françaises de Shakespeare*, 3–4
17. q. *ibid.*, 6–7.
18. Cf. Stendhal, *Racine et Shakespeare*, ed. B. Drenner.
19. Cf. *Berlioz and the Romantic Imagination* (Arts Council, 1969), 41 foll.
20. Cf. *Centenaire d'Eugène Delacroix, 1798–1863* (Musée du Louvre), 96 foll.
21. *The Complete Works of John Keats*, ed. H. Buxton Forman, 111. 254; IV. 50.
22. I owe this reference to Mr. N. Scarfe.
23. I am indebted for this inscription to Mr. H. S. Vere-Hodge.

INDEX

Index

Index

Index